BERDAN'S UNITED STATES SHARPSHOOTERS

IN THE

Army of the Potomac

BY

CAPT. C.A. STEVENS

(HISTORIAN)

Contentions fierce, Ardent, and dire, spring from no petty cause.—Scott.

1892

COPYRIGHT 2014 BIG BYTE BOOKS

Discover more lost history from BIG BYTE BOOKS

Contents

TO SHARP-SHOOTERS:	1
PREFACE	2
UNION VOLUNTEERS	4
FIRST CAMPAIGN	27
SECOND CAMPAIGN	150
THIRD CAMPAIGN.	169
FOURTH CAMPAIGN	188
IN CAMP.	201
FIFTH CAMPAIGN.	211
SIXTH CAMPAIGN.	245
SEVENTH CAMPAIGN.	307
EIGHTH CAMPAIGN.	327
NINTH CAMPAIGN.	346
THE LAST CAMPAIGN	432
APPENDIX	442
BIOGRAPHICAL SKETCHES	449
SHARPSHOOTER MONUMENTS	469

TO SHARP-SHOOTERS:

TO SHARP-SHOOTERS IN THE LOYAL STATES:

GENTLEMEN Many of you are undoubtedly aware that an effort is making to get up a regiment to be composed entirely of first class rifle shots at long distances—and that, in Consequence of my having myself done something in the way of rifle-shooting, suggestions have been , made in the public-press that I should aid- in this effort. I am, moreover; receiving, almost daily, applications by letter and in person to the same effect; and I see so clearly the great importance of the object in view that. I do not feel at liberty to refrain from doing what I can to further it. With thus view I propose that all those gentlemen who have made themselves good shots at long distances, and who are willing to place their skill in this Way at the service of our country un this her great struggle, should send their-names to me with an affidavit showing the ,best shooting they have done at, 200 yards or more. As soon as the necessary arrangements are made for the equipment, etc., notice will be given to all those whose applications shall be approved. No application will be considered in which the average of ten consecutive shots exceeds five inches from the center of the target to the center of the ball at -200 yards. The prodigious efficiency of detachments of such sharp-shooters, armed with our Northern patent target Rifles, needs only to be alluded to to be recognized at once by all who have any knowledge, of the subject. Need I add one word to enforce the duty, of our amateur target shots to make their peculiar skill useful to our country at this time of trial? That skill, the offspring of a manly Northern sport, can he converted into a powerful military instrument so readily that I feel confident the subject needs only to be suggested to insure its being fully and promptly attended to.

Very respectfully, your obedient servant,

H. Berdan;

Fifth-avenue Hotel, New York, May 30th.

PREFACE

The authority for writing this book was conferred upon the author by the Survivors' Association of the United States Sharpshooters, at Boston in 1890 for the First Regiment, and at Detroit in 1891 for the Second Regiment. This task was accepted with the expectation of being generally assisted by contributions of incidents from members of both regiments; but in this I have been considerably disappointed; so that it has occupied the two years endeavoring to obtain facts, especially relating to the "casualties," which have been very difficult to get. Since the work was written I concluded to add the company rosters, and to them refer for casualties not found elsewhere in the book, and altogether so for the Second Regiment. But as I have been unable to obtain anything like complete rosters, *excepting of a very few companies,* and with some of them none at all, I was obliged at the last moment to give that up. Valuable aid, however, has been rendered, for which my sincerest thanks are tendered.

It is a pretty difficult matter to write a history of such an organization as ours, composed of so many companies from different states, and there must be many things left out that would add interest to the work. Nevertheless, the writer most sincerely hopes that in its general character after making due allowance for possible errors, the history will be satisfactory, as it is as impartial and truthful as the historian could possibly make it.

Furthermore, it would be well to state that while this is a history of the Sharpshooters, there has been at no time a desire to make it appear that "we did it all." On the contrary, much pains has been taken to obtain the names of organizations engaged with us in every battle of importance, and to refer to their part as well as our own. By this means, a better idea of the engagement is obtained.

C. A. S.

SHAKOPEE, MINN., Aug. 1, 1892.

ENGAGEMENTS.

BLACKFORD'S FORD,
FREDERICKSBURG,
ELLIS' FORD,
THE CEDARS,
CHANCELLORSVILLE,
PITZER'S RUN,
GETTYSBURG,
WAPPING HEIGHTS,
AUBURN,
KELLY'S FORD,
BRANDY STATION,
LOCUST GROVE,
MINE RUN,
WILDERNESS,
ORANGE ROAD,
TODD'S TAVERN,
PO RIVER,
SPOTTSYLVANIA,
HARRIS HOUSE,
NORTH ANNA,
TOTOPOTOMOY,
COLD HARBOR,
HARRISON'S CREEK,
HARE'S FARM,
JERUSALEM PLANK ROAD,
DEEP BOTTOM,
BURNSIDE'S MINE,
DEEP RUN,
HATCHER'S RUN,
BOYDTON ROAD,
WELDON ROAD,
FORT HELL,
REAM'S STATION.

UNION VOLUNTEERS

The enlistment of volunteers for the Union army during the summer of 1861, was carried on with a patriotic vigor that fully attested the loyalty of the North, and was a ready response to President Lincoln's second call (May 3d). This time it was for three years' service, it having been clearly demonstrated not only to the President, but to the entire North, that it was useless to attempt to put down the Rebellion, now a determined fact, and extending over so large an extent of country comprised in the southern states, with a force of 75,000 men first called out—and for three months only. It was a momentous era in American history—the life-struggle of the nation. Everybody realized the danger, every one saw the necessity of promptly meeting it. The farmer, the merchant, the laborer, the rich and the poor, old men and young men were alike affected; their mothers, wives, daughters, sisters urging them on, their tears mingled with their prayers—prayers for the volunteers, for the Union cause. So earnest had the people become, now that war was inevitable to save the Union, and to put down forever this scheme of secession, that more than double the number asked for had enlisted and been accepted, so that in two months' time the war office in Washington reported 90,000 troops enrolled besides the three-months men whose time would soon expire. But while this great force had a cheering look in print, it was far above the actual number that could be armed and equipped. The government was not prepared for so many; there were not guns enough to go around, and it took time to furnish them. In this respect the Southerners had the advantage, as they had seized all our arsenals within their limits, and were therefore well supplied in this all-important matter. The only gun factory the government could rely on was at Springfield, and they were unable to meet the requirements, so that it was a long time before this increased force could be made ready for the field.

SHARPSHOOTER ORGANIZATION

It was during this time that this organization was commenced, on the proposition of Hiram Berdan of New York, and which was to be composed of companies of picked men from the loyal states. The purpose being to bring together the best marksmen possible of the North, and to arm them with the most reliable rifle made. With such men so armed and thoroughly equipped, it was believed that in the line of special service—that' of sharpshooting and skirmishing—they would become invaluable to the Union cause.

The proposal of Col. Berdan having been accepted by the government, printed circulars were issued by the adjutant-generals of different states calling for companies of Sharpshooters, and setting forth the terms on which candidates for admission would be accepted, and wherein it was ordered that: "no man be accepted who cannot, at 200 yards, put 10 consecutive shots in a target, the average distance not to exceed five inches from the center of the bullseye." Or, in other words, the string measurement of the 10 shots should not exceed 50 inches. Each man was allowed to choose his own rifle, but must justify his selection by the performance of the weapon in his own hands; and for each rifle furnished and accepted, $60 was to be paid therefor, thus insuring the best arms that could be purchased. Many, however, did not avail themselves of this offer, preferring to let the government furnish them.

Berdan's proposition was accepted by the Secretary of War, June 15, 1861, as follows:

The regiment within named is accepted, in accordance with the within proposal, provided the said regiment shall be mustered into service within ninety days of this date. The first detachment to be mustered in within twenty days, and so one detachment after another, as the War Department may order. And provided, also, that said regiment shall come into service armed and equipped, without expense to the government.

[Signed] SIMON CAMERON,

Secretary of War.

The project received the following recommendation from General Winfield Scott:

HEADQUARTERS OF THE ARMY, WASHINGTON, D. C., June 14, 1861.

H. BERDAN, Esq.,

Dear Sir:—The General-in-Chief, under the reference to him of the subject of Sharpshooters, by His Excellency,, the President, and Hon. Secretary of War, as set forth in your letter of June 13, 1861, desires me to say he was very favorably impressed with you personally; that a regiment of such Sharpshooters as are proposed by you, and instructed according to your system, would be of great value, and could be advantageously employed by him in the public service. Respectfully yours,

SCHUYLER HAMILTON,

Lieutenant-Colonel and Military Secretary.

In all the test shooting required before admission there was naturally some fine marksmanship developed, and among the best was that of Charles H. Townsend, at Camp Randall, Wis., who fired five shots at 200 yards with a total measurement of three and three-quarter inches; while, on the target grounds of the different states, two inches to a shot was frequently the average. But it was not always an easy matter to come up to the standard, and many, failing, were thrown out.

The rendezvous was established at Weehawken, opposite New York City, to which place most of the companies were at first ordered, but on or about the 24th of September proceeded to Washington, where they went into Camp of Instruction. With the required number of companies arriving at the Washington camp during the fall and winter, the First Regiment was completed with over 1,000 men, representing five states, as follows:

A, New York, Capt. Casper Trepp.

B, New York, Capt. Stephen Martin.

C, Michigan, Capt. Benj. Duesler. D New York, Capt. Geo. S. Tuckerman.

E, New Hampshire, Capt. Amos B. Jones.

F, Vermont, Capt. Edmund Weston.

G, Wisconsin, Capt. Edward Drew.

H, New York, Capt. Geo. G. Hastings.

I, Michigan, Capt. A. M. Willett.

K Michigan, Capt. S. J. Mather.

The Second Regiment Col. Post commanding, came in later, encamped next to the First, and consisted of eight companies, representing the following states:

A, Minnesota, Capt. Francis Peteler.

B, Michigan, Capt. Andrew B. Stuart.

FIRST REGIMENT.—No written authority to raise this regiment is found, but it would seem that such was given, as on July 30, 1861, Col. Berdan was notified that officers "are ordered to muster your regiment into service provided you do not present more than ten companies, which is the number for a regiment."—*Memorandum Sketch, Adjutant General's Office.*

D. arrived Jan. 3. '62. K, March, '62, after regiment had left, joining us at Hampton.

SECOND REGIMENT.—This regiment was raised under authority from the Secretary of War to Col. Berdan "to muster and organize into companies and regiments all, the men he could raise during the next 90 days from Sept. 28, 1861, and who, on examination, were found equal to the requirements of sharpshooters."—*Memorandum Sketch Adjutant General's Office.*

C, Pennsylvania, Capt. John W. Dewey.

D, Maine, Capt. James D. Fessenden.

E, Vermont, Capt. Homer R. Stoughton.

F, New Hampshire, Capt. Henry M. Caldwell.

G, New Hampshire, Capt. William D. McPherson.

H, Vermont, Capt. Gilbert Hart.

Our uniform was of fine material, consisting of dark green coat and cap with black plume, light blue trowsers (afterward exchanged for green ones) and leather leggins, presenting a striking contrast to the regular blue of the infantry. The knapsack was of hair-covered calfskin, with cooking kit attached, considered the best in use as it was the handsomest, most durable and complete. By our dress were we known far and wide, and the appellation of "Green Coats," was soon acquired. When fully uniformed and equipped, the Sharpshooters made a very handsome appearance, more so upon the whole than many others.

We wore for a time, principally on outpost duty or in bad weather, what were called "Havelocks," a gray, round hat with wide, black visor, good enough around Washington far within the lines, but after our first appearance before the enemy the following spring, they were discarded as endangering a fire from the rear. Certain grayfelt, seamless overcoats were likewise abandoned, although they were good rain shedders, only they became when wet stiff as a board.

The Camp of Instruction was organized for the purpose of drilling and disciplining the vast army of raw volunteers—to mould the citizen into the soldier. The formation of this camp was intrusted to Gen. [George Brinton] McClellan, who was called to the general command from the field of his victories in western Virginia, which in two months' time made West Virginia a loyal state [see *McClellan's Own Story*].

The time was occupied in camp in target practice, learning the company drill and battalion movements, guard, patrol, and camp duties; and, under the instruction of Lieut. Mears, U. S. A., lieutenant-colonel of the regiment, they were soon able to execute the most difficult regimental drills, and were probably unexcelled therein by any other regiment, particularly in skirmishing, a service they were destined to perform at the front, in all the great battles of the- Army of the Potomac up to the time of their expiration of service.

In the target practice, a matter of the greatest importance, many excellent scores were made, and under the supervision of Col. Berdan great improvement was made in their marksmanship; the colonel, himself a noted sharpshooter, putting himself to the test on many occasions, before multitudes of people. One of his targets was erected at a distance of 600 yards, in which he frequently put five consecutive shots within the 10-inch ring, using the telescope rifle. These telescopes were powerful magnifiers, so much so that a small object, not distinguishable to the naked eye, could be seen at a long distance. But the cross-wires within tremble so easily, that it requires a steady hand to hold the cross on the mark, from the shoulder in off-hand shooting. However, as the telescopic rifles used by the Sharpshooters were generally very heavy—from 15 to 30 pounds—they were mostly shot from a rest; in fact, were generally used for long-range shooting. But two companies of the regiment— C, of Michigan, and E, of New Hampshire—were fully armed, having target rifles of different descriptions. The Vermont company also had a few guns. The balance of the regiment were unarmed and waiting for the Sharps improved rifle, military pattern, which had been promised. This was their choice of all the many kinds presented, manufacturers of all sorts of new guns constantly offering the same for trial and acceptance. Besides this, the chief of the ordnance department was very anxious to have the regiment armed with the muzzle-loading Springfield, then the established arm of the United States infantry. As soon as the government recognized the corps officially by mustering the First Regiment into service, Col. Berdan made a requisition for Sharps breech-loading rifles, which proved to be, according to Berdan, "a declaration of war." The newspapers of that date contained almost daily, statements of what Gen. Ripley chief of ordnance, had to say, or Gen. Scott, or the assistant secretary of war Thomas Scott, and Berdan had to fight the whole of them. They took the ground that there was no rifle equal to the Springfield for a soldier, except Gen. Ripley, who went so far as to say that he preferred the old smooth bore with "ball and buck." Gen. Scott, in his indorsement on the colonel's application, said: "Breech-loaders would spoil his command." The old veteran hero didn't live long enough to find out his mistake—to learn of the great revolution going on in this method of improving guns, so soon to be demonstrated by the Sharpshooters after getting into the field.

In consequence of this attempt to turn the Sharpshooters from their original purpose, and force on them the army musket, it was uncertain for a time whether the chosen breech-loaders would be furnished. But through the persistent efforts of Col. Berdan, an order was finally issued for their manufacture. The open-sighted Sharps rifle, using linen or "skin" cartridges, 52 caliber, conical ball, was the best breech-loading gun at that time made, a perfectly safe and reliable arm, combining accuracy with rapidity, just what a skirmish line needed for effective work. To their good judgment in choosing this rifle may be attributed their future success in the field, attaining as they did a reputation that eventually made the name of "Berdan Sharpshooters" renowned in foreign lands as well as our own. The muzzle-loading target rifles—telescope and globe sights—while of great value before fortifications and for special work, would have been useless in skirmishing.

The two companies—C and E—mentioned as being armed with target rifles, not only had an advantage over their comrades of the other companies in the important matter of target practice, but also were the first to experience a taste of active service, and it proved to them a rather hard one for the first introduction to the enemy. Leaving camp under orders to join Gen. Smith's expedition, on the 21st of September they marched to Fort Smith near Chain Bridge, thence forward to LEWINSVILLE, where they took part September 27th in an attack on a small force of the enemy, a foraging expedition, destroying and capturing a great portion of his supplies and defeating their cavalry. Here it was that the first shots of the Berdan Sharpshooters were fired at the secessionists, with good effect while the affair lasted. The march had been a hurried one and the soldiers were considerably fatigued, but obeyed the orders to advance with alacrity, performing the part assigned them in a manner that attracted the notice of the general commanding. George D. Sanford of Company C, was wounded. Having disposed of the enemy in their front, who made a hasty retreat, they moved forward in connection with the infantry in the direction of Falls Church, and again encountered the enemy at MUNSON'S HILL, where they became engaged in a night fight—after midnight—on September 29th. It was a very unpleasant affair to the Sharpshooters, and they were extremely lucky to find, after daylight, they had but one man wounded, Sergt. George W. Brooks of Company E, hit in the leg. The honor of being the first Sharpshooters shot by the rebels belonged to Sanford and Brooks. As was very likely to happen in a fight after dark, particularly in a wooded country, our troops were exposed for a time to their own tire, owing to mistakes made by other regiments. Possibly a blunder, yet apparently an unavoidable occurrence from the way they were situated, being considerably tangled up in the black thickets. It was a good deal like "going it blind" in that affair, for want of proper guides or a correct understanding of the position of the enemy. Quite a loss occurred on our side in some of the regiments, particularly Col. Baker's California regiment and the 69th Pennsylvania. But it resulted in Munson's Hill being evacuated by the enemy, an important point gained by the Union troops. When the Sharpshooters arrived back at camp, September 30th, after this rough campaign they were well satisfied to take a rest, and they got a good long one before-they moved again.

PRESIDENT LINCOLN AS A RIFLE SHOT

During the splendid weather of the autumn months, visitors to the great Camp of Instruction, with which the city of Washington was environed, came in untold numbers; they were constantly crowding in, not only from our own mighty North, but from all civilized quarters of the world. And not the least of the many objects of interest to be noted was that of the rifle practice referred to. The newspapers at the time were full of these target trials, and the shooting of the Sharpshooters furnished items for a long while to the dailies and illustrated journals.

On one occasion the President, with Gen. McClellan, paid a visit to the camp, and were invited by Col. Berdan to the rifle range where shooting was going on. To show what the men could do in rifle-pits, a target representing two Zouaves painted on canvass, was placed at a distance of 600 yards. One hundred men with their heavy target-rifles, were placed in a pit, where each fired one shot. When the target was brought in, it was found that every shot had struck within the outline of the two figures. President Lincoln fired three shots from a globe-rifle belonging to H. J. Peck, of Company F, while Gen. McClellan and some others tried their skill with more or less success. Abraham Lincoln handled the rifle like a veteran marksman, in a highly successful manner, to the great delight of the many soldiers and civilians surrounding. Once, resting his gun on what he called a sapling, he said: "Boys, this reminds me of old-time shooting," when they waved their hats and cheered him. His visit aroused their slumbering patriotism.

After which, Col. Berdan being called on, proceeded to execute some difficult shots, by knocking out the right eye of a Zouave painted full length on half of an "A" tent, and which was done with a James telescope-rifle. He fired three shots, all easily found within the parts selected—the head, right breast, or the left thigh. Referring to this shooting afterward in connection with his efforts to get us properly armed, he said:

"Then occurred one of those extraordinary accidents from which great and beneficial results often follow. Thomas Scott, the Assistant Secretary of War, thought to gain a point by attacking me personally, and asked me what I knew about guns and war that I should set up my opinion against all these officials, and ended by challenging me to fire, thinking doubtless, I would decline, or, if I accepted, to get the laugh on me by my making a bad shot. I at once accepted, and ordered the men to bring out a target; the only one left was the figure of a single man, full size, with the words 'Jeff Davis' painted Above his head. I remarked that I did not think it was exactly the thing to fire at Jeff Davis in the presence of the President of the United States. Mr. Lincoln laughed heartily and replied:

"Oh, Colonel, if you make a good shot it will serve him right.'

"The target was set up and I called for the sergeant major's rifle, which I knew to be correctly sighted for this distance. Thomas Scott then remarked:

'Now you must fire standing, for officers should not dirty their uniforms by getting into rifle pits.'

"I replied: 'You are right, Colonel Scott, I always fire from the shoulder.'

"I stepped forward and began to bring the gun to my face, when he said:

"What point are you going to fire at?'

"'The head,' I replied.

"'Fire at the right eye,' he shouted. I was then taking aim and made no reply, and it is hardly necessary for me to say, that at that distance-600 yards—I did not aim at the eye, but I did fire at the head. The target was brought in, and as good luck would have it, I had cut out the pupil of the right eye. No man knew better than President Lincoln how to turn what he knew to be an accident to good account. He began to laugh, and kept on laughing until he got into his carriage and then said:

'Colonel, come down to-morrow, and I will give you the order for the breech-loaders.'

"Mr. Lincoln visited us once or twice later, and spoke of that 'remarkable shot' as a good joke—a lucky hit."

Prize shooting was occasionally allowed, and usually created a healthy excitement among the men, as well as visitors who were sure to be there. One of the most important of these matches was held Thanksgiving afternoon (November 28th) between members of the target-rifle companies C, E and F, each man firing two shots off-hand at 40 rods, the winner to receive $5, presented by the colonel. The day being fine there was a large attendance of public men and others who came from town to "see the Sharpshooters shoot;" the judges, Capt. Giroux of Company C, and Sergt. Stevens of Company G, awarded the prize to a Vermonter named Ai Brown, his two shots measuring four and one-quarter inches from the center. H. J. Peck of the same company, a prominent marksman, was a close second in the match—almost a tie. Col. Berdan opened the proceedings by firing two specimen shots, making a string of five and nine-sixteenths inches. Later on, other officers tried their skill, and among them Capt. Drew, who, borrowing a rifle, lay on his back and, resting the muzzle of the piece on the toe of his boot, fired four shots within the 10-inch ring at the usual 40-rods distance. This manner of shooting was somewhat novel, if not actually original, and became quite popular years after the war, when Creedmoor was established. It was very pleasing to the Wisconsin men, who with several other companies took no part in these contests, having no guns and but little practice, and that only with such rifles as could be borrowed from the more fortunate ones. At another time a Michigan member proved the winner, his three 40-rod off-hand shots measuring six inches, an average of two inches to a shot.

SHOOTING CHICKENS ON A FORGED PASS

On one occasion a chicken shoot was arranged by a certain number of the men who could get passes to go outside the camp line. During the progress of the affair, H. J. Peck, of Company F, appeared on the scene, and with his globe-sighted rifle—one of the best in the regiment—killed off most of the chickens; it began to be whispered around that he was an interloper, that he had no pass, therefore had no right there; so it was proposed to stop his further entries. But he produced a pass, and it was not until the match was over that it was found to be a forged one. Some of the party called it a good joke, but the sergeant in charge thought it was pretty tough, and even went so far as to "d—n a man who would shoot chickens on a forged pass."

The general routine of duty at the Camp of Instruction was as follows: The day began with "buglers' call "at daylight, to be followed by "reveille," and for miles around the Union capitol could be heard the bugles of rifle-men, artillery and cavalry, the shrill fife and drum of the infantry, making one continuous sound of soul-stirring music. It is simply grand to be in such a camp, and this was a monster camp in and around Washington, and listen to the reveille playing on all sides, on the color-line of each regiment, all going at once at fairly daylight. Then would the orderly-sergeants order their companies to "fall in for roll-call," Company A, C, G, etc. Every member was expected to turn out and take his place in the ranks, excepting the sick and those otherwise detailed. The company falls in, in two ranks facing outward—to the right—come to a "front," and to "attention to roll-call, "which is called in alphabetical order, usually by the last name; where there are more than one, or several of the same name, they frequently go by numbers, as instanced in the following story relating to 'a neighboring infantry regiment:

THE NINE SMITHS

A little stranger lieutenant having a detail of 10 men for special duty, called on a certain company and took their names. The men were in line at attention, when the officer began:

"What's your name?"

"Smith."

To the next man: "And what is yours?"

"Smith."

Down went the two on the list, Smith 1, Smith 2. "Well, what's yours?"

"Smith."

The officer began to look funny and grumbled out something about the—peculiarity of the thing; then again: "What may I call your name, then?" "Smith."

This was getting to be too much of a good thing. The officer's face was getting red and his patience giving out. Four Smiths in succession! He looked the men over:

"Confound you, what do you mean?"

But there the detail stood like so many heroic statues. "Well, blast it," and rushing up to No. 5, the excited officer fairly gasped: "Your n-a-m-e?"

It was no use, however, the same prompt answer came, this time in deep stentorian tones, "Smith."

This was too much for little shoulder straps, and, breaking down the street for the Orderly, he swore like a trooper, as he fancied it was a trick; but couldn't find the sergeant, and back he came in utter despair at the thought of being fooled, for he was an excitable little body, and his own men didn't like him. But the list must be made:

"Well, then, for a change, what on earth is your name?" "Smith."

The officer fairly jumped. Then he ripped and swore and jumped again; but there the statues stood,—old soldiers,—looking straight away, the regulation distance. By this time a crowd had gathered, and the officer began to cool down. So he hurried through:

"And yours?" "Smith."

"And next?" "Smith."

"Je—yours? ""Smith."

Here he broke again: "Great Scott! Here's nine Smiths in a row, and another man left. Guess they must grow up by the acre where this crowd came from. Well, yours, my man?" to No. 10.

"Mine, sir! My name's Brown."

"Good heavens! What a relief. The Smith family is exhausted," and as the detail moved off the assembled crowd roared.

After calling the roll, details were made by the Orderly, such as guard duty, police, water squad, etc., members dilatory in turning out being put on these details; otherwise they were made up in regular order. For guard duty at this camp a sufficient number of muskets had been issued,

The officer of the guard was generally a lieutenant, and the officer of the day was a captain or company commander, detailed by the adjutant. The guard detail, officers and men, were for 24 hours' service. After roll-call, streets were cleaned up, tents put in order, all before breakfast call. With us, the instructor required the company cooks, two in number, who were located with fire, pots and kettles, at the foot of the company streets, to have coffee ready and served the first thing after roll-call, to guard against malaria in the winter weather, which this season was particularly damp and sickly, every precaution being taken to protect the health of the soldiers. At least that was the intention, but sometimes the best of intentions are spoiled by a too rigid discipline for appearance sake. For instance: The peremptory order to have the tents in exact line, close to the ground, shaped and sized to present a general appearance—all alike. After they got into the field this rule was abandoned, and the soldiers built their tents for comfort, wherein boards were used, fence rails and logs, the floor raised from the ground and a better protection assured from colds and disease. This camp suffered severely from sickness and deaths, in consequence of the mistaken strictness of the disciplinarian as long as he remained; but After he left us, through the special efforts of Lieut. Col. Ripley, his successor, a general change in this respect was noticeable, concessions were made to comfort, and the soldiers had better privileges granted them in this important respect, really necessary to their health. It was all well enough during the fine fall weather to have the tents trim and in regulation style, but when winter set in, the rigid rule had to be relaxed, and the men allowed to fix up their quarters for comfort and not for show. The medical director of the Army of the Potomac, Chas. S. Tripler, in his report on the sanitary condition of the troops in the vicinity of Washington dated Jan. 28, 1862, says:

"The Berdan Sharpshooters are also in a bad sanitary condition, and not improving. This camp, however, is badly located. I shall visit this brigade personally." He also recommended the building of "pens of logs and slabs the size of the base of the tents, some three feet high, and then to secure the tent upon this for a roof. The camping ground of Berdan Sharpshooters I think should be changed.

Its drainage is bad. This regiment is suffering from measles, and lately severe lung complications have accompanied the disease. A fresh and dry camp, therefore, is in my opinion decidedly necessary for the command. If a suitable ground is selected and the tents put up the way I have suggested, I should look for favorable results."

And on February 6th he reported further: "Measles, which seem to be scourging the whole army of the United States, still break out from time to time in different regiments. Berdan's Sharpshooters have been and are still severely affected with that disease. It is hoped that hospital and field arrangements already made and in progress will soon abate this evil."

The camping ground, however, was not removed. The report closes with a tabulated return, in which the Sharpshooters are put down as follows:

First Berdan Sharpshooters, mean strength, 745, total sick, 71.

Second Berdan Sharpshooters, 720, 132.

Brigade strength 1,465

It was noticeable in this camp that considerably more sickness occurred among the American companies, than was the case in Company A, the Swiss and Germans. Their commander, Capt. Trepp, explained this in the manner of cooking their food. For while the Americans were great hands to fry everything,—fried pork, fried beef, fried hardtack swimming in grease,—Trepp's men boiled their meats, and, with plenty of vegetables, made soups, rarely if ever, eating fried food. It was really forbidden. This, the captain claimed, was the principal cause of their really small sick list. The others understood this after awhile, and resorted more to boiled food than formerly.

Our calls were all made by the bugle. Each company had two buglers, and a regimental band was formed under the instruction of a chief bugler, in the First Regiment Calvin Morse of Company F; and they became sufficiently proficient to make very fair dress parade music, only occasionally the boys would get out of wind, and then there was a great gap in the notes. This caused a general te-heeing along the line, and the most scathing scowl of the instructor could not prevent it. The bugles were also used in the skirmish drill, both company and regimental, in accordance with the commands of the officer commanding. After breakfast, came sick call, which on the bugle sounded a good deal like singing:

> "I'm—sick! I'm—sick!
> Send for doctor, bring the nurse.
> I'm—sick! I'm—sick!
> Hurry doctor, I am worse—I'm—s-i-c-k!"

About nine o'clock we had guard mounting, and which in good weather is an interesting service well worth witnessing. Drills, company or regimental as it happened, occurred twice a day, and therein the Sharpshooters made a fine appearance, and, as Col. Ripley expressed it, became "wonderfully proficient." But we had a proficient instructor, and also apt and careful company officers. Among them may be mentioned Capt. Drew, who was thoroughly conversant with the tactics before entering the service, and his company was very fortunate in having accepted him for their commander. He was not only very popular with them, but throughout the entire First Regiment.

There were other calls going on through the day, such as "fatigue call" for working parties, "officers' call," the "assembly," the "retreat" at sunset, "tattoo" at 9 p m., and "taps" half an hour later, when lights were put out and all of the enlisted men not on duty abed or supposed to be. Toward the close of the afternoon before "retreat," weather permitting, dress parade was held. This was a popular feature of camp life, witnessed generally by many spectators, and really a grand performance. Here reports were made as to the condition of the companies, whether they were all "present or accounted for," orders were read by the adjutant, and inspections and reviews frequently occurred. How agreeable Col. Mears used to make it for a certain field officer who sometimes persisted in wearing white pantaloons when on duty, especially when some of his lady friends were present. Who would not like to have been sergeant-major in those days? How pleasantly Mears used to ask for the whereabouts of that unfortunate gent! The regimental orders signed "J. Smith Brown, Acting Adjutant," met with little favor at our hands. How beautifully he used to "about face!"

On Sundays we had, besides our regular cleaning up, Sunday morning inspections, which included dress, general appearance, packed knapsacks, etc. Also, during the forenoon on church call brought the entire regiment, excepting those on duty, to the parade ground, where the chaplain officiated. In bad weather these duties and services were dispensed with.

One feature introduced into the drill was the charging across the wide parade ground onto and over the high board fence of "Corcoran's grounds." Mr. Corcoran was a prominent and wealthy property holder living in the district. To climb this fence required a good jump and a secure hold on top. It was exercise that the feeble and sickly had no business with, but was a course of training very suitable for our service. At the command to advance as skirmishers, or to charge in close order, if the fence was in the way, it must be scaled, the men dashing forward thereafter until summoned to halt or retreat, by bugle or otherwise.

A speck of trouble threatened the Sharpshooters because of the breaking away of fence boards and the action of the military authorities thereon, as instanced in the following:

GLENWOOD CEMETERY, Feb. 4, 1862.

Dear Sir:—I regret being again compelled to trouble you in relation to the Berdan Sharpshooters destroying the fence on the place. Since I wrote to you last they have refrained from troubling me much until the last four or five days when they commenced operations again, and yesterday made a decided attack. Will you be kind enough to send an orderly with the bearer, my son, to examine and report to you? Also please send such message to the officers of the regiment as you think will prevent a recurrence of these depredations, and greatly oblige

Yours very respectfully,

G. CLENDENIN, Supt.

To GEN'L A. PORTER.

This document was indorsed as follows:

Respectfully forwarded to Headquarters Army of the

Potomac. A. PORTER, Provost Marshal.

HEADQUARTERS ARMY OF THE POTOMAC, Feb. 6, 1862. Respectfully referred to Col. Berdan with instructions to ascertain the names of the men who, in spite of orders, continue to commit depredations on the Glenwood Cemetery, and to confine them in the Guardhouse and prefer charges against them. The general commanding desires an example to be made of these reported and willful violations of his reiterated instructions.

By command of Major General McClellan,

JAS. A. HARDIE, Lt.-Col. A. D. C.

Whether any of the fence-thieves were ever caught, or whether their names were ascertained, it is useless to ask at this late day. When we left for the Peninsula, however, but little of the cemetery fence remained in "good standing." Even Gen. McClellan was powerless to check the course of the Sharpshooters when they sought food and fuel.

While the men were being steadily drilled in all the movements of the tactics,—excepting the manual, as arms were scarce, although that was practiced more or less by companies with a few guns, not as a regiment,—it must not be supposed it was all work and no play. For, besides the target practice, which was in itself an amusement, other diversions were indulged in of a nature to train them for arduous duty in active service, particularly in marching, destined to be often long and fatiguing. Therefore, foot ball, jumping, racing, wrestling, boxing and fencing, were prominent in the sports, which seemed also to keep up a good feeling among the men, and between the companies. It is worthy of record, also, that in this peculiar organization of companies from different states jealousy was unknown; on the contrary, they were like a band of brothers, imbued with the one feeling of patriotism in their voluntary enlistment for three years, unless sooner discharged. But few came from the same town, and but few were known to each other before enlistment. It was in many respects a remarkable organization. Not that all were as perfect as possible, or their behavior faultless; for no such thing as a regiment or company, without fault-finding and discontent, without grumblers, or without their share of "sorry soldiers "ever existed. This is plainly in the course of nature, and in the volunteer service no one regiment was very much better than another in this respect.

As a fair example, however, of the character of the men composing this organization, I give the following compliment paid the second and third Vermont companies by Col. Stoughton years after the war. First, he refers to the regardful act of the legislature of the state of Vermont, providing for a special allowance of seven dollars per month for their enlisted men, and then says: "About the 20th of November, the second company of Sharpshooters, numbering, officers and men 91, started for Washington, to join the Second Regiment, where it became Company E. To go back to the trip to Washington, I must give the company as high a compliment as any they deserved during the war, and that is, upon arriving in New York City, on Peck Slip pier, 25 East river, on the 'Elm City,' they marched up to Park Barracks where every soldier from New England remembers having once been, where they got their first real army fare, and, upon ascertaining they were to leave Jersey City at four o'clock that afternoon, they with one accord desired a pass to go out into the city, none of them having been in New York before. The captain, much to the astonishment of the regular army officer in command of the barracks, granted the passes with the promise that they should all return in time to march to the ferry. At the appointed time every officer and man was in line, which astonished the commander of the barracks as much as the granting of the passes had done in the morning, and with a single exception, not a man was intoxicated, and he was able to march to the train." The third company raised afterwards (H, of the Second), in which the colonel, then Capt. Stoughton, took part, "was another fine body of men, who were complimented both in New York and Philadelphia as they passed through those two cities." The Wisconsin company also proved their "bringing up," by taking in the city of New York, returning in time to receive their quota of loud-tasting bolognas furnished by the Dutch sutler, as they broke camp at Weehawken for

Washington. They were a fine looking body of men, and so recognized by all who saw them. Thus did the West vie with the East.

As showing how the boys amused themselves even at others' expense, I will give the experience of Company D, on their arrival in camp, Jan. 3, 1862. To go back to their starting point: This company was recruited in the fall of '61, from Chenango, Otsego, Herkimer and Oneida counties, New York. One would-be officer of the company had worked hard for a commission, and was, in his own estimation, at least, better fitted for it than any of his comrades. His modesty was not a candle to his merit. Before leaving Utica he had, in anticipation of his speedy promotion, gotten for himself an officer's outfit. His jaunty cap bore conspicuously in front the magical letters "H. S. S. S." As soon as the company reached Camp of Instruction, the unsympathizing veterans of the hillside thronged to welcome the tired recruits, greeting them on seeing these letters on their doughty champion's cap, with the shout: "Unfortunate Soldiers Sadly Sold." However time-worn this translation of these cabalistic letters may have been to the veterans, it was novel, although humiliating enough to the recruits, foot-sore and weary as they were, though excessively patriotic. The company soon affiliated and were happy as could be with their comrades of the other companies. Their citizen's clothes were at a premium. They had no trouble in lending (?) what little money they had brought with them from home, to their promising neighbors, who gave them much *advice,* but little else for their generosity. What tricks their older comrades used to play upon them during their tours of night guard duty. What a pleasure it was to be corporal of the guard in those days, with the whole chain of sentinels bawling after him at one and the same time for causeless, frivolous pretexts. How enjoyable it was for him, in looking up his relief at midnight, to find their belts on the tent poles misplaced, and to receive a cuff on the ear, or the heel of a shoe in the face, when he awoke the wrong parties, as he was almost certain to do. How enjoyable Capt. Hastings made things for the entire guard and camp when he happened to be officer of the day!

Shortly after their arrival one of the Company D men got into trouble in Washington. It was on a Sunday, and this man whose name was Henry C. Vedder, wanted to hear a celebrated clergyman preach at the capitol, while his two companions preferred to enjoy the sunshine and queer sights of that then somewhat antiquated city. Vedder was persistent, and left the others in disgust to follow out his devout inclinations, forgetting that his companions had the one pass for the three, so that he was soon arrested by the provost-guard who refused to listen to his animated story about the pass, hustling him off to the guardhouse without ceremony, where he remained the entire Sunday, musing no doubt upon the irreverence of his companions to say nothing of his own wretched surroundings, with the certainty of being hounded for at least a week by the tantalizing comrades of his company.

Strictness in military discipline is essential to good order and successful soldiership. Without a proper regard therefor, no army can be relied on in time of need, and therefore the absolute necessity while in camp or garrison to enforce respect for orders, for the observance of which, officers and men alike are held responsible, no deviation therefrom being allowed. "Obey your commands," is the first and imperative duty of a soldier. It is true that in the volunteer service, particularly in its first stages, many things apparently trivial in character were overlooked, until at least the men had been long enough in service to understand they were no longer civilians, and their natural independence curtailed or broken, to fit them for their new condition; so that, while in Camp of Instruction many little acts "contrary to good order and military discipline," were disregarded by even the most rigid disciplinarian. After they got into the field with the enemy before them, it was different, and for what elsewhere (in drill camps) would be considered slight offenses, heavy punishment was often inflicted. A case in point, amusing to the boys, is given to show how reckless the new volunteer sometimes became, regardless of consequences, with the chances all against him.

THE CUSSED VOLUNTEER

In Company F was a well-made, hardy looking six-footer, of a rather uncontrollable disposition, unused to discipline, and especially that kind requiring him to look up to others whose superiority was more in their relative positions in the service than in their physical makeup. This stalwart Vermonter was not always very particular as to how he conducted himself when officers were around, especially if they were really inferior to him in muscle. One morning this man was on guard, and happened to be in one of his too-frequent independent moods,—"a heap of sarcasm,"—when along came one of the field officers in full uniform, just from the city, with gold epaulettes on his shoulders, high cocked hat, and dangling sabre rattling at every step; when, after taking a most tantalizing stare at the officer, deliberately sticking his bayoneted gun in the ground, he mounted a fence rail, and with his elbows stuck down in his knees, his chin buried deep in his hands, called out, as he afterwards claimed, "in a very sociable manner "

"I say! Come over here a moment."

To say that the officer looked astounded at the audacity of the volunteer from Vermont is expressing it too mild. His cheeks turned white, then red in a moment, while his face worked hard and rapid in a desperate endeavor to control his rage, but finally toning down his voice as calmly as it were at all possible, yelled out to the reckless sentinel to explain his conduct then and there. But as the insolent camp guard merely wanted some tobacco,—"to take a friendly chew,"—the officer bolted with rage into camp to headquarters, where Col. Berdan was treated to a specimen *of regular* swearing, at "the damnable impudence of his cursed volunteers."

In most every encampment there is at least one officer who is continually getting into hot water, so to speak. Who seems to be constituted a target for all the rough hits and slang phrases of the camp, caused principally by a too earnest desire to show his authority while on duty. The picture may be recognized in every regiment, wherein the obstreperous martinet is frequently taken down, for trying to fill the guardhouse with men of other companies for very little causes. Such officers soon get to be despised. There are other officers more fortunate in their disposition, for whom the men could not do too much. And yet, the real test was on the field of battle; if the officers stayed with their men, their respect was honorably earned. If they tried to keep out and away from the line of danger, it was deservedly lost.

The regiment was reviewed late in the fall by Gen. McDowell, and visited at various times by those noted war governors of the West and East, Randall of Wisconsin, Blair of Michigan, Ramsey of Minnesota, Berry of New Hampshire, and Sprague of Rhode Island. Also by Senators Wilkinson (Minn.), Doolittle (Wis.), Chandler (Mich.), and Harris (N. Y.), who were looking after the welfare of the volunteers from their respective states.

As the spring-time approached, every preparation was made by all the troops about Washington for a forward movement, from the camps of instruction to active service. The quartermasters were particularly busy, and in the Sharpshooter regiments were the recipients of a large amount of extra clothing, blankets, etc., turned in for safe keeping until needed in the future. Marching orders were getting common, and war rumors became frequent as the spring advanced.

FIRST CAMPAIGN

FROM WASHINGTON TO HARRISON S LANDING.
THE PENINSULA CAMPAIGN.

On the 20th of March, 1862, the First Regiment of Sharpshooters broke camp at Washington in the afternoon, and marching through the city, proceeded over Long Bridge to a point beyond Alexandria, in Virginia, where they arrived long after dark after a very fatiguing march in a soaking rain through a sea of mud,—said to be 15 miles. It was the regiment's first march, and proved a hard one with their backs weighted down with heavy knap-sacks,—extra clothing, blankets, etc.,—making many a lame back and sore shoulder. Added to this, their first troubles, general headquarters could not be found, and considerable standing around occurred before they were luckily piloted to an old camp now deserted, of the 69th New York, introduced to us as "Camp Californy." But notwithstanding this rough introduction to active service, the regiment had started forth with light hearts, for at last they were leaving a long encampment, chafing and fretting with a pardonable impatience to get away,—to "do something or go home,"—for new, more active and warlike scenes. After six months camp life they were anxious to get to the front, and see for themselves what manner of man this enemy was they had heard so much about. They were at last going to have an opportunity to size up a "Johnny Reb."

I will not attempt to describe their feelings as they marched out of Washington; it was a mixture of joy and sadness, hopes and fears, expressed in a merry laugh or a long-drawn sigh. Not a cowardly fear, but that natural anxiety for the ultimate result of the movement, wherein the individual life as well as the Union was at stake. A number unable to march were left behind, some of whom never caught up—being discharged.

The regiment, except the two companies having target rifles, were armed with Colt's five-shot revolving rifles, the long promised Sharps not having arrived. It was thought at first that these Colts would not shoot true, but this proved not exactly the case as they were pretty good line shooters, although there was some danger of all the chambers exploding at once. The shooting qualities of this arm were tested in several instances before getting into action, and some good shots were noted. Andrew J. Peirce, of Company G, a very clean and tasty soldier, while on the way down the Potomac made a trial shot of the five chambers in the presence of the regimental officers, at a buoy bobbing up in the river some 400 yards distant, and the result was thus announced by Col. Berdan, who, with the other officers, were intently watching with their field glasses:

"There, that will do, sir. You have struck the buoy twice, and 'twas well done."

Peirce had not an opportunity heretofore to make any targets, on account 'of the Wisconsin company having no arms in Camp of Instruction, and this, his first chance to draw a bead, was very satisfactory to the officers mentioned.

The regimental officers were now as follows:

FIRST REGIMENT.

Colonel—Hiram Berdan, of New York.

Lieutenant-Colonel—Wm. Y. W. Ripley, of Vermont.

Major—Casper Trepp, of New York.

Adjutant—F. A. Willett, of Michigan.

Quartermaster—W, H. B. Beebe, of New York.

Chaplain—Rev. Gurdon S. Coit, of Connecticut.

Surgeon—Guy C. Marshall, of New York.

The lieutenant-colonel and major ranked from Dec. 1, 1861. "Col." Ripley had seen service as captain in the 1st Vermont Volunteers. Maj. Trepp, formerly captain of Company A, had received a good military education in Switzerland, and was in active service in Europe. The quartermaster was a well-known and once popular hatter of New York city.

Much doubt had been entertained by old army officers, as to our efficiency as a distinctive branch of service—that of sharpshooting and skirmishing. But this feeling changed after the breech-loading system was developed in their first action, and the success there attained never failed thereafter.

SECOND REGIMENT.

Colonel—Henry A. V. Post, of New York. Lieutenant-Colonel—Francis Peteler, of Minnesota. Major—Amos B. Jones, of New Hampshire. Adjutant—Lewis C. Parmelee, of Connecticut. Quartermaster—B. S. Calef, of Boston. Chaplain—Lorenzo Barber, of Albany, N. Y. Surgeon—Chas. P. Hale, of New Hampshire.

This regiment left Camp of Instruction about the same time as the First, being assigned to the army under Gen. McDowell, and they were armed and equipped the same as the First Regiment. As the movements of McDowell's corps was intended to be in conjunction, to co-operate with McClellan's troops in the advance on Richmond, this campaign includes their movements as far as the Second Sharpshooters are concerned, which will be taken up in the interim.

Leaving the "Californy "camp on the 21st, Berdan's regiment embarked in the evening at Alexandria on board steam transport Emperor, and during the night men were detailed carrying supplies and baggage to different steamboats. It being a rainy and very dark night, and many soldiers from the different regiments running to and fro, it was not strange that accidents should occur in the confusion, and several fell overboard to be rescued from their cold bath, one man being drowned. W. G. Smith and Jno S. Tillotson, of Company G, received credit for pulling out two of these men. It was a dangerous place and the wonder is that more were not lost in the darkness, owing for some unaccountable reason to a remarkable scarcity of lights on the docks. Early the next morning the transport steamed down the Potomac in company with many others, some 22 in all, containing the division of Gen. Fitz John Porter of the 3d corps of the Army of the Potomac, and arrived the afternoon of the 23d opposite Fortress Monroe, passing several deserted works *en route*.

It was a beautiful day when they left Alexandria after the drenching weather just experienced, and the soldiers easily forgot the previous night's wetting and their tiresome, muddy march from Washington, in the general enthusiasm depicted on every countenance at the grand pageant before them; as all the steamers having been ordered to pass in review ran first upstream a short distance, when turning downward they passed Gen. Porter's flagship amid the roar of saluting cannon, the waving of flags, cheers of patriots, and bands of music playing on every side. Nor was the excitement abated during their pleasant sail downstream until they approached Mt. Vernon, when all seemed inspired with the one feeling of reverence as hats came off and sudden quietness prevailed, except with the bands changing their lively tunes to more solemn strains, in token of respect for the tomb of George Washington. And it was good to turn their attention from the hilarious to more serious thoughts of home and friends far North, and to peer into the near future with its uncertainties and its forebodings. For, of all places in the hearts of patriotic 'Americans, there is none to produce the same feeling of veneration existing on a visit to this hallowed spot. No matter how many great and worthy men we have had, soldiers or civilians, there can be but one Washington.

On our arrival at Fortress Monroe we found Hampton Roads harboring hundreds of vessels, moving about or discharging troops and supplies, guns and ammunition. The wonderful Monitor had but lately wound up the destructive career of the rebel ram Merrimac, in the greatest naval battle known, and was now riding peacefully at anchor,—an advanced sentinel,—ready to serve the balance of the Confederate navy by knocking them out of existence, should they dare to show up, or threaten our transport vessels.

During the morning of the 24th the regiment landed at Hampton, on the Virginia peninsula, with appetites sharpened, their rations having by some oversight been placed on board another transport. The men were more or less starved on this trip, the invigorating breezes, from the Chesapeake having a very stimulating effect on the rarely failing appetites of the healthy members. In such hungry dilemmas the roughest food often proves very acceptable, and the writer experienced a keen relish for a rind of raw bacon about a foot square, and it proved one of the sweetest morsels ever masticated by this hungry volunteer.

The village of Hampton was deserted and in ruins, having been burned by the rebel Gen. Magruder in August, 1861, to prevent its being used for quartering Union troops. It was denounced as a wanton act, without warning to defenceless inhabitants, forced from blazing beds and homes at the midnight hour. And at the time of which I write, little else could be found there but tall, blackened chimneys towering high above heaps of charred timbers, and burnt and crumbling bricks—a startling picture of war's desolation.

While on Hampton beach the boys waded in waist deep after oysters and other shell-fish, which were served up in all manner of styles, around huge fires started on the shore. There were roast clams, fried oysters, stewed periwinkles and boiled muscles. It was one of the good times enjoyed by the soldiers, and jokes and songs were in order, with long and strong choruses echoing down the rebel shores. And if there were any rebels on the other shore they probably heard the chorus. It was a regular concert. Other regiments had their fun also, for this might properly be called, to many, their first day in rebeldom, the enemy's scouts being not far distant, and as it was uncertain where they would be to-morrow, they were bound to make the most of it. In the singing, the great army choruses were taken up, when they were "Way down south in Dixie", or marching on with "John Brown ". It was catching, and rank and file, the line, field and staff, were alike affected. So they kept it up, until the stern "Fall in! "reminded them of a different kind of fun ahead. But the ever changing character of soldier life would not admit of much time speculating on the future. And it was better so, that military ardor and excitement take the place of deep brooding over useless imaginings. Thus it happened soon after, on the bugle sounding the "assembly," when the Sharpshooters went into temporary camp nearby, in an old cornfield four miles from Ft. Monroe, among a large body of troops. It was the beginning of war.

BIG BETHEL

March 27, 1862.

At an early hour, before dawn, the Sharpshooters left their encampment to take part in a grand reconnoissance by the division of Gen. Porter, which proceeded on two parallel roads, the Sharpshooters ahead in line of skirmishers—one-half under Col. Berdan, the other wing under Lieut.-Col. Ripley. It was the first movement of the regiment in active service, and with light hearts and smiles of joy at the opportunity they sprang forward to their position of honor—the front line. Never were troops more eager to get out into the field of active duty. It was like a holiday excursion for them that day, whatever it might be thereafter. A position was awarded them, that depended upon their efficiency as to whether they would retain it. Their reputation was to be made or lost on this reconnoissance. The eyes of their generals were upon them, and upon them devolved the duty of rendering a good account of themselves—and they succeeded admirably. Their advance through dense woods and entangling thickets, over heavy plowed fields, wet and muddy meadows, breaking down and scaling fences, often fording small streams, was made with an eagerness and rapidity that soon left their supports far in the rear, and several times they were obliged to halt until they came up. Until finally Capt. Auchmuty of Gen. Morell's staff, rode up to enquire with the general's compliments: "If the Sharpshooters intended to go on alone, or would they prefer to wait for support." Even this scarcely checked them, especially after the rebel cavalry came in sight and shots were exchanged. A sort of running fight ensued, the cavalry falling back continually before our advance. On arriving at Great Bethel they found the enemy hurriedly leaving, their rear guard being attacked by the Sharpshooters with some effect, particularly among their cavalry, and several prisoners were taken. The movement was continued three miles beyond Bethel, towards Yorktown, but meeting no opposition—no enemy to contend with—they were ordered back to "Camp Porter," the object of the reconnoissance having been effected. The regiment arrived back to camp during the night after a tiresome tramp of some 30 miles. It was an important affair for them, their conduct being pronounced very satisfactory by the generals commanding. And while it proved the efficiency of their drill and instruction, it also tested their endurance for hard marching, of which this day's work was a particularly severe trial, and but for their constant exercise and training during the past fall and winter months they must have failed to keep up without a long list of stragglers. For an initiatory performance, they could never have done better. They were no longer raw troops, but were fast earning the title of "old soldiers."

An incident occurred while we were lying at Hampton wherein a Company F man, C. G. Odell, distinguished himself as an earnest champion of the defenceless. It was while on picket. The line ran close to a farmhouse, where some U. S. soldiers (regulars) were stationed. The family living between the lines did not have a good opportunity of getting food for themselves, and what scanty fare they did have was spread before the children, the parents serving them first; when one of the above mentioned soldiers was going to sit down and eat the children's portion, despite the expostulations of the parents. Odell tried to reason with the brute, but he would not listen to reason; whereupon the Sharpshooter threatened him with the bayonet and five revolving shots if he didn't desist—"gave him to understand he would have to walk over *my* dead body before he took the food out of those children's mouths." This had the happy effect of forcing the fellow away, for which the deep gratitude of the entire family, freely expressed, was bestowed on Odell. Soon after this occurrence Odell again distinguished himself, in getting outside the lines, away off into a rebel residence, attracted thither by a young lady—gay deceiver—whereby he came near being *captured*. He had previously aided in freeing some negroes, when the girl sailed along and enticed him away. For this episode he was well laughed at by the boys, and scolded hard by the colonel. Yet he declared he had lots of fun, "whether the girl went back on him or not."

On the 3d of April Gen. McClellan arrived, and great preparations were made for an immediate forward movement. The troops in the field at this time according to Gen. McClellan's own report, and which moved promptly the following day, were:

Third Corps, Brig.- Gen. Heintzelman.—Two divisions, Porter and Hamilton; Averell's cavalry, and [General John] Sedgwick's division of the 2d corps.

Fourth Corps, Brig.- Gen. Keyes.—Two divisions, Smith and Couch, and 5th regular cavalry.

Syke's Brigade of regular infantry, together with Hunt's artillery reserve.

In all, 58,000 men and 100 guns, besides the division artillery. Casey's division of the 4th corps was unable to move for want of wagons, and Richardson's and [General Joseph "Fighting Joe"] Hooker's divisions of the 2d and 3d corps had not arrived.

The Sharpshooters again led the advance of Fitz John Porter's division, in the movement commencing on the morning of April 4th. The boys appreciated the confidence placed in them by this repetition of the honor bestowed, and proudly marched forth—officers and men—determined to do all in their power to show that it had not been misplaced. At an early hour before daylight they were up and ready, the regiment taking up the line of march at the head of the column, and passing Bethel halted for the night in a cornfield at a place called Cockletown, 24 miles distant. Although the distance reported for this day may have been somewhat greater than the actual number of miles by direct road, it should be borne in mind that troops do not always follow direct routes: on the contrary often diverge from the same, especially when "feeling their way". This will account for any difference that may hereafter manifest itself in regard to the real distance between given points.

HOWARD'S BRIDGE

April 4, 1862.

Before bivouacking the Sharpshooters had routed on the way a small force of the enemy consisting of 400 Mississippi infantry, two pieces of artillery and some cavalry, at the crossing of a small stream called the Poquosin, where they planted their flag on a small earth-work, capturing some prisoners; one company (B) going forward in line of skirmishers over the field, the others moving up as a support. A few shots from our artillery and a volley from the Sharpshooters followed the retreating foe, who hurried off as our skirmishers deployed out and advanced onto their position. It wasn't much of a fight, but what there was, the Sharpshooters got the glory of it.

Gen. Morell commanding 2d brigade of Gen. Porter's division, in his report to Gen. Porter of this affair, says:

"Pursuant to orders for the advance of the Army of the Potomac, my brigade, composed of the 14th New York, Col. McQuade; 4th Michigan, Col. Woodbury; 9th Massachusetts, Col. Cass; and 62d Pennsylvania, Col. Black; moved from Camp No. 2, near Hampton, at five o'clock A. M., on the 4th current, preceded by Col. Averell's cavalry and Col. Berdan's Sharpshooters, and escorting Griffin's and Weeden's batteries of artillery. I marched to Big Bethel over the same route as in the reconnoissance of the 27th ult. [Abbreviation for *ultimo*, meaning "of last month."] Beyond Big Bethel the cavalry fell to the rear, the Sharpshooters, as skirmishers, continuing in front of my brigade, which had the honor of leading the column. A small body of the enemy's cavalry retired as we advanced, and, though frequently in sight, kept out of reach. As we approached Howard's[2] Bridge over the Poquosin river I threw forward part of the 14th New York, also as skirmishers, and advanced with them and the Sharpshooters to ascertain if the works which I had reconnoitered on the 27th ult. were still occupied. When within a few hundred yards of them the enemy opened fire upon us. Meanwhile the balance of the 14th had deployed to the right. The 4th Michigan by your order, extended on their right to the river, and the artillery had come to the front. The whole steadily pressed forward, and after a slight resistance the enemy retreated."

[2]*General Oliver Otis Howard lost his right arm while leading his men against Confederate forces at Fair Oaks in June 1862. He returned to command and was among the first at Gettysburg in July, 1863. After the war, he commanded forces in the west during the Indian Wars and wrote My Life and Experiences Among Our Hostile Indians.*

While awaiting orders to resume the movement, some of the men did a little foraging, and Eugene Paine, of Company F, tells how they rolled out a hogshead from a building, and covered themselves with molasses, if not glory; a fierce attack being made on the sticky stuff, with their hands and faces and clothes besmeared, some coming out of the fracas with only their cup handles, and all bearing "sweet evidence "of the struggle to get the lion's share. This is related as one of the little recreations the boys indulged in,—when they got a chance,—and while it would not be considered exactly proper according to the rules in force governing the conduct of the troops, it was among the expected things when the opportunity was presented. It was tough on the owner, but that's what he contributed "towards the maintenance of the army" and the amusement of the "boys."

BATTLE OF YORKTOWN

April 5, 1862.

[This day's fight was called by Gen. Porter, the "Battle of Yorktown," the succeeding operations the "Siege of Yorktown."]

The next morning the Sharpshooters again advanced, and rapidly, with a scanty supply of rations, and after scouting awhile through woods and fields the rain at times pouring fast which, though drenching in character, failed to dampen their ardor, at about ten in the forenoon were suddenly fired on by a rebel field-piece in front of Yorktown. The screaming shell passed harmlessly over into a field beyond, and was followed by several others without damage to the men. The first shot, which came quartering over "G" company, well-aimed but a little high, had the remarkable effect of causing almost every man to duck, which movement extended to some of the other immediate companies. Such a droll occurrence, such grotesque dodging, never was seen again in that regiment. But the shell came so sudden and unexpected, and so close with its shrieking noise, the first many had ever heard, that the men, governed by the same impulse, ducked and crouched simultaneously, as if instructed—one time and one motion. The next moment they were up again, and with loud hurrahs, and laughter at each other, they rushed ahead down the road on double-quick. As the riflemen pressed forward the enemy fell hurriedly back and soon after, far in advance, approached within sight of the formidable looking earth-works next to York river, computed by our battery men 1,800 yards distant, and which were well mounted with guns of large caliber. These forces were commanded by Gen. J. B. Magruder.

Leaving the road on the right, the Wisconsin men with the Swiss company deployed out in an open field, the latter on the right of the line, where they remained upwards of an hour in support of Weeden's battery which had hurried up, taken position and opened fire, and which was afterwards joined by Griffin's battery on their right. The shell of the enemy came rapidly over, bursting in close proximity to the riflemen, the pieces striking the ground around them but without injuring them. Not so with the artillery, which had one man killed and several wounded during that time. The balance of our regiment was distributed in different parts of the field on either side of the road. The rebel infantry drawn up in front of the works, were soon scattered and sought cover behind the same. The Wisconsin company was finally assembled and marched to some buildings in a peach orchard on the left of the road, where they rested under arms an hour. Morell's brigade was now in position supporting the batteries behind us, while the other troops were hurrying forward, but did not reach the vicinity until afternoon. Meanwhile the target riflemen had taken position on the left, behind a fence 800 yards from the enemy's works, and were soon joined by men from other companies. New Hampshire, Vermont, Michigan and Wisconsin, were principally represented at that point. While here the Vermonters cried out: "Corporal Peck "(C. W.) "is hit," the first casualty in that company. He received a severe wound but didn't leave to stay, returning for more hard work and honest service. During this time Company B had been surprised by a masked battery ahead, and on receiving a heavy discharge of canister shot were ordered back to a line with the rest of the regiment. Lieut. Albert R. Barret, (formerly orderly sergeant of Company H), says of his company: "In that battle of Yorktown, when we were ordered up, my company (H), in passing to the front to take position on a hill as near the enemy's works as possible, had to cross a slight hollow, and, as we did so, a shower of bullets flew around and over us. We took double-quick and passed safely over, but many of us had bullet marks in our clothes, the balls also striking the ground in front, every step we took."

From the peach orchard fence the Sharpshooters proved themselves. In a very short time they succeeded in silencing a number of cannon in their front, which the enemy were unable to load, so fast and thick did Colt, Sharps and target-rifle bullets come in upon them. Their futile attempts to man their guns, their excited gestures running to and fro, were plainly to be seen by our men, and with cheers they drove them off, or dropped them, whenever they came forward. They were completely silenced, and the Sharpshooters thus demonstrated their efficiency for such an occasion.

There was but one Sharps rifle in the regiment at the time, which was the personal property of Truman Head, better known as "Old Californy," or "California Joe," a member of Company C, and who gave most convincing proofs of his skill as a marksman. This particular Sharps rifle was purchased while at Camp of Instruction, and had a sabre bayonet and single trigger. But the men, after a careful examination of the outfit, while they unanimously endorsed the rifle, decided they would rather have the angular bayonet as less cumbersome, and more to the "point."

After a resting spell and a scanty demand on the haversack, the rebel bullets in the meantime whizzing wildly in and around the yard and buildings, the Wisconsinites and Vermonters took up a position on the right of the road in the field first entered, where they remained until after nine o'clock at night, being exposed during that time to the fire of the enemy's cannon on the right of the works, also to a cross-fire from the left during the latter part of the afternoon, at a time when those at the peach orchard fence had been called off, owing to an anticipated attack from the rebel cavalry, who came out from behind their works, presenting a bold front on the open plain as they drew up in line, threatening to ride down the five-shooting riflemen by the roadside, and cut off those in the orchard. The men with the Colts quietly awaited their coming, and had they made the rash attempt but few-would ever have returned. With five shots from every man at close quarters, death and destruction awaited them. But a Union shell exploded in their midst, scattering them hurriedly, while several well-aimed rifle bullets helped to hurry them back to cover. The officer in command fell,—'twas claimed he received the contents of the Sharps rifle,—his white bosom presenting a blood-stained mark as he tumbled from his horse, which was reported as plainly discernible through one of the strong rifle telescopes brought into use.

On several occasions the rebel shell broke the fence rails above and ploughed through the small embankment where our men lay, throwing dirt over them; once, when the guns of the enemy were rapidly at work sending these shrieking shells closely over, James S. Webster and A. J. Peirce, of Company G, were suddenly, but harmlessly, elevated from the ground by one of these missiles penetrating the bank under and between them, which, landing in front of Lieut. Marble, C. A. Stevens, George Whitson and Wm. W. Sweet, phizzed out. Had the shell exploded, many would have been hurt. It was an exciting time, yet the members of the different companies kept cool, behaving like veterans. At sunset the rebel bands played "Dixie," which they immediately followed up by a terrible cannonading from all points, trying hard to demoralize the Sharpshooters, but failed. Our men kept quiet and took the "fiery shower" with the utmost composure. The Union batteries responded with vigor, and for a time war's music filled the air with all its loud-mouthed, terrific tones.

The casualties this day in the regiment were not large, considering the time—upwards of ten hours—they were under fire of shot and shell, there being but three killed and six wounded, but many very narrow escapes. The first man killed in the regiment was Private John S. M. Ide, of New Hampshire, who, while exchanging shots from an exposed position in front of an old building with a Confederate concealed behind a distant tree top that was toppled over in front of the works, was brained by the enemy's bullet. And it was not until night had closed the day's shooting that his body could be safely removed. On learning of the fall of this man, Col. Ripley, notwithstanding the dangerous approach to the fatal spot, and that his field-duties did not oblige him to thus expose himself, boldly walked down the lane which was at the time completely under the rebel fire. With a quick step, but erect, this good officer advanced, the admiration of hundreds of eye witnesses, while bullets plowed and dusted the ground around him. On reaching the body of the prostrate rifleman he inquired into the manner Ide had been shooting, then picking up the fallen man's rifle, screwed up the telescope one notch, believing that Ide had been shooting under. "I'll try him a shot at one notch higher anyway," he said; then taking position, the man in the tree top was discovered, a quick aim and interchange of shots followed. Ripley escaped harmless as the ball spattered in the log building behind him. But the grey-backed fellow—well, there were no more shots from that tree top. Whether killed or scared to death, it was a sure case of a "gone Johnny." Private David Phelps, of Company H, was killed this day, and later on, Daniel C. Painter, of Company B, and Sergt. James Way, of Company C, were wounded.

At half-past nine P. M., the Sharpshooters, having been all this time thus far in advance of the other troops, were as one of the guards in charge of a considerable amount of camp utensils and stores left there when the troops moved off. He told a story on one of the sutlers who had remained at Hampton with his goods. The latter imbibed too freely on his unsold and now unbottled beer, and getting very patriotic made speeches to the guards and company cooks, to his ultimate loss of a roll of greenbacks, which were found and confiscated by some of the camp followers, the sutler being too drunk to prove property.

From the nature of the ground it was impossible to get onto the enemy's works without considerable preliminary preparations, owing to the swampy woods, the flooded roads, and fallen trees along the line of the Warwick—extending from Yorktown to the James, where the Confederate gun-boats had full sway. Therefore having reconnoitered the enemy's position sufficiently to satisfy him that much loss of life would result from an immediate assault, and with very doubtful success in front of the Yorktown fortifications—strong bastioned works—whatever might be the result to the left, in the swamps, also strongly covered by the enemy's batteries, Gen. McClellan determined to besiege Yorktown, and work was immediately commenced. In his report on this decision McClellan says: "Instant assault would have been simple folly."

Gen. Barnard, chief engineer, in favoring only siege-operations in front of Yorktown, said: "It was deemed too hazardous to attempt a reduction of the place by assault."

Gen. Keyes, commanding the 4th corps, gave it as his opinion that: "The line in front of us was one of the strongest ever opposed to an invading force in any country."

And as showing how quickly the army moved after Gen. McClellan arrived at Hampton, without any delay whatever, Gen. Keyes adds: "Not a day was lost in the advance, and in fact we marched so quickly and so rapidly, that many of our animals were 24 and 48 hours without a ration of forage."

On the 10th of April the Sharpshooters moved back a half mile and made a camp not far from the river. The other troops also encamped in the fields before Yorktown, making one grand encampment known as "Camp Winfield Scott." That of the Sharpshooters was very nicely arranged, cedar bushes and small trees being planted in front of the tents and along the color line, which served the double purpose of shade trees and to conceal their position from the enemy's lookouts, rendering a successful shelling by rebel artillerists an uncertainty. Arches were formed of cedar brush over the entrance to each street, with letter of company in center of same, so that there was probably no regiment in the field that presented a better arranged camp than that of the First United States Sharpshooters before Yorktown.

THE SIEGE OF YORKTOWN

April 10—May 4, 1862.

During the progress of the siege, which may properly be stated to have commenced about April 10th, the Sharpshooters furnished daily details of 60 men, who leaving camp before day break took up a position in rifle pits in advance of the fatigue parties, and watching the rebel works during the day, were relieved at night by other troops and returned to camp. Works were in the meantime hurriedly thrown up, roads built, parallels dug, in fact everything necessary was being done to protect the artillerists and the advance of the troops when the struggle should commence for the possession of the position before them. During this time the fatigue parties were much annoyed by the fire of the rebel cannon, which at times were kept in constant use, especially at night. The Union gunboats in York river were engaged exchanging shots with the forts at long range, also in shelling the opposite shore where the enemy were in possession, particularly at Gloucester Point; while effective shots were frequently made from our shore batteries from one and one-half to three miles distant, dismounting cannon and ploughing deep furrows through the earthworks of the enemy. But little fatigue duty was performed by the Sharpshooters, and that consisted principally in carrying gabions to the advanced works to be prepared for the protection of our gunners. The following named accomplished officers superintended the siege operations: "Brig.-Gen. J. G. Barnard, chief engineer, charged with the selection, laying out, and completion of the approaches and batteries; Brig.-Gen. Wm. F. Barry, chief of artillery, charged with arming and supplying with ammunition all the siege and field batteries; Brig.-Gen. Fitz. John Porter, director of the siege, to whom was assigned the guarding of the trenches, the assembling and distribution of the working parties, etc."

FITZ JOHN PORTER IN A WILD BALLOON

On the 11th of April a great sensation occurred in the Union camp, on the report quickly spreading that Gen. Porter had been carried off by a balloon, which proved to be the case. Prof. Lowe's balloons were near the Sharpshooter camp, and this morning Gen. Porter, impatient at Lowe's absence, went up alone to make observations,— to take a view of the enemy,—when the rope holding the balloon parted below and away she shot high up in air, sailing rapidly over the rebel lines; the general pulled away at the ropes until they were all tangled up, but he couldn't manage the wild thing. Finally, the gas giving out, the machine came down about four miles off with a big bump. Col. Ripley with other officers had mounted their horses and hunted him up. It was a terrible experience, and Gen. McClellan was pretty badly scared about it. He immediately issued orders forbidding his officers taking any more balloon excursions. Previous to that, they used to go up occasionally and take a view of the surroundings, as it was an interesting trip as long as the ropes held it fast to the ground.

But Gen. Porter had a long ladder prepared and erected, standing 100 feet in the air, fastened to a tree. After being placed in position James Winchell of the Sharpshooters was sent up to test it. Taking an officer's field-glass he reported he could see Yorktown and Gloucester very readily, so that it was used by the general officers for a place of observation.

Speaking of balloons, later on the enemy tried their hand at that manner of "observations," and Lieut. Bronson, of Company F, reported that his detail at the front (April 26) [1] fired into this rebel balloon made of an A tent, and brought it down. At the same time the 1st and 11th Massachusetts charged and captured a redoubt near the Yorktown road in the woods.

During the night of April 11th, which was a very dark one, a detail of six Sharpshooters sent out as an advanced picket had a short but exciting brush with a considerable force of the enemy in the old peach orchard. Our men had gone too far forward and occupied rebel ground, and the enemy were determined to drive them back. They were known to be advancing by the noise made, slight as it was,—you couldn't see anything,—but on getting close enough to be 'heard giving low commands, the Sharpshooters suddenly opened fire with their skirmish rifles, and kept it up for a few moments in a lively, resolute manner. This was a surprises, and threw the approaching force into confusion, causing them to come to a sudden halt. Rapidly reloading, the picket waited until they heard them coming again, when another sharp and well-directed volley once more stopped them. Our fire was now returned in earnest, the bullets whizzing by very close, the pickets still retaining their position. As another advance was made by the unseen enemy, firing as they came on, apparently closing in and around the little band, the latter poured in a final round and quickly fell back on the reserve, a long ways in the rear. Owing to the dense darkness but little could be seen, nor were the enemy distinguishable except by their fire, but so close did they come that, as H. J. Peck, of Company F, remarked: "You could hear them breathe." The fire of the Sharpshooters had evidently made them desperate, as they finally came on with a rush, swearing: "D—n you, get out yer," intent on wiping the boys out. It was an exciting time, made doubly so by the

"Bright flashes in the inky night," and the unusually loud report of the guns. California Joe and another Michigan comrade were slightly wounded, the former receiving a bullet on the band of his Sharps rifle, snapping the same, driving it with force against his nose and cheek, causing the blood to flow freely. Peck, of Vermont, had his left hand hurt by a piece of board knocked off an old building they were passing, while several infantry men stationed in their rear were said to have been shot by the elevated balls. On their return to camp the next morning much excitement existed for a time—the camp was wild—at the rapidly-spreading report that "Old Californy was shot." This was increased on the return of another squad (Wisconsin men), who had a fight the same night at a mill near the river, where some sharp shooting also occurred. But our men lying dose, and constantly moving their position after firing, escaped injury; at the same time deceiving the enemy, who might easily imagine a much larger force in their front, they being strangers to the Sharpshooters, their methods, and rapid shooting. Finally, the fighting having ended, they held their ground until near day break, when they retired to the line of works behind them.

CALIFORNIA JOE

There were few persons in the loyal states during the time of the Peninsula campaign that had not heard of "California Joe, the Sharpshooter." The press of the North gave considerable space in noticing his feats of valor and his wonderful marksmanship. Columns of thrilling anecdotes or stories were published, in which this particular Sharpshooter was made the hero. In fact, the names of Col. Berdan and California Joe were for a time linked almost inseparably together, and through them the Sharpshooters became more extensively known during this campaign than would probably otherwise have been the case. Almost everything relating to the Sharpshooters, in the way of extraordinary shooting, was credited to "California Joe." From the description published of this noted person, and of his reputation as a California mountain hunter, one would have naturally supposed him to be some giant-like character, of a wild, fierce nature, with a disposition adapted to cower ordinary persons—even a rebel a mile away in a tree top or rifle pit. Such an impression must have prevailed among the average readers of the stories of his prowess. And yet our California Joe was no such manner of man. On the contrary, he was one of the mildest, I may reasonably add, gentlest of men. It is true this person—Truman Head, of Company C, First U. S. Sharpshooters—was a, great rifle shot, who carried a Sharps breech-loading rifle, that he performed arduous and important service at the front, before Yorktown and on the line of the Chickahominy, whether with his company, or upon some special service as a scout and sharpshooter sent out by Col. Berdan or some of the generals, wherein he discovered the presence of a hidden foe or a masked battery of the enemy, and silenced him. And he never failed in his mission. That he ever "shot a man out of a tree two miles off, just at daybreak, first pop," I can best answer by stating that, if there was ever a time when Truman Head showed a disposition to be angry, it was on reading such stuff. But "Joe," as I must call him, was one of those splendid characters that made him a hero in spite of himself. Entirely free from brag and bluster, an unassuming man, past the middle age, short in stature, light in weight, and a true gentleman in every sense of the word, he was always a special favorite with the entire command. When the regiment was organizing, the breaking out of the rebellion having brought him East from his far west haunts to join the command of Col. Baker, an old friend of his, that gallant officer being killed at Ball's Bluff about the time of his arrival, he obtained permission to join the Michigan company while at the rendezvous opposite New

York city. His sorrow at the death of Col. Baker was often expressed, and in his quiet chats with his comrades, he was always ready to recite the following beautiful poem of that gifted officer, entitled,

To A. WAVE.

Dost thou seek a star with thy swelling crest,
o wave, that leavest thy mother's breast?
Dost thou leap from the prisoned depths below
In scorn of their calm and constant flow?
Or art thou seeking some distant land,
To die in murmurs upon the strand?
Hast thou tales to tell of the pearl-lit deep,
Where the wave-whelmed mariner rocks in sleep?
Canst thou speak of navies that sank in pride
Ere the roll of their thunder in echo died?
What trophies, what banners, are floating free
In the shadowy depths of that silent sea?
It were vain to ask, as thou rollest afar,
Of banner or mariner, ship or star:
It were vain to seek in thy stormy face
Some tale of the sorrowful past to trace:
Thou art swelling high; thou art dashing free,—
How vain are the questions we ask of thee.
I too am a wave on the stormy sea:
I too am a wanderer, driven like thee;
I too am seeking a distant land,
To be lost and gone ere I reach the strand,
For the land I seek is a waveless shore,
And they who once reach it shall wander no more.

When Joe enlisted he executed a will bequeathing $50,000, should he be killed, for the care of disabled Union soldiers at Philadelphia, his early home. For Truman Head was a bachelor, although it has been stated on reliable hearsay that the old gent, when a young man, was once engaged, the girl of his choice belonging to one of the first families of the county; but owing to the opposition of the stem parent—the father—he lost the girl, both being too loyal to disregard the parent's wishes. Head then left his native heath and became a wanderer;—no one knew where,—and crossing the great plains arrived and settled in California. But it appears that though so far separated and his whereabouts unknown the course of true love remained, for Head remained a bachelor and his lady a maid. His service as a Union soldier and Sharpshooter closed with the Peninsula campaign, owing to failing health in which his eyes were affected, he being honorably discharged late in the fall of 1862. Returning to California, he died full of years and honors in the year 1888, respected by all who knew him. The death of the old veteran pioneer and Sharpshooter was noticed in the California press as a great public event, with extended notices of his career. He was buried with Masonic orders, and a monument has been erected to his memory in San Francisco.

On the 19th of April Companies A and C were ordered to report to Gen. Smith's division on the left, where several severe contests had already taken place without accomplishing any successful result. These two companies of Sharpshooters were sent for, to work on the enemy's artillery which was annoying and endangering our troops, and the good work performed by them will be found fully reported further on. The following incident occurred while they were thus detached:

A GOOD SHOT

As it was positively forbidden to shoot off guns while in this encampment, to prevent any real knowledge of our position becoming known to the enemy, therefore when one of the Michigan men failed to resist the temptation to blaze away at a large squirrel in a distant tree top, probably reminding him of old times at home, a guard soon appeared and took the sportsman in charge. Being brought before the general, squirrel in hand, he was put on immediate examination as follows:

"Well, my man! Why did you shoot off your gun, when it is against orders to do so? "

"I know 'tis wrong, General, but I couldn't resist the temptation to try that squirrel's head. 'Twas a splendid mark, and I really believe when I pulled on it, I forgot about orders."

The general scarcely suppressing a smile, continued: "Well! What was the result? Did you bring it down? "

"I did," replied the marksman, "here it is," showing the game.

"What! Shot through the head, off that tall tree? What gun do you shoot? "

"Target rifle, sir."

It was one of the globe-sighted rifles. Looking steadily at the soldier, the general finally replied:

"'Tis well. You may go this time, but if you had missed it, my friend, you would hardly have got off so easy. Cease firing! Do you understand?"

The rifleman assented.

"All right, then, go to your regiment," and William Straw, of Company C, hurried off to his quarters to toast his squirrel before the camp fire, with many thanks to Gen. Smith for allowing him to do so.

Notwithstanding that while on picket duty the men frequently had sharp exchanges with their equally as determined opponents, yet at times a disposition prevailed to communicate, especially when near each other, and the following dialogue between two of our Sharpshooters and a Florida rebel is a fair specimen of the conversation indulged in on such occasions. The parties were separated by a deep swale covered with water and thick brush, and were unable to discover each other's person.

Joseph Durkee hearing a noise on the other side, yelled out in a loud voice: "Halloo, Mike! Have you got any tobacco?"

Secesh (with a strong Hibernian accent): "Yes, be jabers, and whisky, too."

Joe: "Come over, and we'll have a quiet smoke!"

Secesh: "I will meet you half-way." Joe agreed to do so, and advanced some distance through brush and water, then stopped.

Secesh: "Where the divil are ye—are ye comin'?"

Joe: "I'm half-way over now; can't go any further without swimming."

Secesh: "Have ye a boat?"

Joe: "No, I haven't."

Secesh: "Where's yer gun-boat?"

Joe: "Down taking care of the Merrimac."

Secesh: "Then come over in the big balloon." (Much laughter along the rebel lines.)

Joe: "Have you a boat? "

Secesh: "I have, sure, and I'm coming over."

Joe then enquired the news of the day, and if the Johnny had a Norfolk Day Book.

Secesh replied: "I have. Have you got a Tribune?"

Joe answered that he had not.

Secesh: "Where's General Buell?"

Joe: "Buell's all right, and surrounds Beauregard."

Secesh: "Where's General Prentiss?"

Joe: "Where's Johnston?" Another rebel laugh.

Joe: "How about Island No. Ten?"

Secesh: "That's evacuated."

Joe: "How is it you left 100 guns and 6,000 prisoners?"

Secesh: "Sure they were not much account."

Joe: "How about Fort Pulaski?"

Secesh: "That, me honey, was only a rebel sand bank_

But tell me, what made ye lave Bull Run?"

Richard Blodgett: "We had marching orders." This caused great laughter among the rebels, some of them exclaiming: "Bully boy."

Dick: "Where's Zollicoffer?"

Secesh: "Gone up the spout."

Joe; "Why don't you come over?"

Secesh: "I can't get through the brush." At this moment a rebel bullet came whizzing over by our men, and

Joe angrily inquired who fired.

Secesh: "Some fool over this way." An order was then issued to cease firing.

Joe: "Ain't you coming? What regiment do you belong to? "

Secesh: "Eighteenth Florida. What do you belong to?

Joe: "Berdan Sharpshooters." Some of the reb's comrades now warned him to look out.

Secesh: "Would ye shoot a fellow?"

Joe: "No! But I will stack arms and smoke with you, if you will come over." Here a rebel officer ordered the man back, and he refused to communicate further.

REBEL DARKY SHARPSHOOTER

For a considerable time during the siege the enemy had a negro rifle shooter in their front who kept up a close fire on our men, and, although the distance was great, yet he caused more or less annoyance by his persistent shooting_ On one occasion while at the advanced posts with a detail, the writer with his squad had an opportunity to note the skill of this determined darky with his well-aimed rifle. Being stationed at a pit on the edge of a wood fronting the treeless stretch of ground around the opposing works, with sand bags piled up for cover, during the forenoon this rebellious black made his appearance by the side of an officer and under his direction commenced firing at us. For a long time this chance shooting was kept up, the black standing out in plain view and coolly drawing bead, but failed to elicit any response, our orders being to lie quiet and not be seen. So the negro had the shooting all to himself, his pop, pop, against the sand bags on the edge of the pit often occurring, while other close shots among the trees showed plainly that he was a good shot at long range. He became pretty well known among the scouts and pickets, and had established quite a reputation for marksmanship, before he came to grief. Emboldened by his having pretty much all this promiscuous shooting unopposed, the pickets rarely firing at him, he began to work at shorter distance, taking advantage of the ground and scattering trees. This was what our men wanted, to get him within more reasonable range, not caring to waste ammunition trying to cripple him at the' long distance he had at first been showing himself. They wanted to make sure of him. In the meantime our boys would when opportunity offered, without being seen, post a man forward to await in concealment for the adventurous darky. The scheme succeeded and his fate was sealed. The result was finally announced in the "latest from the front," one morning in camp, that "a scouting party having cornered the nigger in a chimney top a quarter of a mile distant, where he had been concealed, finally brought him down," and thus ended his sport with his life. It was said that Sergt. Andrews of Company E (afterwards captain) discovered the fellow in the second story of the old chimney,—standing monument of destruction, of which there were many along this Peninsula route,—and with the aid of his fine telescope, found him firing through a hole in the back of the fire-place.

Details of men from the different companies were frequently sent out at night in charge of a commissioned officer on special service, to assist in protecting the working parties. A party under Lieut. Shepard succeeded one dark night in establishing a rifle pit within 600 yards of the rebel lines. The following morning the enemy discovering what had been done, opened furiously with their cannon but with little effect. Not being able to drive the riflemen away by cannon shot, they tried to drop a mortar shell onto them, by sending up on their curved mission three of those destructive projectiles. The first one fell short, the second was heard to go upward with a slow sound which finally for a brief time ceased, but was soon heard coming rapidly down directly over their heads, and luckily for the crouching party it exploded with a terrific report seventy-five feet above, sending the scattering pieces all around but not among them. A well-aimed shot but a little short.

"By gosh!" exclaimed a Pennsylvania Dutchman nearby; "we'll get hit."

"Hit away, then!" retorted Bob Casey, of the Sharpshooters, who carried a long and heavy hunting rifle brought from Wisconsin. "They can't root us out—we're here to stay." Nor were they "rooted out" or driven away, for after firing mortar No. 3, which came down some distance beyond them, phizzing out, failing to explode, going two feet into the earth, they ceased their mortar experiments and all gave a long breath of relief.

General McClellan reported: Many times towards the end of the month the enemy attempted to drive in our pickets and take our rifle pits near Yorktown, but always without success. As the siege progressed it was with great difficulty that the rifle pits on the right could be excavated and held, so little covering could be made against the hot fire of the enemy's artillery and infantry.

On the 24th, Sergt.-Maj. Horton, temporarily relieved for the purpose, was placed in command of a company of scouts, to be employed at the extreme front in guarding against surprise while advanced rifle pits were being dug, and for such other duties as occasion required. They were employed daily, and occasionally at night, until the evacuation by the enemy—a period of ten days—their service being very severe and full of danger. In the meantime C. A. Stevens, the first sergeant of Company G, acted as sergeant-major.

On the 28th considerable firing occurred and the enemy in front of the scouts appeared to be greatly confused, a number of them having been knocked over during the day. But that blunders should sometimes occur among the troops, and especially in movements after dark, was among the dread possibilities, even with the most cautious. A lucky oversight occurred that night in which our scouts were the chief actors. As it was getting to be quite dark they discharged their Colts rifles, expecting momentarily to be relieved, and wishing to have an opportunity to clean their arms on returning to camp, no firing being allowed there. Horton had left the pit for the reserve to hurry up the relief, and while away the scouts suddenly discovered an unknown body of troops advancing from toward the rebel side, 10 rods distant. Our boys yelled "Halt!" and although the strangers did so, yet came to a full charge; whereupon the occupants of the pit scrambled out running to the rear where, after retiring a few rods, they began to load. This was quickly done, they then watching closely in their efforts to distinguish the force in their front. Suddenly a form passed in front of them and Joel Parker was about to fire, but was stopped lay C. N. Jacobs who yelled: "Hold on! That's Horton." So it proved, who immediately marched them to camp paying little attention to what they said of the "rebel attack; "which proved to be the relief who had gone out in a roundabout direction through mistake, and on approaching the pit had deployed out, not knowing what they might encounter. It was a careless and yet lucky act of the scouts in not keeping their guns loaded. Had they not been discharged some of them would no doubt have been hurt, as the picket would have charged the pit on receiving the Sharpshooters' fire when a fatal fight would have been the disastrous result. After the Sharps rifles were received there was no difficulty of unloading them without firing.

On another occasion while scouting along the river through a grove in the daytime, the scouts came suddenly in close contact with the rebel picket posted in a rifle pit behind a fence. The first intimation our men had of the foe, was a whizzing bullet under Sergt. Joel Parker's ear, whereupon he dropped as if shot. "Down, boys!" he cried in a low tone; and as the rest of the party went down, they poured a rattling volley into the fence which they then discovered sighting a number of heads on the lookout. The enemy were taken aback, and in their confusion the scouts slipped away without harm. Afterwards, they learned from rebel prisoners that their fire had fatal effect on "several of the Johnnies."

THE POWER OF SAND AS AN EXPLOSIVE

While the enemy occupied a good deal of time trying to shell us out, in building the approaches, sending shot and shell at times with great rapidity, our own gunners were by no means idle, both shore batteries and gunboats responding in a manner that showed we were not asleep. So that on some days and even nights, there was a perfect uproar of speaking cannon, sending a network of missiles back and forth. And our shots were just as well aimed as were those of our opponents. In the latter days of the siege, our gunboats succeeded in demolishing several of the big guns as well as a portion of the works of the enemy, plowing great furrows therein, no doubt making it decidedly uncomfortable for the gray coats, and Yorktown' an undesirable place to live in at the time. But one of these big guns of the Confederates, called by our boys, "Petersburg," was literally exploded by our Sharpshooters and in a novel way. It appears that Lieut. Bronson (Company F) had early in the war, while with Grebel's battery, learned enough of artillery practice to understand that sand or gravel thrown into a loaded cannon would be very likely to explode it. And while out one day (April 30th) with a detachment, observing that the muzzle of this gun was surrounded with sand bags, ordered his men to shoot at the sand bags as soon as it was loaded, to throw sand if possible inside. Then after the enemy had fired this particular cannon the thirteenth time, our men still peppering the sand bags, it went into the air, a thoroughly demoralized, "busted thing." The Sharpshooters had really exploded the big gun.

A SHARPSHOOTER KILLED

As the time was now fast approaching when the Union commander would be ready to commence offensive operations, fatigue parties were nightly engaged in preparing rifle pits on different parts of the plain, between the nearly completed works of the Union troops and the formidable ones of the enemy. During the night in question, which was a very dark one, a detail of Sharpshooters under Lieut. Marble, of Company G, were ordered out to protect a fatigue detail of infantry in digging an advanced rifle pit in an important position. The scouts were sent ahead on a knoll, where they lay several paces apart watching sharply through the dense darkness. These scouts were: Sergt.-Maj. Horton, Sergt. Joel Parker, Corp. C. N. Jacobs, Privates John S. Tillotson, Michael Costello and Joseph Durkee, all of Company G. The position they occupied was, at the time unknown to them, within 40 yards of a rebel rifle pit, and as the fearless Joseph Durkee endeavored to reach another position over the knoll, although cautioned by Marble as also the rest, before going forward, not to attempt it, a single shot brightened up the black space for a moment, when the brave scout rolled over in death, shot through the head. The death-like stillness that had prevailed, broken by that solitary fatal shot, was followed by a terrific volley of musketry by the enemy, with rapid discharges of artillery from their fortifications, lighting up the atmosphere in terrible brightness. The scouts and pickets lay flat on the ground, letting the whizzing shots go harmlessly over them. Not so with the working detail, who, throwing down picks and spades, scampered back in great confusion in the track of the murderous fire, towards the Union works. The result was, that a number of them were wounded. But not until after the firing had ceased did the Sharpshooters move from their close position—they knew better. They finally retired when all was quiet, and no farther attempt was made to continue the work that night. The body of Durkee was left on the field with his arms and accouterments, his comrades being unable to bring them off, but was found after the evacuation lying where he fell, and buried on the spot. His Colt rifle had been carried off and a note left, stating the regiment that had it, and their determination to have them all before long. Evidently were they greatly elated to know they had killed a Sharpshooter—the only one they did know of, during the siege. Their boast, however, was of no avail, as the regiment mentioned was badly cut up at Williamsburg during the charge of Hancock's brigade, and the Colt rifle recovered. When the 5th Wisconsin met the 5th North Carolina in that famous bayonet charge, said to be the first effective one of the war, driving back the enemy in confusion, capturing their battle-flag bearing the Southern Cross and fifteen stars, the slayer of Joe Durkee counted one more "lost in action" on the Confederate rolls. The boasting rebel enjoyed the possession of his prize but a short time. A rebellious newspaper, the Petersburgh Express, spun out the following yarn in referring to this affair:

"A McClellan Sharpshooter had been picked off by a Kentucky hunter, at two hundred yards distance, and on approaching the pit where the Sharpshooter lay, it was found to contain a cushioned arm chair, choice liquors and segars, and food of the best description."

Joseph Durkee's death was mourned by his company as that of one of their bravest, yet they were not greatly surprised to hear of it, owing to his predominant daring, amounting at times to sheer recklessness. Unfortunately, he could not restrain his ardor, but was always ready to rush rashly ahead, and nothing but a most imperative command or an effective shot, could stop him when he got fairly started; so it was really but a matter of time with Joe. He had a younger brother left in the company, James Durkee, who with more judgment and a cooler head, made a most 'efficient soldier, and while always on hand in a fight, lived throughout his well-served term.

Individual feats of valor frequently occur in a campaign, particularly so in a service like that of the Sharpshooters, which are not generally known, or if so, are so similar in many respects that they are passed by without credit or record. Others there were, who had distinguished themselves on trying occasions, and it is one of my purposes in writing this history, to give them the credit due them when known to be so entitled; but there were doubtless many incidents unknown to the writer, as the regiment was often scattered in detached companies. Following, we notice an exploit much talked of at the time among "the boys," and noticed in the newspapers.

CAPTURING A CANNON.

Among the famous shots of the regiment was a member of the New Hampshire company called "Old Seth," who was noted for his persistency in using his favorite "telescope" on all possible occasions. He evinced the greatest dislike to laying around camp, and, if not detailed to go to the front, would sulk away to his tent, disappointed and soured at the "blamed luck" that prevented him from keeping his pet rifle barrel warm. For some days this happened, he constantly bemoaning his fate, fearful that the siege would end before his turn came again to go out. Finally in the latter days of the besiegement (May 2d), receiving orders direct from Col. Berdan to "select a special detail of sharp shots for important service,"—which was to get as near the enemy as possible and find out what they were doing, notified the orderly of Company E, that this man was wanted; and he went off, determined to make the most of it. Arriving at the front before daybreak, taking in the Situation of affairs, the scouts deployed out to different rifle pits, Seth selecting one far in advance between the lines, and, moving cautiously along, succeeded in getting there without attracting notice. It proved to be a rebel rifle pit built during the night, the enemy intending to occupy it, but Old Seth got ahead of them before they were astir, and when the Johnnies awoke to the fact that a Yank was in possession, their rage and disappointment knew no bounds, and they prepared to lay him out. But despite their efforts, they never got there, thereafter. For while it would have been impossible for Old Seth alone, with his ponderous muzzle-loading telescope, to have stopped them, although he made his shots count, yet with the breech-loaders behind him, the balls rattled in so fast about the rebel pits, that they soon got sick of it, and became effectually whipped. Having thus silenced the foe in his front, Old Seth turned his attention to larger game, and soon found it in the shape of a frowning cannon which had opened on him, breaking their shells all around him. It was an ugly customer, and the isolated Sharpshooter for once concluded he was in a trap. But they had to load, and as this was Seth's opportunity, instantly he bravely commenced his work; and so successfully did he plant his bullets around the big gun, that it was not long before the firing ceased, and he virtually had the cannon captured. It was to all intents and purposes his gun—they couldn't load it. From that time until the siege was over, two days after, the Sharpshooter held his place, keeping the cannon quiet. Day and night he remained at his post; he had got away from camp and was just in his glory, with plenty of ammunition, and a fresh supply of water and rations furnished him the second day by some of his venturesome comrades, before daylight. But they had to crawl to do it, for the enemy, although quiet, were on the alert, and would doubtless have rushed down on the pit after dark, but were evidently afraid of the five-shooters behind Seth, from the scouts that lay on the ground watching every movement, and listening for every sound—the least noise causing a rifle to crack. It was a daring undertaking, an important capture, as the cannon in question had been one of the most damaging to our working parties at the parallels, up to the time George H. Chase commenced firing with his 32-pounder rifle.

A CONFEDERATE CROW.

On the same day Durkee was killed, before nightfall another Sharpshooter, name and company to me unknown, while on duty in the most advanced rifle pit at the head of Wormsley's Creek, was struck by a bullet in the abdomen and mortally wounded. Col. Berdan coming up, told the Sharpshooters they must put a stop to such work of the enemy. With his field-glass he then discovered a low mound of earth directly in front, but a long way' off, and presently, what might have been mistaken for a crow seemed to be perched thereon. Watching the object steadily for a few moments, he saw it disappear and shortly after resume its place. Pointing out the spot to Lieut. Wm. Elmendorf, of Company B, he immediately detailed six men, and placing them under command of the lieutenant named, gave him the following instructions:

"Advance under cover of nightfall as far in that direction as you deem sufficient, dig a rifle pit for the Sharpshooters, and after placing them therein, return to the redoubt and await the morning light, and the materialization of that *crow's* head above the mound. And, my men, don't fail to let the daylight through it." Or he might as well have said in the language of a war poet:

> "Ah, rifleman, shoot me a fancy shot,
> Straight at the heart of you prowling vidette;
> Ring me a ball in that glittering spot
> That shines on his breast like an amulet."

At the appointed time, it being intensely dark, so much so as to blot out every land mark, the selected Sharpshooters, accompanied by a working detail from a Maine regiment armed with picks and shovels, emerged from the redoubt; passing through an apple orchard, taking the course as well as they could in the almost utter darkness, they-cautiously advanced until presumably far enough and halted, awaiting the approach of the working force which had for some unknown reason not kept up. To dig a rifle pit with bayonets would be no easy job, so Elmendorf accompanied by another officer started back to find the detail, leaving the Sharpshooters in command of a sergeant. The officers having lost themselves soon after, resorted to groping carefully about, not daring to call out, occasionally stopping to listen for footsteps. Not a single star was to be seen, all was inky darkness to them, and the perplexity of the situation began to be very uncomfortable, when voices were heard, then footsteps. Thinking they had at last come up with the strayed fatigue party, they listened again, and to their dismay recognized the conversation of a party of Confederates. They immediately dropped and awaited developments, hugging the ground close. Yet the situation did not improve any, for the approaching footsteps grew nearer and nearer. The cracking of a twig beneath them was followed by a clicking of gun locks, and a moment rater by a shower of buck and ball passing over them. Not waiting for their opponents to reload and try it again, the officers hastily retreated in an oblique direction. Finally hearing more voices they now concluded to ascertain who these new strangers were, taking the chances of an escape should they still prove foes. They couldn't all be rebels on that field. In response to their "Halloo!" came an answer back "distressingly close; "in return they cried out "friends without the countersign." To which "advance one," was quickly retorted, with the admonition to "look out for the trenches." Fortunately for this advice they did not plunge into them in the dark, but let themselves down carefully, when they found they were in the presence of a party of Duryea's Zouaves. They had gone a mile out of the way, and hurriedly retracing their steps, finally found the fatigue party who had in the meantime got up with the advance, their delay being caused by Stopping to relieve themselves of their overcoats and other surplus articles. Advancing somewhat farther, the pit was dug unmolested, although the enemy's shell were continually flying overhead, making a pyrotechnic display that helped to light them in their work. Soon after daylight that "crow's head" showed up under a slouched hat. A second after, a puff of smoke arose from the rifle pit—that slouched hat, or what was inside of it, must have stopped a bullet, as it was the last seen of it. Thus as the colonel's order faithfully carried out, after arduous and hazardous service getting into position. The above incident shows the dangers incurred by the Union soldiers during the siege of Yorktown.

Continuously from nine A. M. till three P. M of the 2d of May, the enemy kept up a vicious shelling from a six-pounder placed in a depression outside their works unseen by , our men, which evidently obtained the range by signals to the gunners from the heights above them. So accurate was its aim that at no time was it safe to arise to a standing position, save when the tormentor was allowed to cool off. The shells would hit the bank, sending showers of dirt over the men, while some would strike inside our works and explode, or skip beyond, tearing through the tree tops, dropping huge limbs, scattering splinters and big chunks of bark.. Visiting the redoubt, Col. Berdan, although warned of the danger, did not leave until he had made his observations, and then not until after a shell had exploded in the redoubt, when with the remark: "That crow fellow's fun did not last him long, did it, boys?" he concluded to leave the rest of the "fun" to "the boys," and retired, after admonishing them not to unnecessarily expose themselves. In fact, it was one of the standing orders the Sharpshooters had, at this place and elsewhere, not to "recklessly expose themselves;" to take "all possible cover," and to "waste no ammunition for the sake of shooting."

THE EVACUATION.

On the night of May 4th the rebel gunners kept up a continual fire from their artillery until midnight, when the cannonading suddenly ceased. From that time until daylight, the Union batteries on the river side fired steadily every five minutes. A heavy explosion was heard within the enemy's works, and it became evident they were leaving Yorktown; therefore, at just daybreak a movement forward was ordered, by the troops on the front line. The scouts being' present, pushed rapidly ahead notwithstanding an objection to their doing so was made by a colonel of some other regiment, who evidently wanted to be there first, but his protest against the Sharpshooters was not allowed to be repeated by Gen. Jameson, who sharply retorted: "The Sharpshooters have been at the front during the entire siege, and they shall not be displaced now."

And so it happened that the six scouts: Wm. H. Horton, Joel Parker, Caleb N. Jacobs, John S. Tillotson, Henry Martin and Oren Vide, of Company G, and Lieut. Martin V. Bronson, of Company F, closely followed by Gen. Jameson and another colonel, were of the first to reach the deserted works. These were examined very carefully, a deserting rebel sergeant informing them of the existence of torpedoes throughout the place. James Winchell, of Company D, says he advanced also at the same time, with a squad of pickets per order of Gen. Jameson, and they went on to the works together, where they sighted the sergeant who cried out: "For God's sake, don't shoot, boys," and as the general was moving forward, yelled to him: "General, do if t take another step, there is a big shell in front of you. The devils have been busy planting them, but I can't tell where they are all placed, but wherever you see fresh earth, lo ok out! "And three more rebels after shaking a white rag, delivered themselves up to this Company D squad, consisting of Lieut. Horace Chase, Sergt. J. E. Hetherington and privates Drake and Winchell. These prisoners told the same story about the evacuation and were taken to the rear. The scouts meantime had gone on to the village of Yorktown and obtained their breakfast. Alter which, on collecting some spoils,—knives, lances, tobacco, cigars, etc.,—they returned to camp, to be received by their excited and overjoyed comrades with the heartiest cheers. Following close after the scouts in the advance on the deserted works, was the regular Sharpshooter picket under Capt. Drew, who also returned to camp well laden with trophies.

The Wisconsin company of Sharpshooters can rightfully claim the honor of being represented by the first ones to enter Yorktown on the heels of the retreating foe, and if they did not raise the flag on the ramparts, it was because it was left in camp, it not being customary for scouting parties to carry "company colors" with them. The flag-bearer, Henry Martin, was, however, present, and as a substitute for planting the colors on the rebel works, he waved his dark green cap and yelled like a Trojan.

Brig.-Gen. Jameson, in his report to Gen. Porter, director of the siege, thus states: "At 3 'o'clock this morning quite heavy explosions were heard in the vicinity of Yorktown, and a very bright fire was observed there. About half-past three A. M. there were strong indications that the rebels had evacuated. Soon after, three soldiers approached our lines under a flag of truce. They stated that Yorktown was evacuated. In accordance with instructions from you, I deployed two companies of the 62d Penn. Vols., together with a portion of the Berdan Sharpshooters as skirmishers, with a portion of the 22d Mass as support, and advanced cautiously towards the rebel works in front of Yorktown.

No signs of the rebels were visible as I approached, and I had the honor of entering the town at about half-past five A. M. Most of their guns were left in their works loaded and spiked."

Among the articles brought into the Sharpshooter camp was a large sized rebel flag by a member of Company F, which was trailed in the dust by the boys through the company streets—up or down each street—to regimental headquarters. The colonel galloping in at the same time with an engraving of George Washington held on high, taken from a deserted rebel house, as he excitedly exhibited the same to the rallying men, cheers loud and long greeted its appearance. It was a glorious and exciting scene, the boys were all happy, hurrahing for everybody and everything in sight. The siege had been an arduous and tiresome one, and the men were anxious and ready to move forward, with hopes of further and greater victories. It was their first great success, and they had no thought of what hard and trying service awaited them.

Gen. Porter writes: "Col. Berdan and Lieut.-Col. Ripley, of the Sharpshooters, deserve great credit throughout the siege for pushing forward the rifle pits close to the enemy's works, and keeping down the fire of the enemy's sharpshooters."

Now, while our men at Camp Winfield Scott are rejoicing over the close of the siege, relating their experiences at the front, around their camp fires, I will record the service performed by the two detached companies, A and C, mentioned before as having gone to the left, under Maj. Trepp, to act as Sharpshooters for the command of Gen. Smith. For this account of the arduous duty they performed I am indebted to the written report of Capt. Rudolph Aschmann, of Company A, translated by Capt. John B. Isler, formerly of the same company.

WARWICK RIVER.

"In the middle of April, Maj. Trepp received orders to report with Companies A and C to Gen. W. F. Smith for duty. Smith's division formed the extreme left wing of the army. It appeared that the generals had learned to appreciate the usefulness of the Sharpshooters, for these two companies were called for, as the troops on the left flank were very much annoyed by the enemy's artillery. Here our duties were very disagreeable and extremely dangerous. On this flank, Warwick creek, a sluggish, unfordable stream, separated the two armies. The enemy had their side strongly fortified, and where a dam crossed the stream, being their weakest point, had planted a battery of artillery flanked by rifle pits, which menaced the position Gen. Smith's artillery had taken, and endangered the picket line in their front. During the night of our arrival, we constructed a rifle pit flanked by fascines as near as 100 yards from the enemy's works. While in this, we had to remain during the day, and could only leave it at night owing to the proximity of the enemy's batteries. Every morning before dawn a detachment of Sharpshooters occupied the rifle pit, and, remaining 16 hours on duty, were retired at night. From this position we watched the movement of the enemy's artillery, and made it impossible for them to serve their guns any longer. We were all the time in a most dangerous position, and lost while performing these duties several of our men, among whom was our second sergeant, N. Sauer, a most excellent soldier, who was -killed in the rifle pits April 25th. Success in war demands sacrifices, but we accomplished our purpose, and thereby earned the thanks of our generals."

And now, by the time the Union batteries—siege guns and mortars—are in readiness for a general bombardment along the line of the Warwick, followed by an attack by our troops, the enemy quietly slipped away during the night of May 3d, and the next morning several deserters under a -white flag gave the news. Pursuit was immediately ordered -with the cavalry in advance, and, at nightfall coming up with the foe, we prepared for battle, our cavalry having made an unsuccessful attack, falling back to the main body.

WILLIAMSBURG.

Gen. Hancock's brigade having occupied two vacated redoubts on the right, being hard pressed and liable to be cut off, Gen. McClellan on reaching the field towards the close of the afternoon, after a hard ride of 14 miles from Yorktown where the guns were plainly heard, ordered three brigades to reinforce Hancock, but, he says in his report:

"Before Gens. Smith and Naglee could reach the field of Gen. Hancock's operations, although they moved with great rapidity, he had been confronted by a superior force. Feigning to retreat slowly, he awaited their onset and then turned upon them, and after some terrific volleys of musketry he charged them with the bayonet, routing and dispersing their whole force, killing, wounding, and capturing from 500 to 600 men. This was one of the most brilliant engagements of the war, and Gen. Hancock merits the highest praise for the soldierly qualities displayed and his perfect appreciation of the vital importance of his position. Night put an end to the operations here. The next morning the enemy's position was abandoned."

Casualties at Williamsburg of the Union forces: Killed, 456; wounded, 1,410; missing, 373; total, 2,239.

Gen. Hancock in his report of the fight, thus speaks of his famous charge, and of his troops in general:

"The enemy's assault was of the most determined character. No troops could have made a more desperate or resolute charge. The 5th North Carolina was annihilated. Nearly all of its superior officers were left dead or wounded on the field. The 24th Virginia suffered greatly in superior officers and men. The battle flag of one of the enemy's regiments was captured by the 5th Wisconsin Volunteers, and sent by me as a trophy to Gen. Smith. For 600 yards in front of our line the whole field was strewn with the enemy's dead and wounded. The troops under my command behaved with a spirit and steadiness unsurpassed by veterans, so much so, that they murmured when ordered to fall back from the first position. Having had to detach so many at various points as I advanced, and also to protect my flanks, my battalions numbered but about 1,600 men when I engaged the enemy. By the evidence of an officer who noted the time, the action continued twenty-three minutes from the time of the enemy's appearance until his repulse. When it commenced, the contest in front of Fort Magruder appeared to have ended. I learned from the prisoners captured that we had been attacked by two brigades of infantry, of six regiments, numbering about 5,000 men and some cavalry. The enemy's advance was commanded by Brig.-Gen. Early, who was wounded during the action. Our troops at night bivouacked in the rain on the ground they had so handsomely won, lying down on the battle field, which was saturated by long-continued rains."

Further extracts are given to show the desperate nature of the conflict. Having been well advanced on the front lines to the right, the 5th Wisconsin was the last to retire, "disputing the ground inch by inch," and Hancock "only waited for that gallant regiment, already sorely pressed by the enemy, to get into position," before again advancing to attack. As showing ho w closely they were followed by a too-confident foe, by the time they had formed in the new line among the other troops awaiting them behind the crest, Gen. Hancock further says:

"At this moment the advance of the enemy was under the crest and within 30 paces of my command. I ordered a forward movement to the crest. The whole line advanced cheering, and on arriving there delivered two volleys, doing great execution. The order was then given to charge down the slope, and with reiterated cheers the whole command advanced in line of battle. A few of the leading spirits of the enemy were bayoneted; the remainder then broke and fled. The want of protection in my rear, and expecting an assault from that quarter every moment, I ordered a halt at the foot of the slope, and delivered a terrible fire along the whole line, expending from 15 to 20 rounds" (per man). "The plunging fire from the redoubt, the direct fire from the right, and the oblique fire from the left, were -so destructive that after it had been ordered to cease and the smoke arose, it seemed as if no man had left the ground unhurt who had advanced within 500 yards of our line. The enemy were completely routed and dispersed."

It is well to state that the part taken by Gen. Hancock's command was the decisive blow, culminating in victory, to an all day's fight in front of the rebel Fort Magruder by Hooker's division, relieved late in the day short of ammunition by Gen. Kearney's troops.

Companies A and C, of the Sharpshooters, on the morning of the 5th were sent to the front and found the enemy well intrenched, with whom they exchanged shots until afternoon, when they were withdrawn and retired to the reserve, being present on that part of the line where Hancock made his charge. During the day and a portion of the night rain fell almost continually, so that everywhere about them water and mud prevailed. Our boys had taken possession of a barn at nightfall and made every preparation possible for Comfort until morning; but they were doomed to disappointment, being turned out to make room for some 200 prisoners. "This treatment," Aschmann says, "was well calculated to rouse our ire, but it could not be helped, and so we had to exchange our comfortable quarters for the open field and its miseries." Had it been for wounded men the boys would not have cared; as it was, they were very much disposed to growl—they were truly

"Uncle Sam's Sorry Soldiers" that rough night. The Sharpshooters had to take their share of the hardships with the rest of the troops; there were no especial buildings for them, but all were treated alike.

"On the following day we marched over the battle field and witnessed the casualties of warfare. Dead and wounded lying uncared for everywhere. A great many of the enemy's wounded fell in our hands, and were brought in by our men. We camped three days in the vicinity of the battle field, marching away on the 9th through the town of Williamsburg headed for Richmond. Following the route the enemy had taken, we witnessed everywhere evidences of his utter demoralization and hasty flight."—Capt. Aschmann.

On the 5th marching orders had been received at the-Sharpshooter camp before Yorktown; all were packed and prepared, but they did not move into the town until the 7th. Marching four miles they pitched their tents within the deserted fortifications in the heart of the village. Before starting they were joined by a new company, L, which had just arrived from Minnesota—a fine looking-body of men, that did great credit to that young state.

A large number of cannon, all their heavy guns and ammunition, had been left behind by the enemy, many of which were spiked. Torpedoes were also discovered in and around the works, brought to light by rebel prisoners; and the spot where the murderous missile exploded and killed the unfortunate Lathrop of the telegraphic service was marked by a large hole in the ground near one of the poles that held the electric wire. These prisoners testified to the shooting qualities of the Sharpshooters, who they affirmed had made fatal work with the enemy, both on the fortifications and in the rifle pits. One old negro expressed his-opinion in this laconic style:

"By golly! Stick up a cap, an' a hole gets in it immejately."

On the 8th the regiment received the long expected Sharps rifles, now needed more than ever, as the Colts were for our dangerous service found defective in many respects, and they gladly turned in the "five shooters." On: receiving the new arms the men were impatient to get again within shooting distance of the enemy. These rifles shot both linen and skin cartridges, of 52 caliber, and also had primers, little, round, flat coppered things, which were inserted below the hammer; but the regular army or hat cap was more generally used, as the primers were not always a_ "sure thing; "also carried the angular bayonet.

While at this place the orderly-sergeant of Company G-returned to his position in his company at his own request, Sergt. Brown, of New Hampshire, succeeding him as acting sergt.-major, *vice* Horton appointed lieutenant of another company and afterwards adjutant of the regiment *vice* Willett, resigned.

York river was at this time full of sailing craft of all descriptions. The scene on the water was simply grand, the trim white sails in countless numbers standing "off and on," while huge steamers moved back and forth, altogether presenting a picture of bustle and excitement deserving the attention and ready pencil of an artist. It was a complete spectacle, and a grand one. Troops were hurriedly embarking for a move up river, whither the gun-boats had already gone, as also the division of Gen. Franklin fresh from. McDowell's corps on the Rappahannock, which had been aboard the transports until after the evacuation, when they were pushed ahead by boat to West Point on the Pamunkey, where on the morning of the 7th they had a fight lasting from 11 to 3, when the enemy retired, "all his attacks having been repulsed."

On the night of the 8th the Sharpshooters left Yorktown by steamer State of Maine, and proceeding to West Point, disembarked the afternoon of the 9th by means of small boats from steamboat to shore, the water being shallow. They went into temporary camp near the landing. It was a sight to see the ship's tackling lift the cattle off the boats and drop them into the water. Down they would go, almost invariably out of sight, but soon their horns and nose would show up, as they swam snorting and plunging to shore in countless numbers. Generally, they would be dropped into the water right side up, but occasionally a slip occurred in their struggles, whereby they went down head first to plunge about and roll over before they came to the surface. But they were patriotic beeves—going to meet their destiny. Hundreds of horses were also unloaded the same way, and the boys on the deck would bet their hard-tack and tobacco on which equine or bovine would get to shore first.

The battle at this place occurred before our arrival, as before stated, and after a sharp action the enemy left. While here awaiting orders to move on, the men were employed in assisting to remove rations and stores from the row boats; the new company, L, occupying the time drilling in the manual, also in skirmishing; and for this latter purpose Capt. Drew was detailed to instruct them, assisted a portion of the time by his first sergeant. Under Capt. Drew's able lessons in this necessary art of the service, the company in the brief time given them made great progress, being highly complimented therefor. On the 13th the regiment took up the line of march, and were destined to experience a full share of the hardships and fatigues the Union soldiers had to undergo during their stay in the vicinity of Richmond.

A TOUGH MARCH.

We left West Point at 5 o'clock the morning of May 13th, loaded down with packed knapsacks and haversacks, canteens filled, gun and ammunition. Falling in behind artillery and loaded wagons, a most wearisome trip commenced, only an imperfect description of which can be fairly given. In fact, only those who have taken part in these trying marches can appreciate the hardship incurred. The first mile was very fair walking, when we were brought to a sudden standstill by the command "Halt! "Five minutes later the bugle sounds the advance, but it is slow traveling now, with road narrow, crowded, hot and dusty; a quarter of a mile further on, halt again for three minutes. Advance 10 rods more—" Halt! "Men begin to rest their aching shoulders by sticking their rifles under their knapsacks, some resting on old tree stumps, others lying down stretched out on their backs. "Listen boys, there goes the bugle "—Attention! "Fall in—Get up there—Keep in your places--Close up, men!" Forward 50 paces and again "Halt! "Now it is down on your back, road side, middle of the road—never mind the dust—anywhere so you get down. Presently we hear: "Open order! '2 for some mounted officers, or maybe a few pieces of artillery. Something the matter ahead—" no further movement for a full hour." Off go knapsacks, some eat, drink and crack jokes—swap lies—others roll over and sleep. All to be startled up into line by that everlasting bugle sounding "Attention!" Then "advance," and away we go, two miles now, halting every 10 rods about two minutes each time, then another halt. Col. Ripley now came along and gave us 20 minutes rest at his own risk, for which he received cheers. After a long 20 minutes, at least 45, we push on 20 rods more and halt again. So it goes all day long, pushing ahead, slow time, common time, quick, and double-quick to catch up, and sudden halting. All mixed up with dust, dirt, sweat and lame shoulders. Towards the close of the day a rumor spread among the companies that the Sharpshooters were to be sent ahead, and that a fight would probably take place. Passing Gen. McClellan and others, at a crossing of roads, helped to confirm the belief of a meeting with the rebels before going much farther. The men began to revive in consequence, the report acting as a stimulant on their tiresome, dusty march. For no matter how worn out and fatigued troops are, when they are about to fight, a sort of superhuman second strength comes to them, and, forgetful of their past trials, they rush in, animated as it were with a new life. But it proved merely a rumor, although it may have originally started on good grounds—perhaps the Johnnies heard the Sharpshooters were coming and ran away. It was nearly sundown when we reached Cumberland Landing on the Pamunkey, after a long day's march of only 12 miles, but about the toughest in all our experience, when we pitched our ponchos in an old cornfield near the river. Companies A and C joined us *en route.*

An instance occurred during this march showing how -easy it is to misjudge the carrying capacity of men by their size. One of the six-footer heavy weights of the company in the right files where the tallest men are placed, had been complaining considerably on account of his sore shoulders, although it was not in a cross manner, he being really one of the best natured of men, when he was jokingly scolded for his grumbling by the orderly, marching to his left—a light weight and much smaller sized man. The result was that another heavy member, known as "Buckshot," who marched in the center of the company, a tent mate of -the orderly, made a wager that the latter had the heaviest load in the company. This the orderly had no idea was the case, although he was carrying besides the usual articles of "extras," shoes, etc., extra ammunition and the company books. However, when they reached Cumberland they weighed up, and sure enough the sergeant's knapsack weighed 28 lbs to 22 for his tent mate, the third heaviest being 17, and that was not the big fellow's either. This is mentioned as showing that it was not always the biggest looking man that stood the greatest "wear and tear." For while it is true that there were some heavy men, and the two above mentioned were among them, who seemed able to stand everything—good marchers, rough and ready campaigners—yet is it also true that the light weights, from 140 down, were unexcelled for all manner of hard service.

We sometimes hear, out of service, of men carrying 70 lbs in their knapack. But no such back-breaking, sidesplitting weight was carried by the soldiers—unless some unfortunate was working out a sentence, walking a beat$_s$ under guard thus loaded; in lieu of the ball and chain, or log substitutes for thumb-tying, the stocks and other hard inflictions. A knapsack must not be shoddy to hold 70 pounds. In light marching order the knapsack, if carried at all, which was hardly the case, had little more within or on top than a rolled blanket, sometimes extra rations, and the balance of 60 rounds of ammunition that couldn't go in a 40-round cartridge box. At other times the knapsack varied all the way from a new outfit—generally with new troops—to the smallest possible kit or supply of extras, principally underclothes, poncho or rubber blanket, and woolen blanket—overcoats turned in. These all told, with the 9 or 10 lb gun, 40 rounds, canteen of water (pretty weighty), haversack packed with hard bread, coffee, sugar, and pork boiled or raw, added, 40 pounds would be more like it with all accouterments; and frequently half that weight was all the boys carried, particularly when off on some hurried service requiring quick movements, wherein the weight of the knapsack itself cut no figure. The average weight of a knapsack with us on general service would not exceed, well packed, 15 pounds.

Here we rested until the 15th, being ordered into line the afternoon of the 14th to be hurriedly reviewed by Secretary Seward from Washington, accompanied by Gen. McClellan and staff. Cumberland Landing, 27 miles from Richmond, boasted of two or three old houses, and was lined in front with many boats while we were there.

On the 15th another extraordinary day's march occurred, over a very wet, muddy road, the rain pouring down all the time, stopping often at long periods, and accomplishing *five miles* from half-past six A. M. to four P. M., at about which latter hour we arrived at White House. The roads were in such a bad state that it often required eight or ten horses to move the artillery, the passing soldiers assisting in pulling the cannon out of the deep mud holes. Owing to the difficulty in transportation, provisions were scarce, and short rations in order.

Gen. McClellan reports: "On the 15th and 16th the divisions of Franklin, Smith and Porter were with great difficulty moved to White House, 5 miles in advance. So bad was the road that the train of one of these divisions required 36 hours to pass over this short distance."

We encamped in a clover field near the White House on the Pamunkey, 20 miles northeast of Richmond. This building, said to be on the site of the one wherein Washington was married, was occupied, and a guard stationed around the premises to keep out intruders. It was the property of the Lees, on a plantation of 1,200 acres, with better soil than we had yet seen, a part of which was sowed with wheat; and were it not for the existing military surroundings would have presented a very domestic appearance. A pretty spot, accessible by steamers and sailing craft from York river; many vessels of different kinds lining the shore close by, loaded with provisions and other necessary articles for the army. The railroad to Richmond crossed the river at this point previous to the destruction of the bridge. We were in the midst of a splendid clover field of many acres, while above us, on the opposite side of the road, was a fine old apple orchard of 75 trees. Numberless small tents, amid which waved the regimental colors, denoted the different bodies of troops that encamped around us. The beautiful growing fields were soon trampled into dust and destroyed, as the Union troops crossed over them. And feelings of pity must have possessed thoughtful minds to see that hitherto quiet and peaceable spot, indicative of the days of joy and contentment when the gallant cavalier George Washington became a loving visitor, now subjected to the ruthless tramp of the armed soldier, the iron hoof of the plunging steed and the deep ruts of the ponderous artillery.

"Oh grief! o'er you fair meads and smiling lawns Must steeds of carnage batten, men of blood Their fell magnificence of murtherous pomp Pavillion in you placid groves of peace."

As an illustration of the fact that it wasn't bullets alone that decreased the army rolls, especially on this campaign, a young man named Isaac M. Barker, of the Wisconsin company, died on the 18th of May at West Point where he had been left with the commissary department when the company moved from there, from the effects of vaccination, his arm having swelled to a great degree. More men died or were discharged from sickness than were lost in battle. The tough marches they had to undergo caused many of them to break down and become unfit for further active service. Later on, they became so inured to these hard services as to appear able to stand almost anything in that line. But it took considerable time to make them so perfect, and many fell by the roadside before that great desideratum of a soldier's life was fairly accomplished.

Striking tents on the 19th the troops moved on towards the Chickahominy, passing by Tunstall Station and Barker's Mills. White flags were freely displayed from the houses on the way, and oftentimes the provost guard were stationed around residences to satisfy the defenseless inmates that no harm was intended or would be allowed by the Union troops; which appeared to gratify as well as to surprise many, as they had been led to believe by the rebel officers and soldiers that we were bound to plunder them. But plunder was not what we were after. Reports had been falsely circulated among these people that the Union troops were driving the women and children from Williamsburg forward; at the same time they admitted that the rebel soldiery did pillage to a great extent before leaving.

At Barker's Mills the regiment encamped from the 22d to the 26th, in a pleasant grassy spot near a heavy belt of timber, with good water easily obtained, and it proved to be a long time before they found such another favorable camping ground. We purchased while at this camp many articles of provisions, such as sweet potatoes $2 per bushel, onions 25 cents a dozen, eggs 50 cents, chickens 75 cents each, and other things at pretty steep prices. The gold and silver paid the inhabitants therefor, they stated was the first hard coin they had handled or even seen for a long time. They did not appear to have a high appreciation of Confederate scrip, some of whom had a large supply of that valueless paper on hand. One of our men, William B. Sandel, visited a house close by, before the provost got his guard stationed, and inquired for eggs. The mistress stated that an officer had engaged all she had, but Sandel, determined not to be put off in that way, said positively that he must have a half dozen, and to her inquiry as to how she was to manage it, replied:

"Well, give me six eggs, and then give the officer if he comes, *all you have*. You need not tell him I had any."

A good-natured looking daughter hereupon with a laugh, declared that a Yankee trick, and gave the eggs.

During the forenoon of the 26th, we went into camp on Gaines' Hill, from the high grounds of which the city of Richmond could be seen in the distance, beyond the Chickahominy river which ran by us at the foot of the hill.

THE VICTORY AT HANOVER COURT HOUSE.

May 27, 1862.

On the 27th of May at an early hour, before daylight, the Sharpshooters rolled out of their tents and fell into line, the rain falling fast; orders being received to march at daylight, with three days' cooked rations and 100 rounds of ammunition. Leaving camp at four A. M., the regiment as part of Gen. Porter's newly organized

5th corps, made a forced march of 18 miles to the right, notwithstanding the heavy rain falling, the deep mud, and swollen creeks which they forded, and arrived about noon in the vicinity of Hanover Court House. The enemy had for several days been posting large bodies of troops on the right flank and in rear of the Union lines, threatening our communications with the Pamunkey and York rivers, whereby he could be in position to help the rebel Jackson; and attack Gen. McDowell should the latter leave Fredericksburg to reinforce Gen. McClellan, as it was expected he would, and whose advance was then eight miles south of the Rappahannock. For the purpose of driving this force back, and to cut the Virginia Central, and Richmond & Fredericksburg railroads, was this sudden movement of Gen. Porter's command decided on.

No movement could have been more quickly executed, and nothing could exceed Gen. McClellan's promptness here; as at Hampton in moving after his arrival from Washington immediately on Yorktown, as also at Williamsburg and at West Point. The critic that intimates tardiness in the movements of the Army of the Potomac on the Peninsula campaign, is false as to the facts, and does an injustice to officers and men. From the first, there was no delay in moving when the order came; from Hampton to Yorktown, from Yorktown to the Chickahominy; and before daylight of the next morning after reaching the last named line, Porter's corps was off on a hurried march 18 miles to the right, through the heaviest rain and deepest mud, to win an important victory. We dare to say that no army ever moved quicker or with more determination, than the Army of the Potomac on the Peninsula campaign.

As a fair instance of how our soldiers suffered by these hurried, fatiguing marches regardless of the weather, to get into action, and which too often occurred when they were better fitted to sleep than fight—but for the martial and heroic excitement that kept them up—we quote Gen. Butterfield on his brigade:

"Our march to the battle field near Hanover Court House was the most severe I have ever experienced. Half an hour before the fight began I hardly thought it possible for my men to pitch camp and prepare supper, so much fatigued were they with the march in mud, rain and sun."

As before said, too often was this the case that our soldiers went into the fight all but worn out and used up with fatigue; nothing but patriotic excitement and stern duty kept them up.

By the time our regiment had arrived at the front, leading Morell's division, and preceded only by a strong detachment of cavalry and some light artillery (Benson's) under Gen. Emory, the rain had stopped and the sun came out hot, which while it dried the soaking water from the soldiers' clothes, brought the perspiration within. It was a veritable scorcher. Advancing through a large field by the right flank, the Sharpshooters halted and formed line of battle on the right of the road at

The distance reported by some officers-14 miles—may have been correct by the map; but by the roads traveled and the time taken we figured it out 18. It might have been 14 miles on horseback, but we guess it was fully 18 afoot. McClellan's chief of staff, Gen. Marcy, reports the march as "more than 20 miles."

KINNEYS FARM, being about 400 yards from the enemy who were in a lane behind a rise of ground covered with wheat, sending down to our artillery a shower of bullets and canister shot. Quickly the Union cannon responded, while skirmishers in front became engaged. As we entered the field, the enemy were loudly cheering over their capture of a company of skirmishers from the 25th New York, sent out with cavalry, while a small rebel flag was defiantly waved from the lane. This was soon lowered, however, and the cheering stopped by the Union guns. Remaining in line some minutes under fire, orders were finally given to move forward, several members of the regiment being hit at this point. Our men were divided; a portion crossed to the left of the road under Ripley, the, lieutenant-colonel, and advancing in skirmish *line* through the wheat field took part in the capture of a rebel cannon. On the right of the road the Wisconsin and Swiss companies deployed as skirmishers through a small wood and into a large field beyond, Company I, of Michigan, following as a reserve, under command of Trepp, the major—Col. Berdan having general command of all the

Sharpshooters. The enemy fled, our men pressing steadily forward two miles further, passing a number of rebel surgeons who were busily engaged with the wounded. The Wisconsin men captured some prisoners, among them a

North Carolina lieutenant who claimed to be "too exhausted to run." We didn't blame him for being frightened a little, for our men came down on them with a rush—there was no halting after they got started. The Johnnies were surprised, it was done so quick—their loss here being 17 killed, 27 wounded, and 31 prisoners.

The cavalry and artillery had in the meantime pushed on in flying style after the fugitives, capturing more of them.. Those members of the 25th New York that had been taken, succeeded in escaping from the enemy during the chase. So far, so good. Everything went off just as nicely as the most ardent patriot could have expected. It was sport for the boys. But it appears that the enemy's main force were some distance to the left of the scene of the first fight, massed for mischief, and after the victorious Unionists had passed by, made an attack on our rear at

PEAKE'S STATION.

The 44th New York, 25th New York, and 2d Maine, under Gen. Martindale, were for a long time hotly engaged at this point, exposed to cross-fires from surrounding woods; but although many gallants fell, yet bravely did the little command hold their ground. On hearing of the attack the advanced troops were ordered back, and away went infantry, Zouaves, artillery, and Sharpshooters at a rapid pace, finally on double-quick towards the woods where lay concealed the rebel force. Regiment after regiment rushed running into line when near the woods, and with a loud hurrah, moving right on, charged fiercely through the timber. The Sharpshooters deployed out double-quick, and entering the wood hurried forward. Some of them became immediately engaged, but the main body were brought suddenly to a halt by a deep ditch before a second piece of woods. Scrambling through this they pushed rapidly ahead. The firing was loud and rapid, while the dense smoke rolled low in heavy clouds rendering objects indistinct. The rebels were driven out from the wood, over the road, down the railroad, through a wheat field, and beyond to another wood a mile off. They were badly cut up—dead and wounded lying all around. The Unionists fought well; the 44th and 25th New York, 2d Maine, 9th (Irish) Massachusetts, 62d Pennsylvania, 5th New York (with their flaming red costume), and the 1st U. S. Sharpshooters (dressed in dark green). Other regiments were on the field and took a prominent part, principally on the flanks; but those above named were in the hottest of the fight, and were the principal ones engaged in the immediate front of the enemy. The Union loss was quite heavy among the three regiments first mentioned, but it was not as great as that of the Confederates.

The rebels were completely routed, leaving knapsacks, blankets and guns scattered promiscuously about, and getting away themselves evidently in much confusion. The batteries were well worked, sending screeching shot and shell after the retreating forces. Capt. Griffin used his guns with great effect; a rebel shot killing one of his horses, from a gun down the road, he turned on it instantly, sighting and firing the cannon himself, putting a shell through their caisson, which blew up, scattering the fragments over the road, causing the enemy to scamper hurriedly. About sunset the battle was over.

A large number of the rebel dead were buried the following day, upwards of 700 prisoners taken, with one gun and considerable amount of small arms and baggage. The Union troops succeeded in cutting the railroads, driving the rebel forces off. The latter at this battle were commanded by Gen. Branch, of North Carolina (an ex-member of congress).

The regimental surgeon, Guy C. Marshall, was taken prisoner at field hospital by rebel cavalry and never returned to the regiment; while his hospital attendant, Charles L. Wood, a New York member of Company G, had a narrow escape from a shower of bullets from the same party, who left him lying on the ground unhurt. In his desperate fix he dropped as if shot, and they thought he was. Charlie was a good one, and like a true patriot didn't want to be captured—and never was to the end of his three years. Dr. Marshall died while a prisoner, after having performed noble service among the sick and wounded at Libby prison. Having been allowed to pass out when needing medicines, he finally, finding his many protests unheeded relative to the apparent neglect and sufferings of our imprisoned soldiers, obtained an audience with Jeff Davis, the Confederate president. Whether on account of his earnest denunciation of the treatment our men were receiving, or in any other manner he angered the chief traitor, his liberty was taken from him and he was closely confined. Even then he did all possible to help his comrades, until breaking down himself, he died a real martyr to the Union cause, a true patriot, an heroic man. He had been very popular in his regiment.

A number of prisoners were captured by the Sharpshooters; among the lot were three captured by Private Benjamin D. Atwell, of Wisconsin, a youth 18 years of age. Pushing through the dense woods with Eli Vincent, they found a chance to shoot from behind a tree, when as Ben was about to fire, he looked back and discovered three rebels capping their guns, with their backs towards him. Rushing close up, he ordered them to "throw down those guns, you rascals, or I'll shoot you!" They obeyed instantly and turning around replied: "We are your prisoners." The trio consisted of a second lieutenant, an orderly sergeant, and a private. Ben had "surrounded them," surely as he laughingly informed me, passing, but what to do with them puzzled him, especially after calling to Vincent to return and help him, who, replying harshly: "Take care of them yourself, I've got something else to attend to," was rapidly moving forward. Ben, however, shouldered their guns and marched them to the rear to the provost guard. His excited companion pushed forward through the timber with long strides until brought suddenly to a halt. An intrenched rebel behind a log a few paces distant had raised his piece and was about to pull the trigger, but being discovered, Eli quickly brought his rifle to his shoulder and fired—stopping but a moment to "mark the shot," he went on.

When the Sharpshooters went into the second fight the heat of the day was intense, and from the effect of their previous exertions in marching and fighting they were very much fatigued; therefore on receiving orders to assemble on the road they were not sorry, as darkness was fast gathering and the fighting was over. It's true a number of them wished to push further on over the open field, but were restrained on the edge of the woods owing to a peremptory order to halt at that place and assemble. The regiment rested for the night in a piece of woods nearby. During the following day many prisoners were brought in by our troops, who were also engaged in burying the dead. The trees, brush, and riddled fences, showed plainly the fierceness of the conflict.

A number of individual cases of self-defense occurred in this battle. One of the most provoking, and also comical, took place in the evening. A plucky little member of the 9th Massachusetts, having been slapped across the mouth and sent reeling to the ground by a large, corpulent looking reb, in response to the Irishman's demand to surrender, got even with the big fat Carolinian, after picking himself up and making a big race for it, by using the bayonet; to use his own phrase: "tickling him in the stomach."

While in this neighborhood, H. J. Peck, of Company F, secured an officer who was hurrying down the road:

"Come over here, colonel, I want you." yelled Peck, and as the officer turned he saw a well-aimed Sharps covering him. It was enough, he came in,—a second lieutenant of the 7th North Carolina,—and the Vermont boy passed him to the rear, after securing his revolver and sword. A member of Company L also captured two men, after the fighting had ceased, while he was hunting for fuel in the woods.

Considerable amusement was caused by a member of Company G, who was known as "Snap Shot," throwing off his coat before entering the last battle, discovering to his comrades a mailed or steel shirt which he hurriedly divested himself of; remarking: "I have carried that weighty nuisance long enough." He had worn it on all the long and tiresome marches, and when he got into the fight, threw it away.

The regimental loss at Hanover was 20 killed and wounded. Among the latter was Sergt. Lewis J. Allen, of Company F, who got a whack side of the head, knocking him Bat in the wheat field. Some of the boys rushed for him, but he got up and ran wildly ahead. He was caught by Peck and brought back, being a little off in his mind just then, but came around all right soon after. He proved a stayer, and remained with his company throughout the enlistment, in all its trials and hardships. Sometime after, he was attacked with brain fever which he attributed to that blow, but recovered.

Gen. McClellan arriving next morning was greeted by the troops with the loudest cheers. While here he sent the dispatch to the war department:

HANOVER COURT HOUSE, May 28, 2 P. M. Porter's action of yesterday was truly a glorious victory. Too much credit cannot be given to his magnificent division and its accomplished leader. The rout of the rebels was complete—not a defeat, but a complete rout. Prisoners are constantly coming in; two companies have this moment arrived, with excellent arms. There is no doubt that the enemy are concentrating everything on Richmond. I will do my best to cut off Jackson, but am doubtful whether I can. It is the policy and duty of the government to send me by water all the well-drilled troops available. I am confident that Washington is in no danger. Engines and cars in large numbers have been sent up to bring down Jackson's command. I may not be able to cut them off, but will try. We have cut all but the Fredericksburg & Richmond railroad. The real issue is the battle about to be fought in front of Richmond. All our available troops should be collected here—not raw regiments, but the well-drilled troops. It cannot be ignored that a desperate battle is before us. If any regiments of good troops remain unemployed it will be an irreparable fault committed.

GEO. B. Mc CLELLAN, Maj.-Gen.

HON. E. M. STANTON, Secretary of War.

Gen. Porter in his report of this engagement thus speaks of his command, which consisted of the following troops: Gen. Morell commanding division composed of Gens. Martindale and Butterfield's, and Col. McQuade's brigades; two regiments of cavalry and a light battery, under Gen. Emory; and Col. Warren's brigade. He reports:

"The defeat and rout at Hanover of Brig.-Gen. Branch's command,—8,000 Georgia, North Carolina and Virginia troops,—with the loss to them of eight officers and more than 1,000 men; the destruction of extensive bridges, railroad and others; cutting off the rebel force in Northeastern Virginia from all rapid relief from Richmond; and the movements of Col. Warren's command from Old Church along the Pamunkey, has caused the rapid retreat to Richmond from below Fredericksburg of Gen. Anderson's command; thus releasing for active operations the large forte under Gen. McDowell, and I think must have relieved the government of all apprehensions of an attack on Washington. Two important military railroad trains were captured and destroyed by Gen. Stoneman's and Gen. Emory's commands, respectively. I desire to express my admiration for the conduct of the officers and men in the laborious march to Hanover; the steadiness with which they turned from the pursuit of a retreating foe to meet the unexpected attack of an unknown force in their rear; the confidence they evinced in their officers; the good order in which they went into action. Specially worthy of note was the firm resistance Martindale's brigade presented to the attack of a superior force, holding it in check till it could be met and routed by the remainder of the division."

CASUALTIES KNOWN.

Co. A—Wounded: Martin Tanner, Jacob Wildz.

Co. B—Wounded: Clinton Loveridge, severely.

Co. F—Wounded: Lewis J. Allen, Benjamin Billings, W. F. Dawson mortally.

Co. G—Wounded: Corp. Hiram N. Richardson, scalp, and one finger lost.

Co. I—Wounded: James Davis.

Co. L—Wounded: Hammond Fallon, Fingor Fingalson.

On the morning of the 29th rations were brought up and dealt out to the very hungry troops, but in the afternoon we marched back to camp at Gaines' Hill, where the sick and guards had been left during the movement, and where we arrived after another fatiguing trip at a late hour at night. Capt. Aschmann relates the following incident of - this tough march:

"The darkness of the night, bad roads, and the many swamps and forests we had to pass, made our march very difficult and dangerous. One of our men, Jacob Bachman, sank up to his arm pits in the mire, and it was impossible for him to extricate himself from his perilous position until the next morning, when some stragglers found him and brought him exhausted and worn out to our camp, where he recovered from the terrible shock to his system only after many weeks of careful treatment."

While at the Gaines' Hill camp we were visited by a terrific thunderstorm, the lightning striking a stack of guns of an adjoining regiment scattering the same, the fiery ball playing along the entire line of shining bayonets, causing some damage to life and property. The rain poured down in torrents, so that tent life was anything but agreeable just then either for health or comfort, and the sick list naturally increased from the dampness and exposure.

Our rations, though not extensive in variety, were generally fresh and good. But it was impossible for some of the men to stand desiccated vegetable. The Wisconsin orderly liked it, and on introducing it at this camp was particular to praise its wholesomeness. But the next morning when he rolled out for roll call, he found himself surrounded with all the camp kettles full of the desiccated soup, contributed by the boys, as they couldn't stand the flavor. It was issued in big, square, pressed cakes about an inch thick, and a small piece made a mess—a little went a good ways. But they had cooked the entire week's ration, a whole square, thus making it too strong,—they could smell it from afar off,—and it took more than a week's scouring of the kettles with a vast amount of cook's swearing, to get rid of the offensive taste. As for the orderly, he had enough to last him for a whole campaign, and didn't draw any more of that kind of ration.

Soon after the Hanover fights, Company L left the regiment (May 31st) and reported to the 1st Minnesota volunteers in the 2d corps, and thereafter remained with, and shared in the glories and honors of, that famous regiment—that gallant 1st Minnesota which, with the brave and undaunted 2d Wisconsin, so ably represented the Northwest at the first Bull Run, where they both, in several notable instances, withstood the brunt of battle, and left that fated field at the last moment unwhipped and with colors untarnished; and although at the time, the eastern press teemed with praises and sensational articles about certain regiments from their immediate localities, without even a bare mention of the two now under notice, yet on the records are they placed, as 'tis due them, among the staunchest there engaged. Probably this apparent ignoring of the western men can be accounted for, because Gorman and Coon "couldn't see" the reporter's demand to "come down "to the extent of $50, before going into the fight. Their reply in substance: "If my men get a name, they must earn it," settled it. They were not heralded after the fight, but they got name and fame notwithstanding, that will last, and they earned it.

On the afternoon of the 31st the guns at Fair Oaks were distinctly heard, and several times was the regiment ordered into line expecting to move forward. On this day the Sharpshooters joined Gen. Martindale's brigade for a short time, and at an early hour on the morning of June 1st they left camp, and, marching a mile and a half to the swamp of the Chickahominy, relieved Stockton's Michigan regiment as pickets, where they remained until noon of the following day, being then relieved by the 4th Michigan. The heavy firing during the fight at Fair Oaks on the other side of the river plainly indicated the severity of the action. On the hills back of the pickets, artillery were in position, and above them in the air were two balloons some distance apart, while in the neighborhood of the swamp fatigue parties were busily engaged building roads and bridges. A squad of men under Corp. Harmon Ellis, of Company G, were employed as guard over the house and premises of Dr. Gaines, nearby. The doctor was under arrest for signaling the enemy across the swamp. He did not get away in time and was caught in his own house, but attempting -to escape, Ellis aimed his gun and stopped him. The doctor complained about the Yankee soldiers ruining his plantation, and his "niggers "not getting enough to eat. He knew nothing civil towards a "Yankee hireling." He was an insolent old fellow and the boys watched him closely. The last Ellis saw of him, on his guard being relieved, he was in the midst of a lot of other prisoners, awaiting under an umbrella for transportation to Yankeedom, where it was hoped he would learn manners. On the afternoon of the 2d the regiment returned to camp.

Considerable excitement was occasioned at times during the ascension of the balloons, inasmuch as they became a target for the rebel cannon posted on high ground across the swamp. The balloons would be sent up from different points, and as soon as the rebel gunners obtained range they would come down, and change their position. A rope attached prevented their ascent beyond a certain distance, and they became a valuable auxiliary for the occasion.

HAIL COLUMBIA ON THE GRAPEVINE BRIDGE.

A comrade sends an account (somewhat lengthy) of how Porter's chief of artillery wanted four men and a sergeant to go on to Grapevine Bridge in the swamp and watch the enemy's movements, and in case they attempted to cross from the connecting bridge over the river, threatening to attack our batteries, to fire a signal shot for our artillery to open their "50 guns" onto the unseen foe as they crowded onto the bridge, Sharpshooters and all, as the artillery officer had kindly informed the detail on setting out that they would all be sacrificed, as "we could not risk a serious disaster to this wing of the army for a few men;" which comforting assurance was probably more to test their courage, but they were picked men, volunteers, and didn't scare worth a cent; besides they undoubtedly were unwilling to believe that our battery men would knowingly mow down Union soldiers to gain a moment's time, while our nimble Yankee boys were jumping and dodging about to get out of range.

The swamp had been flooded by some device of the enemy, either by cutting a dam above or erecting one below, I am unable to say which, and the water was several feet deep over a space of about 400 yards in width on our side of the river at a point where Grapevine Bridge crossed it. -This bridge over the swamp was a floating one, and moored by great grapevines attached to the scattering live oaks that stood about the swamp, in some cases with several feet of their roots out of the ground, like trees on stilts. From the approaching sounds of the battle it seemed probable that the enemy might presently get possession of the bridge over the river, which stream was narrow and deep. The bridge over the swamp, as well as the whole of that over the river, could not be seen from the height where the guns were. After several hours anxious waiting the Sharpshooters observed -that the advancing enemy were being suddenly driven back, in which Meagher's and Sickles' brigades took a prominent part, thus relieving the watchful sentinels of any further danger either from the enemy, or of being blown by our artillery to Hail Columbia.

On the 6th of June orders were received to divide the regiment into detachments to report to different division commanders, four companies remaining at headquarters—D, E, F and K. Company B was sent to Hooker's division, and Company H to Richardson's. Company H reported to Sumner's[1] headquarters at Seven Pines, where the Confederate sharpshooters were annoying our pickets. On arriving there a detail was sent to the front, where, despite the danger incurred at the time from the sharp firing as they approached, they succeeded in discovering the position of the enemy and stopped their shooting. The rebel sharpshooters soon found their match before them, and were thereafter very careful about exposing themselves. One morning soon after, a detachment under First Sergt. Barrett was sent across the "Nine-mile Road" to look after a part of the regular picket line, where several of our infantry men had been shot. Locating the enemy's position, four of our Sharpshooters deployed, two on each side of the road, and advanced carefully through the brush some 200 yards where they lay quietly watching for further developments; but seeing or hearing nothing they rigged up a stick with a hat and coat and shoved it out across the roadway, when instantly a report was heard and a bullet passed through the coat. The puff of smoke seeming to issue from the center of a tree 100 yards distant, the Sharpshooters then crawled forward either side of the road, keeping under cover as much as possible, firing at the right and left side of the tree, the result being of a very damaging character to the concealed Johnny, he receiving his quietus. The company was frequently called on to perform service of this kind, to locate lurking foes and silence their guns.

1 Edwin Vose Sumner was the oldest field commander on either side of the Civil War. He had served in the Black Hawk War and the Mexican War.

Companies A and I, under command of Maj. Trepp, were assigned to Gen. Smith's division on the right wing of the troops, the south side of the Chickahominy, Opposite Porter's corps on Gaines' Hill. Gen. Smith received the Sharpshooters again with a hearty welcome, at the same time providing for them in the best possible manner which told more than words, and the boys thought a good deal of "Baldy Smith "which was right, for when soldiers have the respect of their officers, and officers have the respect of the soldiers, they can be depended upon for the most arduous and trying duties. Stich was the fortunate case here, a mutual respect for each other.

The Sharpshooters occupied a redoubt called Fort Davidson, manned also by a battery of 12-pound Parrot guns. This garrison was placed under command of Maj. Trepp. They were ordered under arms every morning at daylight to guard against an attack on the fort. They also furnished daily 12 Sharpshooters for the picket lines where skirmishing was going on far in advance, with the enemy scarcely 150 yards away—within speaking distance. Artillery duels were frequent, and on several occasions the enemy made ineffectual sorties, being invariably driven back. One of the enemy's guns considerably annoyed Gen. Smith's troops with more or less damage, whereupon that wise officer had constructed a rifle pit for the Sharpshooters, who soon thereafter silenced it. Our troops suffered the most from sickness, "the sanitary condition being deplorable, owing to the fatigues the men had undergone recently, and typhus, dysentery and other diseases of a dangerous type spread with fearful rapidity, so that the sick list swelled to great proportions, and interfered considerably with the efficiency of the men. The field hospitals were rapidly filling up, and more than one-third of the men in our detachment were on the sick list."—Asenmann.

Companies C and G left the regimental camp and, marching several miles to the right, reported to Gen. Slocum for duty. This detachment was commanded by Capt. Drew, of G. Going into temporary camp near the Chickahominy, a scouting party of 10 men was sent out to reconnoiter the front. Picket details were ordered daily to Chickahominy Swamp, and several skirmishes occurred. On one occasion they had a hot time of it, on account of the severe fire of the enemy,—a miniature battle,—our pickets having been caught in the swamp knee deep in water, when the rebel pickets opened on them heavily, causing several narrow escapes, but without loss. The fighting was severe for awhile, our men returning the fire in sheer desperation, and with success. But they came out of the swamp in a sorry condition, wet through and covered with mud. They could fight on fair ground, but to swim and fight was a disadvantage they did not like. During one of these picket skirmishes (June 2d) John S. Cole, of Company C, was killed. Company B also had a sharp fight, later on, near Fair Oaks.

On the 11th the Michigan men, under Capt. Giroux, (Company C), were ordered off still further to the right, to Mechanicsville, leaving Company G alone, who were employed on picket duty at the front until the 13th when, striking tents, they joined Company C at Mechanicsville. This place had been considerably battered by shot and shell, the marks of which were plainly observed on the deserted buildings. It was not a very pleasant camping ground, an unhealthy odor pervading the place.

During this month the regiment lost several members by fever at the hospital on Gaines' Hill; among them, Corp. Gideon F. Jones, of Company G. His remains were taken to his friends in Wisconsin by Thomas McCaul, of the commissary department, who eluded the vigilance of the guards at White House landing, Fortress Monroe and Baltimore, and who, although absent without leave,—he actually stole his lost friend out of camp,—was willing to risk a punishment to have it go through safely. The dead soldier was buried at Fox Lake, and a handsome headstone illustrating the Sharpshooter service, erected by the citizens of East Randolph, where Jones resided at the time of enlistment.

Early on the morning of the 15th the two companies made a movement to the right expecting an attack, but returned a few hours later, and on the 17th camp was changed three-fourths of a mile to the right, between two small hills out of sight of the rebel artillerists, who were watching with their guns planted on the high hills on the south side of the Chickahominy. The church steeples of the rebel capitol could be seen from this point, four miles distant. On the 19th they again broke camp, and, marching with Gen. Taylor's Jersey brigade, after a hot and dusty tramp crossed the Chickahominy at Woodbury's Bridge, on the left of and below Gaines' Hill, and camped at Fair Oaks—a distance of about 12 miles. The division of Gen. Slocum was relieved at Mechanicsville by that of Cen. McCall, lately arrived from McDowell's army on the Rappahannock. The scene at Fair Oaks at the time the Sharpshooters arrived there, was not one likely to afford much encouragement; rather was it of a most appalling nature, with the numerous soldier graves scarcely dug out, so that often their feet and occasionally a head or arm protruded, while the stench was awful. And they were glad to get away from this forbidden spot, when on the 21st they were ordered back to Mechanicsville, where they arrived in the evening and reported to Gen. Reynolds, who commanded a brigade in McCall's division; and were then ordered into camp in a pine grove near that general's headquarters.

The enemy were getting thicker on the opposite hills and in advanced rifle pits, and although everything appeared quiet over there, save the rub-a-dub-dub boom! of the snare and base drums at reveille and retreat, the silence was ominous.

"From camp to camp, the hum Of either army stilly sounds," and our soldiers felt it in their bones, that a storm was brewing; and not much longer were they to wait its coming. Every time that drum pounder came around with his "rub-a-dub-dub, rub-a-dub-dub, boom! "yells and hideous noises from our side greeted the old and weary, and too "oft familiar sound." Some said it was a "nigger on horseback" coming down to tantalize the Yanks, but I guess that was made up.

THE SEVEN DAYS BATTLES.

For several days previous to the fighting to be especially known as the "Seven Days Conflict," considerable firing occurred along the lines, principally with artillery, and it became evident that a crisis Was about to occur. On the 22d Capt. Drew, with a squad of six scouts under Sergt. Benson, made a reconnoissance to the right at an early hour in the morning and returned safely, meeting with no opposition from the enemy, accomplishing the purpose for which they were sent out; and on the 25th the two companies were ordered under arms, heavy cannonading being heard particularly on our left, where on the south side of the swamp Gen. Hooker's division became engaged with the enemy in the action known as Oak Grove.

BATTLE OF MECHANICSVILLE,

June 26, 1862.

The enemy were discovered about noon on the right, having crossed above Meadow Bridge and attacked the Union pickets, driving them in, capturing some of our men, including a number of the noted "Bucktail" regiment of Gen. McCall's division. These Bucktails were Pennsylvanians, and were so called from the deer tails in their caps. At three P. M. the rebels advanced in force with skirmishers in front and made a determined attempt to drive in the

Union troops posted along the left bank of Beaver Dam creek. The Sharpshooters were instantly ordered into line, and held in readiness to move at a moment's notice. Meanwhile, the sick and disabled were hurried off to the left, some in ambulances, others on foot. At this time Thomas McCaul returned from his trip to

Wisconsin dressed in a very unmilitary uniform—straw hat, shirt sleeves, and coarse mixed trousers, with which he successfully escaped the provost guard at Washington. Although employed in the quartermaster's department, he shouldered a sick man's rifle, (I gave McCaul a 19 pound double-barrel rifle, borrowed from Company C,) and fell in for the fight. His absence from the regiment had been *unnoticed*.. He brought with him from friends at home, a bottle of "Bininger "—so it was marked, though some of the boys pretended it was currant wine—and a box of cigars, which Orderly Stevens placed on a stump and marching the company around it, they helped themselves with a smile for the landlord and a puff for Tommy, and Company G went into action smoking a Fox Lake cigar.

About four P. M. the Sharpshooters, under Capt. Drew, were ordered forward, leaving their knapsacks "stacked "in the pines, and crossing a ravine proceeded under fire over an open field in line of skirmishers to a thick wood. A detail from the two companies were stationed in rifle pits on the right of the road under Capt. Giroux, of Michigan, and Sergt. Staples, of Company G, where they remained during the action subjected to a scathing fire of canister shot and shell from the rebel batteries posted on an eminence 800 yards in front, which cut the limbs off the trees over their heads, and frequently plowed the dirt of the pits onto them. They assisted with the Bucktails in preventing the passage of the road by the enemy. The force under Drew on entering the wood commenced firing on the unseen foe, the thick smoke rendering objects a short distance off indistinct. The Union troops became hotly engaged and a severe fight occurred, the rapid discharge of musketry and the booming of cannon making a terrific noise. At nine P. M. after some five hours fighting, the enemy retired, and the Unionists rested on the damp ground for the night. The Sharpshooters without rations or cover, passed an uncomfortable night after their arduous exertions during the afternoon. The fighting was sharply contested but we succeeded that day in keeping the enemy off, the Sharpshooters doing their part; as also did the Bucktails of the Pennsylvania Reserves, six companies of whom came on with Gen. McCall. The troops slept on their arms that night amid the lamentable cries of the rebel wounded, which could be distinctly heard after nightfall along the lines.

During the afternoon a small force under Lieut. Shepard had taken position in advance behind a fence, and while there, suddenly encountered the enemy at close quarters; the latter having approached under cover of the dense smoke through the thick brush, noiselessly and unseen. Having ascertained the character of the force on the opposite side of the fence, the men opened on them through the rails and then fell back over a small field to the woods, before the enemy recovered from their surprise and returned the fire. A number of our boys on falling back, rapidly reloading their easy breech-loaders, turned and fired again, among them Alvin Sherman, who remained at the fence until he had fired several rounds, repeating the same on crossing the field notwithstanding the urgent orders of the lieutenant to hurry away. Among those wounded this day were: W. G. Cronkite, Company C, and C. A. Stevens, Company G, slight in neck.

At an early hour on the morning of the 27th (before daybreak), the Sharpshooters were ordered into the rifle pits on the right of the road, joining the detail under Giroux, and the Bucktails. The Union troops were at the time hurriedly moving away to the left, the commanding general deeming it necessary to draw in his greatly extended lines towards the Chickahominy bridges below Gaines' Hill, to make close connection with the main army. His right wing—Porter's corps—was in the vicinity of Mechanicsville, "too much in the air," too much exposed to a severe flank attack. Likewise his rear, which was now threatened by the rebel Jackson, who was approaching with a large force, and already close at hand, unprevented by our armies of the Shenandoah or the Rappahannock, the latter only 50 miles back,—"waiting for orders,"—said to be protecting Washington 60 miles further to the rear. Besides the line of supply to the Pamunkey river was in danger of being cut off,—had already been raided by the enemy's cavalry,— and Jackson could swoop in there any moment if not brought to a halt. These were the considerations that determined Gen. McClellan to make James river, held by our gunboats, the new base, rather than attempt to protect the lengthy old line, at the expense of his own strength in the face of the rebel army equalling in numbers his own. So it was ordered that the 5th corps should hold Jackson in check that day, the 27th, to gain time to effect the safe removal of the siege guns, wagon trains, the sick and disabled men; also, to prevent his crossing the Chickahominy between the Union army and the James.

The Sharpshooters and the Bucktails now in the rifle pits, on a rise of ground at the edge of a small piece of woods, commenced firing at daybreak on scouting parties of the enemy 600 yards off. Soon after, the rebel fieldpieces opened in their old position and a constant shelling of the rifle pits was the result, which was responded to by long-range shots from our men. About eight in the morning, Brig.- Gen. (John F.) Reynolds rode quietly and unattended to the woods, keeping behind the same in the open field, away from the road so as not to be seen by the enemy, dismounted at the timber and, personally visiting the pits, ordered the men to fall back quickly and in order, without noise, as the enemy were fast getting in the rear by a flank movement to the right, and the Union troops had left the place. His order to: "Fall back just as quickly and quietly as possible, men, as the enemy are upon us," came not a moment too soon, as the riflemen had scarce reached a half-mile away before the Confederates swarmed into the pits and on to the road, capturing a portion of the Bucktails who failed to receive the order to retire; also two Sharpshooters, Dewitt Collins and Richard B. Blodgett, of Company G, the latter dying in the Richmond prison a few weeks later. For this hazardous and noble act on the part of Gen. Reynolds, the Sharpshooters had good reason to feel very grateful and to become endeared to him, saving them as it did from capture if not annihilation, and the virtual breaking up of Companies C and G of the First Regiment. After giving the order, the general hurried back to his horse, galloping quickly off to the bead of his brigade.

Capt. Drew with a small squad of the Wisconsin company being in an advanced position on the left of the road, also narrowly escaped capture and for the time being he was lost to us. The Sharpshooters of Wisconsin and Michigan and the Pennsylvania Bucktails were the last of the Union troops to leave the scene of the sharply contested battle. Hurriedly snatching up our knapsacks as we passed by the late encampment in the pines, we pushed onward to the left, with the enemy close behind. It was an exciting time with little else to think of but get away. Our troops had all been withdrawn from the field before sunrise of the 27th, all but our Bucktails and Sharpshooters, rear guards and a few fieldpieces.

The battle of Mechanicsville was a Union victory, more so than our men imagined at the time. It appears that the Confederate generals had planned to swoop down on Porter's right and turn it in disaster; but the enemy had reckoned without its host, in this well-conceived charge. Its host was Stonewall Jackson, but he didn't come that day.

He failed to connect for once, at least, and as it turned out, the rebels were badly worsted.

The southern generals: D. H. Hill called it a "bloody repulse." Longstreet: "We had attacked at Beaver Dam and failed to make an impression, at that point losing several thousand men and officers. Next to Malvern Hill, the sacrifice at Beaver Dam was unequaled in demoralization during the entire summer."

McCall's division of Pennsylvania Reserves bore the brunt of this fight, although reinforced and assisted to some extent late in the day by Griffin's brigade of Morell's division on the right, while Gen. Martindale, still further to the right,. had been slightly engaged earlier in the day. The Reserves consisted of three brigades commanded respectively by Gens. Reynolds, Mead and Seymour.

Gen. McCall reports: "About noon, the 26th, the enemy were in motion, and at 12:30 P. M. our pickets at Meadow Bridge were driven in, and those along the road were ordered to fall back. About three P. M. the-enemy's lines were formed in my front and the skirmishers rapidly advanced, delivering their fire as they approached our lines. They were answered by my artillery and a rather general discharge of musketry. The enemy commanded by Gen. Lee boldly advanced in force under a heavy artillery fire and attacked my position from right to left. His principal effort was directed to my extreme right. Here for a long time the battle raged with great fury. The Georgians rushed with headlong energy, only to be mowed down by the steady fire of the gallant Second Regiment. The enemy now for a time retired from close-contest on the right, but he kept up during the whole day a heavy general fire of artillery and infantry, which, with the rapid reply of the Reserves, was at times one unbroken_ roar of a stunning depth. For hour after hour the battle was hotly contested, and the rapid fire of our artillery, dealing death to an awful extent, was unintermitted, while the greatly superior force of the enemy enabled him to precipitate column after column of fresh troops upon nay nearly exhausted lines. About sunset Griffin's brigade, with Edwards' (regular) battery, arrived. The former I requested its gallant leader to move to the extreme right, that being the weakest point in my position. Some time elapsed before these troops could reach their ground, and as the enemy ha(advanced, only a portion of this force could be brought into action. Then, a short time before the close of the engagement, the 4th Michigan relieved the 5th Pennsylvania, whose ammunition was exhausted; and two companies of the 14th New York joined the Rifles (Bucktails), and the detachment of Berdan's Sharpshooters. My loss in this action was, as nearly as I have been able to ascertain, 33 killed and 150 wounded. The loss of the enemy was heavy beyond precedent in this war for the numbers engaged. I learned from excellent authority while a prisoner in Richmond that Gen. Lee's loss in killed and wounded did not fall short of 2,000. In the published returns it appears that the 1st North Carolina lost nearly one-half of its effective force, and the 44th Georgia nearly two-thirds. Stonewall' Jackson's artillery was in the battle, although his infantry was several miles to the right."

The government records show a total Union loss of all engaged of 361—killed, 49; wounded, 207; captured and missing, 105.

The companies remaining at the Gaines Hill camp—D, E, F, and K—also came out, and Col. Ripley says of them, that they headed Morell's column, and took part late in the day near a battery, but "had but small share of the fighting."

Their turn was to come next, and very soon. "Some of the men, moved by pity for the sufferings of their wounded enemies left their lines to give them assistance; they were fired on, however, by the merciless rebels and had to abandon the attempt." Remaining on the field all night, they became the rear guard of Morell's division the next morning, covering the retreat—"as daylight appeared they found themselves alone." Quietly the men stole away being "especially cautioned against allowing their tin cups to rattle against their rifles, as the first sign was sure to be the signal for a rebel volley."

Further from Ripley: "As they approached the camp they had left on the preceding afternoon, a scene of desolation and destruction met their astonished eyes. Enormous piles of quartermaster and commissary stores were being fired, tents were struck, the regimental baggage gone and large droves of cattle were being hurried forward towards the lower bridges of the Chickahominy. Halted for a few minutes amidst the ruins of their abandoned camp where, however, they found the faithful quartermaster-sergeant (Edwin E. Robinson) with a scanty supply of rations, very grateful to men who had eaten nothing for twenty hours and expected nothing for some time to come."

When the other companies were sent to different commands early in June for outpost duty, Col. Berdan was ordered to visit the right and left alternately, to make such changes in the position of the Sharpshooter outposts and supports as was thought proper. On the day previous to the opening of the Mechanicsville battle, he says he had ridden out to the right and saw the enemy apparently working on their small earthworks, throwing dirt high in the air about twice a minute, which was all they appeared to be doing, so that he suspected it was only a ruse to make us think they were preparing for defense, when in fact they contemplated an attack at this point. Riding further along, he dismounted to take another look, and as he raised his glass saw a puff of smoke from some bushes at the creek, the ball passing under his right foot, producing a stinging sensation. Mounting his horse he hurried back to Gen. McCall's headquarters, reporting what he had seen, and suspected was the enemy's intention; whereupon the general ordered a brigade sent up in supporting distance of the troops on guard duty at that point, and none too soon, as the enemy threatened our rear and their capture; and, were it not for this brigade of McCall's, might have accomplished their purpose.

As C and G passed the old regimental camp, Robinson and Frank Whipple the thoughtful commissary, aided by the bustling McCaul who rushed in, distributed among us all the coffee and sugar we could conveniently carry, then knocking in the head of a barrel of whisky, threw it over the piled up stores put a match thereto and moved on, Whipple grabbing his rifle, as the flames rose upward.

Maj. Roy Stone, commanding the 1st Pennsylvania Rifles, or "Bucktails," thus reports on Mechanicsville: "Two companies of U. S. Sharpshooters, Capt. Drew and Capt. Giroux, attached to my command during the action, behaved with great steadiness and delivered a most effective fire. At daybreak of the 27th I was informed that the army would retire at once to a new line on Gaines Hill, and I was directed to hold with my regiment and the battery the position I then held until that movement could be effected. I extended the Sharpshooters up to my right and left, to keep up the appearance of still occupying the whole line, and as soon as it was fairly light opened fire upon the enemy, who had advanced under cover of the night and planted new batteries within grapeshot range. Their infantry also came down with apparently undiminished force, filling the road towards the ford with a solid column. The fire of the enemy's batteries was much hotter than the evening before; so much so that it was impossible for the gunners to stand up to load their pieces. As long, however, as their ammunition and my own lasted we were enabled to hold the enemy in check. A little after six o'clock A. M. we were ordered to retire as best we might to the main body, three miles distant. After leaving the intrenchments we were still obliged to go more than half a mile before escaping the range of the same batteries which had annoyed us all the morning. The movement was necessarily hurried, the enemy having outflanked us and pressing closely upon our rear. I posted Capt. Holland with his company about 300 yards from the ford, directing him to obstruct the road and cover the retreat of our main body, and ordered Capt. Wister to destroy the bridge at the mill hospital. These were difficult and hazardous duties, and were performed with the coolness of veterans, and probably saved us from entire destruction. Our loss in the morning's fight and retreat was more than half what remained from the previous day's work. We could not bring off our dead and wounded, and every man who gave out in the double-quick was necessarily captured."

GAINES' MILL.

June 27, 1862.

Shortly after noon the great fight at Gaines' Mill began, and raged hot and furious until after dark. The enemy having been reinforced by large bodies of fresh troops during the latter part of the day, after a most stubborn resistance by the Union soldiers finally succeeded in forcing back the corps of Gen. [Fitz John] Porter and division of Gen. [Henry Warner] Slocum; the Unionists falling back not more surely than slowly and stubbornly to the last. Gen. Porter had at first but 28,000 men, afterwards reinforced by Slocum to 35,000; while the enemy had some 65,000 in line, commanded by Lee in person. During the progress of the battle Gen. Smith's cannon across the swamp, did great execution on our left, near the river, among the enemy's right wing.

"All the heavy guns I could place in position were used in trying to drive back the columns of rebel forces Pouring over Gaines' Hill to attack Gen. Porter's left flank. The long range (two and one-half miles) prevented great accuracy, but the rebels were finally forced to retire to the woods and take a covered road till they got below our view.—GEN. W[illiam] F[arrar] ["Baldy"] SMITH.

At ten o'clock Gen. Porter's line was formed awaiting attack; his purpose being to hold the enemy at bay that day, to enable the main army on the south bank of the Chickahominy to make the movement previously decided on by Gen. McClellan, to the new base on the James river, as free from attack as possible; the success of which depended in a great measure on the success of Porter's battle. At the same time Gen. Porter asked that reinforcements from the other side be held in readiness to support him if it became necessary, in case the enemy pressed him too hard, thus making his situation critical. The 5th corps was posted behind a ravine where the mill stream ran, on the front of Watt's farm a mile east of the Gaines Hill camping ground, forming a semi-circle extending from the valley of the Chickahominy on our left, around to a point near New Cold Harbor, and covering the approaches to the bridges over the swamp. Gen. Morell's first division occupied the left and center of the line in the edge of the woods; Gen. Sykes' second division (mostly regulars) on the right, in an open field; and Gen. McCall's third division forming a second line in rear of the woods, in the field 600 yards behind Morell's troops. Thus formed, the troops rested, calmly waiting for the expected onslaught of superior numbers of consolidated foes massed for the complete destruction of Fitz John Porter and his isolated 5th corps. Never did soldiers more fully understand that there was a storm brewing, a storm of myriad lead and hurtling iron. A storm which they must repel, regardless the necessary sacrifice, the human cost, to save the day. That day must be saved! The 5th corps must hold its ground; and these silent—only whispering—soldiers, all knew it. It didn't come to them in so many express orders; their full sense of the grave situation was sufficient. How many failed to look back home, during these lulling moments? How many failed to realize that this might be their last battle, which it was to ever so many? But when the great struggle commenced,—when the order came to "commence firing,"—such thoughts passed from their minds. Amid the deafening din of battle, surrounded by fire and smoke, they were patriots, and thought only of victory.

The battle opened about noon on Syke's front and right, threatening the flanks, but was readily repelled for the time being, and a lull ensued. But at three o'clock the engagement became general, lasting until dark. At four P. M. the division of Gen. Slocum arrived from over the river and immediately entered into the thickest of the fight, doing great service and losing heavily. Three separate charges were met and defeated by our troops, while the fourth and last effort succeeded only so far as to gain our line, but advancing no further.

Six companies of Sharpshooters were engaged in this battle, Companies D, E, F and K being together under Lieut.-Col. Ripley, in Morell's front, where they were deployed on the further side of the marshy ravine far in advance. Here they remained some time before- the enemy appeared in front, during which time Gen. Griffin rode over to the Sharpshooters' line, and told Col. Ripley that Gen. Porter wished a few reliable men sent out in front to ascertain the movements of the enemy—thus showing the confidence Gen. Porter had in the Sharpshooters. The colonel (lieutenant-colonel) came to Capt. McLean, of Company D, and asked for 10 men with a non-commissioned officer—"volunteers for special work." Sergt. John E. Hetherington was placed in command of the 10 scouts, with instructions to ascertain as quickly as possible the enemy's movements, and report. They were to fire no shots or make any disturbance, unless absolutely necessary for their own protection, or otherwise in the discharge of their duty. The result was that they soon came upon the flank of a marching column moving in the direction of the White House, and found that a great part of their army (Jackson's troops) had taken the road in that direction, under the supposition, no doubt, that the line of our retreat lay in the direction of the Pamunkey, from whence we had originally come. This was a very important matter, and Sergt. Hetherington, having accomplished his purpose, started back to make his report. But before he got back, the enemy had swung well around to our rear, the scouts became engaged with them, and they had some sharp fighting to do. James Winchell was hit in the shoulder, falling into the enemy's hands, Henry Collins was slightly wounded, and C. J. Buchanan just escaping capture. It was in this manner, on this gallant reconnoissance, that the Sharpshooters were the first ones to engage the Confederates at Gaines Mill.

Deserters from their ranks and loyal citizens of Virginia represented that Gen. Jackson, with 50,000 men, had united his forces with those of Longstreet, A. P. Hill, and D. H. Hill, from Richmond, and that they were advancing with the determination to overwhelm and crush the Army of the Potomac. The dust from the immense columns of the enemy could be seen for miles, and soon our scouts and pickets warned us that they were extending over our whole front.—GEN. FITZ JOHN PORTER.

Following close on the return of these scouts, at half past two P. M. Ripley's command, became engaged with the enemy's skirmishers, who came onto the Sharpshooters from the rolling country fronting them. Holding their places until forced back by the severe attack later on, to their immediate right, whereby a connecting regiment was obliged to give way, they retired slowly, still firing, across the marshy ground, half-way up the opposite slope, where they halted. Here reinforced, they assisted in driving back the foe, following after and firing rapidly until they reoccupied their old position, only to be forced back again, the pressure being too great against them; and the enemy held that side of the ravine thereafter.

Berdan's Sharpshooters, under Lieut.-Col. Ripley, were thrown well forward as skirmishers. The enemy approached through the woods from the direction of New Cold Harbor, and made their first serious attack about twelve o'clock upon the right, which was handsomely repulsed by Griffin's brigade. The second attack was made about half past two, and the third about half past five o'clock, each extending along my entire front, and both, like the first, were gallantly repulsed.—GEN. [George Webb] MORELL.

But not until late in the evening, between seven and eight did the rebels break the lines of Morell's division, then only by massing the troops of Jackson, Longstreet, and both Hills, and hurling them with terrible onslaught on our center, which coupled with the demoralization caused by the repulse of our cavalry on the left, whose riderless horses plunged wildly among our batteries causing a natural panic, amid the dust and smoke, noise and confusion, brought about the disastrous result. It was a critical moment, but the enemy had lost heavily, and were themselves too greatly disorganized to follow up their advantage, the Unionists forming new lines covering the crossing of the Chickahominy as darkness settled over one of the most obstinately contested scenes of war.

Porter's demand for axes, made early in the day, to slash down the timbers in his front, thus offering an impassable impediment to the enemy's approach, assuring a most certain and highly important victory for the Union, was not responded to until too late to be of service, although he sent twice for them. Had they been received in time, it must have made a material difference in the result of the battle; the rebel army would have been whipped, which would have had the happy effect of making an entire change in the military situation. The slashing of trees in Porter's front would have slashed the Confederate hopes for the safety of their stronghold; for if half the number of soldiers on open ground could hold twice their number at bay an entire afternoon until nightfall, what other result could reasonably be expected, had we been able to fortify, than a decisive victory for the Union arms? Gen. Porter took in the situation, but was unable to improve the opportunity. What few artillery axes he could use in places, did good service in barricading,. imperfect though it was; nor did he, as it was, have sufficient reinforcements to turn the tide of battle.

Gen. McClellan says: "The objects sought for had been obtained. The enemy was held at bay. Our siege guns and material were saved, and the right wing joined the main body of the army. Our thin and exhausted regiments were all withdrawn in safety. Twenty-two cannon were lost, three of which being run off the bridge during withdrawal."

The Michigan-Wisconsin detachment, Companies C and G, was under the command of Capt. Giroux, in the absence of Capt. Drew, who, with a detail of scouts from both companies, had become separated from us, and crossing the Chickahominy took no part in this battle. The two companies after falling back from Mechanicsville, during the morning rested with the Bucktails on a rise of ground on the road to the bridges built by the Union troops across the swamp. In the afternoon they were ordered into the fight, a half-mile in front, the Bucktails going ahead. On reaching a slope in front of the Union batteries the Bucktails moved off to the right leaving the Sharpshooters under fire on the side of the hill. The battle was now raging in earnest, shot and shell flying fast, the Union batteries on the top of the hill replying vigorously over the Sharpshooters' heads. The stretcher-bearers were kept busy carrying back the wounded, hit in all manner of places—body, arms, legs, head and face.

One unfortunate field officer of a Zouave regiment was led off the field crying aloud at the loss of his nose, presenting a sight not easily forgotten.

After some maneuvering the Sharpshooters moved forward into a piece of woods to the left, where they were suddenly greeted with rebel canister, but without, effect. A body of Union soldiers moving up in their front, and our captain being ignorant of the position of the opposing forces, he soon after fell back with his command a short distance from the woods into the open field, and became subject to the fire of the rebel batteries. Meantime the firing in the woods was a constant uproar, the bullets speeding back and forth by thousands. Nothing in words can better describe the terrific strife than those of Col. Simpson of the 4th New Jersey, which regiment, with the 11th Pennsylvania, were surrounded and captured after a most gallant struggle, when he said: "The hissing of the balls was like that of a myriad of serpents."

The command of Companies C and G having been turned over to the first sergeant of G, the commissioned officers having retired, they were ordered to a position on a side hill covering the road to the bridges, where the two companies assisted greatly in checking the stragglers while falling back; eventually serving as a rallying point from whence stretched out long lines of battle re-formed after the old lines commenced giving away in earnest, especially after the disastrous charge of the Union cavalry and lancers on the river bottom at sunset,—when the great red sun like a big ball of fire was fast disappearing behind the spires of Richmond,—and who were plainly visible with their red flags fluttering in the breeze as they charged fiercely over the plain, to be hurled back from the cannon's mouth in death and disorder.

During this exciting period, when the two companies above named came on to the hill, we found Col. Berdan and Col. Matheson (32d New York—"California regiment") engaged rallying the scattering troops hurrying to the rear. The former said he had stopped them from crossing the bridge below, and had never worked harder, bringing them into line—these scattered men who had lost their regiments. It was at this critical moment, after sunset, that further reinforcements from the south bank of the Chickahominy, consisting of French and Meagher's brigades of the 2d corps, arrived, and with loud cheers pressed forward and checked the farther advance of the enemy in that direction—our left. A fictitious statement by an aide that, "McClellan's left wing was in Richmond," had the desired effect, and it was afterwards learned that the enemy thought that from the great noise made, the cheering by our rallied lines, that heavy reinforcements had come over; also that Lee told the Confederates to "hold their position at any cost," expecting an attack by fresh troops the next morning. The next morning we were not there. After that battle it was an old saying: "That was the last seen of the Lancers in the Army of the Potomac." For good men though they were, it was soon demonstrated that lances belonged to another age, past and forgotten, and were perfectly -useless in this war.

Gen. Reynolds, commanding his brigade while engaged at the front among his brave Reserves, was captured by the enemy late in the day, or rather taken the next morning with his adjutant-general Capt. Kingsbury, having got lost in the woods overnight. He was afterwards exchanged, and lost his life at the head of the 1st corps, about the first man, on the field of Gettysburg.

Early the morning of the 28th the Union troops had crossed over the Chickahominy, destroying the bridges after them. McClellan's army was now for the first time all on the south side of the swamp, while a large body of the enemy were on the north side. Their main force 'twas supposed had been menacing the Union soldiers from the vicinity of Richmond, which proved not so, the main force being together against Porter.

The Sharpshooter detachment fell back with the California regiment during the night, remaining with them until mid-day of the 29th, having unavoidably lost their knapsacks which had been unslung in the evening during the closing charge at Gaines' Mill, and were not obtained afterwards. And this was the last of the hair-covered knapsacks.

When the first sergeant of Company G, as the ranking non-commissioned officer, received his orders from the Michigan captain commanding the two companies, to take command in his absence, recover the knapsacks left half-mile in rear of our batteries, and in the line of the direct fire of the Confederate artillery; that non-commissioned officer (C. A. Stevens, the writer of this history), informed the first sergeant of Company C (Byron Brewer) that he should obey the orders given him, but that when he ordered the combined companies to "left face—forward, march!" he would not look behind him—towards the rebel front. The hint was taken, and as the command moved briskly off rearward, Orderly Brewer, Sergts. Benson and Parker, and Thomas McCaul, of Company G, rushed to the front, down the declivity in front of our batteries, up the opposite slope into the field of battle, under the rebel fire—where they did good work. McCaul becoming at once a suspicious character with his straw hat on, soon found it advisable to cast it off and away, as he went down behind a stump in the field and blazed away. The cry to his comrades from the infantry in line, as to "who that fellow was with the straw hat," brought forth the response: "Oh, he's all right! That's our Tommy!" causing yells of laughter heard over the battle roar. This rather disconcerted our hero who didn't understand it, but with a "—you, what are you laughing at back there in the rear," our Tommy, despite the balls that spattered thick about him, held his ground as long as any others on that part of the field, notwithstanding his greatly exposed position—in advance of the infantry line.

McCaul said it was the only fight he was in where he could distinctly "see the men fall that we drew bead on." Their colors were advanced apparently some distance ahead of their line, at least Tommy thought so, almost to his complete discomfiture, because as the "last man of their color guard" stuck the staff in the ground, he said: "I was fool enough to think of going out after it," and started for it on his hands and knees, when Sergt. Parker yelled him back and so fiercely that Tommy startled, jumped to his feet to look back, as a rebel volley flew all about him, accompanied by derisive cheers. Answering with a defiant cry back: "Get out! Keep your—old flag! This is no place for Tommy;" he came back like a quarter horse, bare-headed, minus his straw hat, lost in the melee.

The casualties at this battle have been reported, for the Union troops 6,837, the Confederates 9,500, thus showing the great slaughter inflicted on the enemy in their futile attempts to cut off our right wing while separated from the main army. The loss of the Sharpshooters under Ripley, were two killed, seven wounded and two missing, which was wonderfully small considering their great exposure. But the Sharpshooters always had orders to take all the cover possible; being armed with breech-loaders they could lie low, and without changing position reload and fire ten shots a minute. A regiment of Sharpshooters in line could play havoc with an approaching column, as was afterwards demonstrated. The superiority of breech-loaders over muzzle loaders was plainly manifest.

CASUALTIES IN THE SHARPSHOOTERS.

Co. E.—Killed: Levi H. Leet.

Co. F.—Killed: B. W. Jordan, James A. Read. Wounded: E. H. Rimes, severe.

Co. K.—Wounded: James Mathews, mortally; Thomas Cliff, slight; Alphonzo Manzer, captured.

Many people, ignorant of the true situation, used to think that McClellan's left wing ought to have gone into Richmond either during the Gaines' Mill battle, or the next day after Porter had crossed and joined his forces, but it was easier said than done. If sixty-odd thousand rebel troops could not conquer half their number on open ground without barricades, how could it be reasonably expected that sixty-odd thousand Federals could, within the short time allowed them, whip half their number behind breastworks seven miles ahead to the rebel capitol—" so near," and yet so far?

Relative to this military conundrum to the unmilitary critic, I will leave it to the commanding general to explain:

It will be remembered that at this juncture the enemy was upon our rear, and there was every reason to believe that he would sever our communications with the supply depot at the White House. We had on hand but a limited amount of rations, and if we had advanced directly on Richmond, it would have required considerable time to carry the strong works around that place, during which our men would have been destitute of food; and even if Richmond had fallen before our arms, the enemy could still have occupied our supply communications between that place and the gunboats. While the enemy had a large army on the left (north) bank of the Chickahominy, he was also in large force between our army and Richmond.—GEN. Mc CLELLAN.

The fact is, McClellan was checkmated, and for the reasons stated. His division and corps generals on the right of the Chickahominy were averse to sparing any troops whatever to reinforce Gen. Porter on the 27th, in consequence of the threatened demonstrations in their respective fronts.

McClellan again: "So threatening were the movements of the enemy on both banks of the Chickahominy, that it was impossible to decide until the afternoon where the real attack would be made. Large forces of infantry were seen during the day near the Old Tavern, on Franklin's right, and threatening demonstrations were frequently made along the entire line on this side of the river which rendered it necessary to hold a considerable force in position to meet them. If, on the other hand, the enemy had concentrated all his forces at Richmond during the progress of our attack, and we had been defeated, we must in all probability have lost our trains before reaching the flotilla."

To show that it was not a new idea of Gen. McClellan to fall back on James river, suddenly determined on, but had been contemplated sometime before, the following additional is given:

In anticipation of a speedy advance on Richmond, to provide for the contingency of our communications with the depot at the White House being severed by the enemy, and at the same time to be prepared for a change of the base of our operations to the James river if circumstances should render it advisable, I had made arrangements more than a week previous (on the 18th) to have transports with supplies of provisions and forage under a convoy of gunboats sent up James river. They reached Harrison's Landing in time to be available for the army on its arrival at that point. Events soon proved this change of base to be, though most hazardous and difficult, the only prudent course.—GEN. MCCLELLAN.

GARNETT'S FARM.

June 27, 1862.

During the time of the Gaines Mill battle, the enemy on the smith side of the Chickahominy were by no means idle. On the contrary they were very aggressive, particularly in front of Gen. Smith's division (second division, Gen. Franklin's 6th A. C.), where more or less fighting occurred all day, in which the enemy admit serious losses. Gen. Hancock's brigade having been placed in the front line early in the morning, bore the brunt of the enemy's repeated demonstrations, but as Hancock had been ordered to avoid as far as possible a general engagement, his efforts were only directed to keep the enemy off, repulsing his several attacks, which he succeeded in doing, as well as silencing from time to time his artillery. In this latter service Maj. Trepp's command of Sharpshooters (A and I) performed a very important part, when in the afternoon being sent forward, they effectually silenced the enemy's guns. This in front of our infantry lines, it being a duel engagement between the rebel artillery and our Sharpshooters. After this affair, in connection with some New Jersey troops they assisted in repulsing a fierce charge of the enemy, the battle lasting about three-fourths of an hour, and Gen. Hancock says of them: "They performed excellent service during the contest, driving back the enemy's skirmishers who threatened an advance towards our left flank. They also did considerable execution on the right of the enemy's force attacking me from Garnett's house." So well did they respond to the desperate attack, that they exhausted their ammunition. The next morning Hancock's brigade had fallen back a half mile to a more favorable position, where he says they were "ready to repel any attempt to debouch troops by Golding's house." The two companies, A and I, remained in Fort Davidson while it was being destroyed to prevent its use by the enemy. Two hostile batteries opened on them, wounding several artillerymen and killing a number of horses.. Having withdrawn the guns from the useless fort, at about ten o'clock the Confederates advanced in great haste, probably supposing there was a full retreat, but in this they were disappointed, for on approaching within about 200 yards of where our troops lay quietly in ambush, a terrific volley surprised them, causing their retreat in great confusion leaving their dead and wounded on the field, which they were afterwards allowed to bury and remove under a flag of truce. Capt. Aschmann says: "With the troops that were sent out to do this duty, we had free intercourse. Among them were many Germans belonging to a music band of a Georgia regiment. They complained bitterly of the bad treatment they received, and would have been glad to remain with us." Lieut Jonathan Sprague, Company L. was wounded and taken prisoner.

GOLDING'S FARM.

June 28, 1862.

Gen. [William Buel] Franklin says: "Finding the enemy (in the morning) in great force at Garnett's, a new battery in the valley of the river and a battery of heavy guns at Gaines' Hill, I withdrew all the force to the edge of the wood inclosing Golding's farm, Slocum's division on the right of the road, and Smith's on the left, connecting with Gen. Sumner's line. We were severely shelled from all of their batteries just before the movement commenced and while it was going on.

Just after the movement was completed two Georgia regiments made an attack upon the pickets. They were handsomely repulsed with great loss with the help of Capt. Mott's battery."

In this affair we captured some of the enemy's attacking force including a couple of colonels—Col. Lamar (8th Georgia), and Lieut.-Col. Towers. Gen. Smith credits the 33d New York and 49th Pennsylvania with being conspicuous in this repulse.

The Sharpshooters were represented at Golding's by Companies C and O, who were moved about considerably from an early hour in the morning to different positions, prepared to meet the enemy at all points, the roar of artillery serving to keep them wide awake for any special emergency. In the afternoon they occupied an important position protecting troops detailed to obstruct the roads and destroy bridges, being subjected to the fire of the enemy's artillery for several hours, their shells bursting frequently among them. The enemy failed, however, to force them away, they remaining until the work was completed. The position occupied while thus posted was one of terrible suspense, especially after darkness had settled around; they being unable to see but little of what was going on, owing to the thick brush and deep woods where they lay, at the same time being almost constantly reminded of the proximity of the enemy by the crashing shell through the tree tops above, dropping huge limbs, and often plowing up dirt and swamp mud among them; while the booming of cannon and rattle of musketry plainly proved that the fighting along the line of the Chickahominy was earnest and severe, especially in Gen. Smith's front, with whose division they were now acting.

Finally at a late hour that dark night which was illumined by the burning of abandoned stores, making the blackened sky lurid with its glare,—a terrible picture of war's desolation,—they moved silently away with the command of Gen. Newton over by-roads and cross-roads, through gloomy woods and black looking ravines, now in a deep gully and again on a hill side, at last striking a well-traveled road, along which they pushed mid other troops, crowded and jostling, heated and dusty, until about daybreak when they halted in an extensive field, helping to swell the already large number of weary soldiers there assembled. Onward, after awhile, towards James river, and about noon the Sharpshooter detachment bidding farewell to the California regiment, left the column and joined the

Pennsylvania Reserves near the Cross Roads. At this place, the Bucktails and the small force under Capt. Drew were found.

BOTTOM'S BRIDGE.

June 29, 1862.

At this point, which was an important crossing of the Chickahominy, batteries from the Pennsylvania artillery had been placed in position as early as the 27th, also at the railroad bridge a half-mile further upstream. On the 28th an artillery fight occurred, the enemy having arrived on the opposite side, and on the 29th orders were received to withdraw the guns and destroy the bridges. Capt. James Brady, of battery H, thus reports the destruction of the railroad bridge, the same being soon wrapt in flames in the face of the enemy across the stream.

This good officer says: "During the afternoon of Sunday, signal was given to clear the track, as the train loaded with ammunition had been fired, and was about being run into the Chickahominy. The burning train, rushing over the bridge, exploded on reaching the creek, throwing fragments thousands of feet high."

Companies A and I, had been sent to Bottom's Bridge that afternoon with a brigade of infantry. The Sharpshooters forming skirmish line, rushed forward exchanging shots with the Confederates who were trying to rebuild the bridge, only partially destroyed, and while so engaged successfully disputed the passage of the bridge by the enemy, thereby giving our moving troops ample time to get beyond that point without being required to make a stand. It was an important matter, and, so rapidly did our boys fire into them, they were completely discomfited and forced to retire from the work. Another telling example of the value of the Sharpshooter service. When the two companies were finally called off, they found their division had gone on, and being unable to find them, passed beyond Savage Station towards White Oak Swamp.

ALLEN'S FARM.

June 29, 1862.

This affair, also known as "Peach Orchard, lasted about two hours, all hard fighting. The battle ground was near our principal supply depot at Orchard Station, where all the government property not transportable was ordered destroyed. While occupying the place the 2d corps, Gen. Sumner, was attacked about nine A. M. in a furious manner with both artillery and musketry by troops from Richmond. Hazzard's, Pettit's and Kirby's Union batteries soon got into position, and after a hard duel eventually silenced the enemy's cannon, while the troops of Richardson and Sedgwick engaged the charging forces with such good effect as to drive them back, after a stubborn fight on both sides. Conspicuous in this battle was the 53d Pennsylvania, which had occupied some farm buildings in the field, and who repeatedly repulsed all attempts to drive them away.

Company H, of the Sharpshooters, had been on picket duty in the vicinity of Seven Pines, said to be the nearest Union post to Richmond, and on this last fateful night were supplied with 100 rounds per man. Here they remained until three A. M. of Sunday (29th) before being recalled and ordered to fall back, when to their surprise they found everything had gone but one battery. Hurrying on past Fair Oaks station, they heard the enemy yelling behind them, the latter having evidently just discovered that the breastworks were evacuated, so the Sharpshooters took to the woods, and following the railroad line came up with Richardson's division here at Allen's Farm. Acting as skirmishers in this contest they moved three-fourths of a mile through woods and fields, performing important service guarding the approach from the Chickahominy, communication between them and the main force being kept up by cavalry pickets. After our troops had all withdrawn they followed the column as rear guard, with nothing in sight but dead men and horses, and a lot of scattered and damaged equipments. On catching up with their division, they reported to Gen. Richardson how they had been left behind in the woods, who laughed heartily and said to them: "Oh, well, I was sure you Sharpshooters knew how to take care of yourselves."

SAVAGE STATION.

June 29, 1862.

At this place which was also one of the depots for our supplies, and where our sick and wounded were lying in hospital, the enemy following close after our troops, appearing in view about four P. M., commenced the attack, which was gallantly met, particularly by Burns' brigade, ordered over the field to hold the woods between the Williamsburg road and the railroad, and Gen. Burns [William Wallace Burns was wounded in the face at Savage Station but survived to fight at Fredericksburg] says:

Before I reached the position a scout informed me that the enemy were in large force on the Williamsburg road. Seeing that both of my flanks would be exposed, I sent to Gen. Sumner for another regiment. Fortunately the enemy did not attack until Lieut.-Col. Miller, 1st Minnesota regiment, reported, and I had time to throw it to the left, across the Williamsburg road, with the left flank retired. I found I still had not sufficient length of line to cover the ground, and was obliged to move Col. Baxter to the right and throw back his right flank to cover the railroad, leaving a gap in the center of my line. These dispositions were in progress when the enemy attacked most furiously with infantry, he having been playing with artillery upon me during the whole movement across the field, which was answered by Gen. Sumner's batteries. The battle raged along the whole line, but concentrated gradually toward my two weak points, the center and the Williamsburg road. I urged more regiments which were promptly sent me. Before these arrived, however, the enemy made a rush on the center, wounded me and killed the captain of the left company of Baxter's (Capt. McGonigle), forced through to the fence, and flaunted their flag across the rails, broke the line for a moment, but the brave men rallied and drove them back. The fight then moved toward the Williamsburg road, when most opportunely the 88th New York came across the field double-quick and cheering. I threw them into the gap on the road, when the enemy opened artillery and infantry upon them, but they never faltered—not only went up to my line but beyond it, and drove secesh before them. The 82d New York then came over the field, and I advanced it to the gap of the center. It too advanced beyond the original line. The 15th Massachusetts coming up, I relieved Col. Morehead with it, and Col. Baxter with the 20th Massachusetts. The 1st California and 7th Michigan coming up, I held them in reserve, looking to the flanks. Col. Owen of the 69th Pennsylvania was led to the left of the Minnesota by my aide, and, still farther to the left, Gen. Brooks' brigade was thrown by Gen. Sumner, on learning the enemy was moving in large force in that direction. The fight closed, however, with the fire of the 88th New York, 82d New York, and 15th Massachusetts. Prisoners reported four brigades of the enemy. Our men showed their superiority, and the victory can fairly be claimed by us. He was the attacking party, and was not only checked, but repulsed and driven from the ground.—

Wm. W. BURNS.

Gen. Lee says his rebel troops consisted of one of Magruder's divisions and two regiments of another. That a severe action ensued, which continued about two hours. These statements are given to show the desperate nature of this battle. After dark, all being quiet again, our troops moved off, leaving a large number of sick and disabled to fall into the hands of the enemy—an unavoidable consequence as they couldn't be taken along. It seemed pretty hard, but there was no help for it. Capt. Hastings' company, H, was with Caldwell's brigade in the second line of battle, but with the exception of receiving the enemy's artillery fire from time to time, were not actively engaged.

During the afternoon of the 29th the two companies under Drew moved off with the greatly reduced Bucktails,—about 150 all told out of six companies that had come to the Army of the Potomac under Maj. Stone,—and, with the regiments of the Pennsylvania Reserves, were placed in position along a particular road in a dense wood on the left flank, where they remained lying on their arms, an ambuscade during the long dark night. Momentarily expecting the approach of some portion of the rebel forces, the men_ were kept in a state of utmost vigilance, and the highest pitch of excitement. Every member of that surprise party had his coat sleeve rolled tip, leaving one arm bared so as to be recognized in case of the appearance of the enemy, and the probable confusion resulting from a close and expected hand to hand engagement in that dark wood. But the graycoats failing to appear, the sleepless night passed away without a brush.

WHITE OAK SWAMP.

June 30,1862.

The fight at this place, which opened in the forenoon, was a contest between a portion of our troops and a heavy artillery fire from several well-posted Confederate batteries-30 guns—across the swamp. This cannonading was unusually heavy, could be heard for miles, and our soldiers guarding that important point, near the bridge, were subjected to it with little opportunity to reply, except our artillery, which did good service. Companies A and I (Sharpshooters), who were here with Gen. Smith's men, report the sudden attack of the enemy's guns had the effect at first of causing considerable confusion among our troops, and it took some time to recover from the surprise.. The battery that had been with them at Fort Davidson (on Garnett's farm) lost 25 horses and 12 men killed and wounded in a short space of time, but nevertheless succeeded, in silencing the enemy's guns. The Sharpshooters occupied an advanced position protecting the center, where they had a lively time with the enemy's batteries, also in skirmishing. The heat of the day was intense, and the men suffered much for want of water. Sergt. Demetrius J. Hays, of Company I, was wounded at this place.

Company H also took part in this fight, and, when the enemy unexpectedly opened with their cannon, the long train of pontoons which were just starting off was stopped and burned, as the mules were stampeded by the firing. Along with them went Capt. Hastings' darky, who had just shouldered the captain's blankets, haversack, etc., expecting to move on, and with the exclamation: "Dis is no place for me, sar," disappeared with his load, never to show up again. This company was sent to the left of and in support of Hazzard's battery, from which place the enemy tried every means to dislodge them. Solid shot would strike the ridge in front, throwing the loose earth in their faces, others would ricochet over their heads, while shrapnel and shell would burst and scatter among them. Edward Lynde and John Acker lying side by side were shocked by a piece of shell striking the ground between their heads, another piece tearing through the blanket roll on Lynde's shoulder; while Capt. Hastings and A. R. Barrett had a close shave from a piece striking the ground between their heads, filling their ears with dirt; it was a very hot place for them, both from the firing and the terrible heat of the sun. Lieut. Barrett says: "We witnessed the wounding of Capt. Hazzard right in our front. Many of the artillerymen were overcome, and their places filled by volunteers from our (Caldwell's) brigade." But this action was only preliminary to the great battle of the day later on.

GLENDALE.

June 30, 1862.

This battle also known as New Market. Charles City Cross Roads, Nelson's Farm and Frazier's Farm, was one of the severest that had yet occurred during the movement then in progress. During the forenoon the Sharpshooters were mustered for pay; shortly after, orders were received to be ready to move, heavy cannonading being heard.

At four P. M. the Sharpshooters, under Capt. Drew, went into action with the Bucktails, the Wisconsin company numbering 51 men. The Michigan company was reduced in about the same ratio, while with the entire Bucktail force they would number in all scarce three minimum companies. Moving forward into a piece of wood fronting an open plain, they remained for a while lying on their arms among the Pennsylvania Reserves, and while there were exposed to a steady canister fire humming by and spattering among them, with an almost constant shelling of the woods by the enemy's guns. They were finally ordered to move to the left, taking a position on a slope of ground in the open field. The Sharpshooters occupied the slope, being on the extreme left of the line, the Bucktails on the right of the Wisconsin company. For a short time, now, the firing ceased, when a very suspicious quietness reigned supreme over that vast plain. But it was only the calm that precedes the storm—a storm that was expected soon to break by our men. A movement had occurred in advance of our position on the right, by which some prisoners had been taken and the firing stopped. A dashing charge had been made over the field by the Reserves under Col. Simmons, at the expense of considerable loss, including that spirited officer, who fell while forcing the enemy hurriedly back, before he could re-form his more or less broken line. This change in the aspect of affairs—this lull in the proceedings—was almost too sudden to be satisfactory, and as before stated it looked very ominous. However, the Sharpshooters had not long to wait before they becalm thoroughly convinced that the battle was not over, being suddenly exposed to a severe cross-fire from their left, caused by the hasty retreat of a regiment in their front, which had been attacked on their left flank by a large force of the enemy. With the rebel soldiers under cover of a strip of wood and the house and out-buildings of a farm, the outlying regiment in the open field was unable to withstand the terrible effect of the attack, therefore made a precipitate retreat to the cover of the woods behind the Sharpshooters, running directly over them, and falling killed and wounded among our men. Pinned to the ground by a big, strapping fellow falling heavily by his side onto his packed haversack loaded with company books, etc.,—no rations those days and no knapsacks—Company G's orderly had hard work to disengage himself; the big blue coat laid there. The rebel balls followed those flying troops thick and fast, striking the ground on the crest of the slope, throwing dust and dirt in clouds in the faces of the riflemen lying thereon, so that it was almost impossible for them to see. Amid the confusion following, the Sharpshooters were kept in their places until all had fallen back but them. Then, while bravely striving to hold the ground, both companies responding to the fire of the rebel troops now preparing to charge, the Wisconsin company suffered the great loss in killed of their gallant captain, Edward Drew, while in the act of reloading a rifle he had been using, obtained from a sick man, and two sergeants, Joel Parker and James W. Staples. Parker was the first man shot, through the head, while on his knees firing over the top of the slope. Capt. Drew on being told of it, also on his knees, had turned to look at "Joe," when a ball struck him in the top of the head as he was pushing in a cartridge to shoot back. This occurred on the left of the company, Staples being shot on the right in his place as a file closer (5th sergeant), behind the position of the first sergeant. No better panegyric could be bestowed on the fallen than for me to assert that these three men, Drew, Parker and Staples, were of the truest specimens of the highest type of American manhood—gentlemen, patriots, soldiers.

The second lieutenant (Shepard) then ordered his men back to the cover of the wood, which was obeyed as quickly as possible, a number getting hit in so doing. Among them was Lyman L. Thompson, one of the company buglers, who went into this fight with his trumpet in one hand and rifle in the other. He was shot while crossing the ditch at the edge of the wood. No longer able to blow the martial blast, he lay down by his bugle and died. The order to fall back was given just in time, as the enemy in force were on the eve of a charge. On reaching the timber the men became greatly scattered, for which they were not to blame, but rallying in squads commenced a desultory fire which was kept up until dark. A portion of the detachment, members of both Sharpshooter companies with some Bucktails, re-formed under Orderly-Sergeant Stevens, who had escaped from the enemy as they swung around through the woods, after releasing himself from the fallen Pennsylvanian previously noted. Another member, William E. Wheeler, failing to heed the call of the orderly to "come on," waited a moment too long to "take another shot," and became a Yankee prisoner.

Capt. Giroux, Lieuts. Baker and Shepard had collected most of the rest and joined the remnant of Bucktails under Maj. Stone. The rebels charged over the ground to the wood, and although afterward driven back, came on again. One of our squads, on deploying through the timber, was particularly noted for its ardor in firing straight shots into rebeldom, and with such rapidity did they discharge their breechloaders as to surprise many infantry officers nearby. Conspicuously engaged in this quick shooting were Thos. McCaul, C. N. Jacobs, Wm. Anderson and Robt. Casey; the latter of whom "executed numerous affidavits" between shots, especially after getting his finger clipped. But that was only natural for

"Swearing Bob," who was always full of "affidavits "when crowded by the enemy. He would shoot and swear, and swear and shoot.

The position assigned to the Sharpshooters and Buck-tails if not actually a blunder was at least an unfortunate one, for had this force on the slope been stationed in the wood before the enemy appeared, the latter would hardly have crossed that field, or if so, not without great loss. But owing to the sudden and unexpected "break to rear" of the regiment on our right front, and consequent confusion on that part of the line, it became impossible for us to re-form successfully on the edge of the timber, the enemy immediately following up their advantage by closing in on front and flank. It is said that large bodies move slowly, but it is not always so, especially in army movements, as it often happens that when once started large bodies of troops move fast. Such was the case at this time, the men falling back utterly regardless of order, when they found themselves flanked in an open field by superior numbers having the advantage of cover. While no blame could probably be attached to the routed regiment under the circumstances, unless that they should have rallied in the woods, yet should the little detachment of Sharpshooters be awarded much praise for the stubborn manner in which they held on, to the last possible moment, and after all others had disappeared in the wooded background. Attempts were made to recover the bodies of the fallen, which were unsuccessful, the woods being full of Johnnies, and Sergt. Benson and Jas. S. Webster narrowly escaped capture in trying to reach the fatal field.

Towards evening Burns' brigade appeared on our left, and taking part in the closing fight of the day which raged for a time in terrible earnest, helped to drive the enemy finally back and off from the road leading to James river, which was thus kept open for the passage of our troops. Some of the Sharpshooters, with the orderly, charged with them, posting themselves on the right. Thomas McCaul also charged with them.

It appears from rebel authority that the enemy were at one time in much confusion, some of their troops being in rapid flight until checked in their course by one of their noted generals, when a determined rally was made, aided by fresh troops, by which they succeeded in making a stand at close quarters, where the bayonet was conspicuously brought into use. A hand-to-hand struggle ensued over the capture of Randol's battery, wherein the Reserves were forced back after a determined resistance. In another part of the field Cooper's battery shared the same fate, but in both instances they were soon after recovered and saved, the enemy being driven off, leaving in our hands a portion of their colors; also, it is said that on this part of the field Jeff Davis and Gen. Lee were present during the afternoon, being with the advance of Longstreet's corps. Cooper's battery was lost finally, as was a portion of Randol's, but unavoidably so, owing to the rushing hosts of foes right up to the muzzles, and the killing of the horses so that the guns could not be brought off. The fighting in front of these batteries was at close quarters, the bayonet being freely used. Randol reported 38 horses shot down by the charging columns, with eight more wounded.

> "Hand to hand, and foot to foot;
> Nothing there, save death, was mute;
> Stroke, and thrust, and flash, and cry
> For quarter, or for victory."

The battle was opened by Gen. McCall's decimated division, barely 6,000 strong, and was maintained until night, holding his own for three full hours until overwhelmed by superior numbers front and flank,—said to be 18,000, under Longstreet and A. P. Hill,—when the troops of Sumner and Hooker on the left with Kearney and Slocum on the right, came to his necessary relief. As McCall was unsupported in the outset, had he not successfully resisted the advancing enemy, the road would have been cut and the rebels have swarmed across our line of march, creating demoralization and disaster. McCall's losses in his Reserves sufficiently attest their gallantry in the unequal struggle: for the third time during this movement, fully proving their staying qualities in the midst of hot work in critical places.

Gen. Porter says: "Had not McCall maintained his position on New Market road, June 30th, the enemy would have cut that line of march of the army."

"It was only the stubborn resistance offered by our (McCall's) division, prolonging the contest until after dark and checking till that time the advance of the enemy, that enabled the concentration during the night of the whole army on the banks of the James river, which saved it."—GEN. MEADE.

And the following high Confederate authority admits that Gen. McCall's troops by their stout resistance that day, kept the enemy off from the road to James river.

Gen. Longstreet said to Surgeon Marsh, 4th Pennsylvania cavalry, who remained on the battle field with the wounded: "McCall is safe in Richmond; but if his division had not offered the stubborn resistance it did on this road we would have captured your whole army."

Gen. Pryor also spoke in the highest terms of the "pluck displayed by McCall's Pennsylvania troops."

Maj. Whaley, 5th Texas, informed Col. Bierer, 171st Pennsylvania, while a prisoner in Richmond that: "he never saw better fighting than that of the Pennsylvania Reserves."

It is true, as Gen. McCall admits, the 12th regiment broke badly and let the enemy in our flank; but they had been unfortunately posted in an exposed position in advance, as before stated, having previously done some good work. But when Gen. McCall stated that he had posted the Rifles—the Bucktails and Sharpshooters—in the edge of the woods, it was an error; for whatever his intention, we had been moved forward onto the open field in front; whereas, had we remained in the woods, there would undoubtedly have been a different and better story to tell on that part of the line.

The Sharpshooter detachment behaved very well in this fight notwithstanding their severe loss—did everything possible, and after deploying through the woods succeeded in capturing a number of prisoners. Henry Lye, company bugler of G, captured several Johnnies in the wood about dusk, among them a lieutenant-colonel, from whom he obtained a fine revolver. This officer in answer to Lye's demand to "Halt! and surrender!" replied:

"Down with your rifle, I'm your prisoner, but—me, if I didn't think these were my men in here."

And Lye thought so too, and therefore hurried away with the officer and an enlisted man, the latter captured and with him when he caught the former.

Frank Smith (G), seated in the midst of a large squad of them after dark, while listening to their conversation, learning their character, found an excuse to move one side and get clear of them. In fact, the woods became full of them, they coming oftentimes in close contact with the

Sharpshooters and Bucktails, who remained in the vicinity long after night had set in. On one occasion, one fellow lay down among them and was captured. The first intimation they had of his character was his statement after remaining some time, that he belonged to a "Louisiana Battalion," whereupon he was instantly throttled by a Wisconsin member and California Joe "within an inch of his life," and disarmed. By the way, the luckless gray-back was so unfortunate as to crawl in between two of the most uncompromising Union men there were in the detachment, and he might consider himself lucky at that exciting time to get off with a little rough handling for a few moments, and also to have thanked Joe for it, as he prevented the Wisconsin man from choking him out of existence.

It was at this place after darkness had come, that the division commander, Gen. McCall, was captured by the enemy on the edge of the wood in question, while Maj. Stone, of the Bucktails, narrowly escaped, receiving a shower of bullets as he flew back to his command, they having been in advance to reconnoiter. The major was thrown from his horse, receiving a slight contusion in consequence. With McCall and Reynolds captured and Meade severely wounded, there was but one general officer left in the division, Gen. Seymour, who succeeded to its command.

Ger. McCall never returned to the army, although exchanged in August, his health failing; then in his 60th year, he resigned in March, 1863. Graduating at West Point in 1822, he had served with distinction in the Florida and Mexican wars. He was an accomplished officer and bravely commanded the Reserves of his native state, on the Peninsula, and his retirement was a great loss to his country's service. He died in 1868.

The force under Giroux and Shepard also received a heavy volley about nine P. AL from down the road, which resulted fatally among the G men, George Lanning being killed. Sometime after midnight they moved on again towards the river, where they arrived at sunrise in the vicinity of Turkey Bend, and where the detachments under the above named officers and Sergt. Stevens, of G, joined together. The Sharpshooters mourned over their losses, which were quite heavy in this battle, particularly in the Wisconsin company which had five killed, six wounded and one taken prisoner, as follows:

Killed: Captain Edward Drew, Sergts. Joel Parker and James W. Staples, Privates Lyman L. Thompson and George Lanning.

Wounded: Wm. o. Clark, hip, mortal; Jonas W. Shepard, head, severe; Henry S. Roberts, back, slight;

George H. Lewis, leg; Robert Casey, finger, slight; John O'Niel, foot, slight. Missing: Wm. E. Wheeler, captured.

The balance of the regiment were more or less engaged along the line on the 30th, suffering loss. In Company H, Lieut. Frederick T. Peet, a fine young officer, was shot through the lungs, supposed to have been mortally wounded, but was afterwards reported among the exchanged prisoners and did not return to the regiment. He had been promoted to a position in the Marine Corps, and was ordered to Washington at the beginning of the Seven Days, but preferred to remain with the company until the fighting in this movement was over. This company went into the fight with the 61st New York of Richardson's division, performing gallant service under heavy fire.

An aide riding up for reinforcements, Col. Barlow, taking off his coat, ordered his men to throw away everything but guns and ammunition, then advanced on double-quick cheering loud to deceive the enemy in the approaching darkness. Going down the road among the thick woods they received a sudden fire almost in their faces. The line recoiled for a few moments amid some confusion, many returning the fire, however, when Barlow, riding up, yelled out to the Confederates: "You are firing on your own men. Cease firing!" Rallying, our men now advanced through the woods and across an open field, where the enemy stopped them at the edge of another wood; here a sharp engagement followed—one of the hottest places, Barrett says, he was ever in. The lines seemed in the darkness to be very close together. After the fight they lay on their arms in the woods a good portion of the night before they left the field.

"Co. H, First Regiment Berdan's Sharpshooters, Capt. Hastings, which had been temporarily encamping near us, gallantly volunteered to go into the action of Monday with us, and did good service. Capt. Hastings behaved very bravely, and after our loss of officers I put him in command of part of my regiment."—CoL. BARLOW.

Capt. Hastings says: "My men stood nobly in the field with the Gist, under a terrific fire of musketry from an enemy concealed in the woods evidently far out-numbering our own force. The conduct of my men was fully satisfactory to me. Lieut. Peet, of my company, though suffering from sickness, entered eagerly into the battle, and conducted himself with great bravery and perfect coolness. He fell wounded while encouraging and cheering on my men."

The regimental command proceeded on to Malvern Hill, skirmishing at times off the main road, particularly on the New Market road near Glendale, where they advanced two miles to watch and delay the enemy should they approach, but met with only small bodies of rebel cavalry easily repulsed and driven off, and having accomplished their purpose were recalled late in the day. They also accompanied Gen. Porter in a reconnoissance at night to the left of the main road over a couple of miles of rough country in the deep darkness, skirmishing and drawing the fire of rebel pickets. They were then withdrawn, rejoining the column. During all this time they had little to eat, often with no water, so that they were pretty well starved out—gaunt, weary, tired and sleepy, but all kept up under the general excitement.

Companies A and I, as before stated, helped to cover the retreat in Gen. Smith's division. Company B was in Hooker's division, following its fortunes and gallant bearing throughout the movement, and lost on the 30th: Wounded—J. W. Kenney, John M. Barton. Missing—Andrew J. White.

MALVERN HILL.

July 1, 1862.

This great battle, the last of the Seven Days, was begun by the Confederates about ten in the morning with artillery and skirmishing; finally, as the day progressed, the opposing forces became engaged in a terrific strife. As darkness spread around, the battle ended, although the artillery fire did not cease until after nine P. M. The result, was a complete victory by the Union arms, repulsing the desperate attempts of the enemy to take the position in every instance. Repeatedly did the rebel battalions swarm out on the plain and with loud, fierce yells rush forward toward the Union batteries which, double-shotted, opened at short range, mowing them down in a terrible manner; while our infantry poured in such staggering volleys, as to render their stubborn and desperate efforts a failure. The gunboats in the river also assisted, by throwing shell into the adjoining forests as big as balloons, but 200 pounds heavier.

The attack was made upon our left and left center, and the brunt of it was borne by Porter's corps (including Hunt's reserve artillery and Tyler's heavy guns) and Couch's division reinforced, by the brigades of Sickles and Meagher. It was desperate, brave and determined, but so destructive was the fire of our numerous artillery, so heroic the conduct of our infantry, and so admirable the dispositions of Porter, that no troops could have carried the position. Late in the evening the enemy fell back, thoroughly beaten, with dreadful slaughter.—GEN. MCCLELLAN.

The Berdan Sharpshooters were well represented on the field of battle. The companies serving with the handful of Bucktails were held in reserve, being greatly reduced in numbers, many unfit for duty, and all exhausted from fatigue and hunger. The following from the commander of the 2d brigade, Porter's corps, illustrates the slim fare and patient endurance of our troops in general:

"The men received but one day's rations from the 27th of June to the 2d of July, yet they made no complaints, but endured the hardships of the march patiently, and fought in every engagement with the courage and impetuosity of fresh troops."—GEN. GRIFFIN.

The battalion of Sharpshooters under Ripley (D, E, F, and K) were sent to the front a third of a mile in advance of the lines of battle of Morell's division, being first deployed by Col. Berdan on the edge of a ravine to the extreme left of the Union forces, bordering on Turkey Run, in the center of a field of wheat to be harvested that day by the sickles of war, and bounded on the farthest extremity by heavy woods. The position of the Sharpshooters was within 200 yards of this timber, where the enemy's skirmishers first appeared and received the first rounds of breech-loading bullets. Thig was about noon. The fire from the artillery on both sides soon became very heavy, the Union shells shrieking by, close over the heads of our riflemen, some bursting behind them sending the scattered fragments over and around them, making their position in advance one of extreme danger. Men in battle can stand a good deal from the front, but when it comes to a fire in the rear, they are apt to grit their teeth and do some tall swearing. Still there was no way then to stop it, so our comrades had to take it, and they did so most gallantly—whether they swore occasionally or not. About half-past two P. M. a heavy line of Johnnies burst suddenly out of the woods, coming on a run. Chief Bugler Morse, of Company F, stationed by the side of Col. Ripley, gave the warning notes to "commence firing." Then the bullets began to fly from our side, and soon the broken advance had to fly back to the cover of the forest. It was a complete victory for our boys for the time being, and as complete confusion to the enemy, their dead and wounded lying all around. But another and heavier line soon appeared, which despite the spanking balls among them to their great slaughter, with undaunted spirit came at our men on a full run, sending their shots before them—firing as they ran. A flanking party of rebel skirmishers appearing closely on their right behind a roadway, forced the Sharpshooters back; the enemy taking possession, won the advantage of the ravine, while our men were catching it in the open field where they had halted beyond the flanking line and continued their firing. Being now in the track of our own fire behind them—the front of the battle line—Ripley was ordered to retire his men and did so, to the rear of the 4th Michigan. Before doing this, they utterly repulsed and silenced the battery of the Richmond Howitzers, their guns being abandoned in the open field without firing a shot; horses and men tumbling over so fast that nothing could' withstand our terrific fire. The battery was composed of some of the most ambitious, aspiring youths of the "First Families of Virginia." whose efforts to distinguish themselves early came to grief, were in vain, their howitzers rendered useless. Gen. Ripley thus describes them:

"Suddenly there burst out of the dense foliage four magnificent gray horses, and behind them, whirled along like a child's toy, the gun. Another and another followed, sweeping out into the plain. As the head of the column turned to the right to go into battery, every rifle within range was brought to bear, and horses and men began to fall rapidly.. Still they pressed on, and when there were no longer horses to haul the guns, the gunners sought to put their pieces into battery by hand; nothing, however, could stand before that terrible storm of lead, and after ten minutes of gallant effort the few survivors, leaving their guns in the open field, took shelter in the friendly woods. A member of the battery in describing it to an officer of the Sharpshooters soon after the close of the war, said pithily: 'We went in a battery and came out a wreck. We staid ten minutes by the watch and came out with one gun, ten men and two horses, without firing a shot.'"

While on this advanced line Private Israel B. Tyler, of Company K, was sent to the extreme left, under cover of some bushes, as a picket to guard the flank. It seemed the enemy had also taken a similar precaution, for Private Tyler had not advanced far before he saw a rebel picket close by, whom he render. He marched back with his prisoner until he met the adjutant who relieved him of his charge, and allowed Tyler to return to his advanced position. His proximity to the prisoner prevented the enemy firing upon him. About this time Col. Berdan cautioned the Sharpshooters to hold their position until they had made a good fight, before relinquishing the ground. So that after they repulsed the first advance of the enemy, still holding on, our battery men were greatly annoyed because our boys were in their way, and prevented them from opening with canister until after they had fallen back.

After the withdrawal of the Sharpshooters from the front, the men and horses in Weeden's battery suffered considerably from the firing in the ravine; so much so, that Ripley was requested to send out a picked force in that direction where they could obtain a favorable position to command the ravine and stop the rebel fire, which was getting hotter and more galling to our artillerists. Adjutant Brown detailed some 20 volunteers in command of Sergt. Richard W. Tyler, of Company K, who was directed to proceed way out to the left, and succeeded admirably in obtaining a good position, which resulted in having the desired effect, besides performing good service on Magruder's right flank as he forced forward his desperate charging columns. They had advanced along the bed of a deep creek at the foot of a slope, where they reached a point commanding at short range the entrance to the ravine nearest the woods. Here the enemy were discovered in force on the slope massing under cover of the oak bushes in this ravine. Espying the danger at a glance, word was at once sent back to that effect by Tyler to Gen. Griffin, and as the former said: "within a few minutes it seemed as if all our heavy ordnance, including the gunboats, had been turned upon this point; "and although the fire from our Sharps rifles into the ranks of the enemy moving along the slope and forming in the ravine, was most deadly, yet that from our batteries in their rear was so effective, the carnage so great, that the position of the Sharpshooters was apparently undiscovered by the excited and suffering foe. The information sent back by Tyler relative to the position of the rebels at this point, was of the utmost importance to our side, and was quickly transmitted by Gen. Griffin to the Signal Corps, which resulted in our fieldpieces and gunboats opening in the terrific manner stated. The notice sent by Sergt. Tyler was received none too soon, for by his prompt action and alertness a serious flank attack threatening disaster was averted.

Gen. Ripley wrote Capt. Tyler some years after the war: "I distinctly remember that Gen. Griffin came to me soon after you went out on the left, and said: 'Your men have sent in word that the rebels were coming down the ravine.'

I heard him tell a staff officer, or orderly, to report the fact to the signal corps, and remember that a tremendous fire was opened on that point very soon afterwards, and that I was anxious lest you got it instead of the rebels."

The position was held by the Sharpshooters during the balance of the day, and on retiring, being at the time outside the Union lines, it became necessary for them to return by a circuitous route which brought them far in rear of the place where they had left the regiment. It was a dangerous duty well accomplished—a critical position for the Sharpshooters. Company E assisted materially in repulsing an attack on the extreme right of Morell's division. Maj. Trepp's command, A and I, were further to the right with Gen. Smith, where they occupied an advanced position protecting the center, having a lively time with the enemy's batteries. The heat of the day was intense and they suffered greatly for want of water.

Not until late in the day were the enemy's heaviest charges made, although the cannonading had been unabated, deafening and terrific—on our side 300 guns playing havoc—the breaking shells scattering all around continually, with damaging results. It was one of the greatest artillery contests of the entire war, and under such a storm of crashing iron there was little ground of hope for any coming' out unscratched or unscathed. Finally, the rebels brave came on in heavy lines of battle, and although driven back with serious losses, tried and tried again, with the same fatal results. The staggering volleys of our infantry, the grape and canister, round shot and bursting shell from our well posted artillery, with the heavy guns of the gunboats, all together drove the enemy, after the bravest of struggles on their part, away from the field a scattered, demoralized mass, whipped out, and useless for any farther attempts.

Gen. Porter in his report makes the following interesting statement: "At about one o'clock P.M. the enemy commenced with his artillery and skirmishers, feeling along our whole front, and kept up a desultory firing till about four with but little effect. During this firing Gen. Sunnier, having withdrawn under the crest of the hill behind Malvern house a portion of his corps, directed me to do the same with mine. I could not at once refer to the major-general commanding (McClellan) then on the right of the line, and protested against such a movement as disastrous to us, adding that as the major-general commanding had seen and approved my disposition, and also Gen. Couch s, I could not change without his order, which could soon be obtained if desirable He desisted and the enemy was soon upon us, compelling him to recall his own corps. The same ominous silence which had preceded the attack in force at Gaines' Mill now intervened, lasting till about six o'clock, at which time the enemy (Gen. John B. Magruder's corps) opened upon us suddenly with the full force of his artillery, and at once began to push forward his columns of infantry to the attack of our positions. Regiment after regiment, and sometimes whole brigades, were thrown against our batteries, but our infantry withheld their fire till they were within short distance (artillery mowing them down with canister), dispersed the columns in every case, and in some instances followed the retiring mass, driving them with the bayonet, capturing prisoners, and also flags and other trophies. The contest was maintained by Morell's and Couch's divisions, the former supported by Sykes, who had thrown some of his regiments to the front and dispersed a large column attempting to take us in flank. A portion of the reserve artillery was also here in action. While the battle was proceeding, seeing that the enemy was pressing our men and accumulating his masses to pour fresh troops upon them, I called for aid from Gen. Sumner, which call was promptly responded to by the arrival of Gen. Meagher, with his brigade, followed by that of Sickles, which Gen. Heintzelman voluntarily and generously sent to complete the contest."

In the closing scenes the Sharpshooters remained on the front lines until their ammunition was expended, when they were withdrawn to the rear of the great battle lines. They had done noble work, well earning a respite in their long and arduous efforts—a glorious close to so many continuous battles. In his report of the action, Gen. Morell thus speaks of a portion of their important service:

"The artillery in front was placed under command of Gen. Griffin. Berdan's Sharpshooters were thrown forward as skirmishers under Lt.-Col. Ripley," who afterwards reported, "that a considerable body of the enemy were stealthily making their way along the valley to attack my (Morell's) left and rear. The 14th New York (under Col. McQuade) promptly advanced to meet them, and after a sharp engagement in which three attacks 'were repulsed, drove them away, and the rebel attempt in that quarter was not renewed."

Their prompt discovery of the situation in front, reported to the general of the division, undoubtedly pre-vented a disastrous flank attack. An instance of many during the war wherein the importance of the Sharp-shooters' service was clearly demonstrated, extended, as they were, in skirmish lines far out in front, awaiting and combating the enemy's advance.

"Simultaneously with the attack on the left of my rear a most determined and powerful one was made on my left front." This was also met and repulsed by Morell's troops, "until they were in turn relieved by part of Sykes' division and the Irish brigade, Gen. Meagher, which having been sent to our aid, was led into action by its own commander and Gen. Porter."—GEN. MORELL.

In this last battle the regiment lost more of the "good and true," among them: Lieut.-Col. Ripley, who was severely wounded and soon after resigned, to the regret of the regiment. Also the following:

Co. E—Killed: Corp. Thomas Ward, George Scales. Wounded: Capt. William P Austin, severe; Lieut. Cyrus E. Jones, mortally; Leroy P Greenwood, badly; and Charles P Shepard.

Co. F—Wounded: Lieut. Charles W. Seaton, Jacob S. Bailey and Brigham Buswell, the latter discharged therefor, the others returning. Bailey was a noted wrestler, and was destined to wrestle more with the enemy—at long range.

Co. K—Killed: Abram Swits. Wounded: Martin S. Goit, severe; Edwin B. Parks, slight.

Col. Berdan in reporting this battle, said: "On Tuesday morning, being unable to find Gen. Morell, and learning that the enemy was approaching, I marched my command to the front and was about to deploy them as skirmishers, when Gen. Porter came along, and he approving my suggestion, I posted them in front of the batteries, where they remained all day, receiving and repelling the enemy's skirmishers, and received the rebel infantry in the afternoon standing firm and firing with great rapidity and coolness until the enemy's line was within grape range of our artillery, when they fell back with the Fourth Michigan, firing constantly. At this period it became necessary to have reinforcements, and at the request of the commanding officer of the Fourth Michigan, Lieut.-Col. W. Y. W. Ripley, of my regiment, went back and got two regiments, first the 12th New York and afterward the 14th New York, which arrived just in time to save the left wing. Lieut.-Col. Ripley behaved with great bravery and coolness."

Col. Berdan before the action commenced, bought some fresh meat, which he ordered cooked and ready for his command as soon as they should be relieved at the front. Nor were the two detached companies with McCall's division forgotten; the colonel having located their position, had ridden over to see how they were getting on. I wouldn't say exactly how it occurred, but some of the company

G men, at least, got part of this beef—maybe they stole it. As rations were scarce, it was a fortunate occurrence for the Sharpshooters that the colonel had been able to get this beef, for as the adjutant had stated they were "hot and hungry."

Prisoners taken at Malvern claimed to have been forced forward in their desperate charges on our batteries, threatened in the rear by the cannon of Magruder, if they faltered. Also, that they were unduly excited by frequent rations of whisky mixed with gunpowder; their canteens, some half full of this stimulant, was reported as conclusive proof that this admixture had been indulged in. Whether or not, gunpowder would have any additional crazy effect, whisky was undoubtedly sufficient to make them reckless.

The enemy lost heavily in this battle, computed at about 4,500—double that of the Union loss. They were finally routed and fell back to Richmond in great disorder, failing to follow up the Federal forces farther; which latter reached Harrison's Landing on James river the morning of July 2d, worn out with fatigue and glad enough to receive orders to prepare camp. They had left the field at Malvern the night before at a late hour, and endured a tiresome march of 12 miles over roads crowded with troops of all descriptions, ponderous artillery, trains of wagons, ambulances full of sick and wounded men, now close together at a slow pace, now stretching out and hurrying to close up, through thick mud, drenched with the heavy rain that fell during most of the night. It was a procession of tired, worn-out, battle-scarred men. Crowded in the line were the lame, the halt and blind; among the latter were California Joe and the Wisconsin orderly who were led away from Malvern during the night unable to see, caused by exposure, the smoke and dust. Many were afflicted on this campaign with their eyes from these combined causes.

Daniel Perry, of Company F, slept in the woods until daylight, when he found the roads and fields full of rebs. Being undiscovered he pushed on as rapidly as possible through the timber, reaching the Landing safely. Owing to his exertions running through the woods and brush, his long fasting, he was very weak and famished; being soon after taken down with fever he was sick for months. He had done good service throughout the day with his company at the front, but when they fell back became separated from them, and while making his retreat in good order over the hill by the "Crews' house," came across Gen. Porter, who probably judging from his size and distinguished bearing, as became only "the tall corporal on the right," concluded it would be to the advantage of the Union cause to have Mr. Perry in a more forward position; so, told him point blank that he was "going the wrong way." Whereupon the tall corporal, head and shoulders above the tallest, joined a new brigade, which went in on a charge; having no bayonet to his trusty rifle and no ammunition, although he had as he said: "received orders direct from headquarters," inasmuch as night was coming on, he withdrew from those ranks—a clear case of "skipped"—not wishing to be caught out after dark in strange company, especially among a lot of noisy charging shouters.

The total loss in killed and wounded during the entire seven days has been estimated in round numbers, for the Confederates 18,000, Union troops 10,000. Porter's (5th) corps lost during this time 7,600, about three times more than the 2d, 3d and 6th corps, the 4th corps losing but 800; and one-half of the entire loss, killed, wounded and missing, which is officially announced as a grand total of 15,849, came from the 5th corps.

The following extracts from a newspaper account of "A Week in Porter's Corps," in Gen. Martindale's brigade, written by Col. Horace S. Roberts, of the 1st Michigan volunteers, so truthfully describes the scene at Malvern, and particularly the trying situation of troops lying in reserve under fire, that I appropriate it, giving due credit to the officer for his word-picture of this great battle.

"All that night other tired troops were coming in, until the whole army was on Malvern heights, where we knew we should have to fight them until night again. About noon they began to feel our position, and we were pushed ahead on a most beautiful ground. I have called the fight at Malvern glorious; it was so to me for its results, and then it was plain, open, fair fight, no woods except what sheltered them, and from whence their infantry came, and to get at us they had to cross the long stretch of open country, where we could see them and be seen, and where we could maneuver and operate. Well. Butterfield's brigade was in front supporting batteries, Griffin's was on the left flank, and we were in rear of and ready to support Butterfield. Our division being off to the left, we formed in double column at half distance, and laid down, and for about four hours we took solid shot, shell and canister, in awful profusion; the roar of cannon was tremendous, our batteries were playing magnificently on them in the woods, the gunboats were hurling their shell over our heads into the enemy, and the 'enemy were doing the best they could, opening battery after battery in new positions. The noise was infernal, and our losses began to be respectable. I do not believe that troops have often lain so long under as hot a fire as my fellows did. It is the most trying position a soldier has to endure, to stand these horrid missiles, crouched low, seeing them strike all about him, hearing them burst all around him, and yet unable to move or do a thing but wait in that awful suspense. Now a pause, and your heart beats quicker, for you know they are getting a new range. *Zim!* now it comes, and they have got a cross fire on you—grin and bear it-shut your teeth and swear and beg for a chance to move on them—anything but this. But no faltering not a bit of it; occasionally, yes, frequently, some poor fellow picks up his leg or his arm, and hobbles off to the rear; then some fellow, less fortunate, has *to be* picked up. Finally, a stop to their shell—and the roar of *our* batteries, and after a little the crash of musketry, tell us their infantry is coming. We are where we cannot see now, but we hear the cannon roar, and now the roar of musketry is prolonged and heavy—now apparently coming nearer, now receding a little, and, our strained ears catch it all. Now the music comes nearer, and even the balls begin to whiz nearer us, and we fear our fellows are getting worsted—a little longer and up comes the aid:

"Colonel, deploy your column!"

I bounded with glad heart to my feet, and in a moment we were in as pretty a line of battle as you have ever seen. Now comes the general.

"Move forward to the brow of the slope yonder, lie down, and if the enemy break our line, charge him."

"All right, sir. Forward! guide center! "and with the cheers of our comrades and our own hurrah, the whole line forged ahead, steady as a clock. *Spang*! go the balls now—thicker, closer they fly. We gain our place;. we cheer and cheer again to give our fellows heart, and then I order them down, arid go along the line and tell them just what I am going to do, and they say they "will do it well." Not long there, when in hot haste from the front comes a messenger from the 83d Pennsylvania, saying that it and the 44th New York were hard pressed, out of ammunition, and must have help. No general in sight. It was just what I wanted. "Rise up! Forward!" and with another cheer we moved on, through fire and smoke, right into the field. I moved by a flank, to gain ground to the left; then to the front again, and they lying down, I moved right over the 83d and 44th, and my line was formed to the front of them. The batteries on our right were thundering on the enemy, as his infantry poured out from the woods, and charged, and charged again, only to be repulsed. I opened fire, and kept it up vigorously until their fire stopped, and they disappeared. They were fearfully slaughtered; they would move up bravely across the field up to short distance before they would have to give back. Everywhere it was the same that day, and finally night came on and the carnage ceased. I lost in that week 210 men, 190 killed and wounded. I verily believe, if we had 20,000 fresh troops the morning after Malvern, we could have pushed into Richmond. They couldn't gain an inch on us, and we *slaughtered* them till we believed they were running to Richmond. They thought they had us—in front and on flank they pushed us. Richmond was close by, and fresh troops could be poured out, but every day they were repulsed—sometimes twice a day, our poor fellows fighting again and again, while they hurled fresh columns against us and yet we came to this point and they couldn't fight us."

Gen. McClellan's panegyric on the efforts of the Army of the Potomac throughout the Seven Days' battles, is here given:

"To the calm judgment of history and the future I leave the task of pronouncing upon this movement, confident that its verdict will be that no such difficult movement was ever more successfully executed; that no army ever fought more repeatedly, heroically, and successfully against such great odds; that no men of any race ever displayed greater discipline, endurance, patience, and cheerfulness under such hardships. My mind cannot coin expressions of thanks and admiration warm enough or intense enough to do justice to my feelings towards the army I am so proud to command. To my countrymen I confidently commit them, convinced they will ever honor every brave man who served during those seven historic days with the Army of the Potomac. Upon whatever field it may hereafter be called upon to act I ask that it may never lose its name, but may ever be known as 'The Army of the Potomac,' a name which it never has nor ever will disgrace."—GEN. MCCLELLAN.

On the arrival of the Sharpshooter regiment at Harrison's Landing a number of men returned to the different companies from the hospitals north, also some recruits arrived from time to time. Gen. Shields' division of troops having arrived from the Upper-Potomac, was sent out to the front. On the afternoon of July 2d a heavy rain fell lasting all night, making the ground very wet and muddy, causing the greatest discomfort to the weary troops who were mostly without shelter, tents or blankets, with little or nothing to eat; who in consequence were anxious to get into comfortable camps so as to obtain the rest so greatly needed, also to provide for the sick and disabled. On the 3d the troops were brought hurriedly into line, crowding the entire plain, and kept standing for hours half-way to their knees in deep mud—virtually stuck fast—exposed for a time to the rapid shelling of a rebel battery that had been run up on a hill behind us, whereby the greatest excitement prevailed owing to the bursting of shells on different parts of the field, throwing mud andiron forward in a manner sufficient to demoralize other troops but those who had seen enough of hard service to grin and bear it. The effect on these soldiers, rather was to madden them, and they would have made it sorry sport for those "rebellious vagabonds "who caused this great rumpus, could they have got them down on that muddy field, in that sea of mud, where not a dry spot could be found to sit or kneel, forcing them to stand up for a half-day. It is true some of our boys spied a dead horse and crowded on to the carcass as if to smother the -very smell of it, strong and offensive as it was. That old horse was a perfect oasis in that desert of mud, whose body could scarce be seen because of the men on top of it. A truly glorious ending it was of this war horse's career, to be thus the means of alleviating the great suffering of the exhausted soldiers, in furnishing them a place of rest. One of the poets astraddle the hind quarters, indited the following, at the risk of being ducked in the mud, but he held his grip and begged off:

Old Horse! Old Horse!

We find you here,

That plunged in battle fully a year,

You neighed for glory, you reared for fame,

To die in the mud on this vast plain.

On the 4th camp was prepared, and in course of time the detached companies were returned to the regiment where Col. Berdan had his headquarters. On the 8th of July President Lincoln came on and reviewed the troops by moonlight. A few days thereafter Gen. McClellan, reviewing the troops, on appearing before the Sharpshooters expressed sorrow at their losses, at their decimated ranks. Riding close up to them, he shook his head saying to an aide: "It's too bad! But they are good what is left of them." Quite a number died at this encampment; among the Sharpshooters were: Company A, Private Christian Schiffman, their first death from sickness; Company B, J. Tatro, said to have been killed; Company F, Benajah W. Jordan and James A Read, who died of wounds received at Gaines' Mill, while W. S. Tarbell died of disease; Company G, Sergt. Shepherd K. Melvin and Private John T. Vincent. They were buried low in the shade of the deep wood, by their remaining comrades, and parting salutes fired over their graves. Gray, blankets were their only shroud, with a network of branches below and above them, the whole carefully covered with earth shaped on top into still another of those little mounds so frequently found along the track of the contending hosts. Private Alexander Merrick also died in hospital at Alexandria.

A number of the sick were hurried northward, greatly reduced, who would no doubt in a majority of cases have died on the banks of the James, had not this change been made. The weather at Harrison's Landing being very warm and sultry much sickness prevailed, although the rations furnished were of the best quality, and included different kinds of vegetables. Loads of lemons arrived, which were very beneficial to the soldiers who munched them down as they would a peach. In this connection reference is made to the morning report of Company G on the 10th of July—and but few of the other Companies could make a better showing:

For duty—First sergeant, 3 corporals, I bugler, and 21 privates. Total, 26.

Off duty—Lieutenant and 25 enlisted men. Extra duty, 5..

About this time (July 8th) the regimental quartermaster, Lieut. Beebe, resigned, and was succeeded by Lieut. George A. Marden, of New Hampshire. Company A also lost their first lieutenant, Magnus Falstich, who had been sick in general hospital and resigned July 15th. Hosts of flies swarmed around this encampment, which were a source of great discomfort, and every imaginable way was tried to get rid of them, without success. The only ones who could stand the pests were the southern darkies with our troops, who would sleep in the broiling sun, their faces covered with flies, just as if they were used to it and enjoyed the nap. But little could be done in the way of drilling, and among the Sharpshooters target practice was indulged in as a recreation. Recruiting parties were sent off to the different states to fill the vacant ranks. It was a good time to go on this service, for while new regiments were forming all through the North, the old ones must be recruited up, it was of more importance to have them filled; besides, the new soldiers learned quicker right in the ranks of the old companies, with a veteran either side of them.

Nothing of importance transpired in the Sharpshooter organization up to the time of the evacuation of the place by the Union army *en route* north, although considerable excitement was occasioned at an early hour on the morning of August 1st before daybreak, by the appearance of the enemy on the opposite bank of the James, who opened furiously with their batteries upon the Union encampment. This unexpected shelling was responded to by our land batteries and the monitor in the river, the gunboats having gone above, when order was again restored, and troops were dispatched across the river to occupy the position which had been taken up by the rebel gunners, they decamping. After burning some buildings which had sheltered the enemy, and slashing down the woods where they had hid, the troops returned; little damage being occasioned and that principally to the steamboats, although some cavalry men and horses were unfortunately killed and wounded near the river.

THE SECOND REGIMENT.

FROM WASHINGTON TO SECOND BULL RUN.

On the 18th of March the Second Sharpshooters, commanded by Col. Post, being attached to King's division of McDowell's corps, crossed the Potomac and went into temporary camp at Fort Ward, where they remained until April 4th. Col. Stoughton says: "We were brigaded with the 14th Brooklyn Zouaves, 22d, 24th and 30th New York Volunteers, Gen. C. C. Augur commanding; and to which brigade was attached Battery B, 4th U. S. Artillery, Capt. John Gibbon commanding; also two regiments of cavalry commanded by Col. Bayard and Col. Kilpatrick. All of these three last named officers were promoted to brigadier-generals before hardly a month had passed." He mentioned this to show the good company the "Second" found themselves in, from the start. Brave boys were they, all of them, from the high private in the rear rank, up through the different grades, to general.

Taking up the line of march, the men being weighted down with heavily-loaded knapsacks, they passed through Manassas; where, as Col. Peteler said, "they encountered the formidable wooden guns left by the rebels," and proceeding southerly encamped at Bristoe

Station from the 6th to the 16th. Moving on by Catlett's, they were ordered to quicken their steps, whereby they became assured that something more formidable than guns of wood would soon confront them.

The first night out the picket guard brought in a man representing himself to be a scout of Gen. Augur. He was dressed up like a Virginia farmer, and the commanding officer wished to know what he had to show he was a Union scoot. He then asked for an army screw-driver, which was furnished, when he proceeded to unscrew the guard of his pistol, discovering, stowed away under the guard, a thin parchment in a recess in the pistol frame, which was a pass from Augur allowing him to go anywhere. In advancing next morning, this scout persisted in going with, the skirmishers, but insisted on keeping ahead of the line some 75 paces in the road, although cautioned by Col. Peteler to keep in line or he would possibly be mistaken for a rebel. Soon thereafter, one of our skirmishers, on the right of the line fully 400 yards off, shot at the scout and broke his leg. The unfortunate man felt terrible about being shot by our own men, said if he had been shot by the rebels he wouldn't have cared. When they took the ball out it looked like a minie ball such as the confederates were using, and which is hollow at the butt; this made the scout feel better over it, but two weeks later another piece of the ball came out, showing that it was a solid bullet, such as were used in the breech-loaders.

FALMOUTH.

April 18;1862.

Here the Second Sharpshooters had their first skirmish with the enemy. Advancing ahead of Augur's brigade they met the Confederate fire with their five-shooters in a manner that evidently surprised the foe, who little expected such rapid firing. The revolving chambers of the Colts were soon heated up, and right here a most favorable opportunity was presented to test these heretofore doubtful arms; and the boys were compelled to admit that they were not so bad after all, having done good work with them. As our men advanced the enemy fell back, crossing the Rappahannock into

Fredericksburg opposite, burning their bridges. From Fredericksburg they were soon driven away, when McDowell's corps entered the city.

The object was to surprise the Confederates and secure the bridges without destroying them. Our cavalry pushed ahead about three A. M., when they ran into an ambuscade in a pine thicket, losing in killed 13 men and 30 horses. Gen. Augur then rode forward with an escort, informing both Cols. Post and Peteler before starting, that if the Sharpshooters were needed he would send back an order. Not very long after, rapid firing was heard ahead, at just before daylight. Going forward, Col. Peteler met Oliver J. Jones who, with Willard Wheaton, both of Company A, were on the picket line, who informed the colonel that they had "killed a—rebel." To which Col. Peteler immediately responded: "You have killed one of our own men! Look for orders in his pocket." Jones searched and sure enough found Augur's order for the Sharpshooters to advance. From this unfortunate affair, an attempt was made to criticise the Sharpshooters for being too eager—shooting too quick. But when it became generally known that the orderly when challenged by our men, drew his pistol and undertook to ride rough shod over the picket, and so was shot—hit five times—the "talk" subsided.

Four companies under Col. Peteler now moved forward as skirmishers, the four reserve companies following under Col. Post. The skirmishing commenced about break of day and was kept up four miles over an open country, the enemy falling back as our men advanced. Reaching the battle field, Col. Peteler fired the first shot at Falmouth, 700 yards distance, at a party of men and horses at a toll-gate. The shot struck in front of them in the road, throwing up the dust. The tollman told the Sharpshooters afterwards: "When that single shot came, the commanding officer said, 'Here comes the—Yankees. Mount!' and as they did so the entire party rushed away."

When our men got up on Falmouth heights overlooking Fredericksburg and the Rappahannock, the rebels were seen retreating even up Marye's Heights beyond the city. Here battery B,

4th artillery fired a few shots, their first firing in the war. From these heights a destructive scene was before them; the four bridges on fire, with four steamboats and 22 schooners, the work of the rebel firebugs.

In the latter part of May they marched 15 miles south of Fredericksburg, expecting to go on to join McClellan's army, but, according to Lieut.-Col. Peteler, "the rebel general, Jackson, was reported to be advancing in four different directions"—wonderful Jackson. Here, after some exchanges between the Sharpshooters and rebel cavalry, driving the latter away, the regiment returned to Fredericksburg and then made a forced march towards Front Royal. On the 1st of June the Sharpshooters were the unfortunate victims of a railroad collision near White Plains meeting with severe casualties-44 men injured. Returning again to Fredericksburg they exchanged their well-used Colts for the Sharps rifles.

ORANGE COURT HOUSE.

July 26, 1862.

On July 24th Companies A and C, under Lieut.-Col. Peteler, took part in a reconnoissance commanded by Gen. Gibbon, making a forced march of 45 miles from Fredericksburg to Orange Court House, where the Sharpshooters gallantly repulsed a rebel cavalry charge that threatened to capture some of our troops, for which good service these two companies were highly complimented by the general officers. Col. Peteler handled his men with much tact, and the line skirmished admirably.

After advancing three-fourths of a mile, one of the men of Company A called Col. Peteler's attention ahead, where they discovered fully 1,500 rebel cavalry across an old field 600 yards wide. A few shots were fired at them when they turned and rode off. Shortly after, hearing a few beats of a drum ahead, Col. Peteler's experienced ear in such matters detected a movement of infantry, who were soon seen advancing to our right and rear, whereupon the Sharpshooters fell back on the reserve—the 2d Wisconsin—who were having a good rest, cooking breakfast, washing in- the creek, bathing their feet, etc.

Col. Peteler at once told Gen. Gibbon that they would be attacked in less than 20 minutes; and told his own command not to go away from their guns, which he ordered stacked while they were trying to get a bite.. A short time thereafter, the noise of clattering hoofs were heard coming down the plank road, which soon developed our cavalry videttes being driven in by the enemy. The Sharp Shooters instantly falling in, wheeled to the right, across the road, where they were ready for the rebs, driving them away. Their shots were found in a number of instances to have trajected over the entire length of a 700 yard field, and prisoners afterwards taken reported we had killed and wounded 30 of their men at that distance.

At the cross-roads, five miles from the Court House, I left the main body obstructing the roads to the right and left, and pushed forward with one regiment of infantry, the Rifles, two pieces of artillery, and the squadron of cavalry, somewhat reduced by detached pickets watching the roads coming in from the left in the direction of Gordonsville and Louisa Court House. We soon encountered the enemy's' mounted pickets, drove them in and pushed on in pursuit.

The country becoming more open, the cavalry showed itself in greater force. Skirmishers were thrown out, and the advance pushed to within one and one-half miles of the Court House, shots being occasionally exchanged between the two. * * * My instructions directed me to run no unnecessary risk in obtaining the information for which I was sent. I therefore proceeded no farther. The enemy's cavalry pursued us and made a dash at our rear guard, but was easily repulsed. * * * I returned on the morning of the 27th. The Second Wisconsin and the Rifles (Second U.S. Sharpshooters) were conspicuous during the march for their well filled ranks, losing very few men by straggling, although the weather was very warm and the marching on the way out rapid.—Gen. Gibbon.

On their return trip, coming back through the Wilderness they took a lunch near a church, when Pony McGaffy (Henry C), of Company A, took it upon himself to officiate as chaplain and preached a sermon in the church, although I did not learn his text, but as near as I could find out from some of the company members, they having had some pretty hard hard-tack, he had considerable to say about B. C, and the 2d Wisconsin stealing corn. He also called for praise, or rather a vote of thanks to Col. Peteler, for having captured a half dozen geese with his revolver while near the Chancellor house; so that the boys were in pretty good spirits after all, notwithstanding their hard usage. August 6th, moving south again from Fredericksburg, the regiment made a reconnoissance with other troops to GUINEYS STATION.

Here they found that Stuart's cavalry were attempting a raid on us, while our cavalry were engaged in the same exciting pursuit on rebel territory. Our Sharpshooters, backing up the cavalry, took part in more or less skirmishing, which had the effect of defeating the plans of the Confederate horsemen. The Sharpshooters also reconnoitered westerly from Guineys to the region around Spottsylvania. Having successfully accomplished the purpose for which they were sent out, they returned and crossed the river to Falmouth.

On August 10th they left suddenly for Cedar Mountain, but were not engaged in that battle—Banks was falling back. Here they encamped until the 19th, when they moved back with Pope's army behind the Rappahannock, being the rear-guard.

RAPAHANNOCK STATION.

August 21-23, 1862.

Gen. Hatch told Col. Post to send Col. Peteler with four companies of Sharpshooters to the river, where it was reported that a battery of rebel artillery and some cavalry were on our side of the stream, a mile away. Peteler's command advanced in skirmish line towards the river, over rolling ground, a succession of ridges, and while going up the last ridge next to the river, casually looking to the right over a corn field the lieutenant-colonel discovered a cloud of dust. Knowing that we had no troops in that direction, the signal to retreat was given, at the same time making a right wheel. Then hurrying to the right of the line, Col. Peteler looking up an old road to the right of the corn field, discovered rebel cavalry as far as he could see; they were closing up when discovered. Cautioning the skirmish line not to fire until ordered, Peteler went back to two companies in reserve commanded by Capt. Caldwell, bringing them into line where they could deliver fire effectively. A rebel shot passed Col. Peteler's knee, they being very close, and struck the ground. At the moment the cavalry were about to charge, our men opened fire with their breechloaders. As soon as the Sharpshooters began firing, the cavalry at once jumped their horses and escaped through the corn field. The corn was high and the whole country about was overrun with horses, only seven men mounted got over the river by an old dam. The Sharpshooters captured the commanding officer; his horse being wounded, ran into our line, and tumbled into a ditch. Sergt.-Maj. Shoup and two others took the Confederate captain out of the ditch from under his horse.

The first thing the irate captain said on being taken out of the ditch was: "I am a captain in Stuart's cavalry and wish to be taken prisoner by a commissioned officer." To which Shoup replied: "Well! Here's Col. Peteler, commanding the line." Then the captain addressing the colonel very politely repeated about his being a "captain in Stuart's cavalry," and undertook to show that he was a person of some importance "down in Dixie," all of which "fine talk" notwithstanding, failed to impress our ready north-western colonel with anything better than sheer disgust at the airs the captain put on. Among other things in their conversation, Col. Peteler asked him where Jackson was? His answer: "You'll hear from Jackson, he'll give you hell in two or three days," made our boys grin at his bombast. He then asked what regiment this was, and on being told they were Sharpshooters, said: "Yes, you d—d fellows: Wounded me at Fair Oaks"—probably Company L, with 1st Minnesota.

As soon as the enemy across the river who were on high ground, saw their own cavalry out of the way, they brought six pieces of artillery right in front, 300 yards off, and opened fire on our skirmish line with grape-shot and shell. The line rallied on the reserve and lay, down behind a depression.

In the meantime. Col. Peteler had told the sergeant-major in 'the rebel captain's hearing and to his disgust, to place him in charge of two privates and march him to the rear, to the provost guard; but before he got away the _enemy's batteries had opened, and the captain had to lay with the Sharpshooters and take the fire of his 'own guns. , thus lying under fire, the boys noticed a dirty white handkerchief hoisted high on a ramrod coming through the corn, and the owner carrying it' cried aloud: "Don't shoot, don't shoot, I'm coming in; "our men hallooing back: "Come in, Johnny! Come along; old boy." He was an old farmer looking fellow of about 45, and when within speaking distance he said: "I'm so glad I'm 'here. I've been) looking for this chance for a long time; "and there lay his captain, who remarked: "Are you here? ""Yes, captain,"-he said half-surprised, "I am here, and—and—I'm d—d glad of it." Then our boys yelled, and yelled again, while the unfortunate captain of Stuart's cavalry, hadn't another word to say.

Considerable amusement was created at this point by a man of Company A named Charles M. Jacobs (soon after killed), who had been complaining that they were drilled too much, at Camp of Instruction, Fredericksburg, etc., after making these sudden and successful movements in the presence of the enemy, exclaiming while on the skirmish line: "Well! By--, our drilling wasn't for nothing."

On the 23d they were sent to the river to prevent the rebels from crossing. During that afternoon, part of the; regiment was near a spring in full view of the enemy on the other side of the 'river, but after dark the entire regiment moved behind a small hill into a pine grove. Company B was on picket along the river, and was instructed to open fire at daylight. During the night the rebs could be heard getting into position, placing batteries, etc., and promptly at daylight they opened with these cannon, while the smoke and fog was so dense that the Sharpshooters could do nothing effective, and found themselves between two armies with 120 pieces of artillery doing their best. The first fire of the rebel battery opposite our position was directed to that spring where our men cooked our coffee the evening before, but now fortunately for our boys they were not there. The firing lasted over two hours, and the Sharpshooters lying in, close column in the pine grove behind that little hill, were literally covered with pine, limbs—to their great discomfort if not amazement—and one tree knocked down by this terrible artillery fire of friends and foes, after it fell and before a word was spoken or 'command given, Henry Page of Company A, spoke up in a loud voice calling to Lieut. Col. Peteler, saying: "Colonel, I want to go home." There were many narrow escapes that morning, before the Confederates fell back from the river.

While supporting 'a battery, Sergeant Preston Cooper, of Company A, had a shell burst on his cartridge box, which took the flesh off the small of his back, and for nine months thereafter he couldn't lie on his back. The same shell killed two corporals and wounded three others in rear of Sergt. Cooper.

SULPHUR SPRINGS.

August 26, 1862.

At this place the Sharpshooters drove a rebel battery off the field. Two of the companies had been on duty guarding a signal station at Luray mountain, which brought the regiment for that morning in rear of the division. The advance, Patrick's brigade, was fighting at Sulphur Springs, when an aide of Gen. McDowell, galloping back to the Sharpshooters then on the way bringing up the rear, ordered them to double-quick to the front. Arriving, they quickly deployed right and left near the river, and in

10 minutes after taking the position the rebel lines on the opposite side of the Rappahannock were entirely silenced. The enemy found good rifles in front of them, and men who knew how to handle them, and they hunted their holes.

This was about nine A. M.; they remaining silent until about four P. M., when a flag of truce came down to the burnt bridge to parley with our officers about a prisoner (a woman); then the rebel line close to the river, rose up and skedaddled over the hill, taking advantage of the truce to get out from under the Sharpshooters' guns.

Cols. Post and Peteler had a narrow escape from Confederate sharpshooters, whose bullets sounded very much like Whitworth's. The two colonels were standing in front of a board fence at the burnt hotel (burned by Sigel the day before); Col. Post with glasses was looking up the hiding places of the rebels, telling Col. Peteler where he thought there was one in a corner of a fence 400 yards off. Col. Peteler, who always carried a rifle, took a shot at the supposed place, but from where he stood couldn't see any one; then, while loading for the second shot and capping his rifle, Col. Post meanwhile looking through his glasses which brought their elbows about six inches apart standing side by side, a rebel ball from off to the right 500 yards, struck the board fence right in rear between their elbows. The boys noticed the shot, and the puff of smoke from behind a pile of rails and went for them, sending the Sharps bullets in around the rails like so much hail. This showed that the Johnnies had some good guns and good shots.

Pushing forward, they approached Manassas, on which field they were again to prove their valor, and effective service as Sharpshooters,

SECOND CAMPAIGN

HARRISON'S LANDING TO WASHINGTON.

About the middle of August the army of the Potomac left Harrison's Landing by land and water for the vicinity of Washington, per orders from the new general-in-chief, Gen. Halleck, against the urgent protests of Gen. McClellan who wished to advance from that point on Richmond, and was about ready to commence the movement when the imperative order came to fall back.

With McClellan gone, Lee at once sent forward his troops to reinforce Jackson who was making every effort to get into Pope's rear. This latter general—now in command of the "Army of Virginia"—was naturally very anxious to get his troops together, and to have that portion of McClellan's army which was to join him, hurry forward—and this they were doing. The enemy were crowding him close, and great excitement prevailed all along the line from the Rappahannock to the Potomac at Washington; while at the same time the people of the northern states were impatiently awaiting the outcome—hoping for the best. Sensational rumors were frequent, and were reported to the people by the press with startling headlines, so that the excitement was at fever heat: "McClellan left the Peninsula—Lee advancing on Washington—Pope in command of the Army of Virginia."

But the greatest sensation of the time, and which spread far and wide through the army, was the affair of the 22d of. August, when the Confederate cavalry leader, Gen. J. E. B. Stuart, in the midst of darkness approached Catlett's Station and suddenly charging thereon under a negro guide, captured a portion of Pope's staff and his dispatch book, thus giving the enemy information of our situation as to need of reinforcements, plans, etc.

Gen. Stuart (official records) gives this report of the raid: "Having," he says, "captured the picket, we soon found ourselves in the midst of the enemy's encampments,. but the darkest night lever knew. Fortunately we captured at this moment, so critical, a negro who had known me in Berkely, and who, recognizing me, informed me of the location of Gen. Pope's staff, baggage, horses, etc., and offered to guide to the spot. After a brief consultation it was determined to accept the negro's proposition, as whatever was to be done had to be done quickly, and Brig.-Gen. Fitz Lee selected Col. W. H. F. Lee's regiment for the work. The latter led his command boldly to within a few feet of the tents occupied by the convivial staff of Gen. Pope and charged the camp, capturing a large number of prisoners, particularly officers, and securing public property to a fabulous amount. The men of the command had secured Pope's uniform, his horses and equipments,. money-chests, and a great, variety of uniforms and personal baggage, but what was of peculiar value was the dispatch-book of Gen. Pope, which contained information of great importance to us, throwing light upon the strength, movements, and designs of the enemy, and disclosing Gen. Pope's own views against his ability to defend, the line of the Rappahannock."

Gen. Pope expressed his indignation at the failure of his own troops to prevent the raid, in words following: "On the night of the 22d of August a small cavalry force of the enemy, crossing at Waterloo Bridge and passing through Warrenton had made a raid upon our trains at Catlett's

Station, and had destroyed four or five wagons in all, belonging to the train of my own headquarters. At the time this cavalry force attacked at Catlett's—and it certainly was not more than 300 strong—our whole army trains were parked at that place, and were guarded by not less than 1,500 infantry and five companies of cavalry. The success of this small cavalry party of the enemy, although very trifling and attended with but little damage, was most disgraceful to the force which had been left in charge of the trains."

Considering, that the night was so extremely dark, the enemy's cavalry, one of the boldest and best of that arm of service North or South, it is not more surprising that this raid succeeded than that we were not betrayed oftener, with so many intelligent contrabands allowed to remain in the camps—negroes picked up on every line of march.

But to my story: On the 14th of August as part of the 5th corps, the Sharpshooters began their march overland, passing through Williamsburg, Yorktown and Hampton, marching steadily' each day, sometimes at night, arriving at Newport News near the mouth of the James on the 18th, a distance of 70 miles. Before starting, knapsacks were turned in to the quartermaster, also surplus baggage— everything done to make light marching possible. Many members were scarcely able to walk at first, from the effects of disability, but as they moved on they improved, and by the time they reached the end of the Peninsula were fast regaining their strength and health. Green fruit found along the line of march helped them greatly; it proved to be better in the worst ˉcases of dysentery than the doctor's pills and powders. What under other circumstances would have tended to cholera-morbus, seemed now a substantial cure for their ailments. Embarking on transports' at Newport News, on the 21st they sailed to Acquia Creek arriving there the morning of the 22d. This was the terminus of a railroad running to Richmond via Fredericksburg, on the south bank of the Potomac. Here again, small boats were used to reach shore, the big steamers being unable to land as the water was too low. It was tedious, and somewhat risky from capsizing. Taking cars for Falmouth 12 miles south, they again resumed the march late in the afternoon, going westerly until two A. M. of the 23d when they halted till daylight, then continuing on until noon, bivouacking at Barnett's Ford. During the day heavy cannonading was heard farther west where Gen. Pope's troops were engaging the enemy while on their way north. The 5th corps remained near the ford to prevent any 'attempt at crossing the stream by the Confederates, should they appear. Twenty-fourth, changed position to points along the Warrenton pike, and on the 25th again , near the river. On the 26th repassing Barnett's, marched all day-and night along the Orange & Alexandria railroad from Rappahannock Station northerly towards Bealeton Station; on the 27th made a particularly hard march of 20 miles, going into camp at five P. M. near Warrenton Junction, in an open field by the roadside, suffering much from oppressive heat and want of water.

At half-past nine P. M. orders were received to draw three days rations, and be ready to march again at one o'clock the morning of the 28th. Promptly at that hour Col. Berdan ordered his regiment in , line, and moved towards the road, but in doing so, was surprised to find troops in front of him asleep, with no sign of their preparing to march. As the colonel marched the Sharpshooters over these regiments in the dark, a great disturbance was kicked up and a good deal of loud swearing, by officers and men of the sleeping regiments. But Col. Berdan kept right on until he reached the road, when he ordered a halt and to break ranks. Now, the colonel received more blame and grumbling from his own men, who did not know that he was not notified that the original order to march at one A. M. had been countermanded. The regiment being one of the farthest from the road in the brigade; had evidently been overlooked, or at least not found by the officer intrusted with the countermanding order; so, Col. Berdan was blamed, first by the sleeping regiments, and again by his own because they too could not have slept. Had he condescended to go amongst them and explain how it occurred, they no doubt would ha excused him, but he says: "it wasn't military," so he "silently took it all, in grief at his command, coupled with feelings of disgust at the result of his efforts to obey orders to march on time." The Sharpshooters had always given him due credit for promptness, but this time they seemed to think he had blundered; probably because of their broken rest in their greatly fatigued condition. Had the aide completed his whole duty, by notifying all the regimental commanders, this unpleasant episode would not have happened.

The regimental commissary, Frank Whipple, of Company C, assisted by Thomas McCaul, of Company G, drew the rations at headquarters, the night being very dark; so dark, that Straw, the wagon-master, accompanied by McCaul, had to go ahead feeling the way, to keep the team in the road to headquarters and back. When they returned they found the order to march changed to three A. M., at which time when the regiment moved into the road it was already filled with troops, also crowded with Pope's wagons—a perfect jam at times *en route—making* the movement a difficult one and naturally much slower than usual, delaying their arrival at Bristoe Station, 10 miles travel, until between eight and ten in the forenoon—that is, the 5th corps was all up and in line by ten o'clock the morning of the 28th. The Second Regiment of Sharpshooters were met with at Bristoe, they having undergone hard service and suffered considerable loss.

SECOND BULL RUN BATTLE FIELD.

August 28 to September 1.

[What is known as the "Second Bull Run," comprised all the conflicts on the Plains of Manassas on different days and at different places, principally the actions at Gainesville, Groveton and Chantilly, and by these names they are known.]

The afternoon of August 27th Hooker's division of McClellan's army was engaged with the enemy at Bristoe Station, the latter falling back from that point during the night.

THE FIGHT AT GAINESVILLE.

August 28, 1862.

Gibbon's brigade of King's division, composed of the 19th Indiana, 2d, 6th and 7th Wisconsin, encountered the enemy in a desperate action on the Warrenton pike east of Gainesville, in the evening, meeting with heavy losses. They were moving towards Centreville at the time, and ran into Jackson's troops. After the battle they held their ground on the turnpike until midnight, then fell back to

Manassas Junction. During the fight they were reinforced by the 56th Pennsylvania and 76th New York from Double-day's brigade, which was following Gibbon in the line of march.

Gen. Doubleday speaks of it thus: "Gen. Gibbon was received with a tremendous fire from a large army in position, under Jackson, Ewell and Taliaferro. Knowing he would be overpowered if not succored, I immediately complied with his earnest request and sent him the two regiments referred to, leaving myself but one regiment in reserve."

The Second Sharpshooters were also in this fight, taking part therein with Hatch's brigade, principally under heavy artillery fire, meeting with little loss. Hatch had led in the column, and returned to

Gibbon's aid as quickly as he could, but not in time to change the result. While the Sharpshooters were 'in advance before Gibbon struck the enemy, Cols. Post and Peteler sent Adjutant Parmelee back to Gen. Hatch warning him that the rebels were in line of battle on our left, but that general refused to believe it, although he came at once forward, saying there were no rebels anywhere near there, and took no heed of the Sharpshooter's report; which if he had, would have doubtless prevented that disastrous action with its great and fruitless loss of life. The Sharpshooters were ahead and saw the enemy—that's what they were out there for. It was not very long thereafter, before it got to be understood that the Sharpshooters' report from the extreme front, was to be depended on.

The Confederate Gen. Jackson said: "The Federals did not attempt to advance, but maintained their ground with obstinate determination. Both lines stood exposed to the discharge of musketry and artillery until about nine o'clock, when the enemy slowly fell back, yielding the field to our troops."

This is high testimony to the gallant manner in which Gibbon's brigade behaved in this action, they also receiving a complimentary notice from their general commanding; thus earning a lasting reputation, second to no other body of troops in the army. A Sharpshooter taken prisoner at Second Bull Run, overheard Gen. Jackson ask a member of the 7th regiment, "what troops were those with the black hats, and how many of them , "and when informed there was but a brigade opposed to his division, the rebel chieftain would not believe it, considering it impossible that his superior force could be held in check by so small a number of men; while the officers generally, admitted that "those black-hatted fellows fought like tigers."

DAWKIN'S BRANCH.

August 29, 1862.

The 5th corps remained at Bristoe all day and night of the 28th, when orders having been received at corps headquarters to march immediately beyond Bull Run to Centreville, Gen. Porter started his command at an early hour on the 29th, eventually passing by Manassas Junction to be halted by countermanding orders from Gen. Pope, who turned him back to the new front beyond the Junction westerly, towards Gainesville. During the day fighting had been going on afar off to our right, in front of Sigel's corps, along an extended line running northward beyond Groveton to near Sudley's Church; with a large interval of forests between these troops and Porter's corps, which formed the Union left, on the Manassas Gap railroad two miles west of Bethlehem Church—Gen. Reynold's troops, nearest to Porter's right wing, being two miles away, which was no connection whatever, but a bad gap. The enemy strongly posted under Jackson, connected on his right with Longstreet, the latter extending down to our left, which was guarded by some 8,000 men of the 5th corps—Morell's and Sykes' divisions.

Porter became aware of the fact that Longstreet was opposing him, from the reports of the Sharpshooters and the 13th New York, who had crossed the Branch in the forenoon in advance as skirmishers; also from the knowledge received through Gen. McDowell from Buford's cavalry that 17 regiments of the enemy's infantry, a battery and some cavalry, had passed through Gainesville three and a half miles west of Porter's position, early that morning, and had moved down on to the line in his front, where our men captured some of his scouts. The Sharpshooters were on duty most of the day in line of battle, with Butterfield's brigade on the extreme left of the corps, having been recalled as skirmishers about an hour after Gem McDowell told Porter he was "too far out," when the line of battle was re-formed on the east side of the Branch, the 13th New York remaining in advance in their original position. Gen. Porter's troops stayed on the field overnight, the skirmishers in front, until about three o'clock next morning when they were withdrawn by order of Gen. Pope, to fall back and take the road to Groveton. The casualties in Berdan's regiment were not very extensive, yet serious:

Co. D—Wounded: Sergt. William o. McLean, mortal. Co. I—Wounded: Daniel Warren.

Co. K—Wounded: Norman Wilson, mortal, and—Loomis, in head by piece of shell.

The position occupied this day at Dawkin's Branch by the 5th corps, previously reduced in numbers by the withdrawal of the Pennsylvania Reserves now under Reynolds, was of the utmost importance to the Union cause, being on the left of the battle-line proper confronted by the enemy, who were thus held in check from a flank movement.

This is the field wherein Pope declared that Porter had betrayed the Union cause. This is the field whereon the Military Board of Review appointed by President Hayes, declared that Porter was the means of saving the Union army from disaster. However it may be; and to the unprejudiced mind I will leave it, to look through nonpolitical eyes for their calm judgment, as to whether Porter was wrong, or Pope was mistaken; I at least can congratulate my comrades of the 5th corps, that no tarnish can be placed on their escutcheon. For, with all due respect and proper credit to the generals, this book is dedicated to the men who handled the instruments that did the fighting. And whoever attacks the reputation of the 5th corps, or the Army of the Potomac, had better be in some other business.

The Second Sharpshooters, in Hatch's brigade of McDowell's corps, were deployed late in the afternoon of the 29th, after considerable moving about that day, and as skirmishers fought with their brigade three-fourths of an hour on the Centreville Road; east of Gainesville, the enemy being found well posted and in great force in their front.

After marching about three-quarters of a mile the Second Regiment of U. S. Sharpshooters was deployed to the front as skirmishers, the column continuing up the road in support. The advance almost immediately became warmly engaged on the left of the road. Two howitzers were then placed in position, one on each side of the road, and Doubleday's brigade was deployed to the front, on the left of the road, and moved up to the support of the skirmishers. We were met by a force consisting of three brigades of infantry, one of which was posted in the woods on the left, parallel to and about an eighth of a mile from the road. The two other brigades were drawn up in line of battle, one on each side of the road. These were in turn supported by a large portion of the rebel forces, estimated by a prisoner at about 30,000 men, drawn up in successive lines, extending one and a half miles to the rear.—GEN. HATCH.

The Sharpshooters were deployed, four companies to the-right of the road under Col. Peteler, and four to the left under Col. Post. Crawling up the hill, when they reached the top they butted against the whole rebel corps, and the colonels commanding reported back the situation, which at first one of our generals could hardly believe, but was forced to soon after. The Sharpshooters held their ground alone and deserted until long after dark when they succeeded in getting away, Company A having six men captured along with the second lieutenant, James E. Doughty. The service on this occasion was very trying and well done. When the brigade went in, one of our batteries was losing a gun; and the 24th New York, later on, just about dark when the fighting was pretty well over for the day, lost their flag. Relative to this capture, Col. William T. Wofford, 18th Georgia (rebel) of Hood's brigade, says in his report published in the Official Records (U. S.): "We captured a stand of colors from the 24th New York regiment, and took 53 prisoners, belonging respectively, to the 24th, 44th and 17th New York." The flag of the 24th New York was retaken by Col. Post in person, who on seeing it going off the field in the possession of only a few men, galloped hard after them, caught the flag-staff and wrenched it from the man, then wheeled and put the spurs to his horse, which was a good Union horse as she gave her heels to one of the Johnnies, sending him sprawling out, astonishing the others so, that the colonel came off with the flag. This most interesting incident connected with that rebel capture, the Confederate colonel failed to' report.

GROVETON.

August 30, 1862.

Owing to a mistake made by Gen. Griffin's brigade and some other troops—along with them Gen. Morell—in missing the road in the darkness and going on to Centreville, the 5th corps was now only about 6,000 strong, which, moving by the Sudley road, arrived at the Warrenton pike at "Old Stone House "east of the little village of Groveton, about sunrise, after a quick march, taking position in the center of the new battle field. The fight commenced in the afternoon on the enemy's left wing under Jackson, by the brigades of Butterfield and Barnes of Morell's division, (Griffin having gone astray), and by the division of Sykes—the Regulars. The enemy's line (Jackson's), extended along an old abandoned railroad from Groveton north towards Sudley Church, with Longstreet to the south on Jackson's right. Gen. Porter's corps was on the left of the Union line and had charged close up to the rebel works, where after a most determined battle, they were flanked by Longstreet's cannon and forced back with serious loss-2, 151 killed and wounded out of 6,000, over one-third, showing the fearful cost of that unequal struggle. It was a brave attempt in the face of every description of fatal missiles from big-mouthed cannon and rapid musketry, spitting fire in deathly music that occupied in its intensity of sound the entire space in front and around them. The air was thick with balls of lead and iron—a perfect raining down from the mounted heights before them. Despite all, they pressed on, pp the fatal slope, until within almost grasping distance of the enemy's flags, and the day seemed ours, when Jackson's fresh reserves came to the front scarce 50 feet distant, adding more thousands to the merciless bullets sent tearing through the Union ranks. The advance was stopped, and our men fell back leaving the field strewed with their fallen.

Warren's decimated brigade made an heroic attempt to stem the bloody tide, but were finally obliged to retire under the terrible pressure to the ridge behind them, where the Regulars and Reserves made a stand that stopped the further advance of the elated Confederates. But though the enemy succeeded in driving us from their works—within almost touching distance—yet as they failed to follow it up by forcing our men from our own ground, where the 5th corps awaited their coming, it may fairly be called a drawn battle, so far as any decisive results were concerned.

The rebel commander, Gen. Lee, thus reports the fight: "About three P. M. the enemy having massed his troops in front of Gen.

Jackson, advanced against his position in strong force. His front line pushed forward until engaged at close quarters by Jackson's troops, when its progress was checked, and a fierce and bloody struggle ensued. A second and third line, of great strength, moved up to support the first, but in doing so came within easy range of a position a little in advance of Longstreet's left. He immediately ordered up two batteries, and two others being thrown forward about the same time by Col. S. D. Lee, under their well-directed and destructive fire the supporting lines were broken and fell back in confusion. Their repeated efforts to rally were unavailing, and Jackson's troops being thus relieved from the pressure of overwhelming numbers, began to press steadily forward, driving the enemy before them. He retreated in confusion, suffering severely from our artillery, which advanced as he retired. Gen. Long-street, anticipating the order for a general advance, now threw his whole command against the Federal center and left."

Col. Berdan was ordered by Gen. Butterfield with whose division the Sharpshooters were acting, to deploy his regiment in front and advance through apiece of woods, when he was to halt his command and report the situation of the enemy in front, awaiting further orders. Having successfully skirmished the woods and finding a large force of the enemy confronting him, he at once reported back to Butterfield, who showed him an order this general had received, to push on through the woods; but as the colonel was persistent in his belief that it would do no good without a strong support, he was informed he might show his diagram to Gen. Porter. When' Berdan returned to the line, after the skirmishers of the 1st (and right) brigade came up, connecting with his left, he notified Col. Roberts, commanding; the brigade, that it would be useless to advance farther as the enemy were already on their right and rear. Col.

Roberts at once seeing the correctness of the statement halted his line, replying: "Colonel, you are right—you are certainly right." He then awaited more support.

In his official report Col. Roberts says: "Upon Saturday, the 30th inst between the hours of three and four A.M. I received orders from

Maj.-Gen. Morell to break camp or bivouac, with as little confusion as possible. My directions were to follow in the rear of Col. Berdan's regiment U. S. Sharpshooters. Approaching near Groveton, I was directed by Gen. Butterfield, in command of the division, to move the brigade to the extreme front. In this position we remained nearly two hours awaiting the movements of the enemy, but, with the exception of a scattering fire from my skirmishers, also from those of Col. Berdan's regiment to the extreme front, and an occasional shell or round shot whizzing harmlessly over our heads, the coming battle seemed to be at a stand. At this juncture, between the hours of eleven A. M. and twelve m., I received through Gen. Butterfield from Maj.-Gen. Porter an order to advance my skirmishers briskly, through the skirt of woods to my front, and following with my command to attack the enemy, take possession of a railroad excavation located just through the woods on my right, to then sweep around to the left, and advance upon the batteries of the enemy posted upon a hill some distance to my left, the above order assuring me that I would receive from the forces under Gen. King (McDowell's corps) a vigorous support on my right. I at once commenced executing the order, my skirmishers advancing through the skirt of woods, the command following them closely. We had passed nearly through the belt of" timber to our front, when upon the opposite edge beyond the wood my skirmishers receiving an exceedingly hot musketry fire from the railroad cut, were obliged to halt. Cols. Johnson and Berdan immediately notified me that unless they could have better support from the skirmishers on their right, it would be impossible to advance farther. Upon going to the front I found that their report was correct; Capt. Spear being wounded at this point by the enemy's cross-fire. Fearing that our skirmishers did not properly connect with those of Gen. King's on the right, I deployed two companies of the 18th Massachusetts to correct the error, if possible, which they succeeded in doing satisfactorily. I then sent Capt. Powers to Gen. Porter, reporting our true position; requesting a more decided support on the right, or else, on account of an enfilading fire from the enemy, it would be futile to commence the attack."

This had been the opinion of the advanced Sharpshooters as represented by Col. Berdan, when the latter called Col. Roberts' attention to the serious aspect of the position. The enemy having full sweep of the fields before them, our men -unless properly backed up, would have been pretty much all slaughtered in a useless attack. This was very obvious to them, as also to Col. Berdan. The men on the front line, could tell pretty near as well as those behind them. Their dearly purchased experience in the past, gave them a good idea of the prospect of success over an open plain enfiladed by a crowding enemy. As it was, when the order to advance was given, Roberts' brigade was badly cut up: "Our brave boys holding the ground but falling in Scores," he says, also adds: "To Cols. Johnson (25th New York) Marshall (13th New York), also Col. Berdan, I feel much indebted for giving me from time to time the true position and movements of the enemy."

The battle proved to be another hot one for the Sharpshooters, who commenced skirmishing in the forenoon in advance, to the line of woods where they remained several hours—B and G in reserve, the balance of the regiment a long way out. At three o'clock these two companies received orders to deploy double-quick to the regimental line. Lieut. Nash (Company B) commanding the left division of the regiment, halting his men for a few moments in a patch of woods, warned them of the probable danger in front, in the following manner

"Now men! If there are any here who think they are going to have an easy time on this skirmish, change your tune now. For when you strike that open field, you'll find the shot pouring in thicker than the leaves over your heads. But mind you! I don't ask a man to go ahead of me, but keep your line and push forward, and if any fall wounded we'll help 'em all we can. So away we go! Now for 'em, boys."

And Nash kept his word, he kept in front—he always did—and the "boys" were with him, they kept right up to their work. Then the whole line advanced from behind, the Sharpshooters going ahead as skirmishers over the open field under the heaviest kind of fire until they reached a shallow ditch 200 yards off, where they took cover for awhile, and poor cover at that, being about 300 yards from the enemy who were posted behind the railroad embankment, keeping up a constant fire at our riflemen, sending their balls down close to their heads. As an instance of the dangers incurred by our men in this position, I mention the case of Sergt. Charles H. Brown, of Company E, one of their best men, he having raised up to fire was immediately shot through the head. There was very little chance for a man to escape being hit at that place, even if he laid very low. Here our men remained until the charging troops came up, using their rifles with great rapidity, when they rushed forward with the line, engaging at close quarters, until finally ordered to fall back from their imperilled position, owing to an advance movement of rebels in force on their left flank, the Sharpshooters being at the time short of ammunition. As the latter retired behind the Union artillery the enemy were driven back by our batteries opening on them heavily. So close did the Confederates shoot while our men lay in the ditch, they' had their knapsacks filled with bullet holes. The rolled blanket of James Ragin

(Company G) was repeatedly bored with deadly messengers.

Gen. Hatch, now in command of King's division, having reported to Gen. Porter, was placed on the right of the 5th corps, going into the fight at that point, the Second Sharpshooters being 'advanced as skirmishers in the woods. In all, this regiment lost 42 members on the Bull Run battle field, including a number captured. Col. Stoughton afterwards speaking of their service said: "They were under fire every day from August 23d to the wind up at Chantilly, August 30th. No men ever bore themselves more gallantly than the Sharpshooters. It is hard at this moment to enumerate the deeds of special daring performed by these men, often called upon to go and find troublesome rebel sharpshooters; and invariably with a good account, the ranks were fearfully decimated, and the rolls showed few men for muster on pay sheet, that were made up on the march to Antietam. At Groveton Company E was the first to encounter the rebels under Stonewall Jackson, and in each succeeding day of that terrible fight the Vermonters vied with the companies from Maine, New Hampshire, Minnesota and Michigan, to see who should do the best work; and on the very front line on the left of where Lee broke, our line, Companies E and H stood their ground with their cannonade, until there was danger of being out-flanked and captured, and then only by the most strenuous effort did they get away."

Col. Post commanding Second Sharpshooters, a valuable regiment, much exposed, and which rendered most excellent service, is' deserving of especial mention for his conduct, amongst others, in the battle of the 30th.—GEN. Mc DOWELL.

When the Second Regiment left Falmouth, they had between 600 and 700 in the _ranks (August 10th); when the first roll was called near Alexandria, September 2d, 127 answered to their names; and during Pope's campaign 200,000 rounds of ammunition was used by this regiment of Sharpshooters. In fact they were all worn out what were left of them, a good many were buried in Virginia, or sent to hospitals about Washington, while some went South to rebel prisons. Quite a number who had been absent returned to the ranks before they reached Antietam. Col. Peteler, hearing of the Indian Outbreak in Minnesota, obtained a leave of absence at the close of this campaign, and while home was placed by Gen. Pope commanding the north-western department, in command of Fort Abercrombie and the military district between Sauk Centre and Pembina, which he retained until the following spring.

The casualties in the First Sharpshooters were severe, with a total loss of 65 out of 290 present, according to the adjutant's, report, but I cannot name them all. Col. Berdan was slightly wounded by a piece of shell.

CASUALTIES.

Co. A.—Five killed, and among the wounded, Capt. Isler who was obliged to leave the field. Corp. Adolph Seunhauser and Private Charles Bieler were among the killed.

Co.First Sergt. Philander Austin, Corp. George Downing. Wounded: Thaddeus Hadden, Corp. John McCaffary, George M. Barber.

Co. C.—Killed: Peter G. Van Etter. Wounded: Capt. Jas. H. Baker, left wrist; First Sergt. Byon Brewer, left side; Norton Fitch, left arm amputated; Thomas B. Gorton, _Osseo E. Sturtevant and John Schoonover, who died Jan. 16, 1863.

Co. D.—Wounded: Sergt. John E. Hetherington.

Co. E.—Killed: Sergt. Charles H. Brown. Wounded: Capt. William P. Austin, severe; Samuel A. Clark, Henry E. Badger.

Co. F.—Wounded: Harrison J. Peck, Ai Brown, W. H. Blake.

Co. G.—Wounded: Corp. C. N. Jacobs, left arm, severe; Privates Thomas McCaul, thigh severe; Robert Casey, throat, severe; George H. Hartley, arm, severe (mortal); John D. Tyler, fingers, severe; A. G. Stannard, foot, severe; George Whitson, foot, slight; William H. Babcock, ankle, slight, George E. Albee, in hip.

Co. K—Wounded: Sidney J. Race, mortally; Richard W. Tyler, left leg; Albert Bills, severe; William A. Henderson and Dwight W. Thompson, slight.

When Casey was hit he jumped to his feet, and swinging his rifle at the enemy in an excitable manner, made use of some rather harsh language for their benefit, until the blood in his throat and mouth prevented farther speech. Then, after firing off what cartridges he had left, standing up in full view utterly reckless and determined, the last shot being fired at a-hog running along at the foot of the embankment, no rebels at that particular moment being seen, and which he laid out, this gritty soldier walked coolly off the field singing a peculiar tune of his own, completely heedless of bullet or shell flying thickly about him. He was discharged after much suffering and a struggle for life.

It is said that Stannard, on receiving his wound, paid his opponent back with interest, by bringing him down from a tree top, after which he hobbled off to the rear.

The next day, Gen. Porter accompanied by his staff, riding up to Col. Berdan's headquarters, complimented him and his Sharpshooters for the manner in which they had been placed on the line the 30th, and for holding their positions so long before reinforcements came to them.

During the night after the battle they fell back across Bull Run to Centreville, as per orders from Gen. Pope, "for rations and to await reinforcements." On the 1st of September the Sharpshooters arrived in the vicinity of Washington, going into camp near Fort Corcoran. They had now got back to their starting point of five months previous, and in the hard service they had encountered in a constant campaign of active warfare, had materialized from raw troops to accomplished soldiers in every essential respect. The calamities of war were no longer new to them, but with an experience seldom attained in the past history of the country in years of service, they had certainly earned through their continuous duty at the front, in battle after battle, often day after day, the proud title of veterans. As an important arm of the 5th corps, they gloried in its triumphs, and had no occasion to feel that at any time had their corps suffered defeat up to this last battle. And there, though meeting with reverse with the entire army, their loss of 2, 151 men—more than two-thirds of those engaged—sufficiently testified to their valor, their devotion to the Union cause.

STEVENS AND KEARNY KILLED AT CHANTILLY.

On this first day of September the divisions of Gen. Stevens, of the 9th corps, and Gen Kearny, of the 3d corps, had a fight with the enemy at Chantilly, between Centreville and Fairfax Court House, in which the two generals named were killed, to the sorrow of the Union; Stevens at the head of his division, and Kearny while attempting to reconnoiter in front of his own. Both sides held their ground overnight, and both met with serious losses in some of their regiments. It has been claimed that the battlefield was held by Birney's division, who succeeded Kearny in command, they having by a gallant bayonet charge driven the enemy off. The Confederates, however, hardly concede this, as per the following extracts from their reports of what they call the battle of Ox Hill.

"By direction of Gen. Jackson I sent forward the brigades of Branch and Brockenbrough to feel and engage the enemy. The battle commenced under the most unfavorable circumstances—a heavy, blinding rain-storm directly in the faces of my men. These two brigades gallantly engaged the enemy, Branch being exposed to a very heavy fire in front and on his flank. Gregg, Pender, Thomas and Archer were successively thrown in. The enemy obstinately contested the ground, and it was not until the Federal generals, Kearny and Stevens had fallen in front of Thomas' brigade that they were driven from the ground. They did not, however, retire far until Tater during the night, when they entirely disappeared."—A. P. HILL, Major-General Commanding Light Division.

"Our line of battle was formed, Gen. Hill's division on the right, Ewell's division in the center, and Jackson's division on the left. A cold and drenching thunder shower swept over the field at this time, striking directly into the faces of our troops. The conflict raged with great fury, the enemy obstinately and desperately contesting the ground until their generals (Kearny and Stevens) fell, after which they retired from the field."—T. J. JACKSON, Lieut.-Gen.

The report of Gen. Birney, who commanded the division on Kearny's fall, gives a somewhat different look to the Union side of the combat; for instance:

"The division reached Chantilly at about five o'clock P. M., under orders from Maj.-Gen. Heintzelman to support Gen. Reno, and found him actively engaged with the enemy. Under orders from Maj.-Gen. Kearny I reported my brigade to Gen. Reno, and was ordered by him to the front. On reaching that point I found the division of Gen. Stevens retiring in some disorder before the enemy, the officers in command of regiments stating that their ammunition had been exhausted. I immediately ordered forward the 4th Maine regiment, and it gallantly advanced, and was soon in active conflict. I successively took forward the 101st New York, 3d Maine, 40th and 1st New York. These regiments held the enemy, and sustained unflinchingly the most murderous fire from a superior force. At this juncture Gen. Kearny reached the field with Randolph's battery, and, placing it in position, aided my brigade by a well-directed fire. I pointed out to the general a gap on my right, caused by the retiring of Stevens' division, and asked for Berry's brigade to fill it. He rode from me to examine the ground, and dashing past our lines into those of the enemy, fell a victim to his gallant daring. I sent forward the 38th New York and 57th Pennsylvania to complete our victory. They advanced gallantly and night closed in, leaving my brigade in full possession of that portion of the battle field in which we were engaged.—D. B. BIRNEY, Brig.-Gen.

When the Army of the. Potomac returned from the Peninsula and advanced through northern Virginia they became a part of Gen. Pope's forces, subject to his orders; Gen. McClellan being placed in command of the territory comprising the defenses of Washington. So that when the troops fell back from Manassas and crossed the Bull Run line, they found themselves again under their old commander; and if there was any spirit prevalent among the men of disorder or demoralization over this retrograde movement, it was quickly dispelled by the wide-spread rumor that Gen. McClellan was at their head again. As a result, they forgot their fatigue and weakened powers, they were strong again --anxious to wipe out the past in victory for the Union, and a good thrashing for its enemies.

In course of time, however, they got used to these changes of commanders, submitting to the same with patriotic grace, and with the hope that the general in command, whoever he might be, would lead them on to everlasting victory. Nor should they be blamed for their confidence in their commanders, which in most cases at least, commencing with McClellan, they could be credited with. And was it not a good trait? For surely when an army—the men that do the fighting—lose confidence in their officers and particularly the higher grades, they naturally become demoralized and unfit for duty.

On the 7th of September Company K was reinforced by.

20 recruits from Michigan under Corp. C. W. Thorp. 13

THIRD CAMPAIGN.

THE MARYLAND INVASION.

On the 12th of September the First Sharpshooters, under command of Capt. John B. Isler (all field officers absent), left camp with their corps, marching through Washington on to the Frederick pike into Maryland, crossing South Mountain, and by forced marches on the 16th came up with and joined the main body of the army, which had moved several days before them, fought the battle of South Mountain, and was now in position on Antietam creek. The weather at this period was very hot, many cases of sunstroke occurring among the troops, resulting fatally in a number of instances. I always found it to be a good plan to drink as little water as possible during these hot marches, and believe that wet leaves in the hat served as a preventative of serious effects of the burning sun. Many were careless, however, swilling down water to an alarming extent. While on this march a number of recruits joined the regiment, particularly from Wisconsin for Company G, also 50 Vermonters for Company F.

SOUTH MOUNTAIN.

Sept. 14, 1862.

This battle consisted principally in assaulting the enemy holding two important passes or gaps in the South Mountain range, and occupied the greater part of the day until night-fall, when the Confederates were forced from their strong positions, retreating down the mountain during the night. Thus had their bold advance towards Philadelphia or Baltimore been stopped.

Gen. McClellan's report speaks of these passes: "The South Mountain Range near Turner's Pass averages perhaps 1,000 feet in height, and forms a strong natural military barrier. The practical passes are not numerous and are readily defensible, the gaps abounding in fine positions. Turner's Pass is the more prominent, being that by which the National road crosses the mountains. It was necessarily indicated as the route of advance of our main army.

"The carrying of Crampton's Pass, some five or six miles below, was also important to furnish the means of reaching the flank of the enemy, and having, as a lateral movement, direct relations to the attack on the principal pass, while it at the same time presented the most direct practicable route for the relief of Harper's Ferry."

The fighting at Turner's Pass was participated in by troops of the corps of Reno and Hooker, under the immediate command of [General Ambrose] Burnside, and began at eight in the morning, after Pleasanton's cavalry had reconnoitered the enemy's position on the crest of hills commanding the National road. The divisions of Gen. Reno opened the battle proper, on the left of the road, driving the rebels from the crest in their front, an important point gained.

The contest here was maintained with perseverance until dark, the enemy having the advantage as to position and fighting with obstinacy, but the ground won was fully maintained. The loss in killed and wounded was considerable on both sides, and it was here that Maj.-Gen. Reno, who had gone forward to observe the operations of his corps and to give such directions as were necessary, fell, pierced with a musket ball. A gallant soldier, an able general, endeared to his troops and associates, his death is felt as an irreparable misfortune.—McCLELLAN.

Later on, Hooker's corps came up, when the Pennsylvania Reserves under Meade attacked the enemy on the right of the gap with great success. Hatch's division was sent for to operate on one of the intrenched hills. "The movement, after a sharp contest on the crest and in the fields in the depression between the crest and the adjoining hill, was fully successful." Ricketts' division late in the day, took part in the closing scene, and relieving Hatch's men remained on the battle field overnight. "The mountain sides thus gallantly pressed over by Hooker on the right of the gap and Reno on the left, were steep and difficult in the extreme. We could make but little use of our artillery, while our troops were subject to a warm artillery fire as well as to that of infantry in the woods and under cover."

By order of Gen. Burnside, Gibbon's brigade of Hatch's division, late in the afternoon, advanced upon the center of the enemy's position on the main road. Deploying his brigade, Gibbon actively engaged a superior force of the enemy, which, though stubbornly resisting, was steadily pressed back until some hours after dark, when Gibbon remained in undisturbed possession of the field.—GEN. Mc CLELLAN.

The Second Sharpshooters, now under Col. Walter Phelps, Jr., commanding the brigade, took an important part in this battle, having been detached from the brigade for special service by Gen. Hooker, and ordered to the right of the line, where they carried the ground to the summit, charging over South Mountain, routing the enemy, capturing two mountain howitzers and a number of prisoners. Lieut. Humphrey, of Company E, says: "Back of the brush fence we counted 27 dead rebels from the 37th North Carolina regiment. On September 15th and 16th we were picking up the stragglers." Col. Stoughton refers to the short rest on Upton's Hill, when "the regiment was again put on the move, and reached South Mountain in time to be engaged freely with the rebels, and in which the companies were complimented for the daring and bravery" (displayed by the entire regiment) "in dislodging the enemy and occupying the ground, from which the Confederates were driven by the Sharpshooters." Their work was a noble one, and praises for the brave are not out of order.

ANTIETAM.

Sept. 16-17, 1862.

This great battle resulted in a Union victory. On leaving South Mountain in pursuit of the retreating Confederates, Gen. McClellan ordered the troops to attack them if overtaken on the march, but if found in heavy force and in position, our advance should form for attack, awaiting the general's arrival. The latter event happened, and when Gen. McClellan reached the field on the 15th, he found Richardson's division of the 2d corps and Sykes' of the 5th, the only ones confronting the enemy, who were- strongly intrenched on the heights beyond the Antietam—to the west.

"Their position stretched across the angle formed by the Potomac and Antietam, their flanks and rear protected by these streams, was one of the strongest to be found in this region of country, which is well adapted to defensive warfare."—MCCLELLAN.

This stream was spanned by four stone bridges several miles apart, a distance altogether of six and one-half miles, but our line of battle was hardly four miles long. Our other troops coming up from time to time as hurriedly as they could, were placed in their respective posit this for the attack, during the evening up to a late hour at night. The battle commenced on the morning of the 16th with artillery on both sides, continuing during the day; and in the afternoon on the right, crossing the Antietam by the upper bridge, by the Pennsylvania Reserves of Gen. Hooker's corps, which lasted until dark, driving the enemy before them, occupying their ground. At daylight the next morning fighting was resumed, which soon became severe and determined on both sides in a general engagement. All day long it was kept up from right to left. On the right, Hooker's troops started in with considerable success, but the enemy rallying, massed their forces, and hurling them on this corps (1st) stopped their advance. Mansfield's corps (12th) was then thrown forward to support Hooker, between them they drove the enemy back. In the struggle Gen. Mansfield was killed, and Gen. Hooker wounded. Finally, Sumner's corps (2d) go up and force the fighting, the divisions of Sedgwick and Crawford after suffering greatly, falling back with both their generals wounded. French and Richardson's divisions, however, held their ground although much exposed, their losses including Gen. Richardson, mortally wounded. At all times the enemy's artillery played havoc with our troops, while our own big guns helped to swell the carnage on the other side. Smith's division of Franklin's corps (6th) coming up at the opportune moment swept over the lost ground, holding it thereafter. But, "the condition of things on the right, towards the middle of the afternoon," Gen. McClellan says, "notwithstanding the success wrested from the enemy by the stubborn bravery of the troops, was at this time unpromising. Sumner's, Hooker's and Mansfield's corps had lost heavily."

Gen. Porter's corps (5th) occupied the center, and did good service holding the front line near the second or "turnpike" bridge, assuring the safety of the artillery and supply trains. Sykes' regulars were at times sharply engaged while Morell's division performed important service relieving and reinforcing other troops. The 5th corps batteries were also engaged with good effect, particularly Van Reed's in assisting Gen. Pleasanton's cavalry west of the Antietam, which battery, after firing some 400 rounds, withdrew about dark. Randol's battery went over and drove one of the enemy's batteries out of range, but was afterwards ordered by Gen. Pleasanton to return across the bridge, owing to the destructive fire onto his position by the enemy's concealed sharpshooters, endangering his horses and annoying his gunners.

In the afternoon Burnside, who was on the left, after a hard contest crossed the third bridge at one o'clock, but much later than McClellan desired, who in his report says: "The attack on the right was to have been supported by an attack on the left "—that is, in the morning, and at least by eight o'clock. That was the intention of the commander of the Union forces. On crossing, Burnside's men after considerable delay succeeded in driving the well-posted enemy away, capturing and holding an important part of his line up to the edge of Sharpsburg, including a range of heights with some batteries. Unfortunately for McClellan's hopes, however, it was too late to do any good, but just in time to meet fresh troops from Harper's Ferry—A. P. Hill's division—whom Lee was anxiously awaiting; and who attacking Burnside's left, finally caused him to fall back after dark to the heights first taken above the bridge, where his command remained until the following night, when they were relieved by Morell's division of Porter's corps. Burnside's troops lost heavily, though they made a gallant fight with the advantages of position against them—concealed rifle pits, strong barricades and enfilading batteries. Their delay, however, first in effecting a crossing, and afterwards failing to move right ahead, unavoidable or not, was fatal to the success of McClellan's plans, rendering our victory in a great sense a barren one.

"The bridge was carried at one o'clock by a brilliant charge of the 51st New York and 51st Pennsylvania volunteers. Other troops were then thrown over and the opposite bank occupied, the enemy retreating to the heights beyond. A halt was then made by Gen. Burnside's advance until three P. M., upon hearing which I directed one of my aides, Col. Key, to inform Gen. Burnside that I de-sired him to push forward his troops with the utmost vigor, and carry the enemy's position on the heights. If this important movement had been consummated two hours earlier, a position would have been secured upon the heights from which our batteries might have enfiladed the greater part of the enemy's line, and turned their right and rear.

Night closed the long and desperately contested battle of the 17th. Nearly 200,000 men and 500 pieces of artillery were for 14 hours engaged in this memorable battle."—Mc CLELLAN.

The official report of the loss of the 9th corps (Burn-side's) during this engagement, shows a total of 2,293: Killed 432, wounded 1,741, missing 120. Surely enough to prove that the soldiers themselves were not to blame for any failure that may have occurred.

McClellan's purpose was to renew the attack on the 18th, but was prevented from so doing owing to the weakened condition of many divisions, which had already suffered severely in the general loss of "12,410," of which less than 800 were among the "captured or missing." It became absolutely necessary to collect the scattered troops and re-form them, to replenish their cartridge boxes and caissons which were about exhausted, to give them a little rest and a chance to munch a few hard-tack, with whatever else might come to them eatable, for they were tired and hungry after their hard fighting and previous forced marches day and night. Both Gens. Sumner and Meade notified McClellan that they did not think their corps "in proper condition" to attack the enemy vigorously on the 18th. This same condition also existed among some of the troops on the left, particularly with the new levies.

The fighting at Antietam was particularly severe; many brilliant charges were made by our troops, with a prestige of success that encouraged the hope that on its renewal a decisive result would be attained. But during the night of the 18th the enemy stole silently away, retreating across the Upper Potomac where his left wing extended, not venturing to hazard another day's encounter. The rebel general, Lee, had the choice of ground and wisely made his stand on the formidable heights from which he could slip away if too hard pushed, and did so completely, getting well into Virginia before he stopped. And this was the result of his threatened capture of northern cities, of his invasion of loyal territory. He made a big rush, but when McClellan faced him his rush was over—he rushed the other way, thanks to the hills and natural defenses that shielded him.

The victories at South Mountain and Antietam were glorious ones for the Union cause, as they forced the defiant rebel army out of Maryland, and frustrated their bold designs on Baltimore and Washington. Besides it required more than ordinary efforts on the part of the Union soldiers to dislodge the Confederates, from the hills and mountains. It was truly uphill work for the Blue Coats, and in its accomplishment they well deserved the thanks of the northern people, particularly those of the Atlantic cities. The soldiers that fought the battles of the Maryland campaign could well be proud of the honor. After the battle of South Mountain, President Lincoln in a dispatch to Gen. McClellan, said:

"God bless you, and all with you."

While, after Antietam, Gen. McClellan reproached Gen. Halleck the general-in-chief, with:

"A spirit of fault-finding, and that you have not yet found leisure to say one word in commendation of the recent achievements of this army, or even to allude to them."

At Antietam the First Regiment of Sharpshooters were held in reserve with other troops of their corps, being at times under heavy artillery fire, holding a perilous position during the entire engagement in protecting the center and supporting the batteries.

The Second Sharpshooters were in it hot and heavy, with a loss of 66 killed and wounded of their always valuable men; among them the accomplished Adjt. Lewis C. Parmelee, Lieut. John J. Whitman and Lieut. John W. Thompson, killed; Col. Post and Capt. Dudley P. Chase, wounded. They were in Phelps' brigade of Doubleday's division of the 1st corps under Hooker, rendering important and trying service in advance, where they captured one stand of rebel colors. Lieut. Humphrey: "Sept. 17th, we entered the historic cornfield at Antietam and helped to fill the bloody lane, at the expense to our company (E) of one killed and 10 wounded. Our captain and four men were left for duty." Lieut. Curtis Abbott, of Company H, tells how "on the 16th they led the advance of Hooker's division on Lee's left, had a slight skirmish at the close of that day, and were in the thickest of the fight in the cornfields at about sunrise the following morning. Loss (in H) five men wounded, one mortally. There was heavy loss throughout the regiment. Their ranks thinned by previous hard marches, their loss at this battle was fully 25 per cent of those present for duty." Col. Stoughton adds his testimony to the important service rendered by the Second Regiment here: "While lying on their faces on the open ground they did more damage to the enemy than any brigade in our front or to our right, we firing obliquely. Into the field opposite and in front of Campbell's battery, were put in one grave, 192 of the enemy. Col. D. Wyatt Aiken, of the 7th South Carolina, was on that field and told Stoughton afterwards that it was as hot as any place he was ever in. The following Confederate authority proves it:

The Seventh, led by Col. Aiken, trailed their progress to the cannon's mouth with the blood of their bravest, and when borne back by resistless force, rallied the remnant left under command of Capt. John S. Hard, the senior surviving officer. Col. Aiken was most dangerously wounded, and every officer and man in the color company either killed or wounded, and their total loss 140 out of 268 men carried in. The colors of this regiment, shot from the staff, formed the winding sheet of the last man of the color company at the extreme point reached by our troops that day.—J. B. KERSHAW, Brig.-Gen. Comdg.

Adjt. Parmelee was shot while trying to carry off a rebel flag he had seized, fastened to a fence post; but unfortunately for him and others, the rebels were behind the fence, and the gallant adjutant had five bullets put in him. Lieut. "Jack" Whitman, as he was familiarly called, fell while leading on and cheering his men, being at the time in command of Company B. One of the rebel flags was captured by a Company A man, who was complimented by Gen. McClellan riding by as the Sharpshooters were coming out of the fight. He ran and grabbed it from the hands of the reb who was holding it on the fence. Silas W. Howard, of Company E, received several gunshot wounds, one through his chest, and notwithstanding he did not expect to survive, and took out the fire block of his Sharps rifle, throwing it far away so no rebel could find it to make use of the rifle against us, with all his wounds he survived and was living at his old home at Royalton, in Vermont, in 1892, or 30 years after the battle.

ADJUTANT PARMELEE.

Two very singular things occurred after the battle in connection with Adjt. Parmelee, says Col. (then Captain) Stoughton. The first: As Surgeon Reynolds and myself were riding along the Sharpsburg pike, arriving at the very place where the adjutant fell, we met a carriage containing a lady. She spoke to us and wanted to be directed to the Second U. S. Sharpshooters, and recognizing our green uniforms, said: "Perhaps you belong to that regiment," to which we replied affirmatively. The lady again: "Do you know where Adjutant Parmelee fell?" We answered: "Yes, ma'am, right there, and the blood stains mark the spot." She continued: "Well, I came from New York on behalf of the lady to whom he was engaged, and who was at my house when the sad intelligence of his death was received."

A few days later, Chaplain Barber and Capt. Stoughton had nearly reached the same spot when they met a carriage containing four gentlemen, one of whom made similar inquiries as the lady, and proved to be the adjutant's father, who was informed: "Right there is the spot and there he was buried;" he then said he had come to take the body away.

Adjt. Parmelee was a great favorite in the regiment, a young man of excellent address and education, having passed through a course of studies at Edinburg, and had belonged to New York city's crack regiment, the Seventh—or National Guard. He could quote all the great poets and prominent authors. An amusing story is told at his expense, in a little trick played on him at Camp of Instruction. It appears that the adjutant had been expecting from his friends East a splendid horse, and had said a good deal about it to his fellow-officers. So, one day, Capt. came across an old bone-yard subject, and had him brought to camp and hid. He then requested Capt. Peteler to engage Parmelee in a game of cards that evening, which the Minnesota captain did, not knowing what was intended, although he looked for a joke. At taps or a little after, some one came around to Peteler's tent, crying out:

"Lights out! lights out! "and disappeared. So, the captain taking the hint adjourned the game, and walked out with Parmelee towards his quarters, who, as he approached his tent, quoting one of his favorite verses, that eastern horse still being in his mind: "A horse! a horse! My kingdom for a"—at this point he had just dodged under the tent flap right onto the skinny bones therein. Then there was a scene, but I draw the curtain to say that the "shocked" adjutant, next day finding the horse had died, got even with his unknown trickster, by ordering a detail from every company in the regiment to assist in burying the old played out horse.

"Having ascertained that the enemy's line was formed with their left advanced, making a crotchet, and that they were in position to partially enfilade our lines, I ordered the Second U. S. Sharpshooters, Col. Post, to move to the right and front, advancing his left, and to engage the enemy at that point. The effect of the engagement between the Sharpshooters and the enemy was to draw a very heavy fire from their advanced line, and I ordered the brigade forward to the support of the line in front. The musketry fire at this point was very heavy—the loss of the 2d U. S. Sharpshooters was severe."—WALTER PHELPS, JR.

There were two companies of Andrew Sharpshooters of Massachusetts, named after their governor, raised for Col. Berdan's Second Regiment, who were sent out as independent companies. Berdan offered them Sharps rifles to march and skirmish with, but they preferred to carry the heavy telescopes. One of these companies was in Morell's division of the 5th corps, and one in Gorman's brigade of the 2d corps. This latter company was badly cut up at Antietam, in a close engagement where rapid loading and quick shooting with them was out of the question, their guns being little better in that affair than clubs, they losing 26 with their captain and a lieutenant among the killed.

Gen. Gorman, 'speaking of their service, said: "Captain Saunder's company of Sharpshooters, attached to the 15th Massachusetts volunteers, together with the left wing of that regiment, silenced one of the enemy's batteries and kept it so, driving the cannoneers from it every time they attempted to load, and for ten minutes fought the enemy in large numbers at a range of 15 to 20 yards, each party sheltering themselves behind fences, large rocks, and straw-stacks."

The Second Minnesota Sharpshooters (Company L) were also engaged here in the same brigade, going into action with 42 men and losing 24, as I am informed, "within a space of time not exceeding 10 minutes."

Gen. McClellan reports: "2,700 of the enemy's dead were counted and buried on the field, while a portion had been previously buried by the enemy, which was conclusive evidence that the enemy sustained much greater loss than we. Thirteen guns, 39 colors, upwards of 15,000 stand of small arms, and more than 6,000 prisoners were the trophies which attest the success of our arms in the battles of South Mountain, Crampton's Gap, and Antietam. Not a single gun or color was lost by our army during those battles." He also computed the Confederate force at 97,445 against a total of 87, 164 Union troops in action. The "estimate of the forces under the Confederate Gen. Lee, was made up by direction of Gen. Banks, from information obtained by the examination of prisoners, deserters, spies, etc."

BLACKFORD'S FORD.

Sept. 19, 20, 1862.

On the 19th the Sharpshooters were ordered to the front in advance of Morell's division, and marching through Sharpsburg met the enemy again at this crossing of the Potomac, having been sent ahead to reconnoiter. Proceeding three-fourths of a mile deployed in line, they skirmished in the afternoon with their rear guard, when a brisk little action ensued, the 4th Michigan following as a support. On reaching the river bank the enemy who had crossed to the Virginia side, opened heavily at first, but were soon completely silenced by our men who had taken possession of an old canal bed then dry, assisted by our batteries from the beginning, the Confederates being unable to load their cannon or to remove them. At half past five P. M. Capt. Isler commanding, received an order from Gen. Porter for the First Sharpshooters to cross the stream and drive the enemy from the bluff—"to repulse them at any hazard." Only a part of the command heard the order, and these promptly responding, ran forward into the water waist deep under a hot fire from their opponents, to our loss in killed and wounded, forded the river with their guns and cartridge boxes held above them, and climbing the embankment put the foe to flight, capturing a rebel battery of four guns; afterwards run down the bluff on to the beach by the 4th Michigan following, which were eventually removed to the Union lines on the Maryland side by a portion of the 5th New York. So that three regiments got the credit of capturing these guns: First, Berdan Sharpshooters; second, 4th Michigan; third, 5th New York.

After the Sharpshooters had captured the cannon—the first and real capture—two of which were discovered by a small force under Corp. Cassius Peck, of Company F, and taken, after driving the enemy off, with one prisoner; our men followed the retreating foe 300 yards, fighting every step. While advancing, Company I came in contact with a line of skirmishers, when a fight occurred at short range, the rebels retreating as the Sharpshooters rushed at them, leaving behind numerous articles of value, among them a case of surgical instruments. Being reinforced, the enemy recharged and succeeded in getting back everything but the doctor's case taken by Sergt. Eli Cook, who, however, lost it during the darkness, having placed it under a bush for safe keeping. During the night the Sharpshooters were ordered to recross the river, although they held the shore from which the enemy had been driven. Before returning, a horse was heard coming at full speed. It was very dark, and the rider a rebel staff-officer, rode right up to our lines, looking for the brigade left to guard the ford, Lawton's brigade of Jackson's corps, for whom he had verbal orders, thus proving the number of men that had been opposed to our small force. This officer was captured by Corp. Sankey (Company B) in Sergt. Cook's picket, and sent to Gen. Porter by Capt. Isler.

On the 20th at an early hour, a portion of the 5th corps under Gen. Sykes, with Barnes' brigade of Morell's division, crossed over and advanced more or less as far as a mile from the river, expecting to be reinforced by more troops and to advance towards Shepherdstown. Being suddenly attacked by a superior force, some 3,000 strong, rising in front from the heavy woods, and the "bushes and cornfields" which had hidden them from view, Gen. Porter at the suggestion of Gen. Sykes, ordered the entire command to fall back across the ford, which was gradually accomplished. A new regiment known as the "Corn Exchange" of Philadelphia (118th Pennsylvania), remaining too long found themselves flanked, and being furiously assaulted on all sides met with severe loss, while hurriedly driven back to the bluff. Our troops on the Maryland side heard the firing, when orders came for the Sharpshooters to fall in, who moving double-quick, were posted in the canal where they had good shelter and a fine place to aim—cruel work, but it was war, and our troops must be protected. Here, the concealed riflemen had a chance to cover the retreat, which was handsomely done, the enemy as they approached the opposite bank being quickly driven away by the shower of bullets whizzing among them. The rebels were making fatal work among the Pennsylvanians, shooting them down fast, until our boys came to their rescue and saved them. Taking cover under the bank mid the rocks and caves, many of them refused for a time to attempt the crossing, fearing to expose themselves while so doing. Our men called to them, trying to encourage them, but without avail. Finally, Calvin Morse, chief bugler of Company F, crossed the stream, protected by the fire of his comrades, to show that it could be safely done. Persuasion and coaxing seemed useless, and many of them were captured. But the Pennsylvanians were not to blame for being driven or for their subsequent actions. They had fought hard at the front before falling back, with an inferior gun, "50 per cent of which could not be discharged," and when men cannot shoot back, they hardly care to be shot at.

"Their arms (spurious Enfield rifles) were so defective that little injury could be inflicted by them upon the enemy. Many of this regiment, new in service, volunteered the previous evening, and formed part of the attacking party which gallantly crossed the river to secure the enemy's artillery. They have earned a good name which the losses of the day did not diminish. (These defective arms had been reported to the General-in-Chief, but all efforts to replace them had failed.)"—FITZ JOHN PORTER.

The Sharpshooter companies as usual did good service. The fighting was often severe both with musketry and artillery, our batteries working hard. Our men felt in the best of spirits at the successful issue of the engagement, the enemy hurrying away during the night. Recruits first under fire were awarded great praise for so gallantly vying with the old members during the battle. An instance is given to show their true spirit: Lieut. Nash, of Company B, having called for volunteers to cross the river and bring in the wounded, Company B went entire, with some of other companies; among them, Albert S. Isham, of G, jumped up, quickly followed by William Heath, a recruit, who, plunging into the water up to their armpits despite the heavy firing, succeeded in crossing over, and recovering one of the wounded returned with him in safety, although the unfortunate soldier died shortly after. Rushing waters had no terrors for such brave soldiers.

Capt. Marble wrote me: "Your recruits, first under fire near Sharpsburg, are doing splendidly." Col. Berdan also wrote: "Stevens, send as many more of the same sort as you can get." These recruits sandwiched in among the old members, soon became proficient soldiers.

Relative to the affair of the 19th, Gen. Porter reports: "The result of the day's action was the capture of five pieces, two caissons, two caisson bodies, two forges, and some 400 stand of arms; also one battle-flag. Our loss was small in numbers, but some excellent officers and men were killed and wounded."

The casualties among the Sharpshooters included, among others unknown to me, the following valuable men:

Co. A—Killed: Henry Logas.

Co. B—Wounded: Joseph L. Stokes, George Griswold.

Co. I—Killed: First Sergt. Marvin P. Raymond. Wounded: Arthur Hamlin, shot through both thighs, mortal.

Co. K—Wounded: Joel Race, slight in foot by piece of shell.

In Company G, Willard M. Isham was struck with apiece of shell on both legs and benumbed, which kept him off duty for some weeks; another instance of the effect produced by a glance shot, or even spent ball, the force of the blow often being more severely felt than if it entered the flesh. Marvin and Hamlin were shot in the river on the 19th.

The rebel general A. P. Hill, in his report of Shepherds-town or Boteler's Ford, the Blackford Ford battle, told

ALBERT S. ISHAM.

Co. I—Killed: First Sergt. Marvin P. Raymond. Wounded: Arthur Hamlin, shot through both thighs, mortal.

Co. K—Wounded: Joel Race, slight in foot by piece of shell.

In Company G, Willard M. Isham was struck with a piece of shell on both legs and benumbed, which kept him off duty for some weeks; another instance of the effect produced by a glance shot, or even spent ball, the force of the blow often being more severely felt than if it entered the flesh.

Marvin and Hamlin were shot in the river on the 19th.

The rebel general A. P. Hill, in his report of Shepherdstown or Boteler's Ford, the Blackford Ford battle, told what a daring charge he had made, how he drove us pell-mell into the river, followed by the "greatest slaughter of blue coats of the war; "the broad surface of the Potomac being blue with floating bodies, etc. He must have been looking through a very large magnifying glass at a respectful distance from the river, as his story was certainly a very great stretch of imagination; and yet it was founded on a pretty good supposition when the illy armed "Corn Exchange" were driven back.

No further attempt being made to cross into Virginia, the troops went into camp in Maryland, that of the Sharpshooters located in a beautiful oak forest near the Potomac. On the 3d of October our corps was visited by President Lincoln, which event, while it afforded them much pleasure, would have been more gratifying had they not been roasted for three hours by the hot sun. The Sharpshooters in common with the other old regiments of this army, were by the vicissitudes of war reduced to less than half their original number, and with their weather-tanned faces, "brown as a berry," their tattered banners and faded clothes, their visages depicting sadness and want, presented a most gloomy aspect, while their depleted ranks bespoke their hardships and suffering. All of which brought forth the fullest sympathies of the President. While at this camp the soldiers were poorly supplied with clothing and rations, the latter causing much complaint, especially the wormy crackers. Paper soled shoes, shoddy clothing, and wormy tack, had the effect to implicitly fix in their minds a fervent wish to catch the army contractor and prod him to the front, where bullets and shell could play around his greedy soul. For a man who would purposely rob the defenders of his country—the struggling soldiers—certainly deserved to have a taste of battle's danger.

The paper soled shoes the soldiers used to draw from the quartermaster, sadly sold by some of the army contractors—soulless sharks—were a "thing of beauty" but not a "joy forever." But they were really not so common among our men as may be supposed, for very few requisitions were filled that way with the Sharpshooter quartermasters, who with an eye to the needs and comfort of the command, wouldn't have them—if they could help it. As for the regular army shoe, it was undoubtedly the best that could be made for ease and comfort, also for marching. With a good tap added to the soles by the "company cobbler," they would last long and wear well. Besides, with shoes, you could plunge through water and keep right on thereafter, as the water would soon work out and the feet soon dry. Whereas, with boots, it was different, and many a comrade was behind in the column, trying to get his boots on, after emptying the water out; so that it was often the practice to cut holes in front, whereby the water could squirt out until all was dry again. Occasionally, trouble would occur among the "play-offs," who would manage, often by swapping, to get a sized shoe too large or small, and then great was the complaint of these "sorry soldiers" because they couldn't get a fit, and so have to be excused from picket or other duty. They were generally, however, brought around to an "eternal fitness of things," by the company officer, for his extra time wasted to procure the proper size. So that it didn't always happen that these little tricks prevailed.

Humphreys' division, now the 3d of the 5th corps, some 6,000 in all, made a reconnoisance into Virginia, going to Leetown on October 16th, and locating the enemy's position in that vicinity, returned the following day. Previous to this, the division of Gen. Cox, 5,000 men, left us, being ordered into Western Virginia. On the 10th, the rebel Stuart made his celebrated cavalry raid into Maryland, taking our own cavalry forces from us, in pursuit, and also some of the infantry organizations. This helped to delay the crossing of the Army of the Potomac into Virginia, and another cause was the length of time taken to obtain necessary clothing for the troops, particularly shoes and blankets, as the men could hardly march barefooted. As it was, some of the corps did not receive these necessary supplies until after they had started south. So it was not until Oct. 30th that the troops remaining near Sharpsburg broke up their camps and resumed the march, moving off during the night on the road along the Potomac in an easterly direction, crossing the Potomac on the following day near Harper's Ferry by pontoon bridge, and camping three miles south near Hillsborough. On the 2d of November left camp and marching all day reached Snicker's Gap of the Blue Ridge range of mountains in the evening. During the night the Sharpshooters were ordered out to climb the mountain as a scouting party to ascertain the whereabouts of the enemy, and to place posts of observation thereon, from whence an extensive view of the country surrounding could be obtained. Notwithstanding the danger of ascent from slipping and rolling to the bottom, owing to the prevailing darkness whereby little could be seen about them, they finally succeeded in getting to the summit, and were stationed there for the night. The next day being relieved of this arduous duty they left their elevated position, and on descending went again to their camp near Snickersville. Nov. 5th, left this place, marching southeasterly, passing through Middleburg, White Plains and other points, arriving on the 9th at Warrenton where they remained over a week. While at White Plains on the 6th, they were treated to a snowstorm an inch deep, which was very unpleasant to the troops anti was the cause of more or less suffering.

Gen. Burnside was now placed in command of the Army of the Potomac, *vice* McClellan *relieved*. And Gen. Hooker was shortly thereafter ordered to command The 5th *corps, vice* Porter *relieved*. On retiring from the field, Gen. McClellan issued the following farewell to the army of his creation:

HEADQUARTERS ARMY OF THE POTOMAC, Camp near Rectortown, Va., November 7, 1862. OFFICERS AND SOLDIERS OF THE ARMY OF THE POTOMAC: An order of the President devolves upon Major-General Burnside the command of this army. In parting from you, I cannot express the love and gratitude I bear to you. As an army, you have grown up under my care. In you I have never found doubt or coldness. The battles you have fought under my command will proudly live in our nation's history. The glory you have achieved, our mutual perils and fatigues, the graves of our comrades fallen in battle and by disease, the broken forms of those whom wounds and sickness have disabled—the strongest associations which can exist among men—unite us still by an indissoluble tie. We shall ever be comrades in supporting the Constitution of our country and the nationality of its people.

GEO. B. MCCLELLAN,

Major-General, U. S. Army.

The recruits joining the two regiments, at different points during the past fall, aided materially in filling the vacant ranks caused by death losses, and the discharge of members on account of disability. October 1st, Company

E, Second Regiment, had but 13 men for duty, but on the 17th they were reinforced by the arrival of 30 recruits, who with a number of the slightly wounded or sick, returning to duty, they became a company again. Company H, same regiment, received 13 recruits, with some of their lately sick and wounded. The recruits were steadily drilled, especially as skirmishers. Col. Post came to the Second Regiment the 9th of November, but finding it much reduced in numbers went to Washington to see if he could not get it recruited up and new companies added. He did not return, but resigned Nov. 18th. Changes occurred in the field among the officers and non-commissioned officers of both regiments, caused by promotion or discharge; among them Sergt. James S. Webster (G) was acting sergeant-major of the First Regiment.

FOURTH CAMPAIGN
UNDER BURNSIDE.

Leaving Warrenton the middle of November, the Sharpshooters reached Falmouth the 23d, encamping two miles from town, where they remained until December 11th, when they received "60 rounds of ammunition and marching orders." The march from Warrenton to Falmouth was attended with many difficulties to the great annoyance and discomfort of the troops. Capt. Aschmann says of it: "It took us seven days to reach Falmouth, a distance of 45 miles, which slow advance was owing to the bad management of the transports, to the fearful confusion among the different commands, and the impaired condition of the road which had become almost impassable through the long continued rainy weather. On arriving at Falmouth we made preparations to go into winter quarters by building comfortable log huts. Our camp was about three miles from the river close to the railroad, and as the adjacent forest furnished good building material we were soon in comfortable quarters. Yet much dissatisfaction was perceptible in the army, rations often short were of bad quality, the clothing and shoes worn out, and it was several weeks before these inconveniences were remedied.. The men had not been paid for six months, which put them in bad humor. To make things still worse, our knapsacks which had been left on the Peninsula in August, were returned in a bad condition and emptied of their former contents, so that many lost many valuables in the shape of presents, journals, etc.; therefore the temper of our regiment was not very enviable."

BATTLE OF FREDERICKSBURG.

December 13-15, 1862.

Gen. Burnside organized his army into three Grand Divisions; the Right under Sumner, the Center under Hooker, the Left under Franklin; about 120,000 officers and men equipped, ready for service—infantry, cavalry and artillery. The "center grand division" comprised the 3d corps Gen. Stoneman, 5th corps Gen. Danl. Butterfield, and Gen. Averell's cavalry brigade. 'The First Regiment of Sharpshooters were attached to the 1st division commanded by Gen. Griffin, (5th corps), the regiment being under command of Lieut.-Col. Trepp. The Second Sharpshooters commanded by Major Stoughton, were attached to the 1st division of the 1st corps, in the "left grand division."

It was the hope of Gen. Burnside to separate the rebel forces, to get between their wings and crush them. For this purpose he sent Franklin's troops several miles below Fredericksburg, where they crossed the Rappahannock after some delay with the bridges on the 12th, ready for action on the morning of the 13th when the attack was ordered. In the meantime Sumner and Hooker had crossed at Fredericksburg, after the most obstinate resistance from the enemy concealed in the houses and streets, who for a time drove the bridge-builders away, so hot and destructive was their fire, so that it became necessary to shell the city, our guns opening from the elevated ground above, causing much damage to the buildings, leaving many of them in ruins. Even then, the enemy would not stop, but with a persistency worthy of a better cause—the Union cause—they blazed away until some of our troops succeeded in crossing in boats and charged on them, taking some prisoners. Then it was a running fight through the streets for a long time before they were finally driven off. Right there, was a battle in itself, as evidenced by the heavy losses incurred.

Gen. Burnside says: "No more difficult feat has been performed during the war than the throwing of these bridges in the face of the enemy by these brave men."

And Gen. Woodbury, commanding Engineer Brigade, in reporting the dangers incurred in this work, said: "It is generally considered a brave feat to cross a bridge of any length under fire, although the time of danger may not last more than a minute or two. How much more difficult to build a bridge exposed for hours to the same murderous fire, the danger increasing as the bridge is extended."

When the battle began in earnest, it was a general engagement all along the lines. The enemy being strongly posted on the high ground back of Fredericksburg extending down past Franklin's front, the advantages were all on their side, their artillery being posted so as to command all our approaches, while their infantry were equally as well distributed to give our troops the hot reception they were destined to receive. Although for a time we met with some success on our left, in crossing the plain to the hills, by Meade's and Gibbon's divisions of Reynold's 1st corps, taking a number of prisoners, the former even occupying a portion of the crest for awhile, it was useless; and after a hard and destructive engagement all day the 13th, with desultory efforts the 14th and 15th, our troops were ordered to withdraw across the Rappahannock, which was successfully done in good order by the morning of the 6th.

The cannonading in this action was deafening and prolonged which, with the heavy musketry, was a constant uproar indicating, more death and wounds to be recorded.

Gen. Reynolds in his report of the battle says: "The gallantry and steadiness of the troops brought into action on the left is deserving of great praise, the new regiments, vying with the veterans in steadiness and coolness. That the brilliant attack made and the advanced position gained by them were not more successful in their results was due to the strong character of the enemy's defenses; the advantage he had of observing all our dispositions, while he made his own to meet them entirely under cover."

Sumner's division on the right, made a futile attempt to effect a lodgment on the heights. Hooker's command; reduced by the withdrawal of the 3d corps, two divisions of which were ordered to reinforce Franklin, and one to relieve Howard in Fredericksburg; now consisting of but the 5th corps, pushed boldly for the crest but was repulsed. Gen. Hooker in his report, says he tried without avail to dissuade Gen. Burnside from making the attack, as from information received by a prisoner he became convinced that the enemy were only too willing to have him come on.

"I returned," he says, "and brought up every available battery, with the intention of breaking their barriers, to enable Butterfield's attacking column to carry the crest. This artillery fire was continued with great vigor until near sunset, when the attack with bayonet was made by Humphreys' division. This attack was made with a spirit and determination seldom, if ever, equaled in war. The impregnable position of the enemy had given them so-strong an advantage that the attack was almost immediately repulsed."

That the gallant 5th corps, unsupported, owing to the withdrawal of the other troops, sustained its reputation as true and reliable fighters, in this unequal contest, with a loss of over 2,000, whereby the corps was forced to bear the: burden which the right and center grand divisions combined could hardly overcome, at least without great slaughter, the testimony above and to follow, is proof-sufficient. For Gen. Butterfield adds the weight of these words in their behalf:

"The enemy was posted on his first line securely behind a stone wall near the foot of a crest which was covered with batteries. The position of these batteries enabled the enemy to direct a severe cross-fire of artillery upon the heads of the columns. The enemy's position was one of ·exceeding strength, and his troops were well protected. During all of the movements and formations the columns were subjected to a heavy fire. While endeavoring to force their way with powder and ball, no apparent advantage was gained. Orders were given to carry the heights with ·the bayonets. Gen. Sykes was ordered to form a column of attack on the right of Humphreys. The attack of Humphreys' and Griffin's divisions was made with a spirit and efficiency scarcely, if ever, equaled in the records of this war; but the attack was made against a position so advantageous and strong to the enemy that it failed."

During this sanguinary battle the First Sharpshooters -were held in reserve. On the 13th they occupied a position on the north bank of the Rappahannock, and on the following day, crossing the river, remained in the town until the 15th, when they were ordered to the front on the picket lines -where considerable firing had taken place; but it gradually quieted down after they appeared on the line, which was 400 yards from the rebel batteries and but 200 from the enemy's picket—the latter firing at every head they could see. The Sharpshooters reserved their fire under orders, keeping up a sharp lookout. Around them were the results of the past days' conflict, the ground being strewn with dead Union soldiers, gallant sacrifices to a better cause than to assault impenetrable heights. Stiff and distorted they lay straightened out, doubled up—in all manner of startling shapes, mangled corpse, nameless to the Sharpshooters, who only knew they were Union soldiers—lost in action.

The Wisconsin men were in reserve during the day, subject at times to artillery fire, also during the greater part of the night; at half-past three on the morning of the 16th they relieved those in front, being selected to watch the enemy at that point while the Union forces were recrossing the Rappahannock. At daylight they fell back in skirmish line to the river, over a mile distant, where they found bridges partly taken up, plank being laid to enable them to cross; taking with them 150 stragglers from other regiments, routed out from the nooks and corners of the streets of Fredericksburg, necessarily disturbing these wearied and worn-out men in their ill-chosen resting places—dispelling their dreams of safety and other happy visions. The Wisconsin Sharpshooters were the last of the Potomac Army to recross the river at Fredericksburg, having covered the retreat of the troops on that part of the line.

Cola Trepp reports as follows: "On the 13th I received an order to march with the division, and was assigned a place in the column in the rear of Phillip's battery and bivouacked for the night near it, about half a mile from the bridge over which the rest of the division crossed the Rappahannock. On the 14th at about half past seven A. M. I received an order to cross the river and report immediately to Gen. Griffin, which order was obeyed, and the regiment entered Fredericksburg at about eight A. m. At about noon on the 15th, by order of Gen. Willcox, four companies of my regiment were sent out on picket duty, under command of Major Hastings, on the left, to connect with Gen. Franklin's pickets, and cover a space not before covered. I carefully examined the ground and personally superintended the posting of the pickets, making perfect the connection between Gen. Franklin's right and the block house by the railroad. This detachment remained on the outposts until it was withdrawn, by order of Gen. Humphreys, at about half past six A. M.

the next day. At about five P. M., by order of Gen. Griffin, I sent two companies, under Capt. Seaton, on picket on the right. These remained on the outposts until three o'clock next morning, when they were relieved, by order of Gen. Griffin. On the 16th, by order of Gen. Griffin, the regiment, excepting the four companies on the outposts, crossed the Rappahannock at about six A. M. at the upper bridge. The said four companies retired as follows: Three companies of reserves under Major Hastings, in column, and one company, the last on the outposts, as skirmishers under Capt. Marble, (Company G), bringing with them a number of stragglers from different regiments. The regiment was in camp at about noon, all present. There have been no casualties in my command during the period."

There was one company of the 91st Pennsylvania unrelieved on picket, from Humphreys' division, who held their advanced post until ten o'clock that morning, when finding themselves in a fix with the enemy swarming down by them, some of whom they fired on with effect, others occupying the town, they fell back to the river above, where boats were sent to cross them, one of their men swimming the stream therefor. Gen. Butterfield in his report speaks of the "gallant behavior of Capt. Lentz and his men," on this occasion.

The Second Sharpshooters performed good service on the left, on the skirmish line in the heat of the action of the 13th, also during the 14th and 15th, and were awarded great praise by brigade and division commanders'. Their casualties were slight.

W. H. Proctor, of Company E, one of the gallant first sergeants of that regiment, furnishes the following interesting incidents: "On Sunday the 14th, as we lay in line of battle on the open plain, the rebels ran out a long-range cannon some two miles or more away on our left flank, and opened with solid shot. The first one plowed dirt several rods directly in front of us and passed on. The next, and the next, were coming still nearer and the regiment was getting uneasy, for it was real "tiresome" to wait so long after we saw the flash of the gun, before the shot made our acquaintance. Major Stoughton told the men to keep quiet. There was another flash, and in due time the shot came. It tore the knapsack from the back of a man named George A. Clay, in Company E, sending the man's clothing, etc., 20 feet in the air, and a pack of envelopes in the knapsack was thrown 70 feet high and distributed in so peculiar a manner as to attract the attention of thousands of troops.. The shot passed under a man named Joiner, raising him about two feet, without injuring him any further than a general shaking up, passing on without doing damage. This rebel gun was finally driven away by a battery of ours on the other side of the river.

"On the last day that we held the field, the picket line on the extreme left was held by a line of infantry, and the firing was so heavy it was feared it would bring on an engagement. We received orders in the afternoon to go out and stop that firing. We deployed and lay down among the infantry, making them stop firing. The rebs were exposing themselves recklessly but were evidently suffering little from the infantry. We were directed to use our ammunition only when it would count. We got in some fine work, when soon they almost ceased firing, and commenced calling to us to stop, asserting that we were shooting our own men, wasting ammunition. An officer riding up to the stone wall falling with a shot in the arm from our fire, a white rag was held up—they wanted to have a talk. So we arranged the matter, meeting in the center of the field between the two lines, our infantry having previously gone back. One of the first salutations I received was: 'We knew you when you first began to shoot. We met you before at Yorktown.' (It was the First Regiment at Yorktown.) They said our guns were too sharp for them, and agreed to fire no more without notice; we then went back to our line and everything was quiet."

Capt. Chase, of Company A, who had been placed in command of the right wing of the skirmish line by Maj. Stoughton, writing after the battle said: "On Saturday the 13th our regiment was deployed on the extreme left flank extending from the line of battle to the river, with the 24th New York for a reserve. We were under heavy artillery fire all day (14th), as well as that of their sharpshooters. About noon we charged on a piece of woods occupied by a large force of rebs which our artillery had been trying in vain for an hour to drive out, but they skedaddled like the very devil when we went in. We killed a large number, took 10 prisoners and eight horses. I secured a splendid gray belonging to a captain of cavalry. It is probable that the next call the captain hears will be from the trumpet of Gabriel. There were more hair-breadth escapes than I ever saw in any previous battle." After referring to the incidents given by Comrade Proctor, he continues: "Another-shot struck within a foot of Pettijohn (Dyer B., first sergeant) filling his ears so full of dirt that he had to go to a brook and wash them out, and strange to say no one was seriously hurt." Capt. Wright (then lieutenant "A") wrote Dec. 26, 1862: "When the retreat was ordered our regiment was on picket, we lost none killed as we know of, but there were four of Company A left behind, whether wounded next morning or taken prisoners I could not say; they were James, O'Neal, Stacey and Ben Hamlet. Our regiment numbers about 121 for duty." George E. James was captured and never returned, Henry O'Neal was also taken prisoner, he returning in May following.

Gen. Doubleday commanding 1st division, 1st army corps, says: On the morning of the 13th relieving Gen. Meade's advanced troops with the Sharpshooters, three-quarters of a mile from the Bernard House; on the other side of a deep gorge or ravine, we pressed on for about, half a mile, driving in the enemy's skirmishers as we advanced. The action of the batteries having prepared the way for an infantry attack, I directed Gen. Meredith to take these woods with his brigade. The 7th Wisconsin volunteers and the 24th Michigan led the advance, preceded by the Second Regiment United States Sharpshooters, and carried the wood in gallant style, taking a number of prisoners and horses."

Col. Walter Phelps, Jr., brigade commander, in his report mentions the Sharpshooters thus: "About three P. M. (14th) one of the enemy's batteries opened upon our left at long range, perfectly enfilading us. The Second United States Sharpshooters were engaged as skirmishers during the day, also two companies of the 30th New York Vols., and succeeded in protecting the artillery and infantry from the severe fire of the enemy's skirmishers. On Monday the 15th I ordered the Second U. S. Sharpshooters to the front as skirmishers, and they engaged the enemy's pickets during the day. I cannot speak, too highly of the commanding officer of the Second U. S. Sharpshooters, Major Stoughton," and others named.

Col. Wm. F. Rogers, brigade commander, among other testimonials of merit, says: "I take pleasure also in testifying to the very efficient service rendered by the Second U. S. Sharpshooters, under Major Stoughton, of Col. Phelps brigade."

All of which shows that the Green Coats were there—on the front lines—doing their duty in a highly honorable manner.

The battle of Fredericksburg was the occasion of severe criticism, by the general public at home, and the military board at Washington; although the people themselves were greatly responsible in their howling demands for "more battles." The stay-at-homes liked too well to see them—in print. The movement of the army was delayed over a month from the time it left Warrenton until the attack, owing to the delay in forwarding the pontoons for the bridges from the Upper Potomac, although the troops fronted the position in ample time to have assured success before the Confederates concentrated in front—all ready to whip us. It only, proves the difficulty too often encountered in carrying out the programme mapped out for action. If some of our generals were blamed for being tardy—consuming too much time in preparation—forgetful of the fact that great undertakings of a military nature cannot safely be rushed too fast, there may be ample cause for the delay. Besides, it is too hazardous where so much is at stake, to hurry away, and renders the reckless movement subject to defeat and demoralization. To get ready, is one thing that often depends on the assistance rendered in the matter of supplies; to go, when ready, is another. Whether Burnside blundered or others were at fault, failing with the pontoons—or both—it will never alter the heart-rending fact, that the battle of Fredericksburg was a useless slaughter—with a loss to the Union army according to government reports of 10,884 killed and wounded, and 1,769 captured and missing. Total 12,653.

Returning to camp near Falmouth the Sharpshooters remained in quarters until December 30th when the First Regiment was ordered on a reconnoissance along the Rappahannock westerly, with their division commanded by Col. Barnes, of the 18th Massachusetts.

ELLIS' FORD.

Dec. 31, 1862.

Marching some 10 or 15 miles they halted for the night at Richards' Ford on the Upper Rappahannock, where on the following morning, the last day of the year, a brisk skirmish occurred with the enemy's cavalry stationed on the opposite bank. A small force of cavalry accompanied the expedition, with a few pieces of artillery. The cavalry being ordered to cross the river, proceeded to do so under the fire of the rebel Stuart's cavalrymen, which was returned with interest by the Sharpshooters posted on the river bank, thus protecting the party crossing, driving the enemy from their position in short order unable to withstand the effect of the close shots fired upon them. The enemy then fell back to the cover of the woods a mile away, the cavalry squad following them up and establishing a picket line on the plain, having taken one prisoner. Three companies of Sharpshooters followed after, approaching the river through a rocky, precipitous washout, the water mid-deep and very cold, chilling and benumbing the men through and through. Charles H. Berner, of Company B, being present, tells how "quite a number fell on the slippery stones, pitched headlong and backward, getting wet all over, while some needed to be assisted in getting up, else would they have been drowned, One unfortunate cavalry man got a complete ducking, being thrown into the water by his horse slipping and falling over." Thus wading the river under fire, and forming line on the other side they remained near our cavalry until a small brigade, its ranks greatly decimated by the casualties of war, joined them. While on the open plain facing the woods in front, they were greatly annoyed by a concealed rebel in a thick treetop on the edge of the wood, who had been amusing himself taking "sighting shots" upon our boys. Finally, Adjt. Horton who was in command, ordered a volley fired, which must have taken the reb by surprise, as he was found on their approach in a sprawling position at the foot of the tree, *pretty much used up.*

This small force with seven cavalry videttes then moved-forward, the infantry keeping the road, while the Sharpshooters went ahead as skirmishers and flankers, Company G being on the flank. The rebel cavalry began to practice their old game of firing at our forces as we moved on, and after emptying their carbines wheeling suddenly, running away_ This was done several times, when Horton ordered a squad of the Sharpshooters to rush forward as far as possible, keeping concealed from view on the wooded roadside, and when the enemy again appeared, to break into the middle of the road and try again the virtue of a rattling volley of well-aimed bullets. This plan was carried out to perfection, the rebels leaving behind one of their number whose horse was shot down, and himself captured after a long chase through the thick brush, he running the gauntlet of many shots as he tried to get away. He proved to be a hard customer who hated to give up. As Kirkham, of G, afterwards expressed it:

"He was as mad as a piper; the very ugliest brute I met with in the army."

His face was torn and scratched so much with briars as to be covered with blood, while one of his hands was singed with a Sharps' bullet. His comrades keep out of sight thereafter, thereby saving their cartridges. The seven cavalrymen were joined by Horton who had previously run down a retreating rebel, and now led by the Sharpshooter adjutant, this small mounted party galloped off in hot pursuit, capturing several more of the gang.

Leaving the river, advancing two miles south, the column changed direction to the right, and moving up stream, after skirmishing upwards of nine miles through thick brush and woods, the infantry keeping the road, recrossed the river about dark at Ellis' Ford, where they rested for the night. On the day following, Jan. 1, 1863, they left the Ford, skirmishing back to the Union lines which they reached in the afternoon, having fallen in with no large force of the enemy while away. The balance of the Sharpshooter regiment held their position at Richards' Ford during the day and overnight, watching well the opposite shore, but with no sign of the enemy hovering about. In the evening all arrived back to camp considerably fatigued but without loss.

While passing through the woods on the return trip, being out as flankers, their line of march ran into a lot of chicken coops that had been hid there. The coops were sent flying out of the path, but not till after each man in B Company at least, got one or more chickens, and some turkeys. As 'chicken roosts were scarce around Falmouth and it being New Year's day, they concluded it would be a good plan to take them in as prisoners.

It was an expedition of importance that required quick movements and forced marching, which at that time of year none but veterans inured to hardships had any business to endure. Wading cold rivers could have but one issue with less hardy soldiers, and that, subsequent sickness with probable serious results. But it seemed as if the old soldiers could stand everything without any apparent ill effects from their hard; fatiguing duties. Their endurance was remarkable, particularly from the short rest required to go again. They were indeed men of iron, that it seemed almost impossible could be worn out. Tired and exhausted they often were, but their powers of revival proved the stamina and good condition of these well trained troops.

The First and Second Regiments were soon after formed into a Sharpshooter brigade in accordance with the following order from Gen. Burnside:

"HEADQUARTERS ARMY OF THE POTOMAC, CAMP NEAR FALMOUTH, VA., Jan. 14, 1863

The regiments and companies of Sharpshooters in this army will form a distinct arm of the service, and will be under the command of Col. Berdan, as Chief of Sharpshooters, who will report directly to these headquarters. Detachments from this force will be sent from time to time to the different grand divisions on detached service, to be used as Sharpshooters."

Previous to this formation, the First Regiment had been divided into two battalions and attached to Sumner's and Hooker's corps respectively, but were soon after ordered together again. While thus temporarily separated, the Wisconsin company furnished another acting sergeant-major, in the person of Sergt. B. D. Atwell.

MUD MARCH.

Taking part in the "Mud Campaign," as Burnside's last movement was afterwards named, our brigade

(excepting "F," First, which remained at headquarters) left camp near Falmouth, Jan. 20th, marching to the vicinity of Banks' Ford, seven miles distant, where they arrived in the afternoon, remaining overnight in the woods, concealed from the enemy who were posted on the opposite bank of the Rappahannock. During the night a heavy rain set in, pouring down in torrents, which rendered the roads impassable for artillery, also prevented the troops from going farther. They were in reality stuck in the mud. And to that extent it seemed impossible to extricate the cannon, but by hard work in which men and horses were exhausted, they finally succeeded and returned to camp on the 23d; the movement being of necessity abandoned, the rain continuing the whole time. This unexpected outcome of the attempt to turn the enemy's position, was very disheartening to the troops, who returned from the expedition discouraged and weary; having been obliged to corduroy the roads to enable them to come back. As an illustration of the difficulties encountered by the engineer corps in constructing roads for the passage of the artillery, the officer in charge, on being ordered to make a requisition for what was necessary to accomplish the work, did so by calling for "50 men, 25 feet high, to work in the mud 18 feet deep."

IN CAMP.

The army now remained in winter quarters, our brigade near Stoneman's Switch not far from Falmouth. Picket duty was in order, and when the weather permitted being ordered out to drill. Company and battalion movements it was very essential must not be forgotten—the soldiers could not be too perfect.

At a meeting of the officers of the two regiments at brigade headquarters early in the spring, a proposition was made by the colonel commanding, to have a celebration on a grand scale on the anniversary of the Sharpshooters' first advance on Yorktown. For this purpose a committee of arrangements was appointed, and a programme prepared. The principal feature being a Grand Shooting Match between the different company champions in each regiment, for a regimental silver medal, the winners of which were to shoot off for a gold one. For several days previous, the members of each company were being tested, the picked men of which were to receive a diploma, with a chance to win the champion medals. On the test shooting a number of good targets were made, according to the terms agreed upon, viz., five off-hand shots at 100 yards, open sight, string measurement—the shooting to be done with Sharps army rifle.

At half-past nine in the morning, after guard mounting, the different companies were marched on to the color line, and after a brief and appropriate address by Col. Berdan,, a new, beautiful flag was hoisted on the flagstaff amid the cheers of the assembled soldiers. The order of exercises being read by one of the committee, they proceeded to the target ground where the shooting began in the presence of a large number of visitors. Capts. Nash, Company K, First Regiment, Guest, B., Second Regiment, attended to the calling off; Capt. Smith, G, Second Regiment, Lieut. Wells, B, First Regiment, the targets; while Capt. McClure, D, Second Regiment, Lieut. Stevens, G, First Regiment, measured the strings. Each man furnished his own target, which was handed in to the committee. The Second Regiment having won the "toss" commenced the shooting, their winner being a Vermonter, Albert G. Culver. The

First Regiment winner was Samuel Ingling, of Michigan. The two winners of the regimental medals then shot off for the gold medal, which was won by the Michigan man. These medals were very appropriate, were made in New York, the design being furnished by the committee, subscription therefor, likewise the prize money, being obtained from the officers of both regiments. The next in order being a three-shot string from a tree top 200 yards distant, for a purse of $10, was won by Lamprey, of New Hampshire, Second Regiment, Joseph Sleeper, of Wisconsin, being ahead in the First Regiment. Several long shots of 1,000 yards were then made by Col. Berdan, Capt. Marble, and other officers with both Sharps and telescopic rifles.

The assemblage then repaired to the running ground to, witness the various pedestrian efforts, Nash and Stevens being the judges. The first in order was a 200-yard race against time, for two prizes, $10 and $5—open to one man in each company of both regiments. Won by Private Bartomey, of Vermont, and Sergt. Lye, of Wisconsin, (both First Regiment). Time, 28^1/2 seconds each. Lye who had been unwell then withdrew, and was awarded second prize.

Next, two 100-yard sack races, creating great merriment. After which, came the 400-yard foot race, $10 and $5, run in pairs. After many exciting struggles showing the activity and strength of the men, the deciding heat lay between Peaslee, of New Hampshire, Gardener, of New York, and Van Buren, of Wisconsin. The "Badger" got the lead on turning the hundred yard stake, but the New Yorker closed up towards the end of the race and won by a yard. Time one minute, six seconds. Van Buren took the second prize.. The greased pole, cock-fighting, wrestling, jumping, etc., wound up the sports.

The greased pole, of course, was as usual the occasion of a good deal of fun, particularly the ludicrous fate of a well-known member of Company B, known as the "Wild Jersey-man." Failing in his first attempt, he pulled off his trowsers, making the second trial in government cotton flannels, and was well on his way to the top where the $5 gold piece was fastened, when the mishap occurred—a beautiful example of the shoddy character of the underclothes the men often drew. They couldn't stand the strain, so down came Jim treble-quick, and amid the greatest of shouts he retired to his poncho. In the wrestling, Jacob S. Bailey, a Vermonter (of Company F, First), obtained the victory—the principal contest being with a tall, raw-boned Michigan der, who after an exciting struggle was defeated by the Green Mountain Boy amid loud applause. In jumping, the Sharpshooter colonel led by several inches with apparent ease, to the great surprise of all, Lieut.-Col. Trepp exclaiming:

"Berdan, he beats der teifel! He takes der rifle and beats der boys, an' now he scoops 'ern jumping."

He did it without weights, too. At dark the men retired to their quarters, well pleased with the day's entertainment. Among the officers present, were Gen. Whipple, division commander, also a number of ladies. It was one of those happy holidays that sometimes occurred in the army, but not very often; which generally ends with the intended effect, as on this occasion, in making all concerned feel better, enlivening them up, dispelling for a time the dull and languid spirit resulting from a lengthy routine of camp duties. Often the troops are rolled out from their lethargic state, hurriedly assembled and marched off many miles, to return to the vicinity, where they build new camps on fresh fields, as often within a half mile of the old ones; which change tends to improve the general health—the sanitary condition of the soldiers. Exercise was what they needed, and plenty of it, to fit them for future hardships on the great marches. Snowball contests were engaged in, there being frequently long lines of battle extending to regiments and even brigades, when it was fun to see the snow fly. It was not always play either, for rough usage would occur, many a sorry looking fellow would get more than he bargained for, 'causing hard feelings, with a frequent desire to "rough and tumble." But as a general thing, it had a beneficial effect—it was good exercise.

Yet, notwithstanding the morale of the troops in general was considered excellent, there was one bad habit, one prevailing vice in all the camps—the passion for gambling—although it was strictly against orders; nor did it affect the enlisted men alone. Every effort to break it up, utterly failed. Not that all, or by any means a majority of the men indulged in it, still there were always enough that did, to make it a common practice in every regiment. The boys would play, yet while this pastime had a bad effect, principally affecting their pockets, it didn't appear to affect their efficiency while on duty. They were good soldiers.

The first sergeants of each company had been furnished with a telescope rifle, to be used only upon special occasions; which were afterwards turned in, being too heavy to carry around, and as previously stated, unfit for general use on a skirmish line. These rifles were all right in a fixed position—a good rest—and did great work at long range, particularly among the enemy's batteries. But for hurried off-hand shooting, skirmishing or in line of battle, the open sights could be brought to the eye quicker, and even the muzzle-loading muskets with which the infantry were armed could be loaded quicker, while the breech-loading Sharps were far ahead of all, for rapid firing. The great improvements made in the breech-loading system since the war of the Rebellion, particularly in the metallic ammunition, have caused the muzzle-loaders to be discarded. A line of battle of breech-loaders lying down can shoot faster and do more execution on a charging column, than heretofore when the bite and tear cartridge and rammer were used, besides causing less exposure to the men. A charging column at the present day must needs be very brave, to face a line of breech-loaders, as they will hardly get there. It was owing to the success attained by the Berdan Sharpshooters, in developing the superiority of the Sharps breech-loading rifle over any other known weapon in use, in point of safety to the men as well as execution in firing, for I never knew of an accident occurring by premature discharge of a Sharps rifle, that caused so soon after the war the substitution of the breech-loading system, improved upon, in all manner of firearms. The American manufacturers opened their eyes to the fact, that a safer and better gun could be loaded at the breech, in shot-guns as well as rifles. To Col. Berdan's persistency in urging the government to furnish his command with these arms while at Camp of Instruction, in response to the demands of the members of both regiments, is the credit largely due for the general substitution after the war of the breech-loading gun.

Notwithstanding the arduous duties often imposed on the soldiers, they could always manage to get up a little fun amongst themselves—even on the most trying occasions.

The little jokes they played on each other served to break the force of their irksome camp life, to lighten the load as it were, of their monotony. While at this camp an old member of an adjoining regiment returned from the southern prisons in a: very shabby condition. Being furnished with a new outfit: of clean clothes, he was requested to go with the boys to the river and take a good wash. So they went down, and got the old fellow in up to his neck, when the boys scrubbed away, after first lathering him with Rappahannock mud, and finally began to get some of the prison dirt off. But were for awhile nonplused at the curious color of his body, when to their surprise they developed an old shirt stuck close to his skin, which he said he thought he had lost long before—had missed it among his scanty wardrobe, and didn't know it was there. He laughed at their taunts, saying he was so much ahead. Yet they didn't allow him, to preserve it as a memento, but east it afar off into the current, and as the owner eyed it floating away, he sighed and walked away as if he had lost an old friend, as the shirt must have been, for it had certainly stuck to him very close.

About this time, Company D lost one of their best marksmen, a man who had made his mark as such, in the person of Cyrus J. Hathaway, who was discharged to accept a commission as second lieutenant in the 114th New York, and though it was a great loss to the Sharpshooter service, was cheerfully acquiesced in by his company, on account of the deserved promotion.

Often during their picket duties exciting times occurred, which at least served to keep the soldiers in an animated condition. On the night of March 27th an event transpired whereby the entire division picket force was aroused and brought into line in anticipation of an attack. It appears that fronting the picket line was a large opening or field probably 1,000 yards across, beyond which at the farther extremity of a wood, our cavalry videttes were stationed. Orders had been given the Sharpshooters who were on the right of the line adjoining an old turnpike, to give notice, by firing if necessary, of any approach of the enemy in our front. The Wisconsin company had the line, and the lieutenant in command was very particular about these orders, instructing the men at their posts to watch and listen intently, the night being very dark, and if any demonstration was apparent in front, to "obey orders." During the fore part of the night some scattering shots were heard ahead where the cavalry were, and what with the distant signal lights bobbing up and down, and the aforesaid orders to keep a sharp lookout, it appeared rather evident that the stealthy approach of the Johnnies was expected, at headquarters. Therefore, when at the midnight hour, a number of shots being heard, followed by a sharp clatter of hoofs on the hard road leading from the extreme front, as several cavalry men came rushing back, more scared than hurt, Post No. 1, fired. As most of the boys were snoozing at the time, those not on duty, a grand hustle was made by the lieutenant and his orderly sergeant (Jacobs), to get the company into line behind the pickets, before "Old Trepp "came rushing up, which he very soon did, accompanied by a number of others, all mounted, from general down. Inquiring closely into the matter, all now being quiet at the front, finally in response to the lieutenant's statement about the orders to fire, the colonel retired, after informing the picket officer to be very careful about firing off the guns as, "it disturbed the whole concern." The "whole concern," which, was the division reserves in our rear, were considerably disturbed that time, for it is doubtful if they ever rolled out from sweet sleep quicker or more excited, before or since, than on that occasion. The boys of Company G couldn't sleep the balance of the night with laughing over it. The next day while returning to camp, the reserves yelled over to the Sharpshooters to know who it was started that alarm, when some of the company wags cried back: "Oh! only a wide-awake lieutenant from Wisconsin." As that officer was napping at the time of the firing (relieved by the first sergeant), and who jumped a good four feet when it occurred, the boys of G laughed in their sleeves. For a long time after, the outgoing pickets from other regiments would inquire of the Sharpshooters, if that "wide-awake lieutenant "was in the crowd, which, however, he most always wasn't.

These picket posts were not generally the pleasantest places to lie in, from the fact that a species of crawlers generating in the army, known by the euphonious name of "graybacks," an amazing extent; the result being

A STRAGGLING GRAYBACK.

A well-known and popular Wisconsin colonel, who deserved to be president of an anti-cruelty-to-animals society, while out on the parade-ground one Sunday with the chaplain, preparing for services, having his attention called by the minister to the fact, that an unusually large grayback was crawling over his immaculate boiled shirt front, instantly grasping the wiggling thing with his fingers exclaimed: "You infernal straggler, go back to your quarters," when he deliberately put it inside his shirt and let it roam within.

Possibly he concluded that if they were so thick as to break out to the front, 'twas no use to exterminate the bold interloper.

PERTAINING TO DISCIPLINE.

Skulking and misbehavior in action, were matters on which all worthy commanding officers were severe. The following incidents, however, will illustrate the manner in which disobedience of orders of an unimportant or trivial nature, were often treated, when the comfort of the soldier was involved. Even the strictest disciplinarian who was not a confirmed tyrant, was disposed to be lenient in certain cases, especially when rations were scarce, and the men undergoing severe service. As a general rule the strict colonel or regimental commander, was the friend of the soldier, and was so regarded by the intelligent and trusty. On one of the long marches when rations were scarce, a man in Company A stole a chicken, notwithstanding the general orders against foraging, and not knowing when he would have a chance to cook it, carried it alive in his haversack. The chicken kept peeping, and as he marched at the head of the regiment, Col. Berdan could not well pretend that he didn't hear it, as the night was still and the chicken had a good voice—a stalwart peeper. So he ordered the man under arrest, and when he came before the colonel's drum-head court-martial with others, the next day, the colonel asked him for what was he under arrest. The man replied: "For stealing a chicken." "Are you sure?" asked the colonel. "Yes," said the man, meekly. "Keep him under guard, at the rear of the regiment," ordered the colonel. In a day or two he was questioned in the same way, giving the same answer. The third time he was asked why he was arrested, becoming more outspoken with his long humiliation, he replied: "For not having cut the chicken's head off." "Go to your company!" at once said the colonel. There were no more chickens carried alive in the haversacks.

On another occasion when the regiment camped for the night where there was no wood for fire to boil the coffee, so that the men were compelled to take fence rails despite orders to the contrary, one of the men in order to save time made a short cut, which took him in front of the colonel's tent. He was at once brought to a halt, and then and there made to march in front of the tent for a half hour with the rail across his back. The colonel then stopped him, asking if he knew for what he had been punished, he promptly replying—for he was a Yank—"Oh, yes! because I did not go behind your tent." "Go to your company," said the colonel. He got well laughed at by his comrades, and the old proverb was made clear to him that, "the longest way around was the shortest way home."

The first punishment for cowardice the colonel inflicted on one of his soldiers, was while lying before Yorktown, because the man refused to advance when the enemy were shelling us sharply. He was frightened and behaved very cowardly. That evening the colonel called him out at dress parade and made a brief address to the command, stating that while some men were constitutional cowards, they were not to blame for it, as it was part of their nature. Then speaking of the incident of the day, called the man to the front, ordering the officer of the day to take his gun from him, and put him on fatigue duty. By the way, a light punishment compared with what a Regular soldier would have received, but in this case it proved sufficient. In a few days the captain of the company asked the colonel to give the man another trial, which he declined to do unless a petition signed by every member of the company to restore him was received. This was furnished and the man restored to his place in the ranks. It had a salutary effect, and no complaint was heard of him thereafter. But Col. Berdan said he anticipated the man's return to the company, in the way it happened, and pursued this course, deeming it more effectual to work on the soldier's pride by demanding the petition. Such discipline was effective in keeping the men up to their work, to give and take shots with the spirit of veterans, which was all that was necessary to make a splendid fighting regiment out of such material; particularly if they found their officers willing to share the dangers with them. Much of the honor gained is due to the special service we had, and the advantage of arms used, coupled with their great skill in handling the rifle, and yet it is but fair to infer that much also is due to the prompt treatment of first examples.

As the fighters never complained of what was required of them under fire, but were ready to respond however great the odds against them, both Berdan and Trepp when in command, and the latter was very strict in the field, were disposed to be lenient with the boys when in camp and subject to trivial offenses. This would naturally have a tendency to inculcate a good feeling between officers and men. "Trouble in camp," however, at times existed among the Sharpshooters as in other regiments, and there were very few that escaped this unpleasant state of affairs—one of the evil results of lying in camp too long. Officers would find fault, often amongst themselves almost to an open quarrel; prevented only by fear of the consequences under the strict rules of the regulations. As it was, arrests were made and courts-martial summoned. Particularly was this the case at Falmouth in the winter of '63, when several officers were under arrest on various charges. Nor did Col. Berdan himself escape; on the contrary, a long list of charges and specifications were preferred against him. But because an officer or enlisted man happened to be court-martialed, it did not always follow that he should have been, or that he was adjudged guilty. It frequently transpired otherwise, and did so in pretty much all the cases in our (First) regiment in this camp, that the accused party received a strong vindication by the court in the verdict of acquittal; and in the case of Col. Berdan, the court after hearing the evidence of the prosecution, stopped all further proceedings by refusing to occupy any further time hearing any evidence he (Col. Berdan) might have to offer, adjudging him "not guilty" on all charges and specifications. And this was about the way they generally turned out. Bad blood enough, no doubt, but worse evidence. The enlisted men, they that handled the weapons that did the fighting, were silent lookers-on, wondering why their officers quarreled so. Was this setting a proper example?

FIFTH CAMPAIGN.
FIGHTING JOE IN COMMAND.

Shortly after the failure of the late movement, *not by the enemy,* Gen. Hooker was appointed to the command of the Army of the Potomac, *vice* Burnside *relieved.* Again the hopes of the soldiers revived, for the gallant bearing of Hooker in all the past campaigns of the Potomac army, in which he had been prominently engaged at the head of divisions and corps, had won for him the respect and confidence of the troops in general. Not that they entertained ill-feelings towards Burnside because of the failure of the movements under his command, as much as they may have doubted his wisdom in fighting at Fredericksburg, yet were they easily reconciled to the change. And now the stirring spirit of Hooker infused new life in the army, as they readily became convinced that the change was for the better, and were determined to prove themselves worthy soldiers of so gallant a leader.

A reorganization of the army followed, the system of grand divisions being abolished, and changes made in the assignment of troops. The brigade of Sharpshooters was attached to the 3d corps, being the 3d brigade of the 3d division, thus parting with the 5th corps with which the First Regiment had been connected from its organization, sharing its glories and sufferings, and getting back to the corps they originally started with on the Peninsula campaign. The brigade was commanded by Col. Berdan, the division by Gen. Whipple, the corps by Gen. Sickles.

The commanding general was now busy getting his troops in proper fighting trim before the campaign opened, and the days were fully occupied in the "general training," included in which was target practice—firing by volleys, firing at will, in every position. Finally, orders came to issue eight days' rations and 60 rounds of ammunition; while surplus clothing was turned in, and the necessary preparations made for the next move on the military chess board. All was bustle without confusion, and Hooker's boast that he had the "finest army on the planet, "seemed to be realized.

CHANCELLORSVILLE.

May 1-4, 1863.

On the 28th of April the Sharpshooters broke camp in the afternoon and as part of the 3d corps marched down the river to the left of the Union army below Fredericksburg, where they arrived during the night and rested under arms. The men were well equipped, carrying 60 rounds of ammunition, eight days' rations, overcoats and rubber blankets. Two men in each company were also furnished with "climbers," to be used on special occasions in climbing trees.

On the morning of the 29th they were distant witnesses to the storming of the rebel rifle pits at Fitz Hugh Crossing, by the sturdy Iron Brigade, which were successfully carried and several hundred prisoners taken.

The Sharpshooters remained under arms near the river -until the afternoon of the 30th, the weather having been thus far rainy and unpleasant. Gen. Sickles having received orders to change his position to the extreme right, at two P. M. that day the corps moved off. Making a detour to the rear to avoid Observation by the enemy on the south bank of the river, marching by the old camping ground, they arrived at and crossed the Rappahannock at United States Ford at nine o'clock on the morning of May 1st, having marched upwards of 20 miles during their roundabout route, resting once, when they obtained four hours' sleep—from two to six A.M.—on the damp ground. While *en route,* some 200 rebel prisoners passed by, they recognizing the Green Coats, remarking as they passed along: "There goes them Sharp fellows."

The weather being warm, and the men loaded with knapsacks well packed, haversacks and canteens filled, with a full complement of ammunition, they became considerably fatigued, many being foot sore; yet there was no straggling, no flinching, or apparent wish to back out from the expected conflict. Having crossed the river on pontoon bridge, which by its swinging motion caused the men to stagger, they proceeded, after a hurried coffee, forward; eventually halting in the afternoon in a piece of woods by the roadside, being in the portion of country known as the Wilderness.

Soon after, four companies were posted as pickets two and a half paces apart, in the thick woods 200 yards from the right of the road, to prevent surprise from that direction; the road being full of teams, pack mules, etc., which jostled along in considerable confusion. While on this service, Company K (First) caught two spies dressed in blue. About sunset they were recalled, and assembling on the roadside proceeded with their division to the front where heavy cannonading and some musketry had been heard. Halting in the neighborhood of the building afterwards used by Gen. Hooker as headquarters-the Chancellor Rouse—they remained in reserve in water and mud, while a sharp skirmish was going on in front—the Union batteries on their left speaking loudly. A squad of rebel cavalry made a daring attempt to capture one of the guns, but were soon scattered by a discharge of cased shot and canister, which riddled their ranks, causing the balance to scamper back by a road through the dense pine forest in a harried manner. During this day the battle was opened by the 2d, 5th and 12th corps (commanded by Couch, Meade and Slocum respectively), who engaged the enemy at a point a mile and a half east, on the road to Fredericksburg, but were afterwards withdrawn to the new lines formed around Chancellorsville. Soon after dark general quietness prevailed along the lines, and the Sharpshooters were allowed to lie down for several hours and to make themselves as comfortable as circumstances permitted. But they obtained but little of the needed rest, owing to the wet state of the ground and the fact that their blankets and overcoats had been left with their knapsacks in the timber by the roadside. At the hour of midnight they returned to this place and rested until early on the morning of the 2d, when after a hasty breakfast, they changed position by moving forward to the left of the "headquarters" building into a brushy piece of woods, where after remaining a few hours during which time works were being hurriedly thrown up by different troops, they left their knapsacks in charge of a guard and moved off in light marching order to the right, being temporarily attached to the first division, commanded by Gen. Birney.

Previous to making this movement Companies E and K were ordered to report to a battery hotly engaged in our front. Soon after, an aid informed Lieut. Thorp that: "Your orders are to advance out on this plank road in the form of a letter V, the point in front, drive the rebel skirmishers in, find their main force and report back." This was done with E on the left side of the road, K on the right.

Before starting, a batteryman gave them the encouraging information that some of our infantry had been driven in three time's, but that "they wouldn't get driven back;" thus showing his confidence in the Sharpshooters. And he was right, for although after emerging from the lopped trees and brush in front of the battery, they were subjected to at least 100 shots, the balls passing through hats, coats, haversacks, etc., tearing up the ground around them, yet strangely hurting none, they pressed on, driving the enemy away until they came up to a full brigade, when they were finally ordered back. On this venture, some sharp duels took place. Among them, Lieut. Thorp using a sick man's gun (John Long), had several close encounters, getting his ear grazed, the seam of his sleeve cut, but invariably bringing down his opponent, and afterwards breaking his gun. The infantry supports keeping too close up, suffered considerable, while the active, dodging Sharpshooters wonderfully escaped. Having rejoined the other companies, they were in the following engagement held in reserve a short distance behind our skirmish line.

FIGHT AT THE CEDARS.

Proceeding a short distance along the Fredericksburg turnpike, the two Sharpshooter regiments filed left onto a cross-road and through a dense thicket of pines. Emerging from these, they reached an opening or small farm which presented a dilapidated appearance, and near the house discovered a battery firing to the Left at the rebel artillerists, who were in turn sending shot and shell into some infantry of the 12th corps stationed at the time on the farm. Among these troops were the 3d Wisconsin, which regiment was passed at the roadside. Crossing Scott's Run, hastily bridged with rails, Col. Berdan deployed his brigade on entering a bushy slope, and soon after skirmishing began. It was not long before shots were exchanged, our men advancing up the slope through the dense thicket, onto the more level ground above—the cover being poor, the cedar trees, although numerous, small in size. The little brigade pushing forward, driving back the opposing force, were not long in sighting the enemy below them opposite the hill, who with a piece of artillery and some teams were hurriedly moving away. A brisk fight then ensued, the Second Sharpshooters on the left commencing the firing, followed instantly by the First Regiment who were on the right, having wheeled to the left on receiving the information quickly passed along the line, that "the Graybacks were on the left below the hill." So rapidly did they fire, advancing at the same time, that but a short time elapsed before a white flag was raised by the enemy, a major and 60 men surrendering as prisoners, the Sharpshooters having cornered them.

The Second Regiment soon after, being threatened on their left flank, Capt. Chase ran down the line and caused Company E to about face and left wheel, to protect that end of the line, and while conducting the movement, this good officer was mortally wounded.

When the flag was first raised, the order to "cease firing" was given, and for a few moments the skirmishers allowed their rifles to cool. But 'twas not so with a party of rebels in the opposite timber, who continued to "blaze away" in a manner that savored of mischief. Whereupon, Private John Ross, a German raw recruit from Milwaukee, vehemently exclaimed:

"Secesh (cease) firing? Mein Gott! Such secesh (cease) firing I never see before!"

And with the discharge of his rifle he left the skirmish line, running rapidly ahead. At this moment the order to advance was again given, and the men hurried forward, but Ross had the lead, and apparently regardless of consequences rushed to a suspicious looking building on the opposite rise of ground. Meantime, the Sharpshooters crowded the enemy so close they were obliged to leave a caisson, one of the horses being shot, but escaped with their cannon and transports. Their wagon train was seen in the distance, so Col. Berdan hurried his men forward in hopes of breaking it up, but it had got too far down the road and escaped. The captured caisson was rendered useless by wrenching off the wheels and upsetting it with its ammunition into a creek nearby. Ross, who pronounced the word *cease,* "secesh," and who afterwards saw the joke when told that in reality the secesh were firing, was lost to view for a few moments; but soon after, he appeared driving a fine horse and *buggy* with a wealthy resident of Fredericksburg by his side. The team and prisoner were sent to the rear, and in the buggy was found under the seat several thousand rounds of cartridges, with which the prisoner was endeavoring to get away when overhauled by the emphatic recruit.

The riflemen had now established their line along the road where the caisson was captured, their center being at the building above mentioned which proved to be a foundry—Welford's Furnace—where the enemy had lately been making deadly missiles to hurl into the Union ranks. In front was an open field, and beyond, four hundred yards distant, was a dense wood. One of the Union batteries taking a position near the old foundry fired away for a while, but their ammunition giving out, they fell back with a number of their men wounded by the enemy's guns, which latter having the exact range sent shot and shell into them very seriously. The rebel battery finally ceased its fire, but the contest along the skirmish line was kept up by the Sharpshooters, and the enemy posted in the opposite wood. And although the shooting was carried on at times sharply, yet if no more damage was sustained by the rebels than was the case on our line, the results in a killed and wounded point of view were immaterial; although there is good reason to believe that the foe had a hot time of it, as our riflemen who had taken cover under the road bank behind a snake fence, sent well-aimed shots at different squads as they passed along the edge of the timber, and a great scattering among them was observable; while on our right 60 Sharpshooters having cornered a body of rebels in a railroad cut discovered by lookouts posted in trees along the roadside, forced them to surrender under cover of our ready rifles. It was sudden. The determined attitude, aiming and ready to fire, had a very demoralizing effect on the huddling Johnnies—caught in their own trap. They numbered some 300, and with those captured before, constituted all of the 23d Georgia regiment (365) excepting their colonel who escaped. These troops were well dressed, and although they did not look hungry, said they came over to "help eat them eight days' rations."

This force when first discovered were creeping up onto our line, but were driven back by order of Capt. James H. Baker after some rapid firing, and forced to take shelter in the cut; Capt. Steele the rebel commander surrendering his sword to Capt. Baker, who sent them to the rear. Lieut. C. W. Thorp received the prisoners and took them back with his company, K, turning them over to the provost guard in the woods, where they met Gen. Sickles who asked who took the prisoners, and the provost officer said he did. "The deuce you did," ejaculated the general, "there's the Sharpshooters, they captured these men." "Yes," said Thorp, "our regiment captured them, and I brought them back with my reserve company; and I learned general, from these prisoners that their troops are moving up to flank us on the right. ""We'll take care of *them,*" said Sickles, as Thorp started back to his former position. This must have been the first positive information Gen. Sickles received as to the intention of Jackson's command.

James H. Galloway, of Company I, of the force capturing the main body at the railroad cut, had a close call for his life, a bullet grazing his scalp knocking him down, but Eli Cook and Frank Dolton of the same company rescued him from the dangerous position where he lay. Lieut. Thorp also carried off from another part of the field a wounded man, Walter J. Christy, the target of scores of shots while performing the humane act.

The casualties in the Cedars are given in full, with subsequent losses. Many had narrow escapes during the afternoon, especially a party of flankers under Sergt. Lye, ordered over the field beyond a small creek, to feel the opposite woods. They soon *felt* the presence of a large 'force of the enemy, whereby they were obliged to retire hurriedly over the creek in which several of the party got drenched, - the bullets flying about uncomfortably close. Among them, B. E. Loomis had his cap box shot away, but luckily his -rifle was well stocked with primers, whereby he could *snap* away. These primers were not always equal to the emergency, frequently failing to explode the cartridge "first pop," whereas the hat-caps were always sure, and were therefore generally relied on.

This particular fight—at the Furnace—was named after the thick, clustering cedar trees and bushes scattered over the field, in honor of the Sharpshooters and their supports, for their conspicuous success therein. Gen. Birney, in his 'congratulatory order to his division, adds the name of "The Cedars" to their battle-flag.

The following from a regular army officer, at the time colonel of the 37th New York, commanding 3d brigade of Birney's division, had this to say relative to the Sharpshooter service at this place. After describing the fight and the part taken by his brigade therein, he adds:

"The enemy's supports to their sharpshooters endeavored, apparently, to escape and serve as rear guard to a train which was moving to our right, but were induced to take shelter in a railroad cut by the fire of our Sharpshooters, where they were soon outflanked, when they surrendered. The whole number of prisoners is reported to be 365, including 19 officers. The Sharpshooters understand the true tactics of skirmishers, are possessed of enterprise and courage, and were maneuvered with great skill and address by Col. Berdan, and I regard it as one of the best organizations of the volunteer service."—SAMUEL B. HAYMAN.

The movements on the 2d of May were hardly expected to result in a great battle, the opposing armies rather feeling each other preparatory to a general engagement, which was looked for by the soldiers themselves, On the next day; although some sharp fighting had been going on along the front lines—on the right, the Sharpshooters in their advanced position doing their part in holding in check a portion of the enemy until reinforcements from our own corps swung around. On the left, heavy firing was heard on Hancock's front, and it was evident that the enemy were closing in for hot work. When therefore after sunset we were ordered to fall back noiselessly, the firing having mostly ceased, and halting suddenly scarce a mile distant in an open field among artillery and infantry, stacked arms and commanded to rest in place, without rations—they having been left with knapsacks under guard—it was not surprising that long faces were met with on every side on learning that we were cut off. Our boys could not understand it. Success had attended their efforts that afternoon, capturing as they did, men and horses numbering nearly as many as their own brigade—pushing the Confederates back and holding them at bay until the supports came up. But the force in front was but a small portion of the rebel army—the rear guard of Jackson's flanking column.

The Union line of battle was a long one, and, the enemy had their choice of any portion of the same to attack in force; and when with persistent fury they burst suddenly at six o'clock on the advanced lines of the 11th corps on our extreme right, the latter gave way, and became greatly disordered as they fell back, until checked—but too late—by the batteries of the 3d corps under Pleasanton and Sickles.

In the 11th corps was the 26th Wisconsin (a German regiment), which although in their first action, stoutly withstood the sudden and powerful attack of the crowding, yelling Johnnies, until almost surrounded, when they were forced to beat a retreat from their position, suffering considerable loss. 'Twas unavoidable, and impossible for them in face of the overwhelming numbers that rushed upon them, to do otherwise than fall back. The 119th and 58th New York also made a gallant resistance.

Gen. Carl Schurz, commanding 3d division, shows the desperate nature of this conflict: "The 26th Wisconsin, flanked on both sides and exposed to a terrible fire in front, maintained the unequal contest for a considerable time, nor did it fallback until I ordered it to do so. There is hardly an officer who has not at least received a bullet through his clothes. Had it not been for the praiseworthy firmness of these men the enemy would have obtained possession of the woods opposite without resistance, taken the north and south rifle pits from the rear, and appeared on the Plank road between Dowdall's Tavern and Chancellors-vine before the artillery could have been withdrawn."

On some portions of the line the men of this corps were filling their haversacks with hard-tack from boxes lying broken about, and while eating the same in supposed security from sudden attacks, were thus surprised, having scarce time to seize their guns from the stacks and scamper off, with the rebs close after them. The result was confusion confounded, the rebels having all the fun there was in it to themselves. 'Twas a very unwelcome surprise to us all. Our right was turned, Jackson fell on Sickles' rear—far within our lines—an entering wedge of cold steel threatening to split us up. It was a well-planned and better executed movement on Jackson's part—but it proved his last victory.

Notwithstanding the "half-moon" men, as the 11th corps was known by its badge, were blamed for this reverse, which undoubtedly was the main cause of the failure of the campaign, it is doubtful if other troops under the circumstances, could have held their ground; owing to the extreme position held by this corps—afar out—with its right or northern wing unprotected, with dense woods around them concealing the stealthy advance of the foe to within charging distance—backed up by 30,000 Confederate troops. For even if it is true that pickets were not thrown out, which has been denied, the men in the ranks were not responsible for any neglect of their officers, whether field or general; for Hooker had given explicit orders to scout well the front, and had it been well done a couple of miles in advance, the enemy would have been discovered forming for the charge. That's where the Sharpshooter service would have counted again—skirmishing far enough in advance, whereby in the battle given the enemy, timely warning would have been received by the troops behind; as was the case where the Sharpshooters were used, before and after. As to the failure of the men to rally until they passed behind the main army, it is simply one of those too frequent results attending a panic.

Gen. Sickles made a gallant fight in his efforts to check the furious onslaught, and was obliged to withdraw the divisions of Birney and Whipple from their advanced position across' Scott's Run and near the Wilderness foundry, using his batteries with great effect. When he first heard of the disaster he refused to believe it—we had not heard their guns—and was about to push his corps reinforced on to the rear of the enemy's column, when direct word came from general headquarters, at almost the same time he saw the exultant enemy come down his front, with the 11th men in full retreat. The 8th Pennsylvania cavalry were sent by Gen. Pleasanton to break the enemy's advance, and to their credit, "brilliantly was the service performed, although with fearful loss."

Major Huey, commanding says: "We moved off briskly to the right. The enemy's skirmish line had crossed the road on which we were moving, throwing us between their skirmishers and battle line. The whole regiment made a desperate charge on the main column of Jackson's corps who were crossing the road in our front, completely checking the enemy, losing Major Keenan, Capt. Arrowsmith and Adjt. Haddock, with about 30 men and about 80 horses. I immediately re-formed the regiment to support the Reserve artillery."

Gen. Sickles thus describes the situation: "I confided to

Pleasanton the direction of the artillery time was everything. The fugitives of the 11th corps swarmed from the woods and swept frantically over the cleared fields, in which my artillery was parked. The exulting enemy at their heels mingled yells with their volleys, and in the confusion which followed it seemed as if cannon and caissons, dragoons, cannoneers; and infantry could never be disentangled from the mass in which they were suddenly thrown.

A few minutes was enough to restore comparative order and get our artillery in position. The enemy showing himself on the plain, Pleasanton met the shock at short range with the well-directed fire of twenty-two pieces, double-shotted with canister."

Gen. Pleasanton reports: "They advanced in silence, and with that skill and adroitness they often display to gain their object. The only color visible was an American flag with the center battalion. To clear up this doubt my aide-de-camp, Lieut. Thomson, 1st New York Cavalry, rode to within 100 yards of them, when they called out to him, 'We are friends; come on!' and he was induced to go 50 yards closer, when the whole line, in a most dastardly manner, opened on him with musketry, dropped the American color, and displayed 8 or 10 rebel battle-flags. Lieut. Thomson escaped unhurt."

Gen. Sickles again: "The heads of the columns were swept away to the woods from which they opened a furious but ineffectual fire of musketry. Twice they attempted a flank movement, but the first was checked by our guns, and the second and most formidable was baffled by the advance of Whipple and Birney, who were coming up rapidly, but in perfect order, and forming in lines of brigades in rear of the artillery, and on the flanks. My position was now secure in the adequate infantry support which had arrived; the loud cheers of our men as twilight closed the combat vainly challenged the enemy to renew the encounter. After dark, the enemy's line could only be defined by the flash of his musketry, from which a stream of fire occasionally almost enveloped us. As often as these attacks were renewed, generally with fresh troops, and aided by his artillery, they were repulsed by our guns, now directed by Randolph on the flank and by Osborn in front. Ascertaining the enterprise of cutting us off from the army to be hopeless, the enemy suddenly withdrew to the line of rifle pits and breastworks formerly held by the 11th corps. Several of our guns and caissons were immediately recovered from the woods the enemy had occupied, and to quote the felicitous observations of Gen. Pleasanton: 'Such was the fight at the head of Scott's Run—artillery against infantry at 300 yards; the infantry in the forest, the artillery in the clearing.' War presents many anomalies, but few so strange in its results as this."

In the meantime, Sickles' 2d division commanded by Gen. Berry, which had been in reserve near Chancellor House, was ordered by Gen. Hooker to a line on the Plank road where in conjunction with their artillery they aided in the discomfiture of the advancing foe. In this, they were assisted by a division of the 12th corps which had been severely engaged that afternoon under command of Gen.

Williams. That officer says that the casualties in his first brigade (Gen. Knipe) the afternoon of May 2d, included besides the large number of men, killed, wounded and prisoners, the further loss of every regimental commander in that brigade; that many of the reported missing after dark undoubtedly fell under the heavy fire of the enemy concealed in the woods and rifle pits. Gen. Knipe's brigade certainly had hard luck, being at one time within speaking distance of the enemy, who came very near cutting him and his entire command off. He tells the story thus:

"The advance to our original position was made after dark; arriving behind the barricades without meeting any opposition and without the knowledge that the enemy bad at any time had possession of them. I had just taken this position when some half dozen of the enemy came forward through the bushes, unarmed. Upon being asked who they were they replied, 'We are Confederates, coming in to give ourselves up; we are tired and hungry.' I at once sent them to the rear. Immediately after this, I observed another party approaching. I hailed them, asking what troops they were. The answer was, 'We are friends.' I became pretty well satisfied by this time that the prisoners in my hands had been sent forward as a decoy. I was then asked by the parties in my front what troops we were. I answered, 'We are Confederates,' and the response was, We are Confederates.' I asked of whose command, and received an answer, 'Gen. A. P. Hill's.' I told them to come in, intending to make prisoners of them as fast as they came over the barricades. At this time my attention was called to a movement on my right and rear. I immediately rode in that direction, and hailed the party approaching by asking who they were. The answer received was, 'Do not come any farther, or we will fire.' I replied, 'Do not fire; we are friends,' and immediately wheeled about and directed my command to move off by the left flank, stooping, so as to be sheltered from the enemy's fire in front. At this instant the enemy opened upon my line from both front and rear." Here he says, he lost one company, K, 128th Pennsylvania with their colonel and lieutenant-colonel, cut off on the right and captured, and also lost three valuable officers from the 46th Pennsylvania.

The 2d corps also did good service during the day, in front of Chancellorsville, in defeating the attempts of the enemy to break their lines; the skirmish line of Hancock's division, under Col. Miles (Nelson A.), repulsing a sharp attack of two columns, inflicting upon the enemy severe loss. But to the timely action of Gen. Sickles at the critical point, should be awarded the praise of saving the army from an almost certain general disaster. It was "fight!" with him, and gallantly was it done, notwithstanding the limited means at his command—for which, well does he deserve the title of the Hero of Chancellorsville.

The Sharpshooters lay all night in order of battle, tired, hungry and full of excitement. Several night attacks by portions of the 3d corps occurred during that eventful Saturday night, Berdan's men remaining in their places under arms. But little sleep was obtained, the sudden charges on the enemy's line, awaking the country around with the deafening noise, and lighting up space with the bright flashes from the weapons of death, bringing each man to his feet and his hand to his rifle. Besides, unpleasant reflections would crowd the minds of those remaining in line awaiting orders, on the prospect of the morrow. Then again, would the hardy veterans of many hard-fought battle fields banish dismal thoughts, and cheering up, laugh and chat together—for the last time with some—occasionally telling some anecdote of previous campaigns, seemingly caring but little for the next movement; on the contrary, had their minds made up, and when the time came for action they would be on hand. Surely 'twas a time that "tried men's souls." Not a living man to-day, present on that occasion, can ever forget the exciting times prevailing that fiercely warlike night, when our brigades at the near front charged and recharged through dark wood and thicket, with an occasional glimmer of the moon to light them on in the path of death.

DEATH OF STONEWALL JACKSON.

It was in this vicinity where the Confederate cause sustained a heavy shock in the loss of their famous leading general above named, by the severe wounds then received, resulting shortly in his death.- Early in the evening after darkness had settled around, Gen. Jackson rode out in front of his lines to reconnoiter, intent on getting between the Union army and the crossing at United States Ford; but was soon greeted by a shower of bullets from Gen. Berry's brigades of the 3d corps. Turning back, his own troops mistook him and his aides for Union cavalry and poured in a fatal volley, killing and wounding most of his escort, and shooting Jackson in three places. Placed on a stretcher, while being carried to his lines, one of the stretcher-bearers was killed by a Union shot and others driven away. Another man stumbling, the stretcher fell, and the wounded general was further injured by the severe shock received. Amid bursting shells and pattering balls singing their requiem around him, they succeeded in getting him within his lines after considerable effort. He died a week later, on May 10th.

Notwithstanding the bad outcome of the Chancellorsville campaign, our soldiers felt partly recompensed in the thought that they had gained at least a half-victory when they learned that Jackson had fallen. For it is the game of war to cripple your adversary as much as possible, and in Jackson's death the Confederates were the sufferers, having lost a leader whose place could not easily be filled. As a skillful general in marching troops, and in holding them together in battle, he had no superior—whereby he got the name of "Stonewall." His military career must always place his name among the foremost in American annals.

SUNDAY'S FIGHT AT CHANCELLORSVILLE.

At a very early hour Sunday morning, May 3d, before sunrise, Gen. Sickles withdrew his troops to a new line, called Fairview, when the fighting commenced again—destined to be terrific in character and severe with slaughter—the decisive engagement at Chancellorsville.

Soon were they at it, with all the known missiles of war on their deathly mission from gray to blue, from blue to gray. It was "give and take" with all the fury of determined foes, striving to destroy—to win the victory. The first onslaught was on one of Sickles' brigades, that had not yet fallen back, which repulsed an effort to charge, before retiring to the new position. Our troops now connected, had not long to wait before their great lines were seen coming, perfect in alignment, with firm step, as if courting death which was so soon to play havoc in their ranks—to destroy their formation, to demoralize the living remnants. The soldiers of Birney, Whipple and Berry, the division of French, and the corps of Slocum, awaited the onset. In another moment the crash came, the lines of gray and butternut melted away under the storm of lead from thousands of muskets, the crashing; mangling shell and shot belched forth from loud-mouthed, flaming Union cannon. And, what with the uproar, the long, steady rolling of the infantry, the reverberating artillery, the shrieks of the wounded, the yells of the gray, and the cheers of the blue, it was simply infernal! Fresh columns came up and renewed the attempts to break the Union ranks, with no better success. Thus the contest raged for hours—thus the carnage continued.

The Sharpshooters hurriedly left their resting place of the previous warring night, and moving along the right edge of the open plain passed in the rear of the batteries that had already got to work. The enemy's fire was hot and heavy in reply, and through it Berdan's command had to pass, but none were harmed. Marching then by "file left" into the dense timber, they deployed out, the Wisconsin men in reserve.

Corp. James H. Galloway, of Company I, of the First Sharpshooters, with three other comrades, was sent to the front in a piece of woods. The corporal afterwards said: "As I could see no danger, we set our guns against trees to eat our breakfast of hard-tack, when we saw a line of infantry coming on a by-road. The outside men were dressed in our uniform, but the rest had the gray on, which we could not see. I supposed they were our men. I told them to come on, no one would harm them, when to our astonishment the officer in charge told us to surrender or he would shoot us. I told him I would not. I got my gun and kept dodging so he could not get aim on me. One of my comrades, Jerry Brandolph, was shot in the mouth before he could turn. The other, Alvin Smith, was shot through the hips, and died the next day. The third one, Dwight Ford, received a bad wound. I succeeded in getting back to our reserve." Corp. Galloway was gritty, and bound not to surrender, but returned in time to the supports to stop the enemy's farther advance.

Lieut. Thorp, now commanding Company K, (Capt. Nash being detailed for staff duty), was ordered with his company to support a fresh battery, where he dropped four Men to each gun, who picked off the enemy's gunners in front, completely silencing their battery. A line of battle now came on, and their orders: "Prepare to charge," were distinctly heard; but they were repulsed, and as they fell back, Company F went in, advancing as skirmishers 80 rods, to the edge of the woods.

Bullets and shell were soon flying thickly around, and the skirmishers became engaged. After awhile, stragglers from other regiments began to fall back, when Company G was ordered more to the right, the line ahead having moved that way. Soon after executing this new movement, this company got into the fire, and now again came the time to try their metal; but although a sudden sharp volley of bullets at very short range, not over fifty yards, came into them wounding several, yet did they hold their position, returning the fire with interest until a support could be brought to their relief, none being near at hand, which was finally obtained through the exertions of Col. Trepp commanding the First Regiment. It was impossible to see far through the thick under-growth, with the enemy close to the ground with which their clothes frequently corresponded, and often the flash of their guns only discovered their presence.

Some other troops having broke under the severity of the fire; running by our men, for awhile the latter were subjected to shots from the Union cannon in the rear, the artillery supposing none but the enemy were left there. Of being informed of their mistake by an officer sent back for that purpose, they withheld their fire until the Sharpshooters got out of range; including our surgeon, Dr. Brennan, who was close behind attending to the wounded, and who called to the officer as he passed by: "For God's sake, stop those guns, till I get these wounded men away; "when they had full sweep through the "bush."

A portion of the First Regiment going ahead as skirmishers, having ran pell-mell on to a body of the enemy in the thick wood, on the order of Lieut. Gardner B. Clark (afterwards captain), of Company C, to- "charge," forced them hurriedly to retire, capturing several prisoners, with some loss to themselves in killed and wounded. Here again was presented a sorrowful example of sudden death, that shocked the living witnesses even in the heat of the fray. Harmon Wise, a private in Company C, a good natured, ready soldier, nicknamed by his comrades "Rough," being one of the foremost in the charge, rushed on to a small party of the enemy and demanded their surrender. "Yes," cried one, "I surrender; "but as he said the word he pulled off his gun shooting Rough through the heart, then throwing down his piece gave himself up to his captors, who would not retaliate on an unarmed foe but sent him to the rear. The charging party stood aghast for a moment, but for a moment only, as time was precious and they were obliged to push on, leaving poor Rough their late comrade where he fell, to be seen by them no more.

This Sharpshooter charge of 80 men, was made with unfixed bayonets, so eager were they to follow up their advantage; the troops driven back proved to be the "Stonewall Brigade," as was afterwards learned through prisoners and confirmed by Lieut. Judkins on detail in the ambulance corps, while on the field a few days after, looking for the wounded. The charge was so sudden and unexpected, immediately after delivering a rattling volley, that the enemy concluded a larger force was onto them, and fell instantly back in disorder to their lines. They boasted that it was the first time they had been driven.

In the afternoon Col. Berdan marched his men to the rear, after falling back from the woods where our artillery swept through, that they might rest and procure rations, the most of them having lost theirs with the knapsacks, the woods taking fire and the enemy afterwards occupying the ground. The most heart-rending picture of the whole battle field was the fire that raged, whereby such of the wounded that may not have been carried off the field, were suffocated and burned. Fortunate were those who had to die, that they did so before the holocaust began. Towards night, the dense smoke on some portions of the field, hung like a pall over the men, stifling and blinding them at times—a fearful sight.

Many of the members of both regiments becoming separated from their companies, remained at the front overnight; their duties thereby becoming extra arduous. Col. Berdan reported some 325 prisoners captured this day, which with the number taken at the Cedars, made a total of about 700 to the credit of the Sharpshooters. He also says:

"On Sunday afternoon, a detachment of about 120 men was posted near the building occupied as a hospital, under the command of Capt. Wilson, and at the request of Gen. Barnes, of the 1st division 5th corps, it drove the enemy from the woods and established a picket line for a portion of the 5th corps. He was afterwards ordered by Gen. Sickles to move to the left and establish the line in front of the 3d corps, which was done. He was relieved on Monday morning by my Second Regiment, and the remainder of my command was stationed behind slight works, thrown up by themselves, like the rest of the forces in the vicinity."

These picket lines were established by the Sharpshooters in the midst of heavy firing; without faltering, but with a quick, determined step, they advanced their line in perfect dress—preserving their intervals as beautifully as on a prize drill. These movements were watched by officers and soldiers behind them, whose opinion of the Sharpshooter service can best be judged by the following excerpts:

Gen. Sickles: "The Sharpshooters, under Col. Berdan, supported the First Brigade on the right, throwing out a strong line of skirmishers to the front in the woods. These splendid light troops rendered the most effective service. Major Hastings was severely wounded while upon this duty with his battalion."

Major Hastings of the First Regiment was wounded in the hip, having had two horses shot under him, one being killed. The major did not return to the regiment, being afterwards detailed on duty in Washington.

Capt. Dalton, A. A. G. 3d division 3d A. C.: "The U. S. Sharpshooters were placed on the right of the 1st brigade to prevent the enemy from flanking our right. They were deployed in the woods and did most-excellent service."

Col. Ellis, 124th New York, reporting the Sunday fight, after being ordered to the right to protect the battery, says: "Here we found some Sharpshooters under Major Hastings, and as we advanced in line of battle through a thick wood we were opened upon by a large force of the rebels on our front and right flank, and a severe engagement of about an hour's duration ensued, the enemy in force trying to drive us and capture the battery. Our men fought like tigers, cheering loudly and falling fast. Three color-bearers were here shot down in succession, but the colors never touched the ground." In about an hour's time, the battery being withdrawn, and troops on the left retiring, he fell back to escape "certain capture."

Caldwell's brigade of the 2d corps during the morning advanced through the woods where the Sharpshooters were, driving the enemy, under heavy artillery fire and musketry, meeting with considerable loss, particularly in the 148th Pennsylvania, but were finally forced to retire, owing to a threatened flank movement of a superior force.

Gen. Barnes, commanding 1st brigade, says: "Capt. John Wilson, commanding two companies of Berdan's Sharpshooters, advanced handsomely, deployed to the front, and occupied the woods in advance."

Nor should the hard fought batteries be forgotten, many of which were subjected to a terrific exposure from the enemy's cannon, as also their small arms. The Union artillerists often had a hard time in battle, and particularly was this the case at Chancellorsville, owing to their exposed positions.

The following from Gen. Slocum, commanding 12th corps, shows in brief how they suffered: "At about nine A. M. the troops on the right of my command fell back, which was soon followed by a portion of my line. The enemy at once gained a position which enabled him to use his infantry against our batteries. The artillery, however, held its position until two battery commanders, Capt. Hampton and Lieut. Crosby, were killed beside their pieces, until 63 cannoneers were killed or wounded, and until 80 horses had been shot in the harness. The batteries were then retired to a position in rear of our second line without the loss of a single piece."

Gen. Hancock of 2d corps: "Notwithstanding that my flank was entirely exposed, our 14 pieces of artillery prevented the enemy from advancing, although his battle-flags were within a few hundred yards of us. The troops, however, suffered heavy losses from the enemy's artillery.

Leppien's (5th Maine) battery of five guns, on the right of the Chancellor House, lost all its officers, cannoneers, and horses for the guns. I made a detail of men who removed the pieces by hand to a place of safety."

Gen. Couch the corps commander thus speaks of Gen. Hancock: "I express my thanks to this officer for his gallantry, energy, and his example of marked personal bravery." He also compliments Gen. French and his "fine troops," and Gen. Gibbon and his 2d division.

After the campaign, Gen. Hancock succeeded Couch in command of the 2d corps, and was to receive still further renown as a brave, faithful and popular commander. During the morning, Gen. Hooker narrowly escaped death from a cannon ball striking a pillar of the Chancellor

House, while leaning against the same. As it was he was completely stunned, remaining insensible for over an hour.

During this important period Gen. Sickles had applied for more troops to help him and his 3d corps, while sorely pressed by the enemy, from before whom he was finally obliged to fall back with his ammunition exhausted; the expected relief not coming to his assistance, although there was at the time a large force of troops not engaged, to draw from—three corps—none of the other generals seemingly wishing to take upon themselves the responsibility, hoping that Hooker would soon recover. During the day Gen. Hiram G. Berry, commanding 2d division, was killed.

'T was a hard contest, the brunt of which fell on the lines of the 3d and 12th corps, also a portion of the 2d corps. Their "lost in action" in this Sunday's fight, helped largely to swell the total for the campaign. The commanding position which the enemy's artillerists obtained in the morning, after we fell back to Fairview, completely enfiladed our lines, placing the troops of these three corps under a series of cross-fires exceedingly difficult to withstand—thus giving the Confederates a great advantage—which only the most determined resistance, prevented their superior numbers from inflicting a disastrous defeat. Had the 1st corps—one of the best in the army—been allowed to go in, followed up by Meade's reserves—the Fighting Fifth—striking the enemy on the flank, not only was a great victory assured us, but the prospect of Lee's signal defeat if not entire destruction, seemed inevitable. This fresh attack of fresh troops at the opportune moment, would have demoralized the whole rebel host. Then, Hooker's name would have risen to the clouds.

In a public address many years thereafter, Gen. Sickles speaking of "Fighting Joe," said: "When Hooker stopped, few would go any farther," was a quotation applying to Hooker, and that described his character. Regarding Hooker at Chancellorsville: The proof of the skill with which the battle was planned, was in its being considered of so much importance, that it was used at West Point for study, as one of the best plans of battle of the late war.

SHARPSHOOTING. AND SKIRMISHING

During the night the Sharpshooters rested near a hospital—dreaded place—and in vain the tired soldier lulled to sleep, 'mid the groans of the wounded around him. But nature's sweet balm conquered at last, nor cries, nor shrieks, could prevent sound slumber during the final hour, when he was to be aroused for further duty.

The next morning, May 4th, they again moved up to the front, after witnessing the shelling of the Union wagon train across the river before daylight, by a rebel battery which was soon captured. Col.

Berdan having been placed in charge of the outposts, took out a detail of 10 volunteers to the skirmish line, for the purpose of silencing the rebel sharpshooters who were sending their shots over to our lines and into the reserves; and advancing the skirmishers firing, drove back those of the enemy, holding the ground thereafter. While *lying* in reserve behind the artillery, one battery of which was composed of men from the Iron Brigade, the division commander Arnie! W. Whipple, who had been busy superintending the movements in front, was shot by the enemy's pickets a half mile distant, while among our Sharpshooters; being struck near the spine and mortally wounded, dying shortly after. He was greatly respected as a brave and efficient officer, much sorrow being evinced at his fall. But no place was safe from shot and shell there. Several others were wounded by these stray bullets. After Berdan's line had driven the rebels off, their firing was stopped, although the shells and cannon shot continued on both sides.

The regimental adjutant, Wm. H. Horton, acting aid to Col. Berdan, was severely wounded in arm and side, while with gun in hand he was rushing forward to capture some rebel scouts. He was formerly the leader of our scouts at Yorktown, when sergeant-major of the regiment. Once more he was performing the same duty, having with him these Wisconsin members: Jacobs, Albert Isham, Armfield, Stokes, Alvord, and the present sergeant-major, Ben Atwell; some of whom had served under him at the former place. The adjutant was a brave, gallant officer, and a great loss to the service. He deserved a better fate, his arm being amputated;

This day the Second Sharpshooters were on the picket line; the First Regiment lying a half mile back in reserve where they threw up breastworks, being subject to stray rebel shot, and in the afternoon to rebel shell—a brigade having roused the enemy by a sudden charge through the woods within sight of our position. Not much fighting, however, going on to-day. During the night the heavy booming of cannon heard from down the river served to keep the boys reminded of the probabilities of another clash of arms on the day to follow. It appears that the 6th corps under Sedgwick, after having captured the formidable Marye's Heights at Fredericksburg the day before in a hard fight, being now surrounded on three sides by a large force of the enemy at Salem Heights, while attempting to connect with the main army, were obliged to recross the Rappahannock at Banks' Ford, after a gallant contest in which the enemy were repeatedly repulsed in their efforts to cut Sedgwick off, losing 9 pieces of artillery and 1,400 prisoners captured by our men—but at the fearful cost to the Union of over 3,000 killed and wounded.

A very important reconnoissance was made on the 4th towards Fredericksburg by Charles J. Buchanan and Edwin E. Nelson, volunteers for the purpose, which disclosed the fact that the enemy had left; at least from that particular front where the commands of Capt. Wilson and Capt.

McLean were stationed. The enemy had evidently gone in the direction of Sedgwick's position, to attack the 6th army corps, and it was believed by many of our officers and men afterwards, that had the information obtained by the two Sharpshooters named, and reported to army headquarters, been appreciated and acted upon, it might have changed the face of things that day. However this may be, the incident is interesting, as it proves our service to have been distinctive in character, not only in sharpshooting and as skirmishers, but as watch dogs right in the face of the enemy to note their movements. Going into action as skirmishers five paces apart (oftener ten), and frequently in brushy places or thickets out of sight of the comrade right and left, often far ahead of the regular battle line, each man looking out for himself, making of each skirmisher a separate and distinctive body or force, taking the place in a measure of a company, is a performance that brings out to the fullest intensity all the perceptive qualities of the individual; while the enemy in the largest possible formation, watches this isolated skirmisher with the same degree of interest for the time being, as they do afterwards the approaching columns. So that the skirmisher becomes a very much noted character in spite of himself. The orders given these two intrepid scouts were to go as far as possible without firing if they could avoid it, that is, unless attacked. Pushing through the heavy brush and timber, deployed within sight of each other, they moved cautiously on, feeling their way, starting at the slightest sound, even the flutter of a bird, or the jump and run of a rabbit, for a death-like stillness prevailed, and noting everything about them. All this care was very necessary, as these woods the night before had concealed a strong force of the enemy, with a heavy picket line. Buchanan and Nelson went a long distance, finding no enemy in their front nor elsewhere, the rebels having entirely withdrawn from the front of this particular position, and were then fighting the 6th corps, in their efforts to beat the Union army in detail. This information was promptly reported to McLean and Wilson, who sent the same to headquarters, but our army at Chancellorsville was hardly in condition to avail itself of the opportunity to advance at that time.

Before daylight Tuesday morning May 5th, a portion of the First Regiment were sent to the front. They were posted on picket in a swampy thicket, the enemy being close by, concealed under heavy timber. Here the Sharpshooters remained at their posts 17 hours, most of them without eating, keeping a careful lookout ahead. Behind them on an open field the Union batteries were in position; still farther behind lay the Union troops in intrenchments hastily made with spade and pick. After daylight, sharp firing commenced and was kept up at intervals until dark. Several times during the forenoon did they attempt to drive us in, but to no purpose. The right of the picket line gave way for a time as the enemy apparently in force appeared, which let the Union batteries play into them through the timber. This kept them quiet on the right, but not long after, a move was made on the left of the Sharpshooters where were posted some infantry troops. The Wisconsinites were in the center and kept firing when a good opportunity occurred—when they saw anything to shoot at. The movement on our left was for a time successful; the enemy were heard advancing, their orders to "close up on the right," and "oblique to the right," also to "look out for breakers on the left," passed along their line, were plainly overheard. It happened that their left if they didn't oblique well, would bring them in contact with our center in the swamp where the Wisconsin company was stationed, which they seemed to wish to avoid in their movements. They succeeded in driving in those on the left of the Sharpshooter line, advancing on that side until they got beyond and within Company

G's line, when our artillery opened on them from another point, sending them back again; the Wisconsin men who held their ground behind trees putting in a heavy cross-fire as they decamped. Opposite Company K's front the enemy tried to get their men to "go in there," using some big oaths, but they failed to come "in there." Their moves were probably feints to blind our generals, but whether concluding that their maneuvering was useless, or having found out something they wished to know, they finally resorted to picket firing the balance of the day.

Shooting was in order until late in the afternoon, many close shots being received from the concealed foe. George W. Griffin had an open duel with a rebel target shooter who had watched our men closely, the least exposure bringing forth a bullet. It was some time before he was discovered, but finally Griffin stepped out in the open space and brought him to light. Their pieces cracked simultaneously, Griffin receiving the bullet through his pants below the knee, while his opponent—well, if he was not in fitting condition to continue his shooting others were there to take his place, which was an important position covering an approach along the narrow road by which the pickets entered the swamp. During the morning the heat and smoke of the burning woods was at times intense, but the Sharpshooters refusing to be smoked out, remained at their posts until relieved. A heavy soaking rain set in during the afternoon, making the roads wet and muddy, while a small sluggish stream that ran meandering through the swamp and across the lines, was soon swollen into a torrent. 'Twas late at night when relieved, and marching back to the reserves who were waiting in water and mud—all drenched to the skin—orders were finally received to fall back; they, after a muddy, tiresome tramp, reaching the river at U. S. Ford at daybreak on the 6th, recrossing soon after among a large body of troops. The 1st corps which had arrived from Fredericksburg the morning of the 3d, taking position on the right of Chancellorsville but not engaged in the big battle, now formed a line behind the army to protect the crossing.

That the Sharpshooters performed well their allotted part in the Chancellorsville campaign, there can be no question—earning further renown for their military behavior.

Thus ended the Chancellorsville campaign; one of the hardest fought, one of the most disastrous of the whole series. One in which the hopes of the soldiers were high for success on starting out, but were low enough on their return. Not that they blamed any one, but fortune seemed to be against them; the Confederates still remained a power unbroken. And they well knew more severe trials, more hard battles must follow, with the usual sad losses, before the crowning victory came—as come it must. They were determined on that; they never gave up that ultimate conclusion.

The Union loss is figured up in killed, wounded and missing during the seven days' campaign. The "missing" includes those captured by the enemy, with others doubtless killed in the heat of battle in the thickets or after dark, unbeknown to their comrades. Of those who may have eventually returned, it is but proper to state that for the time being, they were lost to the service—thus reducing to the aggregate number, the ranks of their several organizations.

Cavalry killed and wounded	43, missing	98
1st Corps," "	238,	54
2d Corps,[id]	1193,	732
3d Corps,	3023,	1096
5th Corps,"	541,	159
6th Corps,"	3105,	1485
11th Corps, "	1438,	974
12th Corps, "	1701,	1121

                                           11,282 5,719

Making a grand total of 17,000—surely enough to test the patriotism of our soldiers.

Among the killed were two good officers who were noted for their brave and manly 'qualities in time of danger viz: Lieut. Byron Brewer, of Michigan, killed May 3d by a cannon ball through his body. He had been wounded at Gaines' Mill, Glendale, and three times at Second Bull Run where he was left for dead on the field, was taken in charge by the enemy, exchanged, and after several months joined his company, C, to die in its line. His was clearly a case of unsubdued patriotism—he enlisted for the war.

Capt. Dudley P. Chase, of Minnesota, Company A, Second Regiment, wounded in the arm May 2d at the Cedars, suffered amputation and died not long after. His company joining the left division of the First Regiment, the writer was talking with him a few moments before he was shot, and left him on moving forward, full of patriotic hope for the future. He was an estimable officer.

Col. Berdan makes praiseworthy mention of these officers, as also Marble, Nash, Wilson, Rowell, Stoughton and others of his brigade, including Adjt. Horton of First and Adjt. Norton of the Second. These two adjutants were among the tallest and finest looking officers in the corps, were very active, and energetic in the heat of battle. In mentioning the faithful services of our surgeons, Drs. Brennan and Williams, he says of the latter, that although wounded "by a ball passing through his arm, he did not leave his duties for a moment."

The chaplain of the Second Regiment, Lorenzo Barber, also received great praise, and who well-earned the name given him by the men, as the "Fighting Parson." On the skirmish line he was earnestly engaged with his telescope-rifle, being one of our best marksmen, and on account of his exposure and bravery in the late battle where he was not obliged to go, from that time on he never failed to have a large audience when he officiated as preacher. As the boys expressed it: "That chaplain practices what he preaches. He tells us what we should do, and goes with us to the very front to help us in battle."

The loss in both regiments in the Chancellorsville campaign was about 90 killed and wounded, of which the following are known to me of the First Regiment:

Co. B—Wounded: Sergt. Thomas Smith, Charles H. Thompson, Mathew Morgan, Joseph Marr, William M. Fitzgerald, James H. Byers-6.

Co. C—Killed: Lieut. Byron Brewer, Sergt. John G. S. Evans, Corp. Henry A. Hood, Privates W. S. Parker, John Price, Harmon J. Wise. Wounded: Capt. James H. Baker, left breast, slight; Sergt. E. A. Wilson, hand, slight; Sergt. Porter W. Barker, hip, leg amputated, mortal; Corp. E. J. Southworth, left side; Corp. Leonard Bissel, abdomen, mortal; Corp. Dexter Field, leg and hip; Privates James I. Vanderburg, side, mortal; Henry A. Gilchrist, foot; R. S. McClain, upper arm; Stiles H. Wirts, leg; Fred. Jarvis, arm; James Dillabaugh, shoulder; George R. Brown, Charles H. Johnson. Missing: Martin J. Watson, slightly wounded; Joshua Robinson-22.

Co. E—Killed: Daniel Morse, Jr. Wounded: Edwin J. Peaslee, Alfred A. Rollins-3.

Co. F—Wounded: Edward Trask, Almon D. Griffin, Michael Cunningham, Jacob S. Bailey, E. M. Hosmer, Martin C. Laffie, John Monahan-7.

Co. G—Wounded: Capt. F. E. Marble, knee, slight; Sergt. John D. Lemmon, finger, slight; Corp. William Babcock, hip, slight; Corp. Albert S. Isham, knee, severe; Privates, Michael Costello, arm, severe; George T. Cottrell, neck and shoulder, severe; H. B. Denniston, arm, severe; Frank Meyer, hand, severe; Martin H. Wiltse, arm, severe; Abner Johnson, face, slight; William H. Woodruff, forehead, slight-11.

Co. I—Killed: Martin L. Wetmore, William E. Close, Alvin Smith. Wounded: Capt. James F. Covel, neck; Jeremiah Brandon, left shoulder; Albert G. Austin, cheek, slight; Dwight Ford, abdomen, mortal; Daniel McArthur-8.

Co. K—Wounded: Walter J. Christy, left lung, mortal.

Having recrossed the Rappahannock the troops proceeded to their respective camps through rain and mud; and notwithstanding the prevailing disappointment—to put it mildly—at the result of their hard efforts on the late field of action, the opportunity to rail at one another jestingly was not neglected. For no matter how weary and dejected the boys were, there were some always ready to revive their drooping spirits in this cheery manner. As one body of troops passed another resting, the uproarious greetings and bantering expressions would be sure to come. "There's another played out set! Go lay down in the mud, will you?" comes from the marchers, to be retaliated thus: "Oh, you're pretty fellows to be falling back; "to be replied from the column: "Turn out the provost-guard and pick up these stragglers;" when another mouther would sing back: "There goes the home guard, emancipate them—send them to their mammy—give them some soft bread—black your shoes—boil your shirt," etc. So, it continued along the line of march back to camp.

Loud cheers were frequently given when some particular regiment or brigade passed by. Especially when, while resting on the roadside for coffee, the 1st corps came along with the "full moon "on its banners, and as the great Western or Iron Brigade passed, looking like giants with their tall black hats, they were greeted with hearty cheers by the Sharpshooters. And giants they were, in action. Yet, how vain to boast, for cold lead brought down the best of men, and of that entire brigade in all its just pride and "fierce panoply of war," bat a few weeks were destined to pass, before their decimated ranks proved too truthfully that even they, were not invulnerable. With a large proportion of that Iron Brigade they were soon to start on their last war-path, soon to lose their greatest strength to become a crippled and weakened battalion. When I look back and see that famed body of troops marching up that long muddy hill unmindful of the pouring rain, but full of life and spirit, with steady step, filling the entire roadway, their big black hats and feathers conspicuous;

and remember how soon they were to be swept away by bullets and shell; the pride of looking upon a model American volunteer, which they so truly represented, turns now to utter sadness, at what hard fate befell them in the next battle.

Falling in, soon after, Berdan's brigade pushed on to their old camp at Falmouth, where they arrived before dark worn out with fatigue, and considerably downcast at the unfavorable result of the late movement. But although affairs looked gloomy for awhile, yet did the troops soon regain their old-time lively spirits,—for the Boys in Blue couldn't mope long,—and, as the days passed by, were preparing themselves for another move on the enemy's lines, including drill and reviews, with the usual picket duty when their turn came—often miles away.

Soon after returning from the field, Gen. Hooker issued the following congratulatory address to the troops, which as a recognition of their services at the front was acceptable, but it had little effect in changing their views of the late campaign. For, between Fredericksburg and Chancellorsville they had little to praise. It was all hard knocks for them, piling up losses, with the Union cause so much the worse for it—through no fault of the soldiers. In fact, but for their patriotic spirit, demoralization must have followed. But they had no thought of giving up; all they wanted was to be led to victory—reverses had come too often.

General Orders. HEADQUARTERS ARMY OF THE POTOMAC,

No. 49.CAMP NEAR FALMOUTH, VA., May 6, 1863.

The major-general commanding tenders to this army his congratulations on the achievements of the last seven days. If it has not accomplished all that was expected, the reasons are well known to the army. It is sufficient to say that they were of a character not to be foreseen or prevented by human sagacity or resource. In withdrawing from the south bank of the Rappahannock before delivering a general battle to our adversaries, the army has given renewed evidence of its confidence in itself and its fidelity to the principles it represents. In fighting at a disadvantage, we would have been recreant to our trust, to ourselves, our cause, and our country. Profoundly loyal, and conscious of its strength, the Army of the Potomac will give or decline battle whenever its interest or honor may demand. It will also be the guardian of its own history and its own fame. By our celerity and secrecy of movement, our advance and passage of the rivers were undisputed, and on our withdrawal not a rebel ventured to follow. The events of the last week may well swell with pride the heart of every officer and soldier of this army. We have added new luster to its former renown. We have made long marches, crossed rivers, surprised the enemy in his intrenchments, and whenever we have fought have inflicted heavier blows than we have received. We have taken from the enemy 5,000 prisoners; captured and brought off seven pieces of artillery, fifteen colors; placed *hors de combat* 18,000 of his chosen troops; destroyed his depots filled with vast amounts of stores; deranged his communications; captured prisoners within the fortifications of his capitol, and filled his country with fear and consternation. We have no other regret than that caused by the loss of our brave companions, and in this we are consoled by the conviction that they have fallen in the holiest cause ever submitted to the arbitrament of battle.

By command of Major-Gen. Hooker.

S. WILLIAMS, Asst. Adjt.-Gen,

It soon became evident they were not to remain in camp long, and expected to march forth much sooner than they did. In the meantime, Gen. Hooker was kept busy, as the enemy were known to be moving away from Fredericksburg, although a force still remained there, well-fortified on the hills and capable of making a stout fight if attacked, as was ascertained by troops from the 6th corps, which had crossed over, below town, early in June. In course of time, assured by his scouts—particularly through Pleasanton's cavalry, who had successfully engaged the enemy's cavalry at several points, capturing some prisoners—that Lee was on the march up river, concentrating at Culpeper with the bulk of his troops, Gen. Hooker says:

"Learning that the enemy had massed his cavalry near Culpeper for the purpose of a raid, I dispatched Gen. Pleasanton to attack him on his own ground. Gen. Pleasanton crossed the Rappahannock June 9th at Beverly and Kelly's Fords, attacked the enemy, and drove him three miles, capturing over 200 prisoners and one battle-flag. This in the face of vastly superior numbers, was only accomplished by hard and desperate fighting by our cavalry, for which they deserve much credit. Their *morale* is splendid. They made many hand-to-hand combats, always driving the enemy before them."

He was now anxious to make a dash on the Fredericksburg column, cut it off, and advance rapidly on Richmond. But to this plan the authorities at Washington objected, as Lee was evidently working northward through the Shenandoah region, menacing Washington again. In a telegram to Hooker on the subject, President Lincoln said:

"In case you find Lee coming to the north of the Rappahannock, I would by no means cross to the south of it. If he should leave a rear force at Fredericksburg, tempting you to fall upon it, it would fight in intrenchments and have you at disadvantage, and so, man for man, worst you at that point, while his main force would in some way be getting an advantage of you northward. In one word, I would not take any risk of being entangled upon the river, like an ox jumped half over a fence and liable to be torn by dogs front and rear, without a fair chance to gore one way or kick the other."

Another time he telegraphed: "If left to me, I would not go south of Rappahannock upon Lee's moving north of it. If you had Richmond invested to-day, you would not be able to take it in 20 days; meanwhile your communications, and with them your army, would be ruined. I think Lee's army, and not Richmond, is your sure objective point. If he comes towards the Upper Potomac, follow on his flank and on his inside track, shortening your lines while he lengthens his. Fight him, too, when opportunity offers. If he stays where he is, fret him and fret him."

There was evidently "music in the air"—grim-visaged music—and the soldiers were quick to realize it. The quiet of the camp was not to last long. Nor did they have long to wait when the month of June came, especially after orders came to send the sick and disabled away. None were wanted who were not fully able to march; such ones, unfit for duty, were sent to the Potomac Creek hospital, where a large number of sick and wounded were being cared for, to be removed north by train to steamer on the 14th, the army having mostly left.

SIXTH CAMPAIGN.

THE PENNSYLVANIA INVASION.

On the 11th of June, participating in the general movement of the army, the Sharpshooters broke camp, having been under marching orders several days. The two regiments were now assigned to Ward's 2d brigade of Birney's 1st division of the 3d corps; the 3d division having been consolidated with the 1st and 2d. Moving northward, for miles could their lines be traced by the clouds of dust that enveloped them, many to meet a soldier's death—face to the front. On the 12th, after marching 25 miles, they bivouacked for a day, Company A being detailed for outpost duty, watching the enemy who appeared in force on the left bank of the Rappahannock. Thence pressing hurriedly on via Catlett's Station, they reached the dry and parched plains of Manassas on or about the 15th, suffering greatly from the effects of the sun's heat, causing at times sunstroke and debilitation. It was reported that more than 200 members of the 3d corps were suns truck. Water being scarce, also added to their troubles; for while on a hot march it could be drank too freely to their injury, yet was it a great and necessary relief, when used in moderation. By the time they halted near Fairfax and Centreville, the troops were in need of rest after their hurried and exhaustive march. About this time, June 17th, Pleasanton's cavalry had another brush with the enemy, at Aldie, of which that good general reported:

"I have driven Fitzhugh Lee's cavalry from this place, and they are going off in the direction of Snicker's Gap; nine commissioned officers and 54 privates have been captured in a charge, and their killed and wounded is very large. They also lost heavily in horses and arms. They opened four guns. I had only Gregg's division up at the time, and Kilpatrick's brigade did the fighting. Among the prisoners taken was a company of sharpshooters, which accompany each brigade of their cavalry. These men are thrown out as skirmishers, to pick off our officers."

For several days thereafter, our cavalry were kept busy fighting and driving those of the enemy near Middleburg and Upperville, inflicting considerable loss, suffering also themselves; in which attacks they were assisted by Barnes' division of the 5th corps. Our cavalry fought bravely, making some important captures. Gen. Hooker was proud of them, taking great pains to make efficient this important arm of the service, as he also did with all others. He was a grand officer in this respect. He loved good soldiers, and believed he had them. The most important feature of these dashes, was to discover if possible where Lee was. Our troops had been hurrying north under the supposition that the enemy were doing the same, but whether to repeat the experiment of offering battle east of the Blue Ridge and close to Washington, or to cross the Upper Potomac as in the Maryland campaign, and raid the northern states, was what Gen. Hooker was endeavoring to find out. Gen. Pleasanton, however, assured him that "no rebel infantry was this side of the Blue Ridge; "also that their camps "two miles long" had been seen on the Shenandoah. So that it soon became apparent that a bold invasion on free soil was their purpose, and he at once prepared to meet it.

The army was again put in motion, the different corps being pushed forward to different points from time to time—gradually feeling his way.

The 3d corps moving on the 9th to Gum Spring, rested in that vicinity until the 25th, when they marched to Edward's Ferry that day,—said to be over 30 miles,—where they forded the Potomac, crossing into Maryland near the mouth of the Monocacy. Then proceeding via Point of Rocks on the 26th, they marched to Middletown the next day. On the 28th they crossed the Catoctin mountain range at Turner's Gap, halting near Woodsborough. On this day Gen. Hooker surprised the army by resigning his command, and Gen. Meade was appointed by the President to take his place. Hooker was dissatisfied with the refusal of the general-in-chief at Washington, to allow him to control certain bodies of troops, particularly to abandon Harper's Ferry and reinforce the army with the troops in that locality, about 10,000 in number. He had visited that post and concluded—as others had before and after—that it was a useless appendage to the military situation, That Lee's army could go back and forth without regard to it, and if they wished could easily capture the place, as they did before. Therefore when met with a decided refusal to call off those troops, he sent in his resignation, which was immediately accepted. Here is what he said to Halleck, dated June 27, 1863:

"I have received your telegram in regard to Harper's Ferry. I find 10,000 men here, in condition to take the field. Here they are of no earthly account. They cannot defend a ford of the river, and, as far as Harper's Ferry is concerned, there is nothing of it. As for the fortifications, the work of the troops, they remain when the troops are withdrawn. No enemy will ever take possession of them for them. This is my opinion. All the public property could have been secured to-night, and the troops marched to where they could have been of some service. Now they are but a bait for the rebels, should they return."

This was followed by another dispatch—his resignation:

"My original instructions require me to cover Harper's Ferry and Washington. I have now imposed upon me, in addition, an enemy in my front of more than my number. I beg to be understood, respectfully, but firmly, that I am unable to comply with this condition with the means at my disposal, and earnestly request that I may at once be relieved from the position I occupy."

Notwithstanding Halleck wouldn't let Hooker have his own way about Harper's Ferry, he gave Meade full authority to use his own judgment in the matter, and to act accordingly. The appointment of Gen. Meade was a surprise both to himself and to the army. For the soldiers at that time would hardly have chosen him in preference to Slocum, Hancock, Sickles or Reynolds. But they became better acquainted before the war closed, as Gen. Meade proved to be the last commander of the Army of the Potomac.

On the 29th after a march of some 20 miles, the 3d corps reached Taneytown, and on the following day they camped overnight at Bridgeport near Emmitsburg. The next morning heavy firing was heard at a distance-10 miles away—beyond the Maryland border, warning them that the enemy had been found, that a battle was in progress, and that afternoon they pushed towards it on a forced march, often at double-quick, over a horribly muddy and tiresome road, difficult to travel—away into Pennsylvania.

GETTYSBURG.

FIRST DAY.

The battle of Gettysburg opened unexpectedly at half past nine in the morning of July 1st, by the advance of Heth's division of the enemy along the Cashtown road, northwest of town, where our cavalry under Buford met them and stubbornly resisted their progress, throwing their advance in confusion, holding the force in check until our infantry could get up, yet some three miles distant. The cavalry were dismounted and used as infantry, thus deceiving the enemy, while our batteries were managed with great effect. Gallantly did they maintain the unequal contest against the accumulating lines now hurrying forward, almost enveloping them. Gen. Reynolds commanding the right wing consisting of the 1st, 3d and 11th corps, on hearing the firing hurried ahead of his troops and quickly taking in the situation, urgently appealed to the hard-pressed cavalry to hold on a short time longer, until the infantry which were hurrying on, arrived; when he proceeded to make dispositions for them—directing their course and placing them in position—and while so engaged, to the great loss to his country, and sorrow of the entire army, this grand officer in less than 30 minutes after his appearance at the front, was killed by a shot through his head. Thus fell one of the noblest spirits engaged in the Union cause, whose ability to command placed him among the foremost in the army. The Wisconsin company of Sharpshooters and the Michigan Company C had additional reason to regret his fall, for it was as before said this general, while we were serving with his command at Mechanicsville, who saved these companies from capture if not destruction, by personally coming to them to the front and warning them to immediately retire. From his position in the rear, as his brigade was moving away, discovering the isolated position of the Sharpshooters and Bucktails, without hesitation, his staff being gone, he rode forward and saved them—taking all personal risks to save his troops. 'What more unselfish spirit than his, could be found? And it was where he might have been expected to be killed—on the front line.

The advance of the 1st corps, Gen. Wadsworth's division, came running up at ten o'clock. Cutler's brigade leading, hurried over the fields, going in on the Cashtown road with the 2d Maine battery on their right, three-fourths of a mile northwest from town, where warm work was in store for them—the enemy close up and the fighting desperate.

While this was going on, the Iron Brigade (Meredith's) the 2d Wisconsin leading, immediately formed in line of battle to the left of Cutler's force, and in front of the cavalry which had fallen back to their artillery west of town. Advancing over the open field a short distance to a rise of ground, they met with a terrible reception, the enemy (Heth's division of Hill's corps) pouring in a deadly volley at short range, cutting down the regiment to a fearful extent, killing and wounding 30 per cent., among them Lieut.-Col. George H. Stevens, who was shot in the groin and mortally wounded. Changing direction, the regiment moved rapidly into a piece of woods to the right, where they met a strong force sending into them the bullets thick and rapid—leaden bees humming by. With the men falling at every step, they pressed forward with death-scorning valor and, gallantly charging, the rebel lines were broken by the Black Hats, who captured a large number of prisoners including their commander, Gen. Archer. The 7th Wisconsin, 24th Michigan and 19th 'Indiana having come up on their left, assisted in this charge, and between them 1,000 prisoners were taken. In the meantime Col. Fairchild lost an arm, when the command of the. 2d devolved upon Major John Mansfield.

Cutler's brigade meanwhile was severely engaged on the Cashtown road. It was at this point that Gen. Reynolds fell. Now, owing to the approach of -two lines of battle in their front, lapping their right flank, they were obliged to fall back to the woods on the ridge behind them. The battery and the 147th New York falling back later, were badly cut up, the 147th losing 207 out of 380, during the space of 30 minutes; while the artillery being left for a time unsupported, the commander, Capt. Hall, after using his canister with good effect on the charging column, retired his battery by sections; one gun having four horses shot was drawn off by hand, and another piece left behind was afterwards recovered. At this critical moment the 6th Wisconsin, which had been held in reserve, was ordered to the right to repulse the attempt of the enemy to get in rear of our troops, and successfully did so in a desperate charge in conjunction with the 14th Brooklyn and 95th New York, where they captured in a railroad cut the 2d Mississippi in the face of a destructive fire. In this charge, the 6th lost 160 men—a startling example of the character of the fighting that day. More hard fighting ensued, in which the 1st division was alone engaged for nearly two hours before the balance of the corps came up and got into line.

Rowley's division (3d) was divided, Biddle's brigade taking the extreme left, facing open ground and grain fields, with a piece of woods opposite, 1,000 -yards off, held by rebel infantry. Remaining in position about three hours exposed to artillery fire and that of a skirmish line in their front, they were severely attacked by a division in line coming from the woods directly on to them. They held their ground for upwards of an hour, when flanked on the left along with the heavy fire in front, were obliged to give way.

Coming out of this contest with less than 390 out of 1,287 engaged, shows how well they sustained their part. Two companies of skirmishers from the 20th New York militia, which had been sent out in the morning to some buildings 200 yards in front to contend with the rebel sharpshooters, which they held several hours, fighting hard, until almost surrounded by the advancing forces, with the buildings on fire, narrowly escaped capture but succeeded in getting away.

Stone's Pennsylvania brigade was sent into an opening between Meredith and Cutler upon the low ridge in front of Seminary Ridge, enacting a most important part thereafter, repeatedly repulsing the enemy and holding their position until the whole line retired. In this sharp contest Col. Stone was wounded, as also Col. Wister who succeeded him in command. Roy Stone was complimented by officers and men for the intrepid and skillful manner in which he handled his brigade on the most trying occasions, changing their formations under the hottest fire to meet emergencies. His ability was unquestioned—a feature that was early developed in the war, when in command of the Bucktails on the Seven Days.

No language can do justice to the conduct of my officers and men on the bloody "first day;" to the coolness with which they watched and awaited, under a fierce storm of shot and shell, the approach of the enemy's overwhelming masses; their ready obedience to orders, and the prompt and perfect execution, under fire, of all the tactics of the battle field; to the fierceness of their repeated attacks, or to the desperate tenacity of their resistance. They fought as if each man felt that upon his own arm hung the fate of the day and the nation. Every field officer save one was wounded and disabled. Col. Wister, while commanding the brigade, though badly wounded in the mouth and unable to speak, remained in the front of the battle, as did also Lieut.-Col. Huidekoper, commanding 150th, with his right arm shattered and a wound in the leg; and Lieut.-Col. Dwight, commanding 149th, with a dangerous gun-shot wound through the thigh.—ROY STONE.

The 2d division (Robinson's) was also separated for a time, the 1st brigade being held in reserve near the seminary, building barricades; Baxter's (2d) brigade advancing almost immediately to the right of the 1st division, with a wide gap between them and the 11th corps men who had come into action still farther to the right, with cavalry on the flank. Later on, the 1st brigade was brought up and went in. Before this, Baxter's troops were twice flanked in their exposed position, making several changes to meet the attack, repulsing the enemy each time; finally making a determined charge, capturing many of the Johnnies with three of their flags; when after two hours' hard fighting, suffering much, getting short of cartridges, this brigade was withdrawn and supported a battery. The division was engaged more or less at this point, four hours.

No soldiers ever fought better, or inflicted severer blows upon the enemy. When out of ammunition, their boxes were replenished from those of their killed and wounded Comrades.—GEN. ROBINSON.

Gen. Paul, in command of the 1st brigade, was shot down severely wounded, as were the three colonels succeeding him: Leonard (13th Mass.), Root (94th N. Y.), and Coulter (11th Penn.) This division lost 1,543 enlisted men and 124 officers, out of a total of less than 2,500. This command, with many others that day, suffered greatly while falling back beyond Gettysburg, from both artillery and musketry. For nearly four hours did a portion of the 1st corps hold the field before the 11th arrived; two divisions of which finally joined the 1st on the right, the Confederates in their front being the forces of Gen. Ewell—the left wing of the rebel army.

The 1st and 3d divisions of the 11th corps under command of Gen. Schurz, got into position about two P. M. north of town, a considerable distance away from the 1st corps line, the 1st division being on the right. This latter division under Gen. Barlow having advanced their line, was subjected to severe cannonading, while a heavy force of infantry came down on to them out of the woods in, a long line of battle overlapping the extreme right, doubling it up in bad shape, causing the men to break away. At this time the accomplished Gen. Barlow went down 'mid a "shower of shells" seriously wounded, and was succeeded in command by Gen. Ames. There were too many intervals on this part of the field, the enemy rushing into them to our ultimate discomfit. We hadn't troops enough to go around the lengthy semi-circle, they had too many for a fair fight. Their artillery was continually at work bursting shells among our troops with more or less serious effect. According to Gen. Schurz, two of these batteries on a hillside opposite the 3d division opened on them fiercely, at the same time enfilading the 1st corps. Dilger's battery (I, 1st Ohio) dismounted four of their guns, scattering two rebel regiments below the hill. Capt. Dilger lost during the day 14 men and 24 horses. The loss of the 11th corps has been estimated at 3,000, many of whom were taken prisoners; some of the regiments were badly cut up. Being finally outflanked, about four o'clock the corps was ordered by Gen. Howard, who arrived at

Gettysburg in the forenoon and assumed command on hearing of the fall of Reynolds, to retire from their advanced position to a new line he had established south of town, on another conspicuous height called Cemetery Hill.

The 3d division had meanwhile to sustain a furious attack. According to orders it fell back towards the town in good order, contesting the ground step by step with the greatest firmness. In this part of the action, which was almost a hand-to-hand struggle, officers and men showed the highest courage and determination. Our loss was extremely heavy. The 2d brigade, 3d division, lost all its regimental commanders; several regiments nearly half their number in killed and wounded. Being flanked right and left, the situation of that division was most trying.—CARL SCHURZ.

Capt. Heckman's battery (K, 1st Ohio) had a short but hard experience, having gone forward at the last moment east of town to check the enemy while the corps was coming out, and was almost immediately confronting a sharp attack which he resisted for a half hour, sending into their ranks 113 rounds of canister, when the yelling foes rushed through the dense smoke on to his guns, despite his rapid discharges; in the confusion ensuing he succeeded in getting away with the loss of one gun, 13 men and nine horses.

That portion of the 11th corps posted beyond the almshouse had fought with great obstinacy until its right flank was turned by Early's division, and further reinforcements had been hopeless. It then fell back to the town, and choked up the main street at the very time Paul's brigade was attempting to pass. This resulted in heavy loss to the brigade. -GEN. DOUBLEDAY, commanding 1st corps.

On the left, the line had previously been ordered back to Seminary Ridge where a stand was made. The 2d Wisconsin in retiring, turned once upon the enemy and became nearly flanked by them on their left, their sanguine opponents rushing up in overwhelming numbers. Occupying the new line at the ridge another hard contest ensued, the enemy crowding in close. Major Mansfield was now wounded in the knee, and obliged to leave the field, Capt. Otis assuming command of the regiment. Biddle's and Meredith's brigades, aided by Cooper's 1st Pennsylvania and Stevens' 5th Maine batteries, held the ridge until the last possible moment, covering the retirement of the rest of the 1st corps. At this point a South Carolina brigade lost 500 in the assault, the 1st and 14th rebel regiments from that state losing more than half their number.

The shattered remnants of the Iron Brigade also fell into line. From behind the feeble barricade of rails these brave men stemmed the fierce tide which pressed upon them incessantly, and held the rebel lines, which encircled them on three sides, at bay until a greater portion of the corps had retired. Capt. Holton Richardson, acting assistant inspector-general, of Meredith's staff, rode up and down the lines, waving a regimental flag, encouraging the men to do their duty. The troops, with the assistance of a part of Stewart's battery, under Lieut. Davison, poured in so deadly a fire as to wholly break up and double the first line of the enemy approaching from the west; but the other lines pressed on, and soon commenced a flank attack, which it was no longer possible to answer. When all the troops at this point were overpowered, Capt. Glenn (149th Penn.) in command of my headquarter guard, defended the building for fully 20 minutes against a whole brigade of the enemy, enabling the few remaining troops, the ambulances, artillery, etc., to retreat in comparative safety. The batteries had all been brought back from their advanced position and posted on Seminary Hill. They greatly assisted the orderly retreat, retarding the enemy by their fire. They lost heavily in men and horses at this point, and, as they retired to the town, were subjected to so heavy a fire that the last gun was left, the horses being all shot down by the enemy's skirmishers, who had formed line within 50 yards of the road by which the artillery was obliged to pass.—DOUBLEDAY.

Col. Wainwright, commanding the brigade artillery of the 1st corps, claimed a loss of 80 officers and men and 80 horses during the day, a large proportion of the latter shot while falling back from Seminary Ridge to Gettysburg. The infantry also suffered considerably in their movement towards town, particularly so the 7th Wisconsin which, brought up the rear. Col. Robinson says: "It was here I met with the heaviest losses from the regiment during the day." Col. Robinson assumed command of the Iron Brigade after their arrival at the cemetery by order of Gen. Wadsworth, occasioned by Gen. Meredith having "sustained severe injuries by the fall of his wounded horse." This officer did not return to the brigade.

Surely the people of Gettysburg that day had an opportunity to learn something about war. A great battle had unexpectedly surrounded them in their peaceful homes, even to their very doors, and on all sides could be heard the noise and fury of mortal strife. The burning houses, the shattered trees and splintered fences—limbs and rails flying about—horses and cattle wild with fright, the people distracted; such was the effect of this sudden, unwelcome rebel visitation. The excitement was up to the highest possible pitch; born of hope in the morning when they saw their defenders go forth, with the cheers of the populace and their prayers following them; full of dread and despair in the evening when the invader came to make them prisoners. If ever a town was "painted red" it was Gettysburg— the dead and wounded lying about the streets, in houses, gardens and fields. A gory picture of patriotic valor. The falling back of the 1st and 11th corps through the town occasioned the greatest excitement and confusion, and proved a dangerous undertaking; the troops becoming mixed up, crowding through, eventually got to their proper commands after leaving the place. The enemy entered the town as the last of our men were leaving it, thus adding to the terror of the affrighted citizens. The bustle and hurry of our soldiers, the firing, of shots by the rebels, the din and confusion, the smoking muskets, the yelling Johnnies, the shouting Yanks, and the general uproar; all served to make the 1st of July a day the oldest inhabitants would never forget, and future generations will ever refer to.

A considerable number of our soldiers were captured in town and a good many killed, particularly among the troops covering the rear. Among these was the 45th New York of the 11th corps. Col. Dobke thus describes the awful scene:

"In a short time all sorts of missiles found their way through houses, fences, and gardens, and it was evident that to stay much longer would be certain destruction, so the regiment was ordered to follow the column which had passed, when, marching a few blocks, suddenly a few regiments of the 1st corps were thrown in the way, and our regiment headed to the left to gain the other main streets. When about the middle of the square, a sudden panic arose in a column on the street we were to gain, throwing themselves in our column and into the houses. Not to become mixed up, the 45th turned again to the street just left, marched two squares down, and turned again to the left for the before mentioned roads. About the middle of the block our column was received by the enemy's infantry fire, when the column headed into an alley leading to the direction we had to follow. Unfortunately this alley led into a spacious yard surrounded by large buildings, which only offered an entrance but no way to pass out, excepting a very narrow doorway, to freedom and to heaven; but the enemy's sharpshooters had already piled a barricade of dead Union soldiers in the street in 'front of this doorway. About 100 of the 45th extricated themselves from this trap, ran the gauntlet, and arrived safely at the graveyard. The remainder were taken prisoners, as meanwhile the whole town was surrendered and the enemy in possession of Gettysburg. Only one-third of the equipped men of the 45th assembled at the cemetery behind the stone fence, and two-thirds of the regiment were lost."

Capt. James D. Wood, assistant adjutant-general on Meredith's staff, was the last man on horseback to pass through the town, after making every effort to keep the ranks closed up in the different columns, to prevent confusion. On getting away himself, while in the open field, his horse was killed under him, receiving six distinct wounds.

Capt. Wood also performed important service at the front during the day, in his position as aid to Gen. Meredith and Cpl. Robinson.

The losses in the Iron Brigade in this day's fight were of the most serious character, suffering severely in officers and men. In the 2d Wisconsin all the field officers were shot, with 14 of the line among the killed, wounded and missing.. Out of a total of 302 engaged, their loss was 233, or 75 per cent., leaving 69 for duty. In the 24th

Michigan the three field officers were also badly wounded, one staff and 18 line officers among the killed and wounded, and three taken prisoners; while 294 enlisted men fell, with a number missing—or 363 out of a total of 496. The 19th Indiana lost 210 out of 288, leaving 78 for duty. The loss of the 7th Wisconsin was 178. The total loss of this brigade during the entire battle, principally on the first day—their casualties thereafter being very few—was 1,153; and with the other brigades of Wadsworth's 1st division 2,155; Robin-son's 2d division 1,690; Rowley's 3d division 2,103; artillery 106; making a total including staff and cavalry of 6,059. Of 8,200 in action July 1st, the 1st corps was reduced to 2,450—a net loss of 5,750.

Gen. Doubleday in his report of this day's fight, says: "The 2d Wisconsin in this contest, under the gallant Col. Fairchild, was particularly distinguished. It accomplished the difficult task of driving superior numbers of rebel infantry from the shelter of the woods, and to it also belongs the honor of capturing Gen. Archer himself. He was brought in by Patrick Maloney, of Company G. It is to be lamented that this brave Irishman was subsequently killed in the action."

But for this worthy feat of Private Maloney capturing the rebel general, it would never have been known in public history that he was killed in the battle, as but few enlisted men were ever mentioned. One brave act oft gives wide reputation.

Gen. Doubleday also tells about John Burns, an aged citizen of Gettysburg, over 70 years, who shouldering a musket offered his services to Col. Wister (150th Penn.) who advised him to fight in the woods where there was more shelter, but the game old patriot preferred the skirmish line in the open field. He afterwards fought with the Iron Brigade and was wounded three times.

> He was the fellow who won renown,—
> The only man who didn't back down
> When the rebels rode through his native town.
>
> He wore a broad-brimmed, bell-crowned hat,

White as the locks on which it sat.

Close at his elbows all that day, Veterans of the Peninsula,
Sunburnt and bearded, charged away.

While Burns, unmindful of jeer and scoff,
Stood there picking the rebels off,—
With his long brown rifle, and bell-crowned hat.

And some of the soldiers since declare
That the gleam of his old white hat afar,
Like the crested plume of the brave Navarre,
That day was their oriflamme of war.

Col. Morrow (24th Mich.) wounded and taken prisoner says : "During the time I was a prisoner I conversed freely with distinguished rebel officers in relation to the battle on the 1st inst. and, without exception, they spoke in terms of admiration of the conduct of our troops, and especially of that of the troops composing the 1st army corps. One of them informed me that Lieut. -Gen. A. P Hill said that he had never known the Federals to fight so well." And from a major on Gen. Hill's staff he was informed that, "the rebel army present at Gettysburg was about 90,000 strong, and that their line of battle was estimated to be eight miles long. The death of Major-Gen. Reynolds was well known to the enemy, and the highest opinions of his skill and bravery were freely expressed."

The first day's fight Was one of the hardest of the war for the number engaged on our side; the 1st corps going in with 8,000 muskets, which from the first onset Were constantly decreasing, so that probably at least one-third that number were lost in action by the time the two corps came together; while the two divisions of the 11th with only about 6,000, made in all at no time probably over 12,000 (if that many) on our side, contending in the battle. But one brigade of the 2d div. 11th A. C. which was in reserve at Cemetery

Hill, came into action, and that only at the last moment in support of the artillery, holding the enemy for a short time while Barlow's division was coming off the field. On the other' side, the Confederates were constantly bringing forward accumulating troops, at all times more than double our force. Gen. Doubleday again:

"When that part of the 11th corps adjacent to us fell back, a force of 30,000 men were thrown upon the 1st corps."

When the troops commenced falling back, Gen. Buford hurried a cavalry brigade over to the left, to check the enemy's pursuit, and dismounting them, they made rapid and effective use of their carbines, completely breaking up the enemy's front line. No cavalry troops ever fought better than did those of Gen. John Buford, and to their honor and everlasting glory be it said, by their bold and unflinching resistance to the rebel advance during that eventful morning assisted by Tidball's U. S. battery, prevented the seizing of Cemetery Ridge and its prolongations before our infantry came up; which eventually resulted in the glorious victory that has made Gettysburg famous among the greatest battles of the world. After the infantry came to their relief, many of the cavalrymen dismounting, rushing in with their carbines, fought with the greatest gallantry. The entire action from the time the cavalry first started in, lasted about 10 hours—an all-day fight. The battle had been precipitated by our cavalry running into their infantry, and was continued by our infantry against overwhelming odds, until ordered to retire.

It was not expected by Meade to have a battle there, but rather farther' o the east on ground he had hoped to occupy, before Lee came up. It was too late, however; the die was cast, the success or failure of the rebel movement was to be decided on the field of Gettysburg, and he probably could not have found a better place to settle it.

This preliminary battle had the most important bearing on the results of the next two days, as it enabled the whole army to come up and reinforce the admirable position to which we had retreated. Had we retired earlier in the day, without co-operation with the other parts of the army, the enemy by a vigorous pursuit might have penetrated between the corps of Sickles and Slocum, and have either crushed them in detail or flung them off in eccentric directions.

There were abundant reasons for holding Gettysburg, for it is the junction of seven great roads leading to Hagerstown, Chambersburg, Carlisle, York, Baltimore, Taneytown, and Washington, and is also an important railway terminus. The places above mentioned are on the circumference of a circle of which it is the center. It was therefore a strategic point of no ordinary importance.

There never was an occasion in which the result could have been more momentous upon our national destiny. -DOUBLEDAY.

Such a disastrous result must have followed its abandonment, had this engagement not been persisted in; although, notwithstanding its importance relative to the final outcome, coupled with the desperate character of the contest, it has been over-shadowed by the still greater achievements of the united army.

Late in the afternoon Gen. Hancock arrived, ordered forward by Gen. Meade to assume command of that wing of the army, on learning of Reynold's death. Hancock at once proceeded to establish his battle line, in connection with what had already been done by Howard, along the northern edge of Cemetery Hill and its prolongation easterly, thence curving to the south and rear to a point called Culp's Hill. The enemy approaching from the east side of town towards the Baltimore pike, Wadsworth's division of the 1st corps with the 5th Maine battery were sent to the eastern extremity of the ridge, a wooded sloping height, from the crest of which they checked the rebel advance, remaining at this point during the remainder of the struggle; the balance of the 1st corps being with the 11th on the hill just south of Gettysburg. Meantime, the first division of the 12th corps, arriving, was placed to the right on Culp's Hill in rear of Wadsworth, fronting Rock Creek close by; while the 2d division under Geary, coming up later was posted temporarily by Hancock further south near Little Round Top.

From this time until morning, other troops were hurrying in; the 3d corps arriving about dark on the 1st, resting for the night behind the lesser Round Top—the 3d brigade left at Emmitsburg, coming up next morning. So that soon after daylight of the 2d, Meade's line of battle was formed with the right fronting Gettysburg, prolonged to Culp's Hill, his left extending southerly to the Big and Little Round Tops, a distance of three miles, which was occupied by the different corps in order following: The 12th corps on the extreme right (Geary's division having joined), 1st corps extending to the eastern spur of Cemetery Hill, 11th corps opposite Gettysburg; thence extending along the crest of the rock-ribbed ridges which gradually fell away until they approached the rising Round Tops, were the long lines of the 2d and 3d corps; and later on, in the afternoon, the 5th corps relieved by the 6th in reserve, occupied the extreme left.

The enemy were posted on an opposite range of hills extending from Seminary Ridge south; at a distance of a half-mile on the right, varying to a mile and a half towards the left—the armies facing each other east and west. The frowning heights on either side were crowded with cannon, although in many places owing to the rough nature of the hills, the Union artillery could not get in position. Between these embattled ridges were wooded groves, and a number of cleared farms, fields of grain, orchards and gardens—destined to be soon laid waste by the tramping of troops and the hurtling implements of death and destruction.

An instance of the general feeling existing among our soldiers on meeting the enemy on northern soil is given: John W. Coates, formerly first sergeant of Company B, transferred to Company I with same rank, and afterwards promoted to second and first lieutenant of the latter company, took an important part in the battle, he being a thorough fighter. During the night of the 1st of July he was complimented by Col. Berdan, for his encouraging remarks to his company after their arrival on the field, when he said, speaking of the enemy: "Boys, we have got them on our own ground now, let us give them a good lesson."

SECOND DAY.

During the fore part of the day, our troops occupied the time strengthening their respective positions, particularly at the weaker points; barricades being erected in some places, and all possible defensive arrangements made for a warm reception of the enemy should they deign to attack. In the meantime skirmishing was going on in front, with the artillery feeling the positions to and fro.

The 3d corps went into line early in the -morning, Gen. Birney's division on the left, resting at Little Round Top, relieving Geary's command posted there overnight; Gen. Humphreys' 2d division to the right, connecting with the 2d corps. At a distance of about a mile in front, the Emmitsburg road ran along the crest of a ridge sloping easterly to our lines, and westerly towards the enemy concealed in the woods beyond. Six companies of Sharpshooters (A, B, C, G, H and K) were deployed in skirmish line about eight o'clock in detached positions afar out, under Capt. Marble, Winthrop and Baker; Capt. John Wilson being detailed acting major or field officer, relative to whom Lieut.-Col. Trepp reported: "The regiment was posted with instructions to protect the left flank of the 3d corps. Soon thereafter the dispositions were changed, and I received an order to send 100 men on a reconnoissance in front of the right of the corps. This detachment I conducted in person, and deployed them. The command was given to Capt. John Wilson, a very efficient officer, and I returned to the regiment."

Companies B and G, under the immediate command of Capt. Marble, were together in an open field behind a fence, 200 yards in advance of the Emmitsburg road in the vicinity of the Rodger House, with the 1st Massachusetts on their right, and Company C on their left, at the brick house, where they all soon became engaged, the firing being kept up without intermission until the middle of the afternoon when the action became general, on this part of the line. As our scattered force was too small to hazard the attempt to skirmish the front, on that part of the field—exposed to the destructive fire of evidently overwhelming numbers—Col. Berdan reported to Gen. Birney his inability to discover what force the enemy had ahead of us; stating to both Birney and Sickles his belief that they were concentrating behind the woods for a demonstration on our extreme left—to attack our corps on the flank—and suggested a reconnoissance. Gen. Hunt, chief of artillery, being present, was of the same opinion, and thought the Sharpshooters should be sent over there, to find out what they were doing. They were too suspiciously quiet, and evidently bent on mischief. Whereupon about noon Gen. Birney, after further consultation with Gen. Sickles, ordered the colonel to take a detachment of 100 Sharpshooters, with the 3d Maine (200 muskets) as a support, to the extreme left, to reconnoiter the enemy's right, and discover if possible his movements. Capt. Briscoe of Birney's staff, an excellent officer, was sent out with the reconnoissance, also Capt. Nash, of Company K, (mounted) who rendered valuable assistance, Col. Berdan being in command of the entire force.

PITZER'S RUN.

Moving down the Emmitsburg road beyond the Union lines, the Sharpshooters deployed through a peach orchard northwesterly, past some farm buildings towards a piece of woods through which they were to skirmish. Here they met a small boy who warned them of the vicinity of the rebels. To quote from Comrade Buchanan, referred to later: "As we approached these buildings a lad then living there, who had just returned from an errand to a neighbor's close by, seeing our handful of men about to attack a large force of rebels concealed here, whom he had seen but a little while before as he was returning to his father's house, remarked almost with a sneer, in the hearing of several of us: 'Look out! there are lots of rebels in there, in rows '—pointing towards the woods. We ridiculed the boy's remark and discredited his statement, thinking that he knew nothing about war and was talking nonsense. It is now stated that the lad, young as he was, had been at Antietam the year before, witnessed a part of that battle, and was not, consequently, so unsophisticated as we thought him to be.

At any rate, the words were hardly out of his mouth before we advanced rapidly into the woods, and were almost immediately briskly challenged and disputed by the rebel pickets."

They soon struck the enemy's skirmishers, driving them under a telling fire 300 yards, when they suddenly ran on to three columns of infantry, in rear of the woods—on the west slope of Seminary Ridge at or near Pitzer's Run—who were about making a move towards the Union left. It was a trying occasion for our men, but Col. Berdan, riding in front of the line, quickly took in the situation, and knowing that time gained then was everything, dispatched Capt. Briscoe to our generals, Birney and Sickles, a mile away, to warn them of the danger—the threatened assault upon our left. He then ordered his men to "advance firing," when they attacked the enemy on the flank, throwing them into confusion, pushing close up to them and doing great execution with their reliable breech-loaders— catching it hot meanwhile from the volleys received. The 3d Maine now came into line and fought side by side with the Sharpshooters.

By order of Col. Berdan, I advanced double-quick to the line they occupied, and instantly formed my regiment under 'a heavy fire from the enemy.—CoL. M. B. LAKEMAN.

For awhile our boys held their position, stopping one regiment coming up on the right, despite the efforts of their mounted commander who fell wounded from his horse, while his men were unable to rally. For the time it, lasted it was a desperate affair for Berdan's command, confronted as they were by such overpowering forces, our men falling fast; but there was no shirking, each one firing rapidly to ward off as long as possible the inevitable result— retreat or destruction. Under the circumstances it could not last long, as they soon rallied and made a rush for our little band almost surrounding them, attacking them severely, to our loss. The action lasted 20 minutes, when Col. Berdan seeing the hopelessness of the contest withdrew his command, the enemy pursuing a short distance, the 3d Maine giving then a couple of parting volleys as reminders of what their generals termed: "a most audacious and bold venture." They were completely surprised to find so small a force coming so far from our main lines to assault them. But our boys showed their ability, as also their agility, to get away, as well as to advance.

The enemy showed himself in overwhelming force; but so well did we hold our position that his advance was much checked and very disastrous, and not until ordered by Col. Berdan to fall back, did a single man leave the ranks.—Col. LAKEMAN.

Here is another instance of what might have been accomplished had Berdan's two regiments in their original strength been there. For if 300 men firing 10,000 rounds in 20 minutes, could stop the forward movement of 30,000 foes, it is reasonable to suppose that 1,800 Sharps rifles would in all probability have broken them up to that extent, as to have disarranged all their plans for that day and prevented the desperate assault that followed; the chances being that the Sharpshooters in their combined force would have virtually whipped them on their own ground. As it was, Gen. Longstreet afterwards admitted it delayed them 40 minutes; whereas if it had only delayed them 35 minutes, he says his army would not have *been* repulsed.

"That five minutes saved the day for the Army of the Potomac; "and as Little Round Top was only secured by Vincent's brigade not a moment too soon to drive the climbing enemy away, there is not much exaggeration in that statement. "Five minutes" was a good deal then. All the generals who went over the historic field at a meeting of ex-officers and soldiers 23 years after the battle, declared that the spot where Col. Berdan's command attacked Long-street was the turning point of the war. Of course there will always be a dispute on this point among ex-soldier's. The "turning point of the war," and the "high water mark of the rebellion," are high-sounding claims over which there will always be a disagreement, at least among the living participants in this great struggle. But as an impartial historian, at least as much so as it is probably possible for a Sharpshooter to be, after making due allowance for a natural soldierly pride in the gallant deeds of his comrades—they that handled the weapons that did the fighting, the men of active service—I believe there is very much justification in the claim, backed up as it is by the best military authorities, composed of those that were present during the conflict, and whose opinions are here given.

Longstreet especially gives this as his opinion: "If we had got around to Round Top we would have held the key to the situation and could have cut the Union force in two parts, which could not help each other, and then by the force of a sweeping charge we could have won the day."

Gen. Sickles in his Gettysburg oration, testified to the invaluable service rendered the Union cause by the Sharpshooters and their supports, the 3d Maine, in the contest at Pitzer's Run "where Longstreet was massing his tens of thousands, and where Col. Berdan pushing through the curtain of woods, hurled his dauntless little band directly against the force intended to crush in our left flank and seize the Round Tops:" which statement was endorsed by Gen. Hunt, present, on his personal knowledge of the circumstances leading to and following the Sharpshooter movement.

In a subsequent speech, Gen. Sickles said: "In 1886 I met many Confederate officers at Gettysburg, and in conversation with Gen. Longstreet, asked him what his intentions were on that day.

"To take possession of Peach Orchard and the ridge,' was the reply.

"'What prevented your taking that position at once?' "'Your Sharpshooters, who smoked us out of the woods on your flank.'

"When I asked him what would have been the result of his possession of the ridge and peach orchard without resistance, he said the Confederates would have won the battle of Gettysburg. He also said that when he reached the ridge and peach orchard his loss was so great by my defence of that position that even with his reinforcements he was not strong enough to win."

Some years ago, during an exhibition at Boston of a cyclorama of Gettysburg, according to Sergt. Curtis D. Drew, of Company E, the position of Berdan's command was pointed out as saving the day, that: "Berdan's Sharpshooters fought desperately, and if Berdan had 2,000 more men like his Sharpshooters, Longstreet never could have driven him a foot, and when Berdan finally retreated, Longstreet was afraid to follow him up." As the statements made by the cycloramic historian are an important part of the exhibition, comprising the history of the battle, such then must have been the prevailing impression in the Eastern states at least, of the value of the service rendered by the Sharpshooters at Pitzer's Run—and rightly so.

It was a very important affair, and the result awaited with anxiety by our generals. For the timely suggestion to make this reconnoissance, and the gallant manner in which the command attacked and discomfited the enemy, holding them in check sufficiently long to enable Gen. Sickles to anticipate the movement—the capturing of the Round Tops—Col. Berdan is entitled to credit, and his command, Sharpshooters and 3d Maine, to all the renown that can be accorded to the faithful and brave. Later on in the day, Gen: Hancock recognized the importance of this service, as being largely instrumental in defeating the enemy's intentions, while Gen. Birney in his report said:

"Col. Berdan of the Sharpshooters, and Capt. Briscoe of my staff, deserve mention for their services in leading the reconnoissance before the battle, and for the valuable information derived from it."

The heroic deeds of Leonidas and his 300 Spartans, betrayed and slaughtered by the Persian hosts, has for ages been recounted in verse and story. But no greater display of heroism, no more self-sacrificing spirit of patriotism can be cited in the annals of war, than was this courageous attack of Berdan's 300 on the marching columns of 30,000 foes. And surely, it may be fairly said to be a turning point in the Rebellion.

The Sharpshooter companies engaged in this daring attack were D, E, F and I, representing New York, New Hampshire, Vermont and Michigan. The enemy were of Anderson's division of Hill's corps. The position attained where the fight occurred, was the farthest advance of Union troops on the field of Gettysburg.

The loss of the Sharpshooters in this short and sanguinary contest numbered 19; the 3d Maine, 48. But as Col. Lakeman of that regiment has reported that when his men advanced into line, they were at a disadvantage as they had to take the intervals between the trees occupied by the Sharpshooters, it must account for his greater loss, although not so long engaged.

Of the Confederates, Gen. Wilcox commanding the rebel brigade attacked, admitted a loss of 10 killed and 2& wounded in the 10th Alabama; 18 wounded in the 11th Alabama, six or eight severely, including the major (R. J. Fletcher); making a total in these two regiments alone of

56—how many more, might easily be imagined when it is fully understood how our men peppered them in a heap, at close quarters. It is known that 40 of their dead lay in one small space together, and the one rebel grave at this place was afterwards found to be over 100 yards in length. Gen. Wilcox speaks of our small force of 300 guns as "two Federal regiments,"—naturally enough deceived by the immense number of shots fired by the breech-loaders, and the length of time they were engaged.

A spirited musketry fight ensued between the 10th Alabama and these two Federal regiments. Having continued for some 15 or 20 minutes, Col. Forney gave the command to charge and led his regiment in person.—GEN. Willcox, C. S. A.

Col. Herbert of the 8th Alabama, in the fight, wrote Gen. Berdan after the war: "It was a very gallant fight you made that morning. The result was very important to the Union side, showing the presence of Confederates at that point."

Among our casualties we had an accomplished officer killed: Capt. McLean of Co. D. Referring to him 26 years after, Chas. J. Buchanan, in a beautiful oration delivered at this spot, at the dedication of a monument to the Sharpshooters by the Empire State, feelingly said: "Capt. Charles D. McLean of Co. D, was mortally wounded in this encounter, and but a few paces from where we now are. He was one of the best officers in the regiment, and a braver soldier and nobler man never lived. Smith Haight and Edwin E. Nelson of "D" company, both excellent soldiers, were also severely wounded here. Haight lived but a few hours." Died July 2d. Buchanan was at the time, a prominent noncommissioned officer of the company, afterwards rewarded with a lieutenancy. He was person ally known to me to be one of the completest soldiers in our organization, always neat in his appearance, prompt and brave, always ready for duty in every engagement of his company, and always with them from muster-in to muster-out. Capt. McLean was a most worthy commander of such worthy men, and his loss was mourned by them all. He died in the hands of the enemy July 4th.

Peter H. Kipp, of Company D, makes the following statement: "When we received orders to retreat, we had fired on an average to a man, 95 rounds. We had gone but a few steps to the rear when I saw Capt. McLean fall; I called to our orderly-sergeant and to Lieut. Hetherington. They came back with Edwin Nelson; we got a blanket and started to carry our captain off; but Nelson was wounded before we had gone a dozen steps, when Alexander Ferguson took his place at the blanket, but had gone but a few steps when the captain told us to leave him and look out for ourselves or we would all be shot. So we laid him down; after I had got some little distance away, Lieut. Hetherington told me to go back to stay with the captain. When I got back to where he lay, the rebel skirmishers were just passing him, three Johnnies had stopped to look at him. I told them who he was, that I had come back to stay with him. They told me I must go to the rear with them, but when I refused they pricked me with their bayonets drawing blood in three places, then a rebel lieutenant came up and stopped them, telling me he would get an ambulance and take the captain off, that I should stay with him. We started for the rear, and passed through where Longstreet's men had halted. It is impossible for me to describe the slaughter we had made in their ranks. In all my past service, it beat all I had ever seen for the number engaged and for so short a time. They were piled in heaps and across each other. When I got to where the surgeons were dressing the wounded, I found hundreds of wounded men there. The doctor would hardly believe that there were so few of us fighting them, thought we had a corps, as he said he never saw lead so thick in his life as it was in those woods. But when I told him who we were, said that accounted for it, as he claimed "the Sharpshooters were the worst men we have to contend with." Furthermore, I had been a prisoner about a half hour, when Gen. A. P. Hill came up with his whole corps, forming line of battle a little to the right of where we had the fight.

Lewis J. Allen, first sergeant of Company F, on the right of the line, had his rifle-hammer shot away, and as he said, "swapped" with a wounded man hobbling off using his rifle for a crutch. Amid the great noise and smoke, in his efforts to keep up the music on his end of the line, he failed to notice the withdrawal of his comrades until almost left alone, when suddenly realizing his danger, he bid valor sleep for awhile, and broke for the rear. On getting out of the woods when he struck the plowed ground his wind gave out, sharp pains ran through his side, his long legs refused to go faster than a walk, and that with difficulty, owing to sheer exhaustion while running the gauntlet of southern marksmanship, the bullets flying around him, with every moment expecting to be his last. In fact, this lineal descendant of "Ticonderoga Allen" was just about petered out—not unlike a foundered horse—when he reached a farm house and pushing through the gate fell exhausted on the green sward. To use his own words: "The two women of the house came out. The Irish lady, seeing my convulsive clasp on my side and struggle for breath, ejaculated: 'Lord save us, he's shot!' They ran into the house, crying: 'Where's the butcher knife?' and to my horror, she brought a huge knife like a seaman's cutlass, cutting off my belt, knapsack, haversack and canteen. At last I managed to gasp: "Don't cut any more, I'm not shot!' She fiercely turned with: 'Ye blathering divil ye, ye're making all that divil's fuss and not shot? 'I looked up, to see a squad of rebs coming through the gate as I had done, and, making a hasty grab for my traps that lay as the old lady had strewn them about me, I went out of the front gate 'on the fly,' and turning left on the road ran in the direction of Little Round Top, near where I could see the 3d corps headquarters flag, with Gen. Daniel E. Sickles and staff. The rest of our regiment were there near the general. As I joined them, I saw the reb skirmishers coming down the slope towards- Little Round Top. I saw Gen. Berdan report our work to Gen. Sickles, and our troops by brigade and divisions, double-quicking to the line on which the battle was fought from our side."

Eugene Paine, of the same company, one of the original members, had a similar experience. His position as third man from the left, brought him down in a gully, which offered fair protection, from whence he did some rapid firing from a rest, holding his rifle low on the advancing line, coming from the stone wall 200 yards in their front. The leaves and small limbs from the trees cut away by the flying balls, falling about our men, while slivers and bark, Paine said, filling his ears and face, almost prevented sight. When the bugle sounded the retreat, his greatest troubles began, although he put in three more shots before he got up to run back, whereby he came very near being too late. Passing by a number of killed and wounded, he refused to stop and give up to the rebel shouters behind him, cursing him for a "Yank," which only made him run faster, "the whizzing bullets, bark and splinters" all around him, while his clothes were cut in three places by balls. Finally, reaching the wheat field he sank down exhausted, and while near an old barn shattered by a shell, where he had fainted from the effects of his desperate exertions, coupled with the great heat, some shots close over his head arousing him, he jumped up in time to see an unfortunate rooster fall—for crowing over the boys' retreat.

Allen afterwards said, that of the time this reconnoissance was made and for a long time thereafter, the men generally could not see the importance of the movement; rather, did they consider it a reckless, foolhardy venture. But even if it was so, and all the reports of the generals connected with the reconnoissance prove to the contrary, I must say in the light of the revelation made by Gen. Long-street, Gens. Sickles, Hunt and others, as quoted, that the "venture "inured to the lasting benefit of the Union cause.

Another discerning soldier, writes from Concord, N. H., under date of Feb. 10, 1891, relative to this affair, thus: "I remember the 2d of July, 1863, and what transpired in that belt of timber, just as plain as though it happened but yesterday. We arrived at Gettysburg the night of July 1st, lying in a piece of woods until the next morning, when, at -about ten A. M., I should say, four companies' of-us-were ordered to the front. We knew then that if there were any rebels within 10 miles of us, we should find them; because when we used to go to the front, the troops would say: "There goes Berdan's men, they will soon stir up a fight," and they were right, every time. How still everything seemed when we started out that morning. No one would have thought that two mighty armies lay so near each other, ready to do battle at the first opportunity, but such was the fact. We went up past the peach orchard and crossed over the Emmitsburg road, down another road past a smith's shop, into another piece of woods, and halted. Soon the order came to deploy, which we did at once. Then Col. Berdan rode out into the woods and was gone a short time. He soon returned, and in a very short time the order came to advance. We met the enemy in great numbers before we had advanced far, and we four companies of Sharpshooters, with the 3d Maine, who gave us hearty support, held the whole of Longstreet's division for 15 or 20 minutes; long enough for Meade to get his troops into position, to better meet Lee's army which so soon dashed against our left, in order to get possession of Little Round Top, the key to the situation."—GILMAN K. CROWELL, (CO. E. 1st S. S.)

The name of "Pitzers Run," is as much entitled to be inscribed on the Sharpshooter banner, as are other separate, distinct actions, wherein these riflemen were the chief actors. For this movement was similar to the one before Chancellorsville at the "Cedars,"—so named by Gen. Birney in our honor,—both being to discover the enemy's movements, far away from the main lines, both successfully accomplished. As well also, the first day's battle at Yorktown as distinguished from the siege. These separate, isolated affairs, are usually awarded to other organizations, so that the Sharpshooters are justly entitled to count—and I claim it for them—the name of Pitzer's Run, among their list of engagements.

In after years, on the memorial occasion referred to, Gen. Sickles, in a letter to the survivors, said: "It is not too much to declare that you were able to develop and disclose enough of the position, force, formation and movements of the enemy, to warrant the belief that the battle would be fought on the left, and to justify the dispositions made by me to meet the enemy there. This reconnoissance is historical. It deserves commemoration. It was not only a brilliant feat of arms, it was of inestimable advantage and value to our cause, contributing, as it did, to the-decisive victory of July 2d, from which the enemy never recovered."

Lieut.-Col. Trepp, who accompanied the expedition, in his report (July 29, 1883,) says: "On examining the ammunition of my detachment (after their return), I found that we had not more than about five rounds per man. With the balance of this command, I was then posted as a support to Capt. J. H. Baker's line of skirmishers from this regiment, in front of the center of the Third Army Corps. As Capt. Baker is now wounded and absent, I am unable to furnish the details concerning the detachment under his command, but I am informed that he took his position without order, following the instincts of the true soldier, the sound of the firing, and that at one time, when the enemy pushed his skirmish line to and across the road, he charged with part of his command on the enemy, driving them across the field. I have to call especial attention to the good behavior of this officer in all the engagements, and I would respect fully recommend him for decoration or honorable mention. The same of Privates Martin V. Nichols and William H. Nichols, Company H, who distinguished themselves on this and on former occasions by bravery and intelligence."

THE EMMITSBURG ROAD.

On receiving the information from Berdan, so plainly indicating the enemy's intentions, Gen. Sickles made his dispositions accordingly, to await and meet the now certain attack. His line was advanced a mile to the crest in front near the Emmitsburg road [a controversial move, as it detached his right, that Sickles would defend for the rest of his life], Gen. Humphreys' division occupying the crest facing westerly; while that of Birney swung around to the south, his right under Gen. Graham resting at the peach orchard, connecting with Humphreys', the brigade of DeTrobriand in the center, his left under Ward at the Little Round Top. The batteries were brought up and put in position all along the line. Gen. Meade thought Sickles was too far out, but while "discussing with him the propriety of withdrawing," the enemy's columns appeared, preceded by a general discharge from their cannon. In making this move forward, to meet the enemy as it were to quote the words of Lieut. Buchanan: "It in all probability forced Lee to attack the 3d corps when and where it did in its advanced position, making certain the glorious result accomplished here, under which the rebels groaned and staggered, and from which they never rallied."

And while the 3d corps, as a result of the great battle that began a couple of hours after Col. Berdan's return, became almost decimated in its terrible losses, in the struggle to keep the overwhelming enemy off, sufficient time was gained to throw supports and reinforcements from right to left, including the 5th and 12th corps, enabling them to present a barrier around Round Top mountain that the enemy could not break. The struggle was terrific, the cannonading awful in sound and fury, while the little balls hissed by the thousands, in or about the forms of the contending forces, often invisible 'mid the dense white smoke that enveloped that part of the field.

The casualties early assumed fearful proportions, continuing to a frightful extent before the battle was over. In one regiment, 141st Pennsylvania, which took into the field 200 guns and nine officers, the loss was 145 enlisted men and six officers. This regiment, as a part of the 1st brigade of Birney's division, was in the thickest of the fight. But men fell on all sides, everywhere, in all the commands engaged. Officers, high and low, seemed to vie with the men in sealing their devotion to the cause of the Union, with their life, or through all manner of wounds. Gen. Graham, commanding the 1st brigade, 1st division, was wounded and captured. Gen. Sickles here lost a leg—his last appearance on the field of active service. On his fall, Gen. Birney assumed command of the corps and gallantly—but the sorrow of the survivors went out to their late commander, whose undaunted courage and ability had stood the test of the many past hard-fought battles, gaining for him a renown that must ever remain attached to his name—the heroic Daniel E. Sickles.

Meanwhile, B and G, under Marble, encountered the enemy in force debouching from the woods 300 yards in their front, who advanced in line of battle across the plain halfway, where they were twice badly broken up and scattered by the Sharps rifles concentrating on them from all points,. causing them to fall back in great confusion; some taking cover behind trees, from which they were shot down by both direct and cross-fires from all our detached companies. The service performed by the Sharpshooters here, was of the most-heroic character, as they were in constant danger of being cut off by the increasing forces in their front. But for their-persistent determination to hold their ground, the enemy-must have crossed the Emmitsburg road before our infantry-were in position to check them. Company K, posted on the Emmitsburg road a half-mile or more to the right of Little Round Top, met the charge at that point with the same persistency and patriotic behavior. It was not until five o'clock that our boys were obliged to fall back, after being repeatedly signalled to do so, with their ammunition expended, during the time of the severe struggle at the Round Tops,, with a heavy line of battle coming on them in front. The Sharpshooters resting behind the artillery, the big guns opened, and with the assistance of our troops in compact line, finally sent the steadily approaching foe staggering back with heavy loss, discomfited and defeated for the d ay.

These companies on the, line of the Emmitsburg road and the peach orchard, particularly the commands of Baker (C) and Marble (B and G), by their stubborn fighting in keeping off so long the superior force confronting them,. made it possible in a great degree for the reconnoitering party to Pitzer's Run to accomplish their mission, as in a measure auxiliaries thereto, and should be awarded not a whit less credit for the part they performed. In fact, all the Sharpshooters, of both regiments, became by force of circumstances accessories before and after the movement under Col. Berdan.

Humphreys' division had maintained the unequal contest at the Emmitsburg road for a considerable time, with, both flanks exposed, and when finally ordered back to the original line connecting with the 2d corps, the movement was closely followed by the enemy; our men retiring slowly, contesting stubbornly every foot of ground. The loss in the division that afternoon, according to Gen. Humphreys, was over 2,000 out of 5,000 engaged. The division really had but two brigades in front, during the heavy fighting, Bur-ling's (3d) brigade having been detached to aid the 1st division. The artillery suffered greatly: Seeley's battery (4th U. S.) lost 23, with 25 horses. Turnbull's battery (3d U. S.) also lost 23, and 44 horses killed. Both of these battery commanders were among the wounded. The 15th Massachusetts and 82d New York made a stout fight at the Emmitsburg road, suffering greatly themselves, hurting the enemy as much. Their colonels, Ward and Huston, both fell while here in advance. Lieut. Thomas commanding a battery, was highly praised for his gallantry in serving his guns, contributing greatly to the enemy's defeat.

Prominent in this grand repulse was a portion of Stan-. nard's Vermont brigade, the 13th regiment of which, under direction of Gen. Hancock who followed up the movement in person, recaptured four guns of the regular artillery, which had been unavoidably left in the extreme front through the shooting of all the horses and the severe loss of the batterymen; which regiment shortly after, again distinguished itself by taking two rebel fieldpieces with a number of prisoners. Col. Randall says this last success was accomplished by a single company, who charged the battery from the Emmitsburg road. This brigade of five regiments was a new acquisition, having joined the army the night of the 1st, after marching, Gen. Stannard says, seven days through rain and mud, from their encampment on the Occoquan river below Washington, at an average of 18 miles per day. They were assigned to the 1st corps, and proved themselves worthy in all respects to occupy a position in that veteran organization.

The 1st Minnesota (Gibbon's division, 2d corps), after being subjected to severe artillery fire during the forenoon, also distinguished themselves in a charge made late in the day, driving a rebel regiment off in a very demoralized condition, inflicting great losses and capturing their colors. It was a very important point, a break in our lines, through which the enemy were trying to pass under cover of a wooded front, when the veteran 1st Minnesota met them with gleaming bayonets and smoking muskets, at a cost to themselves of two-thirds of the command from the withering fire they encountered. Gen. Hancock mentions them in this affair thus:

"I cannot speak too highly of this regiment and its commander, in its attack, as well as in its subsequent advance against the enemy." All the field officers, Col. Colvill, Lieut.-Col. Adams, and Major Downie were severely wounded, while a large number of line officers, also the adjutant, were injured, some fatally. Company L, transferred from Berdan's regiment at Fair Oaks, was at the front doing duty as sharpshooters.

During this contest in which the enemy stubbornly persisted in his desperate attempts to break our lines at this critical point, the field batteries of the 2d corps became the center of one of the hottest fights of the day, their gunners being continually shot down by their pieces, yet did they serve them well to the very last. Brown's battery lost a portion of its guns for a time, but the 19th Maine coming to the rescue, eventually saved them after a hard fight. This battery had 24 horses killed and several guns disabled, while the commanding officer, Lieut. Brown, was severely wounded.

Col. Heath, 19th Maine, was attacked with equal desperation, the enemy at, one time obtaining possession of three of the guns of the battery on his left. These guns he retook and carried from the field, most of the battery horses having been killed and wounded.—GEN. HARROW.

Major Curtis, 7th Michigan, in his report, thus refers to the action at this place: "As soon as the enemy came within range, a rapid and destructive fire opened on them along our line. The enemy continued to advance boldly until within 30 or 40 yards of our line, where, partially protected by the rocks and shrubs, they continued to pour in a galling fire. The artillerymen belonging to the batteries being nearly all killed or wounded, the guns were silenced. Advancing boldly to the battery on our left, the enemy took possession planting a battle flag upon one of them. Their triumph, however, was short. A deadly volley was poured upon them at not more than 30 yards distance. Their color bearer fell, pierced by a dozen bullets. Many others were killed or wounded, and they were forced to fall back to their cover, and the battery was saved. During the hottest of the firing many of the enemy were seen to throw down their guns, and, creeping along the ground to our lines, surrendered as prisoners. The enemy, failing most completely in their attempt to carry our line by assault, retreated in considerable disorder." The rebel General Barksdale was mortally wounded close to our lines.

Near the close of the day, a portion of the 1st corps (2d and 3d divisions) ordered from their position on Cemetery Hill, were hurried down by Gen. Doubleday to fill the gap to the left of the 2d corps. It was at a critical time in the engagement when these troops were called upon, but they did not become extensively engaged. The 12th corps was also ordered to the extreme left, although not needed when they arrived there. The 6th corps which arrived on the scene late in the day, after a lengthy march, was moved in detachments to different points on the long line, as a reserve force, and were at no time during the entire battle seriously engaged.

THE ROUND TOPS.

While a great battle raged along the west front of the 3d corps, which extended along the lines of Graham's and' De Trobriand's brigades of Birney's division from the peach orchard southeasterly, the "key" of the entire engagement—as it has been so generally termed—was the contest in front of Little Round Top. Here, Ward's brigade—the extreme left of the 3d corps—rested on the rocks of the little mountain. And when the skirmishers (2d S. S.) sent out by Gen. Ward a half-mile in his front, discovered the enemy's approach, as they appeared issuing from a wood in long lines of battle, Winslow's and Smith's batteries opened on them a well-directed fire, which was answered by the enemy's field pieces posted near the Emmitsburg road. The yelling of the approaching Johnnies at first was not unlike the music of a flock of brant in the air preparing to alight; but as they came nearer, the yells and shouts grew louder and more distinct, so that by the time they got within 200 yards of the brigade, rising above the cannons' roar,

> These piercing, frenzied shouts, Struck terror to the soul.

But the souls of Ward's soldiers refused to be struck that way. They had heard it before, and they knew how to stop it. And right there those demon cries stopped short—completely cut off by the volleys that greeted them.

"Their rising all at once was as the sound of thunder."

The enemy reinforced by supporting columns running up, another and more serious attack was made, with an attempt to gain the stone fence between them. Amid the thick of the fight, covered with smoke and bleeding from their wounds, the musket balls and bursting shell whizzing, singing; hissing and crashing back and forth, blue coats dropping, grey coats falling, for upwards of an hour and a half the opposing forces tried to hold this substantial ready-made breastwork—this stone wall—without success on either side. During this hard battle the losses were getting heavy—Yanks and Johnnies falling at every fire—when the brigade out of ammunition, withdrew on being relieved by troops from the 2d and 5th corps. Previous to this, Egan's "Mozart regiment," the 40th New York, coming to their aid rushed gallantly forward through a wet marsh, knee deep in water and mud, to attack the Confederate lines, suffering very much from shot and shell.

Gen. Ward says: This brigade, with the exception of Antietam, has been engaged in every battle fought by the Army of the Potomac, and has been frequently mentioned for its gallantry, but on this occasion it eclipsed all its former actions. The immense force opposed to them was at one time almost overwhelming. The number of effective men in the brigade when they engaged the enemy was not 1,500, while the loss is nearly 800. Out of 14 field officers, we lost eight. The 3d and 4th Maine, 20th Indiana, and 99th Pennsylvania Volunteers, the veterans of this brigade, to their world-wide reputation have added new laurels, and, if possible, excelled themselves. The First and Second U. S. Sharpshooters and the 86th and 124th New York Volunteers, recently assigned to this brigade, have richly earned the title to wear the "Kearny patch." To the officers and men of my command, without exception, my thanks and the thanks of the country are eminently due. For nearly two hours my brigade was opposed to at least 10,000 of the enemy, in line and *en masse*. I would particularly call the attention of the major-general commanding (among others named) to the gallant conduct of Col. Berdan, 1st U. S. Sharpshooters; Col. Lakeman, 3d Maine; and Major Stoughton, 2d U. S. Sharpshooters, who vied with each other in doing their whole duty. The total loss in my brigade was 46 officers and 712 enlisted men.—J. H. HOBART WARD.

Every man engaged strove hard to win, their hot guns in constant use, encouraged at all points by the presence of their officers close up and urgent. The regimental commanders attested their share of the dangers with the rank and file, in the severe loss they sustained. Of the eight field officers shot down—more than half present—Col. Wheeler, of the 20th Indiana, was shot through the head; Col. Ellis and Major Cromwell, 124th New York, were both shot through the head, while their lieutenant-colonel, Cummins, went down wounded; Col. Walker and Major Whitcomb, 4th Maine, suffered severe wounds; also Major Lee, 3d Maine, and Lieut.-Col. Higgins, of 86th New York. Upwards of 50 per cent of that devoted brigade bled for the Union in that sanguinary contest. On the fall of Gen. Sickles, Gen. Ward succeeded Gen. Birney in command of the division. Col. Berdan then commanded the 2d brigade.

The 5th corps also made a hard fight, as usual, Gen. Sykes commanding. They were on the extreme left at Little Round Top; which important point had been recognized by Gen. Warren, of Meade's staff, and formerly of the 5th corps which he, later on, commanded. Here on this height after a most gallant and successful effort in resisting the, crowding enemy, fell one of the brave soldiers of the war, Col. Strong Vincent, while at the head of his brigade in Barnes' division. From this point the 20th Maine, after driving the enemy away from their front, following a prolonged contest disputed inch by inch on both sides—in which the gray divided the honors with the blue, in point of bravery, meeting death alike—drove the gray coats out of the ravine between the mountains, charging up and over the greater Round Top, holding it thereafter. This was late in the evening and virtually closed the struggle. Gen. Weed, one of the brigade commanders, and Lieut. Hazlett of the artillery, were killed in this contest.

Caldwell's division of the 2d corps, also ordered to the left, filled a gap between the right of the 5th and left of the 3d, and advancing, drove the enemy in his front through a field of wheat, after, another stubborn fight, and so far, as to get in advance, breaking the connection of the troops on his left; and before he could be supported by them, was obliged to give Way, the rebels getting in his rear, so that with difficulty he got by them. His loss was heavy, among them Gen. Zook and Col. Cross, brigade commanders. Sweitzer's brigade of the 5th corps in an effort to reach him, had to fight its way back at close quarters, the 4th Michigan and 62d Pennsylvania having a hand-to-hand conflict with the foe, in which Col. Jeffords of the 4th, was bayoneted and killed—a savage thrust— while trying to save his colors.

To describe the efforts of all the commands in this engagement, would fill the space of a large volume; I will therefore close the account of this day's battle, by noticing the part taken therein by the 2d Sharpshooters, under Lieut.-Col. Stoughton; after referring to the night attack on our extreme right, wherein an effort was made to capture, the position at Culp's Hill now held by only Gen. Greene's brigade of the 12th corps. Here, after a sharp struggle of nearly three hours in which several regiments of the 1st and 11th, corps finally took part, the troops of Ewell having, penetrated our vacant lines, were forced back from Greene's intrenchments, although when, the action ended at half-past nine the enemy remained in possession of the trenches on the right—the only lodgment effected by them during the entire day. During this attack on, Greene,, Wadsworth's and Ames' divisions became engaged, the enemy making a bold attempt to capture Wiedrich's battery, when, according to Gen. Howard, "the men with sponge staffs and, bayonets forced them back." About this time, Col. Carroll's brigade from the 2d corps reinforced our men, deploying into position on the right of the 11th, "just in time to check the enemy's advance."

Col. Carroll says of this affair: "We found the enemy up to and some of them in among the front guns of the batteries on the road. Owing to the artillery fire from our own guns, it was impossible to advance by a longer front than that of a regiment, and it being perfectly dark, and with no guide, I had to find the enemy's lines entirely by their fire. For the first few minutes they had a cross-fire upon us from a stone wall on the right of the road, but, by changing the front of the 7th West Virginia, they were soon driven from there."

In the morning Col. Stoughton's command was put in position on the extreme left of the 3d corps, posted so as to cover the ravine between the Round Tops, as that noted officer says: "by putting Company H on the brow of the hill, with videttes overlooking the ravine; and Company D in the ravine near the woods, to watch the enemy's movements in that direction. Companies A, E, G and C formed a line perpendicular to the cross-road that intersects with the Emmitsburg pike. Companies B and F I held in reserve." Here they remained until two o'clock, when the regiment deployed in front of Ward's brigade, passing through the woods into the open field, a half-mile away. Col. Stoughton riding forward, saw the enemy's skirmishers coming in on his right flank, which being exposed, caused him to retire his men under fire, to a new position, where they did some good work, silencing one of the rebel cannon at t e Emmitsburg road, and peppering their lines of battle following up their skirmishers. One of their regiments broke three times before they would come on, under the well-aimed fire of the Sharpshooters. And not until the gray coats were within 100 yards of them did they fall back, firing as they did so. Col. Stoughton again: "My left wing retreated up the hill and allowed the enemy to pass up the ravine, when they poured a destructive fire into his flank and rear. Here, Adjt. Norton, with about a dozen men, captured and sent to the rear 22 prisoners. Special mention should be made of this officer for his coolness and bravery during this day's engagement. The right wing fell back gradually until they mingled with the regiments composing the 2d brigade and remained till night, when the brigade was relieved." He also reports a loss of 28; among them Capt. Rowell (acting major), Capts. McClure and Buxton, wounded, and Lieut. Pettijohn taken prisoner. The important service rendered by Stoughton's command, consisted in discovering the approach of the enemy for the attack, and in guarding the ravine up to the last moment. Also, in holding in check a portion of the rebel column in their efforts to gain the Round Top, until too late for them to profit thereby. As a recognition of this fact by the enemy themselves, I herewith submit a letter received by Col. Stoughton after the war, from the Confederate officer in command of the troops that were crowding him out of their way.

ABBEVILLE, ALA., Nov. 22, 1888.

COL. H. R. STOUGHTON:—My regiment, 15th Alabama, was on the right of the Confederate line of battle. The position from which we advanced was at or near an old hedge row, north of the pike Emmitsburg, I believe, and right at the brow of the ridge south of Round Top. My orders were to guide to the foot of Round Top and hug to its base, keeping to the west of it and passing up the valley between it and Little Round Top, to find the Federal left and turn it if possible, and to go as far as I could. The lieutenant-colonel, Bulger, commanding the 47th Alabama regiment, was directed to keep close to me. This line of advance was a converging one, and had it not been disturbed by the presence of your command when it first appeared would have strengthened as we advanced, and our losses would not have produced any gaps or breaks in our line. The advance began, and when the right of my regiment approached the first foot of Round Top,, we received your fire nearly in flank; our advance of 150 yards further without change of direction would have presented my right flank to your left, had your line been parallel; but as your right was retired in conformity to the ground, you had partly a front and partly a right oblique fire on me. Receiving no orders, I did not vary my course until you gave me a second one, which wounded several of my men, among them my lieutenant-colonel, Isaac B. Feogin who lost a leg, and he now lives at Union Springs, Bullock county, Alabama. I then, knowing that it would not do to pass and leave you on my right and rear, gave the command, "Change direction to the right," and swung around far enough to advance on you, and the 47th Alabama swung with me. My advance dislodged you, but as you fell back up the south front of Round Top, you kept up a lively fire on my advancing line, which returned it but without much effectiveness, as your men, being trained sharpshooters and skirmishers, kept well under cover, taking advantage of the bowlders which line the mountain side. When over half-way up your fire ceased, and henceforth to the top I did not see one of your men. I halted and rested for two or three minutes on the top of Round Top. My men were fainting with fatigue. We had - marched 25 miles that day before going into the battle. I then advanced down the north side and to the east end of Vincent's Spur, where lay Vincent's brigade, the left of the Union line of battle, which I attacked and drove back upon the center, and my fire killed Gen. Vincent; but just as my ammunition was getting short, and when I was within 120 yards of Little Round Top, Lieut.-Col. Bulger (who now lives at Dadeville, Ala.; Mike Bulger is his name; he is now quite old and feeble) fell, severely wounded, and his regiment, which had suffered severely, broke and retreated in confusion. A moment later you appeared directly in my rear and opened fire on me. I then occupied the ledge of rocks from which I had driven the 20th Maine. That and a New York regiment assailing me in front and you in the rear, forced my thinned ranks to face and fire in both directions, which we could not long endure. Half my men still able for duty were without ammunition. Two of my captains came and suggested a retreat. I ordered them to return to their respective companies and sell out as dearly as possible. But a little reflection made it appear as my duty to order a retreat, which I did, and we ran up the mountain and halted on the top for some time, and at deep dusk we moved back to an old house near the line of our advance, where we bivouacked for the night. Mine was the largest and best drilled and disciplined regiment in Hood's division. It went in with two field officers, 42 company and staff officers, and 644 men with arms in hand, and got out with one field officer, 19 company and staff, and 221 efficient men.

The great service which you and your command did was, first, in changing my direction, and in drawing my regiment and the 47th Alabama away from the point of attack. You drew off and delayed this force of over 1,000 men from falling on Vincent and the Union left at the same time of the attack of Law's other three regiments, the Texas and two Georgia brigades in front, and but for this service on your part I am confident we would have swept away the Union line and have captured Little Round Top, which would have won the battle for us. Again, when Vincent had fallen and I was within 150 yards of the top of Little Round Top, you forced me to retire by appearing in my rear and opening fire on me. The foregoing is substantially my recollection of you and your command at the great battle of Gettysburg. You and your command deserve a monument for turning the tide in favor of the Union cause. But after all, if Bulger had not fallen when he did, or if Longstreet had possessed less love for the fray and been at his proper place to have seen that we had Round Top, and had thrown a force on it and fortified it that night, the battle had been won for the Confederates. Meade testified that "with that which was the key-point in possession of the rebels, I could not have held any of the ground which I subsequently held to the last." Victor Hugo said: "Two great armies in battle are like two giants in a wrestle; a stump, a projecting root, or a tuft of grass may serve to brace the one or trip the other; on such slender threads does the fate of nations depend."—WM. C. CATES.

Capt. H. P. Smith says: "My company, G, deployed as skirmishers, was almost directly in front of the charging column, but we didn't stay there, neither did we kill the whole of Hood's corps. We certainly made it interesting for some of the Johnnies, and we were soon in as much danger from the fire from our own men and artillery (behind them), as we were from the enemy. The 3d corps fought that day when all the chances seemed to be against them."

With such stinging effect did the Second Regiment pepper the Confederates up and down the mountain sides, from behind bowlders and trees, and finally from across the ravine, that some of the rebel officers termed it "a perfect hornets' nest of sharpshooters," which was the most significant term that could have been given. And were it not for their obstinate defense of the position and the pass between the mountains, contesting every inch of the way, Oates' boast to have been able to take little Round Top might possibly have been a true one—although we had some pretty good men up there and they would pretty much all of them had to be killed off first, for they were there to stay.

The battle for the day being over, our troops rested as well as they could in their different positions, on the rocky ridges, the wooded hill-sides, and on the open plain. Worn out with fatigue, it mattered little to them if it was only a stone for a pillow, as long as they could stretch out and snatch a few hours' slumber; replenishing first their cartridge boxes, the ammunition being brought to them.

But there was no uncertainty about the rest and sleep of the countless ones in their front, needing no blanket or coat for evermore. Their hardships were over, their service was finished. They were at peace with each other, the blue and the gray, lying side by side. While behind the lines, where the little red flags flaunted, the "good doctors" held their receptions—some of the field-hospitals being in buildings, some behind stacks of grain.

"The barns that once held yellow grain

Were heaped with harvests of the slain."

THIRD DAY.

The battle was resumed at the first break of day in front of the 12th corps, to regain their position on the right; and after seven hours obstinate fighting—from half-past three to half-past ten A. M.—the rebels were finally driven away and the corps won back all its intrenchments, forcing the enemy beyond its original line, taking from him over 1, 100 prisoners, half of whom were disabled, 5,000 small arms and three stand of colors. It is said that nearly 1,000 gray coats were afterwards buried by our troops on this part of the field, while their wounded can be estimated in the usual proportion. Neill's and Shaler's brigades of the 6th corps, and two skeleton regiments from Cutler's brigade of the 1st, (14th Brooklyn and 147th New York,) assisted in this important repulse. It was a red-hot fight all through, several desperate charges being made on both sides, with equal determination and spirit, the enemy seemingly determined to uphold the boast of Gen. Ewell to capture the place or lose the last man; while our soldiers were equally as determined they shouldn't succeed. When the final charge was made by the Boys in Blue, many of the enemy were glad to duck under their glistening bayonets, and give themselves up.

Gen. Geary in his graphic report of this contest, says: "Everything being in readiness at half past three A. M. (early dawn) a simultaneous attack was made by artillery and the 2d and 3d brigades. This attack was most furious, but was stubbornly met. Our artillery fire continued, by previous arrangements for 10 minutes. This tremendous assault at first staggered the enemy, by whom it was seemingly unexpected; but, rallying as my troops charged at the dose of the artillery fire, Johnson's division of Ewell's corps, followed by Rodes', and that supported by Early's, each division massed in three lines, advanced, charging heavily upon our front and right, and yelling in their peculiar style. They were met at every point by the unswerving lines and deadly fire of my 2d and 3d brigades, our men cheering loudly and yielding not an inch of ground. Line after line of the enemy broke under this steady fire, but the pressing masses from behind rushed forward to take their places." And their last assault is thus described: "At twenty-five minutes past ten o'clock two brigades of Johnson's division, having formed in column by regiments, charged upon our line on the right. They met the determined men of Kane's little brigade, which though only 650 strong, poured into them so continuous a fire that when within 70 paces their columns wavered and soon broke to the rear. The 1st Maryland battalion (rebel) was in the advance, and their dead lay mingled with our own. This was the last charge. As they fell back, our troops rushed forward with wild cheers of victory, driving the rebels in confusion over the entrenchments, the ground being covered with their dead and wounded. Large numbers of them crowded under our breastworks and begged to be taken as prisoners. Among these were many of the celebrated Stonewall Brigade, who, when ordered for the last time to charge upon Greene's breastworks, advanced until met by our terrible fire, and then, throwing down their arms, rushed in with white flags, handkerchiefs, and even pieces of paper, in preference to meeting again that fire which was certain destruction. As they threw themselves forward and crouched under our line of fire, they begged our men to spare them, and they were permitted to come into our lines. The commanding officer of a regiment raised a white flag, when Major (B. W.) Leigh, assistant adjutant-general of Johnson's division, rode forward to order it down, and fell, pierced by a dozen balls, his body remaining in our possession."

Thus ended one of the most desperate and futile attempts to turn the Union position ever made in the war. Their aim was to get possession of the road running to Baltimore, which crossed our lines. But, while they came on with an ardor unsurpassed, it is evident that the men who had to do the fighting, had less confidence of success than their *gen*eral, from the fact that they came prepared with white rags to shake at us, to forgive their boldness, and allow them to pass meekly to the rear, when it became too hot for them.

As the heavy musketry died away on the right, an ominous silence unexpectedly followed for several hours along the rebel front. Our officers and soldiers, however, were not to be deceived, as it was to them but a precursor of another, and if possible, more desperate attempt to break our lines. This was finally developed by the opening at one o'clock, at an average distance of 1,400 yards, of the most galling cannonade from 150 guns from all parts of the rebel heights—right, left and center—that our troops had ever been exposed to.

"About one P. M. on the concerted signal, our guns in position, nearly 150, opened fire along the entire line from right to left.—
GEN. PENDLETON, Chief of Artillery, C. S. A.

The air was immediately filled with shot and bursting shell, the latter breaking continually over and among our men, so that no possible cover was safe from the myriad of dangerous missiles flying about. The fields behind our ridges were swept of all living things, on all portions of our extended line, the cracking, ragged iron was continually searching for mortals to destroy. This dreadful sounding, direful racket, this storm of raining projectiles with their demoniac sounds—shrieking music—in all its terrific grandeur of flash and crash, peril and destruction, was kept up continuously for at least two hours; our cannon replying more or less for a time, until by Gen. Meade's order they gave no further response. From which, it appears, Gen. Lee concluded he had effectually silenced our batteries; wherein he erred, as his deluded, though faithful troops soon found out, to their everlasting sorrow and injury. On some points in our line, the most exposed places, considerable loss occurred both among infantry and artillery. Men, horses, cannon wheels, axles, caisson boxes, were literally piled up—fearful evidences of range and destruction.

Shells burst in the air, in the ground to the right and left, killing horses, exploding, caissons, overturning tombstones, and smashing fences. There was no place of safety. In one regiment 27 were killed and wounded by one shell, and yet the regiments of this corps (11th) did'-not move excepting when ordered.—HOWARD.

PICKETT'S CHARGE.

At three o'clock this terrific artillery prelude as suddenly ceased. Now the rebel purpose was at once developed, for from- out their hiding places in the wooded covers, as if by magic, appeared long lines of battle, stretching, across almost the entire plain. Opposite our center, where Hancock was, stationed with the 2d and 3d corps, to which point their wings gradually converged, came a handsome looking line of battle well closed up, as steady as if on review: 15 regiments of Virginians—Pickett's division of Longstreet's corps—equally divided into three brigades under Gens. Garnett, Kemper and Armistead. These fresh arrivals, for they had come up that morning, represented' the "first families," and as they advanced on, chanting their battle songs, they were for the moment the admiration of thousand of patriot eyes; but for a short time only, for soon' those "silenced batteries!" of ours began to play havoc in their ranks, and amid the great smoke and fire, their formation was for a time lost sight of. On they came, regardless of exploding shells, to be followed at shorter range by the raking canister as they crossed the Emmitsburg road. Soon coming within short range, our troops were "up and at them," their songs turned into yells, and with a grand rush unmindful of results, heeding not their shattering ranks, they poured down on our center. Now the contest waged furious, both sides closing in, striving to repel; continuous streams of fire from rebel muskets dropping Union soldiers fast, while great gaps were cut into the solid ranks of the Virginians by our responding shots, to be closed up by others behind—to meet the same fate. Union cannon from right to left, mowing down their lines, contributed to the slaughter.

"Cannon to right—Cannon to left—Cannon in front—Volley'd and thunder'd."

And yet, with the withering musketry on all sides, oblique and direct, it seemed only to make them more determined to break our lines. Perfectly reckless of life they dashed on, forward to the fence, to the stone wall at the foot of the hill. Here it became hand-to-hand. Bullets and bayonets,. even the musket butts were used; the enemy struggling to cross the fence, to scale the wall. Officers and men tumbled over continually, whole lines fell. On their left, Kemper goes down, then Garnett on the right, and finally Armistead in the center of a handful of men, falls dead within our lines, his hands on Union cannon. For a moment there had been a grave doubt, the enemy were piercing our lines—crossing the fatal stone wall—but with loud cheers heard above the' noise and fury of battle, our men dashed into the breach and the danger was over.

"Amaze and terror seized the rebel host."

Their colors went down, the stars and stripes waved aloft, they broke and were driven back dismayed, a scattering remnant of a mighty host, while thousands of their dead and wounded stretched far along their path. Though defeated, they were brave foes, and were awarded the highest praise by our troops, for their gallantry displayed in this daring assault.

"Their valor shown upon our crests to-day,

Hath taught us how to cherish such high deeds,

Even in the bosom of our adversaries."

The brunt of the main attack was on the brigades of Webb, Hall and Harrow, of Gibbon's division, 2d corps. Webb's men were for a time driven in, but rallying, led on by Webb in person, they joined with Hall and Harrow in the final charge. The great struggle lasted an hour, in that time this division lost 1,600 out of 3,800 engaged, capturing 2,500 of the enemy. Alex. Hays' division claims to have brought in 1,500 with 15 battle-flags.

This brigade captured nearly 1,000 prisoners, six battle-flags, and picked up 1,400 stand of arms. The conduct of the brigade was most satisfactory. Officers and men did their whole duty. The enemy would probably have succeeded in piercing our lines had not Col. Hall advanced with several of his regiments to my support.—GEN. WEBB.

Capt. Coates, of the 1st Minnesota, in Harrow's brigade, says this regiment captured 500 of the enemy with the colors of the 28th Virginia, they again meeting with heavy loss. "Company L was detached as sharpshooters to support Kirby's battery, where it did effective service."

The Vermont brigade, which was stationed in a grove, some distance in front of the left center, performed an important part in the repulse as the enemy came up, by obtaining flank and oblique fires on their right, sweeping them down, the enemy, however, simply breaking to the rear from that side, closing in behind without stopping in their forward movement. The Vermonters lost in all, 350 men, Gen. Stannard being among the wounded, although he hung on. The 20th New York (militia) also of the 1st corps, rushing through the slashing on the slope at the critical moment, closed in on the enemy in gallant style up to the fence, where after a give-and-take contest, they greatly assisted in forcing them back, capturing many of their opponents.

The Excelsior brigade of the 3d corps, composed of New York troops, also lost very heavily, particularly on the second day, as per the official report of the commander:

The strength of the brigade at the commencement of the action was 1,837 officers and men, out of which we lost 778, being nearly 45 per cent of the entire number, showing the terrible fire to which we were exposed.—WM. R. BREWSTER, Col. Commdg.

Col. Stoughton of the Sharpshooters was standing by Gen. Stannard when the latter was wounded, The same spherical shot, he said, that wounded Gen. Stannard, killed a Dartmouth college student named White, of his regiment. Speaking of the services of the Sharpshooters, Stoughton said' of Col. Berdan—"to whom the country is indebted for raising this most efficient corps of men."

One of Company E's men (Second Regiment), Eli A. Willard, of Vermont, a crack shot, failing to discover a certain rebel sharpshooter, a dangerous customer, came to Gen. Stannard, requesting the loan of his glass, saying as he took it: "I guess now, I'll find that fellow." He soon reported back: "I've found him," pointing to a tree near the Emmitsburg road. Willard then went out in front of a large bowlder, took careful aim and fired—there was no further annoyance from that quarter. The first sergeant of this company, W. H. Proctor, credited Willard with having fired 100 rounds that afternoon. He also relates another incident, which is in substance as follows:

Gen. Birney sent an aid to the Second Regiment, lying at the time behind the 14th Vermont of Stannard's brigade, to obtain volunteers to silence a battery out near the Codori House, whereupon the whole regiment jumped up ready to go, but the aid said he would take only forty. These were at once furnished by detailing five from each of the eight companies, placing them in charge of an officer. They were deployed, starting for the battery with a rush and a yell. The battery loaded with canister expected to mow them all down, but as soon as our men came in range, they dropped from view, crawling forward to sheltered positions to put in their work. Soon every horse with the battery was either shot or run back; a few minutes later the gunners fired their canister—hit or miss—then ran away, abandoning the battery. Our men kept those guns quiet all that afternoon.

Company B distinguished themselves assisting Daniel's battery during a critical period of the fighting, handling the guns in changing position, obtaining new range, etc. It was a purely voluntary, act, in which state pride was naturally enough one of the causes, all being Michigan men.

Among the many sad events, was the death of Lieut. Cushing, commanding a battery in connection with Webb's brigade. Although wounded in both thighs, he refused to leave the field while his ammunition lasted.

Lieut. Cushing, of Battery A, 4th U. S. artillery, challenged the admiration of all who saw him. Three of his limbers were blown up and changed with the caisson limbers under fire. Several wheels were shot off his guns and replaced, till at last, severely wounded himself, his officers all killed or wounded, and with but cannoneers enough to man a section, he pushed his gun to the fence in front, and was killed while serving his last canister into the ranks of the advancing enemy.—COL. HALL.

In the midst of the battle, Gens. Hancock. Gibbon and Doubleday were wounded. Gen. Hancock, however, remained on the field directing the movements in his front until the fighting was over, when he retired. He said he had been struck with a 10-penny nail. Luckily for him and the army, it wasn't an ounce bullet or a fragment of shell; as it was, the wound was a serious one.

But while this savage battle was going on in the center, the troops of Pettigrew and Trimble of Heth's and Pender's divisions of the Confederate army, advanced on the left of Pickett, towards the lines of the 1st and 11th corps on our right, and were driven back with great loss—the rout was complete.

The whole mass gave way, some fleeing to the front, some to the rear, and some through our lines, until the whole plain was covered with unarmed rebels, waving coats, hats, and handkerchiefs,, in token of a wish to surrender.—Cot. SAWYER, 8th Ohio.

A thoroughly dejected mob. The 8th Ohio was well advanced to the front for two days, having been detached from Gen. Carroll's command, posted to the left of the 11th corps line; where they got in some stunning flank fires at 100 yards distance, breaking the line, swooping on to them with wild hurrahs, taking in 200 prisoners and three stand of colors. It was one of those individual instances of great gallantry and determination. The regiment lost heavily in the two days' fight, their casualties running up to 100. They captured the colors of the 34th North Carolina and 38th Virginia, having another flag stolen by a staff officer, who ought to have been cashiered.

The 3d corps had been kept in reserve as a support to both 1st and 2d corps, Birney's division behind the 1st. Gen. Newton commanding 1st corps, says: "I made arrangements with Gen. Birney to draw upon him for such support as might be needed, and express my obligations for the cheerful and handsome manner in which he responded to every call made on him." Although the corps rested on their arms subject to call, the Sharpshooters were out to the front in different positions. Companies C, I, and K, under Capt. Baker were protecting batteries of the 5th corps, on our left, and Col. Trepp says: "On this occasion, Corp. Wellington Fitch, of Company C, distinguished himself by making a bold reconnoissance alone, which resulted in capturing a squad of rebel sharpshooters that greatly annoyed our artillery."

Lieut. E. A. Wilson, who was in command of Company C, says Baker's orders were to clear the front of Little Round Top of the enemy's sharpshooters, which was done, driving them off and capturing a lieutenant and 30 men.

THE "DEVIL'S DEN."

This forbidden spot was situated in the hillside fronting Little Round Top about 300 yards distant, with a marshy interval or swamp intervening; and consisted of a hole in the rocks, or cavern, with a small opening, with blasted, barren surroundings. A fitting resort for witches, freebooters—and rebel sharpshooters, who occupied it that day, with whom the Michigan men scattered behind the bowlders at the foot of Little Round Top were kept busy exchanging shots for a long time, as also with other Johnnies lodged behind bowlders in the vicinity of the den.

Finally, having expended a great deal of ammunition, it was determined to stop their firing at all hazards, our artillery above being considerably annoyed, suffering loss from this continual shooting. For this purpose a detail of 20 men was made by Richard W. Tyler, at that time a sergeant of Company K, a gallant soldier who had distinguished himself on previous occasions. With a rush these brave fellows ran across the marsh, and having routed the enemy's pickets in front of the hill, closed in upon them capturing the entire party. There were 20 of them caught in the cave, a number being wounded, and they assured our men that their fire from the Little Round Top had made them prisoners all day. It was made too hot for them to attempt an escape. They were a sorry looking crowd, being very hungry and about famished for want of water. They were much alarmed at being caught, because as sharpshooters they expected no quarter, and begged lustily for their lives, nor would they scarce believe Sergt. Tyler's assurance that they would be treated as fairly as other prisoners, until they learned that their captors were Berdan Sharpshooters, when a sudden change came over their dejected spirit to one of undisguised happiness. That old idea that sharpshooters would be strung up, was discarded by our men after the Peninsula campaign.

This sortie by our boys (every one of whom would be mentioned if I knew their names) was a most gallant and dangerous undertaking, and it was singular that notwithstanding the brisk fire under which they advanced none were hurt, but narrowly escaped the fast-flying bullets, one man being saved by his frying pan (for they carried their cooking kit always), another by his rifle stock, the ball flattening on the barrel, while others "just missed it." But our Sharpshooters were fleet travelers—to and fro—and reeked not of danger, when the order came to "go." As it afterwards transpired, they incurred a still greater risk than most of them ever knew. For in after years, when all: was quiet at Gettysburg—the voice of war but an echo of, the long past—with peace North and South, Gen. Manning of the late Confederacy visiting the place, informed Tyler, now a captain in the regular army, that at the time of this affair at Devil's Den, his brigade was in line of battle but a, hundred yards in rear of the hill, and that the men we had captured were of his old regiment.

In the afternoon, the Wisconsin company was ordered to the extreme front, assisting in repulsing the attempt of the enemy to break the center, in which affair a rebel brigade, being badly cut up, was captured with their colors. Amon Satterly (Co. D) remembers how, on the third day, Col. Berdan taking a body of Sharpshooters out, confronted a line of the enemy, and waving his hat to "come in" and give themselves up, they did so.

On the next day, the 4th of July, although affairs were comparatively quiet, very little effort being made to resume the contest on either side, the Sharpshooters were again thrown out, in the vicinity of the peach orchard, and were engaged in exchanging shots with the enemy's picket lines. Company A formed part of a detachment sent out to bury the dead and bring in the wounded, which duty occupied the entire day, over 1,200 soldiers being found and buried, Lieut. E. A. Wilson (Company C) was ordered by Col. Berdan to take charge of a burial party, and found no dead Union soldiers as far off as were those of the Sharpshooters; these being in the woods near Pitzer's Run, where Lieut. Sheldon fell.

The Second Regiment advanced to the Emmitsburg road, several hundred yards to the left of the cemetery, when Col. Stoughton deployed four companies to skirmish the field and woods in front. The enemy were driven to their earthworks, 200 yards distant, and the position gained was held by our men throughout the day, subject to sharp firing from the foe, with a loss to the Second of three killed and eight wounded, among the latter, Lieut. Law, of Company E. On the morning of the 5th it was ascertained that the rebel army had retreated, hurrying as fast as they could towards the Potomac—they had enough of free soil fighting. The Sharpshooters were immediately sent forward to reconnoiter and report their movements, which was effected after going three miles, when they rejoined their brigade, having discovered unmistakable evidence of their hasty retreat, with many of their wounded left behind in farm houses and sheds along the now deserted road.

The Union loss at Gettysburg was 23,000. That of the Confederates, although at first figured up by Gen. Lee soon after the battle at only about 20,500, has since been ascertained to exceed 30,000. That they should have sustained a greater loss than the Union army is quite reasonable to suppose, considering the fact that they were the attacking party. They had an opportunity to learn what Fredericksburg and other important battles were to us, where our soldiers attacked them in their strongholds.

The result of the campaign may be briefly stated in the defeat of the enemy at Gettysburg, his compulsory evacuation of Pennsylvania and Maryland, and withdrawal from the upper valley of the Shenandoah, and in the capture of three guns, 41 standards, and 13,621 prisoners; 24,978 small arms were collected on the battle field.—GEN. MEADE.

Our casualties were severe, including many brave men and an unusual proportion of distinguished and valuable officers.—LONGSTREET.

Among these officers, were the following named generals, killed and wounded: Hood, Fender, Trimble, Heth, Semmes, Kemper, Armistead, Scales, G. T. Anderson, Wade Hampton, J. M. Jones, Jenkins, Barksdale and Garnett. Gen. Longstreet was much opposed to the reckless assault on the 3d.

The order for this attack, which I could not favor under better auspices, would have been revoked had I felt that I had that privilege.—LONGSTREET.

One of the brigades of Pickett's division, according to Major Peyton of the 19th Virginia, "went into action with 1,287 men and about 140 officers, and sustained a loss of 941 killed, wounded and missing, and it is feared that those reported missing were killed or wounded." He also states that his men suffered terribly from our cannon from the Round Top—" a mile away "—frequently 10 at a time being killed by a single shell.

Col. Berdan reported a total loss of 89, saying: "We went into action with about 450 rifles. During the three days we expended 14,400 rounds of ammunition."

The two regiments of Sharpshooters under Col. Berdan and Major Stoughton, were of the most essential service in covering my front with a cloud of Sharpshooters, and pouring a constant and galling, fire into the enemy's line of skirmishers.—D. B. BIRNEY, Major-General, commanding division.

The greatest excitement prevailed through the North while the battle was in progress, particularly in the eastern cities, as it was looked upon by many as a decisive engagement that would settle the fate of one of the armies. While it didn't end that way, as the Confederacy was still a lively concern, Lee having strength enough left to get away and continue the war nearly two years longer, it was a decision against further invasions. The people became wild with joy when the struggle was over, and the news spread far and wide, of the victory for the Union on the great, glorious field of Gettysburg.

CASUALTIES, FIRST REGIMENT.

Co. A.—Unknown.

Co. B.—Wounded: Lawrence McGraw, Lewis J. Bills, Henry L. Conkling.

Co. C.—Wounded: Lieut. G. B. Clark, Harrison O. Higby, mortal, died July 18; S. K. Roosa, mortal, W. W. Colwell, Don Henry Fuller.

Co. D.—Killed: Smith Haight. Wounded: Capt. Charles D. McLean, mortal; Edwin E. Nelson. Captured: Peter H. Kipp, James H. Reed.

Co. E.—Wounded: Charles Thatcher, mortal, died July 22d; John B. Rand, Harrison Robertson.

Co. F.—Killed: Sergt. A. H. Cooper. Wounded: Capt. E. W. Hindes, George Woolly, arm amputated; W. H. Leach, L. B. Grover, Charles B. Mead.

Co. G.—Killed: Sergt. Henry Lye, Privates Wm. H. Woodruff, Eli J. Fitch. Wounded: Privates Eli S. B. Vincent, mortal, in shoulder;

Orris D. Hawley, left shoulder, severe; John P. Hauxhurst, left hand, severe; Levi Ingalsbee; shoulder, severe; Abner Johnson, finger, slight. Missing: Private Samuel Hall, captured.

Co. H.—Wounded: Sergt. John T. Schermerhorn, severely, but would not accept a discharge, preferring to serve his term out, which he did.

Co. I.—Killed: Lieut. George W. Sheldon, Lewis Girich-ton. Wounded: Lieut. H. C. Garriscin (commanding), Sergt. Henry Burrows, Edwin Cramer.

Co. K.—Wounded: William Clelland, right hip, severe; Ed win B. Parks, slight.

The regimental surgeon, Dr. John W. Brennan, was severely wounded while engaged at his duties on the field. Col. Berdan had his horse shot under him.

Lieut. Dyer Pettijohn, of Company A, Second Regiment, who was taken prisoner on the afternoon of the 2d, remained in the hands of the enemy until the close of the war. In this officer's case came up a question of rank with-out muster. It appears that just previous to the Gettysburg battle he had received a second lieutenant's commission, but had been unable to muster, therefore when captured was still a first sergeant. When he came home, the claim for second lieutenant was allowed and paid in full.

Col. Berdan makes especial mention in his report of the following officers coming under his notice, preceded with the statement that "the entire command, with very few exceptions, behaved most gallantly." Officers mentioned are; Col. Lakeman and Major Lee, 3d Maine, for their services on the reconnoissance, also Capt. Nash; Major Stoughton and-Capt. Baker for their -judgment and skill in, handling their troops under fire; also Lieut. Norton.

While this battle was pending, Col. Peteler was in Washington intending to join his command, where he arrived June 24th, and, reporting to Gen. Halleck, was told he could not just then get to his regiment, owing to Stuart's -cavalry raid, so ordered him to report to

Gen. Heintzelman in charge of the defense of Washington. To describe the feeling existing at the capitol at that exciting period of war times, Col. Peteler was told by some Union officers in the -city, that if he wanted to find his regiment, all he had to do was to wait a short time in Washington, the regiment would come to him; showing that they did not look for the glorious victory that followed. Finally, he received notice through the war department that one of the last acts done by Gen. Hooker as army commander was to accept his resignation June 23d, which he had tendered the winter before, but at that time was refused. This news was disappointing to Col. Peteler who had wished it was lost or destroyed, -as he had been trying to withdraw it.

The 3d corps left Gettysburg at three A. M. of July 7th, commanded by Gen. French, with a third division added, making nine brigades in all of infantry, besides the usual artillery brigade. Our troops were now rushing after Lee, who had a good 48-hours start, and was as anxious to get back to Virginia as Meade was to prevent him.

The Sharpshooters were not well pleased with the treatment received at the hands of some of the Pennsylvania farmers, notwithstanding the rebel guns were plainly within their hearing; while the Marylanders cheered them on and "treated the boys splendidly." They not only sold them food at reasonable rates, but contributed many things—often took no pay. This difference in disposition and feeling seemed very strange to the soldiers, and the only way they could account for it, was, in the language of one of the "phunny phellows" of the regiment, "all owing to the way the human twig was bent."

The marching now averaged about 20 miles a day, via Emmitsburg, Frederick and over the Antietam battle field *en route* to the Potomac. The enemy succeeded in crossing at Williamsport the night of the 13th—nine days after leaving Gettysburg—without a battle. This was just as disappointing to the troops as it was to the northern public. It is true that a portion of our army ran into them near Williamsport, where on frowning heights they awaited our coming, and where the Second Regiment were anxious for another fight,—begged to get up to the enemy's position,—but, as no attack was made, they slipped away into Virginia, their own chosen ground; and there our army contended with them ever after. There were no more northern raids—that much was accomplished.

On the morning of the 5th, it was ascertained the enemy was in full retreat by the Fairfield and Cashtown roads. The 6th corps was immediately sent in pursuit on the Fairfield road, and the cavalry on the Cashtown road and by the Emmitsburg and Monterey Passes. July 5th and 6th-were employed in succoring the wounded and burying the dead.

Major-Gen. Sedgwick, commanding the 6th corps, having pushed the pursuit of the enemy as far as the Fairfield Pass in the mountains, and reporting that the pass was a very strong one, in which a small force of the enemy could hold in check and delay for a considerable time any pursuing force, I determined to follow the enemy by a flank movement, and accordingly, leaving McIntosh's brigade of cavalry and Neill's brigade of infantry to continue harassing the enemy, put the army in motion for Middletown, Md._ Orders were immediately sent to Major-Gen. French at Frederick to reoccupy Harper's Ferry and send a force to occupy Turner's Gap, in South Mountain. I subsequently ascertained Major-Gen. French had not only anticipated these orders in part, but had pushed a cavalry force to Williamsport and Falling Waters, where they destroyed the enemy's pontoon bridge and captured its guard. Buford was at the same time sent to Williamsport and Hagerstown. The duty above assigned to the cavalry was most successfully accomplished, the enemy being greatly harassed,. his trains destroyed, and many captures of guns and prisoners made. After halting at Middletown to procure necessary supplies and bring up the trains, the army moved through the South Mountain, and by July 12th was in front of the enemy, who occupied a strong position on the heights of Marsh Run, in advance of Williamsport. In taking this position several skirmishes and affairs had been had with the enemy principally by the cavalry, and the 11th and 6th corps. The 13th was occupied in reconnoissances of the enemy's position and preparations for attack, but, on advancing on the morning of the 14th, it was ascertained he had retired the night previous by a bridge at Falling Waters and the ford at Williamsport. The cavalry in pursuit overtook the rear guard at Falling Waters, capturing two grins and numerous prisoners."—GEN. MEADE.

On the 17th of July the Sharpshooters crossed the river at Harper's Ferry, and marching along the base of the mountains by Snicker's Gap and Upperville, proceeded to Manassas Gap where, as skirmishers, they took part in the battle known as

WAPPING HEIGHTS.

July 23, 1863.

This was a brisk action; the First Sharpshooters were in it to the extent of 60 rounds per man, during which time they drove the enemy back over a mile to their main force on the hill. Here they halted in the thick brush as they could proceed no farther, having fired away all their ammunition, being afterwards relieved by infantry. A brigade (the Excelsiors) then charged up the hill, driving the foe off, obtaining and holding their position. The Second Sharp, shooters supported the first in the fight.

Companies F and K were together, and advanced on the extreme left of our line. After going 100 yards into the woods they met the foe stuck behind trees, waiting for our boys to come up. The enemy failed to hold their ground, retreating a half-mile through the wood, out into a timothy field containing scattering trees which they were glad to take advantage of. Some sharp shooting now took place, in which Lieut. Thorp—always grabbing a gun—Corp. Israel B. Tyler and a Company F man distinguished themselves, to the *loss* of the Johnnies, along with six prisoners sent back by Thorp in charge of Corp. Hall. Driving the rest away, the line advanced down a hill, across a ravine to the top of another hill where they halted, while the infantry charged over and beyond them.

Gen. Ward commanding 1st division says: "I ordered a portion of the 1st and 3d brigades for-ward to support the skirmishers and drive the enemy out. This order was countermanded, and the 2d (Excelsior) brigade, 2d division, was ordered to report to me for that purpose. The enemy could now plainly be seen in three heavy columns, moving southward by the flank."

Col. Farnum, commanding Excelsior brigade: "Arriving near Wapping Station, we were massed by divisions, and, taking the hills upon the right side of the road, advanced to the crossing at that station; then, crossing to the left range of hills, we were advanced close upon the line of skirmishers of the 1st division, 3d corps, arriving and halting at about four P. M. At about five P. M. we were informed by Gen. Spinola, commanding the brigade, that he had received orders from Gen. Prince to march the brigade through a defile up to the skirmish line, for the purpose of assaulting the enemy on a hill in our front. On the promulgation of this order, the brigade, marching left in front, proceeded to the designated position, and was there formed in line of battle. The order was given to fix bayonets and charge the line in front of us. Arriving on the crest of the hill, driving the enemy before us, we found the work but half done, the enemy being in strength on two hills in front of us, the farther being held by their artillery. The brigade charged on, returning the *enemy's* fire, taking prisoners, and carrying all before it. At this time Gen. Spinola fell seriously wounded, and the command of the brigade devolved upon me by seniority."

To show the strait the Sharpshooters were in with their empty guns, while awaiting the approach of the supports-the charging brigade—the following anecdote is given:

A BLUFF THAT COUNTED.

Lute Harrington, of Company F, a short, stout, well' rounded little fellow, full of fun and high spirited, having finished his shooting for want of cartridges, went to picking blackberries which hung in endless quantities on the bushes about them, for the boys would shoot and pick, and when their ammunition was gone went for the berries with both hands, their rifles slung across their shoulders. A foreign, officer noticing this through his glass, exclaimed: "Mine Got! vat kind of men have we got up dere to pick blackberries on der skirmish line?" Well, Lute was helping himself to the berries with his rifle slung behind his shoulder. Moving through the thicket, casting quick glances along the line to be sure he was in his place, he suddenly came out into an open space slap upon a couple of Johnnies, one of whom was in the act of firing his piece as Lute surprised them—and himself too. But without an instant's hesitation; he aimed his rifle at the one whose gun might be loaded (he had just seen the other empty his), and in stentorian tones ordered him to "drop that gun or I'll make a hole through you, big enough to run a freight car." The man standing with the muzzle of his musket in his hand, the butt on the ground, let it fall at once, when the other reb was made to do the same. Now said Lute: "Gee about here! and be quick about it." He drove them around faced to our rear, marching them back to the provost guard. Twice on the way the larger man of the two stopped, as if minded to clinch the little fellow and wipe him out; but Lute walked right up to him swearing he would let daylight through him. The reb took a look into the black muzzle of the Sharps rifle, and fancying he could see a load coming out, concluded to keep on. When the provost was reached, the one who had given the most trouble, turned fiercely upon our little game-cock, shook his fist and shouted: "You little—Yankee, if I had a charge in my gun you would never got me here." "And if I had a load in mine," said Lute, "I'd never asked you to come here." "Wasn't your gun loaded? "faltered the now crestfallen rebel. Lute held up his rifle and threw down the breech block, not a sign of a load there. They had been tricked—captured by a boy with an empty rifle. Unutterable rage swelled the forms of the two prisoners, as with clinched teeth they cursed all Yankees and Yankee tricks, while the little bluffer went back to the line, roaring happy.

Capt. Aschmann in his German report makes the following interesting statement: "The enemy were moving on the west side of the Blue Ridge towards Richmond, while our army were following' on the east side, for the purpose of either forcing him to a stand, or to interpose between him and his capitol. The march was very exhausting, the heat intense, and several of our company (A) were sunstruck. On the 20th July we entered Upperyille, a small village, where our cavalry had an engagement a month before, and we had to bury a number of dead horses before we could select a camping ground. In the afternoon of the 22d our army corps resumed its march to Manassas Gap, a mountain pass, where from information received, the enemy was contemplating a passage, we arriving there after excessive fatigue about ten o'clock at night. The next morning our regiment was pushed forward to sound the enemy's position, and we soon discovered his outposts,—a strong position protected by bowlders and stone fences,—and a spirited engagement of nearly two hours' duration took place. The enemy offered a most stubborn resistance, and was only put to flight after a desperate hand-to-hand encounter, whereby we lost many of our companies' best men. An assault by our infantry finally put an end to the carnage, driving the enemy into retreat. It appears that only a small portion of the hostile army had been engaged, put forth for the purpose of giving time to enable their main body to get away with the rich plunder in horses and cattle carried away from Pennsylvania, part of which was, however, recovered by our cavalry near Ashby Gap."

During this engagement, Private Wesley Annfield, who had been detailed in the Pioneer corps, not liking that way of serving his country, left them in the rear, and rushing to the front, passed to the flank of his company (G), proceeding to a house in the distance. Soon after, he returned with several prisoners having, he said, "cut off their communications with his axe." He then reported to his company for duty, and with several others a short time after, received promo Lion.

CASUALTIES.

Co. B.—Killed: Thomas E. Carey. Wounded: Charles W. Dutcher.

Co. C.—Wounded: Capt. James H. Baker, left foot.

Co. G.—Wounded: Sergt. William Babcock, left eye, lost; William E. Wheeler, slightly in right arm.

Co. I.—Wounded: Albert J. Sisson.

On the 24th they marched along, encamping three miles from Warrenton on the 26th. They again moved on the 31st and encamped in the vicinity of White Sulphur Springs, where the troops, exhausted by a fatiguing campaign of over 50 days, obtained that rest so greatly needed.

"The Confederate army retiring to the Rapidan, a position was taken with this (Union) army on the line of the Rappahannock, and the campaign terminated about the close of July."—GEN. MEADE.

In this camp they remained over six weeks, with drills and picket duties to occupy their time. A sharp watch was kept at the outposts for prowling cavalry, or as they were generally termed, bands of guerrillas. Sickness again prevailed and in consequence, a number of men were lost to the regiment by being sent to northern hospitals, or by discharge direct. The sulphur springs were frequently visited by the men, who drank of its waters, but generally with wry faces, and if it did them no good, they said it was as tasty as sutler's eggs— to the loss of the sutler. Changes occurred in commissioned and non-commissioned officers in rank and position. In First Regiment Lieut. Aschmann, Company A, became acting-adjutant, Capt. Marble, of Company G, field officer, under Col. Trepp commanding (Col. Berdan having left for Washington soon after Gettysburg), while Lieut. Stevens assumed command of the Wisconsin company.

SEVENTH CAMPAIGN.

RACING WITH LEE.

On Sept. 15th at six P. M. we broke camp, and, after marching two hours slowly, halted after dark in a piece of woods near the road. On the following day marched right along until after dark, resting in a cornfield near Culpeper, having forded the Hedgeman and Hazel forks of the Rappahannock. Many fell out on this day's march from fatigue, rejoining their companies the next morning. It is just possible that foraging had something to do with it, as a number of turkeys were found in the regiment—and the boys took good care of them. They were protected—from the gaze of the officers, so they didn't have to divide. On the 17th marching beyond Culpeper two and one-half miles west, they encamped on the right of the Sperryville pike. At this camp a large amount of green clothing, with overcoats (which were the regulation blue) and blankets formerly turned in, were received and distributed. While here the First Sharpshooters left Ward's 2d brigade, being assigned to the 3d brigade commanded by Col. DeTrobriand—the Second Sharpshooters remaining with Ward. In the history of Company A in "Minnesota in the Civil War," is related the following incident occurring on this campaign, but it is an error in saying the general was Hancock, who was absent from the army during the fall of '63, account of his Gettysburg wound.

"In the fall of 1863, while advancing towards Culpeper Court House, the regiment having the skirmish line moved too slowly. Gen. Hancock stated to the officer in command that the army was waiting on them. The officer replied that he doubted if any other regiment could do better. Gen.. Hancock ordered Second Sharpshooters to the front. Riding to the side of the regiment he said: 'Boys, I have promised that you would go through there; I think you will.' One hour later the general sent his compliments, requesting that they slacken their speed, as the army was not keeping in supporting distance. The rebels never liked the Long range rifles."

The Union telegraph was extended as the troops advanced, being put up by experienced hands in a rapid manner. The lines were kept right up with us. Good log cabin and board shanties were built in this vicinity by the men, which served at least for exercise, but not for use long—three weeks being the length of their stay in this section.

THE ROGUE'S MARCH.

"Poor old soldier, poor old soldier, Tarred and feathered

And then drummed out,

Because he wouldn't soldier."

At this camp an unfortunate soldier who had been dishonorably discharged by court-martial, was drummed out of service by members of his company to the tune of the "Rogue's March," in words as above. This disagreeable duty to the company comrades, who generally dislike to go through the performance, is ,conducted in this manner: The culprit is marched through camp between two files of soldiers, with inverted bayonets—arms reversed—in the front rank reaching almost to the doomed man's body, and a full charge bayonet from behind. Sometimes the man's head is shaved, the U. S. buttons always cut off, and in very serious eases he is branded.

While in this vicinity the members of Company B on picket were considerably agitated over the loss overnight of their second lieutenant, Theodore Wilson, who was known to have strayed outside the lines. As he came back at just day-break, it was rumored and became a standing joke on that officer, that his search for chickens turned to, playing Romeo to some Confederate Juliet; but discovering that the latter enticed him on for the purpose of his capture, he too loyal to be thus tricked, started back, though too late, and had to lie in the bush until daylight. As it rained hard and there was considerable mud, the officer evidently fared hard, from the sorry plight he presented on appearing before his company—and that's where the laugh came in.

FROM THE RAPIDAN TO BULL RUN.

From about the 17th of September to October 10th,. the Army of the Potomac had advanced as far as the line of the Rapidan. At the latter date we became convinced that another move was in order on the military chess board, by the sounding of the long roll by drum and bugle, followed by an order to fall in, quickly. So hastily packing up, we were soon ready to march, and not long after, left our new camp,—one of our best ones,—and, being maneuvered about some little time in the woods as picket scouts and skirmishers, were finally drawn up in line of battle in an open field west of Culpeper prepared for an attack. Here we remained all night without much sleep, under strict orders to be ready for whatever might transpire.

The next morning (11th) at an early hour, we began retracing our steps toward the Rappahannock. While resting a few moments on the way, we were disturbed by a shot fired on the left flank. Soon after, more followed, and hastily falling in, we were sent out as skirmishers, rebel horsemen having been discovered prowling around. Companies G and B were used as a support to the left of the line. After feeling our way about a half a mile through the brush and open field we were assembled, on learning that a small body of rebel cavalry had passed by, which were no longer to be seen. We captured one man in gray uniform.

Not long after, we were again in the column marching on, whither, we knew not, although apparently falling back. The roads were good, the weather cool, therefore notwithstanding packed knapsacks and haversacks with 60 rounds of ammunition weighed heavily, the men made good time, crossing Hazel river by pontoon late in the afternoon, fording the Hedgeman knee deep at night about ten o'clock; finally resting a mile beyond on a hill-side tired, hungry, somewhat wet and many muddy, having been so unfortunate as to slip on the muddy sides of the numerous streams we crossed, causing a fall, which while loaded down as stated, tried their utmost patience, especially should a rifle hammer or muzzle hit one on the head, as was sometimes the case. The following morning (12th), we were astir early and after marching a short distance, northerly, retraced our steps, taking up a position on, the bank of the Hedgeman, near the ford. Some firing was heard during the day, right and left, fighting evidently going on. The day previous we witnessed from a distance Kilpatrick's cavalry charge, away to our right, easterly; but notified that he could take care of the force pressing him, that we had better keep moving, we left him and his troopers to worst his opponents—which he did effectually.

Left the Hedgeman early on the 13th, moving back towards Warrenton Junction, leaving Sulphur Springs to our left. On several occasions were ordered to be ready to meet the enemies they were known to be moving with us, their cavalry hovering on our flanks; at one time drawing up in line of battle, and the 5th division of the Sharpshooters—Companies G and B—were sent out over a wide, open waste or plain to another road at a point of woods three-fourths of a mile from the main body, which latter were finely posted on an elevated position. As the ranking officer, I had orders to "hold that point against any approach in that direction." Good enough to tell, if they didn't come too thick for the small force sent so far away to hold "all corners at bay." On reaching this isolated position, we found ourselves reinforced by two companies of Marylanders, giving us a better show for resistance. Here we remained for a short time, watching well the front, when we were signaled to return, as the enemy were reported ahead. Not long after, firing was heard, and the booming of cannon told us that a fight was in progress. So we again pushed on, hurrying back to the main road on double-quick to catch up,—a very fatiguing performance loaded down as the men were with ammunition and equipments—our regiment being a good ways ahead.

SHARPSHOOTERS' CHARGE AT AUBURN.

Leaving the road by file left; we were soon after drawn up in line of battle, Gen. French ordering the regiment in on a charge, none coming up that: "These are Sharpshooters, general," he replied: ,"Well, no matter, those fellows can fight any way." So; immediately fixing bayonets, we were soon off over an open field towards a piece of woods 300 yards away, from whence shots were being rapidly fired; our loud war cry adding to the general excitement, evidencing a determination to get there.

When Companies G and B arrived, they came in on a run—it made them puff—and passing the balance of the regiment waiting for them, without relaxing speed formed into line in their places on the left, when the regiment immediately moved forward taking up the double-quick and keeping that lively step across the open field until they struck the woods; firing as they ran. It was a good line, and the general was pleased at their promptness and hurried movements.

Entering the wood driving all before them, the Sharpshooters kept on to the top of a hill yelling and shouting, where after some difficulty hearing the command, they were halted and scouts sent ahead. The enemy had fled from this part of the field, and soon after the firing on our right also ceased. Three rebel dead lying in the woods where we entered, showed that we had been engaging dismounted cavalry. A large body of them mounted were to be seen across the open field drawn up in line of battle, whereupon several Wisconsin men gave them a few rounds at 300 yards, when they skedaddled.

Our loss was slight, two wounded in the regiment, one of whom was Jonathan H. Breed in right leg, a Company K man, who would have bled to death but for his comrade Joel Race binding his handkerchief around same, twisting it with a bayonet, until the surgeon took Breed in charge. The torn and ragged regimental colors received three more bullet holes through them. The advantage of breech-loading rifles was again made apparent, our men continually firing as they ran after the retreating Johnnies. Their line was completely broken up, and they scattered and scampered off in a hurry. Had this affair occurred earlier in the war, placed in the hands of an eastern reporter, it would probably have been written up as—

"A grand charge of a beautiful line of dark-green riflemen, and handsome repulse of gray-jackets and butternuts."

But it was too late in the war to become prominent, besides there were no- friendly reporters about, to give us our just dues; which, no doubt they would have cheerfully done, had they been present to see for themselves the importance of the service performed, and by the Sharpshooters only, at that particular place.

Again we were moving on, until late at night did we continue to march, the night being dark, the men fatigued and foot-sore, but there was lid straggling—it was a poor country for stragglers. The Sharpshooters were out on each side of the road as flankers, a portion of the way. We finally rested at Greenwich; two Wisconsin men, Jacobs and Moore, who had got ahead of their company, being the first to enter the place in company with an infantry officer. We had marched that day over 26 miles, besides skirmishing and fighting. Had our troops not been well trained, inured to hardship, therefore in fine condition to travel, they could not have withstood these long, forced marches, but would have been left by the hundreds scattered along the road for miles.

The 2d corps under Warren, bringing up the rear, had a sharp skirmish at Auburn the following morning, where Lee tried to cut them off, but failed. The importance of this action was in the detention of Lee's advance several hours, by Warren's successful maneuvering and final escape, cutting his way through the accumulating enemy, bringing off all his wagons, ambulances and ammunition—with the Confederates behind him. Lee was detained one day at Warrenton (13th) provisioning his troops; so that when his advance struck Bristoe the next day, the Union army had passed that station, with the exception of the 2d corps—the rear guard. Gen. Meade afterwards admitted that he should have given the enemy battle at Auburn, but was misinformed of the relative position of both armies, supposing Lee was ahead of him.

"Notwithstanding my losing a day, I had moved with more celerity than the enemy, and was a little in his advance. If I had known this at the time, I would have given the enemy battle the next day, in the position I occupied at Auburn and Greenwich."—MEADE.

It was now rumored about, that the rebs were giving us a hard race for position near Bull Run and Centreville, and the next morning, 14th, we were quickly marching on; the Sharpshooters again out as flankers—a very important service, as a guard against ambuscades or other surprise;. but we were recalled on reaching the more open and extensive Manassas Plains. Crossing Broad Run, filing to the left and rear, we again drew up in line of battle; but soon after, left and finally crossed Bull Run at Blackburn's Ford, the old earthworks used when the 2d Wisconsin went into their first fight, still to be seen. Arrived on the heights near Centreville in the afternoon, where we found a large portion of our army already in position, having arrived by different roads. Here we remained overnight. Late in the afternoon we could see plainly the flashes that preceded the cannon's deep roar, in the battle then going on at Bristoe Station, in which the 2d corps were actively engaged checking the enemy's advance.

On the 15th they marched to Fairfax Station, resting in the timber. That evening the 3d corps turned out without arms to receive their late commander, Gen. Sickles, forced to leave us on losing a leg at Gettysburg. He rode by the lines in a barouche and was received with loud cheering. The 3d corps liked Sickles, and heartily sympathized with him in his misfortune. He was a brave commander, and such officers had the respect and confidence of their command.

On the 16th in the afternoon, the regiment was ordered out to witness the fate of a deserter, the first one to be shot in the corps. The first division, of which the Sharpshooters formed a part, was formed in two lines making three sides of a square. Between these lines the doomed man surrounded by the provost-guard, was marched solemnly behind his coffin, the band in front playing the usual march. He appeared resigned to his fate, walking firmly along to his last resting place. His looks, as he closely scanned the line's on his death-march, seemed to bespeak a farewell to the soldiers; seemed to indicate the justness of his sentence, and his own deep disgrace; that he was reconciled to his fate, realizing that he was—

"In the lowest deep; but a lower deep Threatening to devour me, opens wide."

His lips moved not; and except his glances right and left, a piercing look, he strode slowly along and erect, to his doom. After a short prayer by the chaplain attending him his eyes were bandaged by the provost marshal, when he-seated himself on the edge of the coffin which was by the side of the grave. -Soon after, 12 muskets poured forth their contents at a distance of six paces, and he fell dead into his coffin pierced by 11 bullets, one gun containing a blank cartridge. The different regiments then returned to their respective camps solemnly impressed with the scene just witnessed.

At this place considerable fault-finding existed among the men owing to the desperate state of the hard-tack.

It was *hard,* for certain; but when on behalf of the company I went to headquarters full of complaints, I found Col. Trepp and Capt. Marble seated at a cracker box table, having just finished their supper.

"Well, Stevens, what's the matter now? Considerable grumbling, eh?
"

"Yes, sir. The hard-tack don't suit the boys."

"Eh! What's that about the hard-bread—what's the matter with it? "

"Well, with us, what tack hasn't been monopolized by worms, is full of bugs."

"Oh! That's all, is it. Why, look here, my friend, see what Marble and I are about; "and he caused me to scan closely that table. "There," said he, "that white worm is Marble's, and this hard shell bug is mine; and I've bet him the cigars that my bug will get across the table first."

Of course, I had no more to say, for there sure enough was the bug and worm "making time" over the table, the fiery end of cigars hurrying them up from "the fire in the rear." I didn't stop to see which came out ahead, but leaving our "field and staff" laughing at me, "made tracks" myself *en route* to the company street where I reported accordingly. And so we bad to eat the hard tack or go without, as no other was to be obtained. It was only what I expected. We had got the best to be had, and it happened this time to be a hard lot; and our soldiers were not used to that kind. On the contrary, as a general thing, Uncle Sam's rations with us were good; and, although we sometimes got big round crackers, hard as flint,—the boys called them "B. C.'s," from their ancient appearance,—the smaller square ones were usually fresh and brittle, and free from crawlers. They didn't mind the worms so much, but the bugs gritted their teeth.

FROM BULL RUN TO THE RAPIDAN.

At four o'clock A. M. Oct. 19th, we were aroused from our sleep by the shrill bugle sounding the *reveille* and *general*. Falling in, rapidly, the troops at daybreak moved off southerly, following the line of the Orange & Alexandria railroad until near Bristoe Station, when they halted for the night:

While on Manassas Plains we found a number of persimmon trees, and in consequence of the hastily bitten fruit many of our men puckered up their mouths to a laughable extent, as it was not quite ripe. They thought they had struck a bonanza, but didn't stop to carry it all off after they had got a few good bites. They were, however, paid for getting sold, in the fun they had over it, and considerable chaffing followed, which served to keep them in good spirits for many a mile after. They were always glad to find fruit on their route, as it generally did them good, but they didn't run after any more persimmons.

On the 20th, pushed on, fording Kettle Run waist deep, and by mistaking the road waded another stream twice; finally halted for the night beyond Greenwich—Companies G and B being immediately detailed for picket. Moving forward the next day, after several changes of position they took up a new one near the picket lines at Cedar Run on the 26th, considerable fatigue being endured at times by the troops, the roads being dusty and weather very warm.

The enemy having destroyed the railroad by burning the ties, bending the rails—twisting them around trees—as they fell back, the Union troops were employed in repairing the same; details being sent out daily from the different companies for that purpose. This caused much delay, and it looked very much as if Lee had fooled us—as he certainly foiled us—in getting away so easy, and apparently at his leisure. It was a great disappointment to the loyal North, also their soldiers at the front; there being no general engagement, although our troops were never in better fighting trim than at that time. It was fine weather, and no better opportunity could have been offered to test the fighting capacity of the two great armies, as also the abilities of the respective commanders, maneuvering on open ground. It would probably have saved us a good deal of hard marching, and subsequent rough campaigning. And it proved to be the last chance to bring them together face to face in an open, fair fight. For Lee now retired to his breastworks beyond the Rapidan, to reach him thereafter we had to fight him on his own ground, attack his breastworks—it was pretty much all breastworks thereafter—until the closing scenes occurred a year and a half hence.

On the 28th I distinctly remember to have labored under many difficulties making out pay rolls, on a cracker-box desk in a leaky shelter tent, the rain pouring down in torrents coming through the little canvas, there was no escaping the big drops. It was decidedly tough, but it had to be done if at all possible, and I succeeded after much patience, warding off the rain by holding a piece of board over the paper with one hand while I wrote with the other. On the 29th, strange as it may appear so early in the season, we received orders to "prepare for winter quarters." But we had heard of such orders before, only to be "sold," as we were on this occasion. And yet old soldiers would rather be on the go, than to be drilling, two or three times a day, for above all things, the volunteer soldier dislikes these daily drills—as a general thing he would rather fight than drill; particularly knapsack drills and battalion movements.

On the 30th they made another move along the railroad line, halting in a large field where they remained several days. On the 3d of November the Wisconsin company voted for state officers, it being election day. The polls were opened on the picket line, each man voting as he saw fit; the Union ticket headed by James T. Lewis for governor, getting pretty much all the votes. The company officers were the judges, passing the ballot box along the line. There was no intimidation.

'Twas an infernal lie, That copperhead cry.

At half past two the morning of November 7th, the 3d -corps broke temporary camp near Warrenton Junction, and started off at daybreak towards the Rappahannock. The Second Sharpshooters led the 3d brigade, taking what our French brigadier told Col. Stoughton was "de post of de honor," the First Regiment being out as flankers. After a quiet and steady march along the road leading towards Falmouth, they left the same at noon and striking off on another road leading towards the river, made a temporary halt; but were soon after sent down the hill where the Sharpshooters formed in line of battle in advance of the other troops.

KELLY'S FORD.

Nov. 7, 1863.

At half-past one in the afternoon the two regiments deployed out in skirmish line, and advancing over the open plain in front, soon became aware of the presence of the enemy by the whistling of bullets about them. The order to double-quick being given, away they went, driving the rebels pell-mell over the river, where they jumped into rifle pits and behind works and commenced to shoot. Pressing on to the river bank under sharp fire from the opposite side, temporary cover was obtained. It was now "blaze away" on both sides in good earnest. After some sharp exchanges' reinforcements were observed coming down on a run, towards a large brick building opposite the right of the, regiment. They instantly became the object of our immediate attention, but although the fire of the riflemen was sharp and quick, yet many succeeded in gaining this place of cover. One of these fellows began shooting at our men from a window above, his first—and last—shot being at Lieut. Thorp of "K," whose tall form as he rested on one knee in his company line, made him a conspicuous object. The shot was well made, striking a twig four feet in front of the officer's breast. The lieutenant at once grabbed Orville Parker's rifle and held for the window. When he put his gun and head out again, Thorp pulled on him. Parker said the reb's gun dropped to the ground outside, while the Johnny fell inside. They soon "skedaddled" from there, however, for between the rattling of the Sharpshooters' bullets and several Union shells from a battery that opened on the building with effect, the place became too hot for them, causing them to scatter out,—like so many bees from a hive,—receiving a close and heavy fire from the First Regiment, which made them run the faster. The B and G men being on the left of the line and immediately opposite the rifle pits, had long-range shots at these runaways, but occupied their attention mostly with those in front—these were vicious fellows and fired to kill.

A DOUBLE-SHOTTED JOHNNY.

A remarkable instance of fine shooting occurred at this time. Corp. Johnson, of Company G, upon being urged to give the retreating rebs a shot, although he considered the chances poor hitting his man at that distance, running off as he was, finally exclaimed: "By great! I'll try him," and allowing two feet for windage, drew up his rifle at 700 yards raise of sight and fired. At the same time Lieut.. Thorp of the adjoining company, K, asked George J. Fisher if he could "down that fellow." Answering: "I guess I can," Fisher shot just as Johnson did, and the man threw up his hands and went down. The fallen rebel was afterwards found wounded in two places, he stating that both shots came the same instant, one through the right thigh, the other the left hip. All of which, simply showed what our marksmen could do with the breech-loaders.

The regiment was finally ordered to cross the river and charge the pits on the bank, the firing having slackened. Two Michigan companies, C and I, led the way, covered by B and G, who kept up a sharp fire, but soon after rushed down the slope headlong after them through the rapid water,—waist deep,—when the rest followed, under a galling fire from the enemy, whereby a number were hit while struggling against the swift, bubbling stream. Among them was Lieut. Frank S. Wells, of Company B, who received a stunning wound in his breast, and would have fallen but for S. C. James, who helped him back to the water's edge, where others took him out. Corp. James then rushed straight ahead through the splashing water, over a sand bar to a redoubt near the river. Mounting the same he received the surrender and sword of a North Carolina captain. Orville Parker, of Company K, fired into a pit just as the inmates had commenced waving their hats, to surrender. The ball passed through one man's head and into another's shoulder, killing both; a terrible illustration of close fighting. The Michigan members had run forward in advance, closely followed by other companies, and when within 10 feet of the first pit in their front, the enemy rising up, fired a volley, but, being above, fortunately shot too high and but few were struck. Our men at once charged on to them, capturing at this place about 80—"packed in the bottom of the pit like sardines." Or of them, a sergeant, shouted in vain for them to pick up their guns and fire again—to "drive the Yankees back!" He was gritty, but it was his last chance to show it, as he was shot down a moment after. It was a lively scrimmage; but more so at the next pit, where through fire and smoke, mid groans and shrieks of wounded men, some bayoneted, others blown through by opposing rifles, the work was carried. Planting the worn and tattered regimental colors on top of the pit, the occupants of the same were forced to surrender. The Vermont company, Capt. Merriman, came down on them in a body, the captain himself in advance, ordering the surrender. As he was alone at the time, they were disposed to bring him down from the top of the works, but when he called on "F" to "come up here," that settled the business. In all, 500 prisoners were taken, including several officers of high rank—all there were in their front—a number being captured in the bushes and in the building on the right, by individual members of the different companies. Those in the building under a major's command, were considerably surprised by Lieut. Judkins, who, approaching the house noiselessly, suddenly burst in the door, and bringing down an axe which he carried with him, heavily to the floor, demanded in stentorian tones their immediate surrender, which was at once granted. Before crossing the river, Jacobs, Webster and Van Buren (Co. G), tried a flank movement on a rebel, but it was no use, they could not obtain a crossfire on the fellow from that side of the stream: Webster finally gave him a polite invitation to come out' of his hole and give himself up. But he rather roughly declined to comply with the request, though he was obliged to succumb to the force of circumstances soon after. The three soldiers above named, with others, were busily engaged after crossing in hunting up these scattered fellows, who were generally found burrowed in small holes among the bushes. At one point the writer was covered by a rebel musket front one of these holes, 50 yards distant; but Van Buren from the right and front coming along with his Sharps ready for any emergency, the Reb concluded, as he afterwards admitted, that he had better not shoot, but responded readily to the demand to "Get out of that hole, lively, and give up your gun," as the brave corporal charged on him. This stopped the deadly intent, and they sent him to the rear, with the other prisoners.

Lieut. Connington and George H. Smith (K) discovered and captured seven in a ditch at the left of the ford, while "Little Park" (as he was called), Frederick Park, Company K, caught five in an old cellar, threatening to "shoot 'em all" if they didn't surrender; which he could hardly have done, as he afterwards discovered he had no load in his gun. But they surrendered. While crossing the river Andrew Kirkham just dodged ,a well-meant shot by jumping aside, and with a warning "look out, Abner," Johnson turned as the "critter pulled trigger," thereby escaping with a heavy whack on his back, the bullet striking his knapsack flattening up inside. Soon after, a Swiss member of Company A got the bottom of his frying pan knocked out on the back of his knapsack while faced firing to the left oblique. This-made him very mad and he swore a lot of foreign oaths, worse than a trooper. For, if there is anything that will make a good soldier swear, it is to lose his cooking kit.

All the companies performed well their part, and had good reason to feel proud of their great victory, which belonged to the Sharpshooters, the First Regiment doing the fighting, connected on their left by the Second Regiment; which though not so actively engaged, held an important position along the river below the Ford. Some of them joined the Wisconsin company, stating that there was not enough game below to keep them in sport, although (Lieut.) Charles H. Foote, of the Michigan company, ".B," did his part by undressing, more or less, and plunging into the deep water swam the river, going out to a rifle pit where he-took charge of the only Johnny left, not shot or who didn't run away, and in all his nakedness brought his captive-back through the turbulent, waters, amid the cheers of his end of the line.

The prisoners were sent back across the river and turned over to a New York regiment, who it appears got the credit of capturing them by some partial, or at least mistaken, Eastern journals. Gen. DeTrobriand, however, our brigade commander—who was right there superintending the fight—knew better, and gave the Berdan Sharpshooters the credit to which they only were entitled, and who were highly complimented by that officer for the gallantry displayed in the affair. By the time that New York regiment or any other infantry regiment crossed over, the Sharpshooters were a mile ahead, and had formed a long skirmish line over the open plain facing westerly. It was virtually Greenback against Grayback—the Blue Coats being in reserve.

Among the many field officers gallantly engaged was Capt. Nash, who was constantly riding the entire line, both horse and rider presenting a bold mark for rebel bullets flying thickly around him, but harmless—although he had a horse killed under him.

"Never mind 'em, boys," he cried, "we'll get' em bye and bye."

Also, Col. Trepp, Capt. Marble and others, were conspicuous for their cool demeanor, and readiness to close into chose quarters with the enemy, despite the uncertain river and, other disadvantages. Lieut. Aschmann, acting adjutant, had a horse shot under him.

Having captured all at the river, the men pushed ahead and formed a long skirmish line fronting a piece of woods, the right resting at some rude and dilapidated breastworks. Soon after, a force of the enemy came out of the woods, advancing towards these works on the right. They didn't come far, however, the firing being too sharp for them, while the artillery from an eminence sent into their ranks shot and shell. They soon deployed out in skirmish line and lying 'on the ground, remained in that position until after dark. Some cavalry appeared far to our left, as if intending to sweep behind and cut us off from the main force at the river, but a dozen or more of our best long-range shots soon scattered them..

Sergt. Allen, of F, tells of a Sharpshooter whose record in the past had been so good that until this day he had never shirked any duty assigned him, who hung back when we charged over the river, but came over with the fourth line, lying down in the first rifle pit after its capture; so following us a little behind until we were at the last earthwork, where he lay sheltered from the enemy's fire. He started up when the men were called for the long-range firing on the cavalry, but immediately dropped back under cover as if afraid. Presently, muttering to himself: "I may as well try a 900 yard shot too," he half arose with his rifle to his face, looking towards our left. The instant the side of his head appeared above the work a ball passed through it, and he dropped at our feet—he was dead. All day he had a premonition of this, and struggled in vain to overcome it. When he showed fight his time came.

After our regiment had crossed the Ford and formed new lines in advance, the main body crossed over in force, and soon the plain behind was full of troops. After dark; being relieved, we retired to a side hill to eat and rest, all suffering more or less from the cold weather. The fight ended with darkness. The regiment lost three killed and 12 wounded.

Some of the men lost their supper that night, and Sergt. Allen tells how it happened: "On being relieved we went back to a deserted house; a party of us going up-stairs started a fire in the fire-place, for the house was adorned with one of those old-fashioned Virginia chimneys with fireplaces on every floor. The coarse shake fencing had been built up cob-house fashion and the pyramid was covered with the boys' cups of coffee. Set my cup on, and leaning back with folded arms against the far wall mentally reviewed the events of the day. Suddenly an explosion rent the air which was at once full of coffee, cups, fire-brands, ashes and smoke, the chimney was demolished, the boys piling down stairs with more haste than grace. A shell from one of our batteries in the morning entering the back of the chimney without exploding, became buried in the ashes, and we had kindled a fire over it with a very natural result.

Fortunately no one was seriously injured, but we lost our coffee."

CASUALTIES.

Co. B.—Wounded: William M. Fitzgerald, mortally; Matthew Morgan.

Co. C.—Killed: Henry Townsend. Wounded: Edward J. Southworth, leg amputated.

Co. D. Wounded: James H. Reed, mortally.

Co. E.—Killed: Samuel-D. Munroe.

Co. F.—Killed: Patrick Murray. Wounded: Eugene Mead, Watson P. Morgan, Fitz Green- Halleck.

Co. I.—Killed:, Elbridge Jewell. Wounded: James Cramer.

Co. K.—Wounded: Corp. William A. - Henderson, right arm, severe.

During the night -the rebel force in front left, but was reported to have been captured by the 6th corps about four A. M. of the Fifth, they having effected a crossing and gained a victory above us at Rappahannock. Station, in which action the 5th Wisconsin took an active part, their brave and fearless commander, Col., Thos. S: Allen, being again wounded.

Two days after, Gen. Meade Issued this complimentary Order: "The commanding general congratulates the army upon the recent successful passage of the Rappahannock in the face of the enemy-compelling him to withdraw to his intrenchments behind the Rapidan.

"To Major-General Sedgwick and the officers and men of the Sixth and Fifth corps participating in the attack—particularly to the storming party Under Brigadier-General Russell—his thanks are due for the gallantry displayed in the assault on the enemy's intrenched position at Rappahannock Station, resulting in the capture of four guns, 2,000 small arms, eight ,battle-flags-, one bridge train, and 1,600 prisoners.

"To Major-General French and the officers and men of the Third corps engaged—particularly to the leading column, commanded by Colonel De Trobriand—his thanks are due for the gallantry displayed in the crossing at Kelly's Ford and the seizure of the enemy's intrenchments, and the capture of over 400 prisoners.

"The commanding general takes great pleasure in announcing to the army that the President has expressed his satisfaction with its recent operations."

Accompanying the above was the following by command of Major-Gen. French: "The Major-General commanding the Third Army Corps, in promulgating the complimentary order of the general commanding-the army, deems it a proper opportunity to express his admiration of the high soldier-like qualities of the officers and men of the corps exemplified in the forcing of the passage of the Rappahannock at Kelly's Ford on the 7th instant. To the fact that the river was in front of the enemy, and not in their rear, they are indebted for their escape after the storming of their intrenchments, saving, by a precipitate retreat over the open country behind them, their flags and cannon."

On the 8th, the troops pushing on towards Brandy Plains, the First Sharpshooters were sent for to clear the way—the enemy being in front, and the skirmishers of the leading division failing to start them—the aid calling aloud for "the regiment that crossed the river the day before." As ˙we' had been in the lead the day before, Gen. De Trobriand didn't feel as if we ought to be double-quicked a mile or more ahead from the middle of the column to take the advance, and so the Second Regiment was called up and went to the front, driving the enemy away and occupying

BRANDY STATION in handsome style, making for themselves a creditable victory. They went through with a rush, and sent the foe flying out of sight towards the Rapidan.

When our regiment reached the Brandy Plains a grand sight was presented to their view; the different corps with their various flags and banners, marching on to the plain at the same time from different roads, thus showing the ability of Gen. Meade in handling large bodies of troops. It having been extensively rumored about, shortly after leaving the Rappahannock, that the Army of the Potomac were to unite in the afternoon at Brandy, for once, at least, the report was correct. As the head of the approaching columns entered through the openings on to the broad plain in front, the humorous Armfield expressed his opinion aloud, that it was "a fine sight for a special artist," and notwithstanding the thick dust that enveloped the soldiers as they moved along the road, "an occasion in which he could see particularly well."

Arriving at Brandy, they halted for the night among the various corps collected together. After several changes, on the 10th of November the regiment went into camp on the farm of John Minor Botts—the once famous Virginia statesman—where winter quarters were quickly erected. So rapid were the movements of Gen. Meade across the Rappahannock, that the Confederates, taken by surprise, hurriedly left their log quarters in this vicinity, and as Mr. Botts—our informant—expressed it: "Hurried back in great confusion to the Rapidan, more like a drove of sheep than men."

Mr. Botts seemed to occupy a neutral position in the war, although expressing strong Union sentiments to our soldiers. Relative to this once prominent Virginian, the following article was taken from a Wisconsin paper in 1865:

JOHN M. BOTTS.—This gentleman employed a portion of his time during the war in writing a book, which he proposes to publish, entitled: "A History of the Secession Movement, and its Public and Secret Advocates, North and South, since the Days of Calhoun." When Mr. Botts was thrown into prison, Jeff Davis sought to obtain possession of the manuscript, but the author refused to surrender it unless Davis would agree to publish it. The publication he desired because it would produce a revolution within a revolution, in which he could take part. Davis did not agree to the terms; the war being over, Botts proposes to publish it on his own account.

Mr. Botts informed Lieut. Judkins, acting quartermaster of our regiment, that he offered to give Jeff Davis the manuscript in question if he would publish it word for word in his leading paper, and would pay him a large sum for so doing, but Jeff refused the offer.

EIGHTH CAMPAIGN.

MINE RUN

On the 26th of November the troops left the Brandy camp to test the virtues of a winter campaign, crossing the Rapidan in the evening. The Sharpshooters (3d corps) crossed at Jacob's Mills after dark, halting nearby, until morning, the weather being very cold. The next morning they moved on, and late in the afternoon went into action at the battle of

LOCUST GROVE.

Nov. 27, 1863.

The fighting had already commenced before they arrived on the field, at a place called by the Confederates "Payne's Farm," several miles from Locust Grove. Advancing in line of battle through thickets of brush and timber, under fire, they reached a position behind a rail fence on the edge of the timber, in connection with the 17th Maine, 68th Pennsylvania and 5th Michigan of our brigade, with the 3d Michigan and 40th New York in reserve, close behind, relieving Carr's division of our 3d corps. The enemy in front were posted on the opposite side of a small clearing, less than 200 yards away, also behind rails. The fighting was hotly con 41, and the Second Sharpshooters (in Ward's brigade) on our right, eight. Company H of that regiment had four men injured by a pine tree felled upon the company by a shell bursting in its trunk. Gen. Birney ordered Ward to the front to relieve Carr's right. "He did so, however, without pressing the enemy." Egan was a fighting commander. The boys called him "Tommy Nogan."

"The musketry fire was incessant, and the enemy made constant efforts to break through my line. They were driven back, and the ridge was firmly held by us. Prince's division not advancing equally with us "(the extreme right) "enabled the enemy to plant a battery on the right, that completely enfiladed my line. At dusk I advanced, my line of skirmishers holding the battle field. During the night the enemy retired, leaving their dead, wounded and hospitals."—GEN.

BIRNEY.

The conduct of the officers and men of the Third Corps engaged, deserves the highest commendation. Opposed to the best troops of the rebel army, in superior numbers, and reduced by detachment, they maintained the high character which they have always held in the Army of the Potomac. The sanguinary loss of the enemy, and their repulse, leaving their dead and wounded in hospital upon the field, exhibit the prowess of the corps beyond any terms which it is in my power to express.—GEN. FRENCH.

This battle was the result of a collision between our 3d corps (except one brigade absent), and Johnson's division of the enemy, while both were hurrying towards Robertson's Tavern by diverging roads, the one to connect with Warren, the other to reinforce Rodes of the Confederate army. Our skirmishers had run into the rebel ambulance train, sending them back in confusion onto their infantry, Steuart's brigade, who at once came forward and engaged our line, driving it back a short distance, when Prince's division, deployed in line, opened the fight. At the first onset Steuart's men obtained temporary success and tried to capture one of our batteries, but failed. The enemy's loss at this place counted up nearly 600, some of their regiments suffering severely, including valuable officers. The Union loss was over 800. Warren at Robertson's Tavern encountered Rodes, but contented himself with feeling the enemy, with French not up, making a show of strength to prevent an assault; Rodes being apparently of the same mind regarding Johnson. Their respective losses conclusively show this, Warren claiming only 50, and the enemy admitting but 20.

Gen. Meade had intended if possible to strike the enemy on the flanks of his position, as "an attack in front had long been impracticable." But this day's work did not result as he had anticipated. Delays occurred in the movements of the 3d corps: First, at. Jacobs' Ford with the pontoons, and the inability to cross the artillery there, owing to the steep bank opposite, with one pontoon short, necessitating a hastily-made trestle to reach the shore, which was too weak for the batteries, causing them to be sent around by another ford, only a portion of which came up the next day, "after laboring all night over almost impassable roads, with jaded, unfed horses." Again, on the 27th, for "want of a guide after crossing the ford to conduct the column upon the route which was subsequently followed (but which was not designated on the map furnished for my guidance, the roads marked down there being entirely wrong and calculated to mislead), the imperfect reconnoissance which caused Jacobs' Ford to be selected as a place of crossing, and the subsequent unavoidable contact with the enemy, resulting in a serious engagement, are the causes to which are attributable the inability of the Third Corps to arrive at Robertson's Tavern sooner than it did." The statement quoted is from Gen. French's answer to Gen. Meade's call for reasons why the 3d corps did not connect with the 2d corps at the time expected.

Gen. French continuing (to Meade): Had your communication been simply confined to calling from me this statement, my duty would have ended, but it has been thought proper to state, that: "Through the delays and failures specified, an opportunity was lost of attacking the enemy before he had Concentrated, and that this had a powerful influence upon the result of the movements of this army." Now I assert that without losing an unnecessary moment the enemy was attacked, and in very large force, before he had concentrated. That Gen. Warren, whom your dispatches to me reported as in the presence of the enemy during that day, had the same opportunity, while my corps was engaging them, to have done the same thing. That during the engagement prisoners were taken from Rodes' and Johnson's divisions in my front, showing that I was fighting two-thirds of Ewell's corps, and that within supporting distance of Gen. Warren, who was within sound of my guns. Had he thought proper to have made a vigorous attack upon those in front of him, my opinion is that the result of the movements of this army might have been entirely different, but that confining himself to one single idea, rejecting the vicissitudes of a march resulting from obstacles over which the best generalship may sometimes have no control, his movements were made my objective point regardless of the rules and principles which all experience shows are necessary to success. I claim that from the moment I met the enemy my order was executed; that the junction with Gen. Warren was then made, as intended by the general commanding the army; that this corps fought the enemy and defeated him, and had the battle been fought by the Second Corps against those troops in its front, and had it succeeded, as I believe it would have done (in conjunction with the operations of the Sixth Corps known to have been within supporting distance), the occasion for this report would not have arisen.

Gen. Warren in his report stated that he had a brisk little contest along his front, "in which Col. Carroll's brigade behaved very handsomely, driving the enemy down the turnpike to his main line of battle, and capturing numbers of Gordon s brigade of Early's division. Though it was impossible to say how much force was near rue, the prisoners from two divisions of Ewell's corps, and the report that the other was near, required caution on my part. Gen. Ewell was probably as ignorant of my real strength as I of that of his corps opposed to me; else, by rapid concentration, it was in his power to have over-whelmed me and cut our army in two. About—P. M. information was received that Gen. French had met and engaged the enemy, and that his advance was checked, his distance being still some 4 miles from me, and his exact location uncertain. About one hour before dark, when I could afford to venture, trusting to nightfall to cover me if I met superior force, I again advanced my skirmish line, strongly supported. The enemy resisted stubbornly and could be driven but a little way. The woods which he occupied prevented the efficient use of lines of battle, concealed his force so as to require caution in advancing, and furnished him the means of rapidly constructing breastworks, which he had done. The day closed without any material change in my position as first taken up, and without a junction of my force with any other. My loss was about 50 killed and wounded."

Extracts from Gen. Rodes' report of his position in front of Warren: "A complete examination of the ground developed the fact that an assault upon the enemy's position would be attended with heavy loss, and must be made in force if at all. My division remained in position the remainder of the day. During the day the enemy fired a few shells at my troops but without damage. The casual-ties during the day amounted to about 15 or 20 killed and wounded. Late in the afternoon, under orders, I sent Gen. Doles' brigade to Gen. Johnson's assistance.

The preceding reports are given, owing to the blame that was attached to Gen. French by Meade, for not proceeding faster, and failing to reach Warren's lines before the enemy came up. It is apparent, however, that the failure of the movement was in a great degree the result of a want of proper information regarding the strange country they were operating in, with its numerous cross-roads—blind paths—and dense thickets. But whether any general was to blame or not, no possible fault could be found with the soldiers. The fight of the 3d corps was the only battle of the campaign, and they cannot be held responsible for its failure. For surely, they all suffered enough before it was over. It is but justice, however, to mention that Gregg's cavalry on the same day had a spirited engagement at New Hope church, several miles in advance and south of Robertson's Tavern, in which they drove the rebel cavalry back a Mile, unmasking a line of infantry who were also driven off by our cavalrymen dismounted, to the cover of a dense woods, and there held until the 5th corps came up and relieved them. In this affair Gen. Gregg's 1st brigade, which did the fighting, lost: Killed, 2 officers, 17 men; wounded, 5 officers, 59 men.

SHARPSHOOTER CASUALTIES-FIRST REGIMENT.

Co. A.-1 killed, 3 wounded.

Co. B.—Killed: J. W. F. Chidsey. Wounded: Sergt. Charles E. Graves, Sergt. Philip E. Sands, Privates S. McNeil, James Wiley.

Co. C.—Killed: Travis T. Doty. Wounded: Rascelus S. McClain, Abial D. Richardson,' Lewis M. Beebe, Edwin J. Farnsworth.

Co. E.—Wounded: Corp. Clarion H. Kimball, Private Henry A. Sanders.

Co. F.—Killed: E. S. Hosmer. Wounded: A. C. Cross, Eugene Paine, Sherod Brown, Charles M. Jordan.

Co. G.—Killed: Corp. John W. Johnson, Private Frank L. Smith. Wounded.: Wesley Armfield, arm, slight; Charles W. Baker, mouth, severe (spit the ball out); George Whitson, cheek, slight.

Co. IL—Wounded: James H. Fisk.

Co. I.—Killed: Leander Ballard. Wounded: James Cramer, Henry Alchin.

Co. K.—Killed: First Lieut. Thomas Connington, Corp_ William E. Showers. Wounded: Corp. Edwin C. Goodspeed, left arm; Louis C. Bitten, shoulder, slight; and two others unknown.

The following morning before daybreak the 3d corps moved away from the vicinity of Payne's Farm, marching through a heavy rain to the left, and in the afternoon the First Sharpshooters were sent ahead as skirmishers along with the 68th Pennsylvania and 5th Michigan, to discover the enemy's position, forming a line in front of the one eventually taken up by the corps, east of Mine Run.. Nothing transpired the next day, Sunday.

MINE RUN.

Nov. 30, 1863.

The enemy at this place were found to be well posted, their works presenting a most formidable appearance, with a large open plain in front. Gen. Meade had decided on an assault, front and flank, "one on the enemy's left flank with the 6th and 5th corps, one on the center with the 3d and 1st corps, and one on the enemy's right by the force under Gen. Warren, consisting of the 2d corps and one division of the 6th." In front of Birney's division of the 3d corps (the 2d and 3d divisions being detached to support Warren on our left), a provisional brigade was formed for this, day's work, consisting of the First and Second Sharpshooters, 3d Michigan and 124th New York, under command of Col. Pierce of the 3d Michigan. A storming party was ordered, Pierce's brigade to go ahead as skirmishers, forming the first line. Before daylight they moved down to the Run, and deploying out waited for the signal gun which was to be fired at eight o'clock. At this hour the artillery opened; the Sharpshooters advancing with their connecting regiments, rushed across Mine Run and over the large opening in front, the Union batteries playing over their heads in the meantime. Companies B and G were on the left of the First Regiment line, having advanced a portion of the way through a thicket of brush and timber, in the direct course of the fire of our batteries. Emerging from the timber on to the plain, they came suddenly on to a rebel force and drove them back to their works, taking a few prisoners. Reaching a position on a slope 300 yards from the fortifications which were frowning with cannon, sharp firing occurred on both sides, the rebel artillery being ominously silent. Several of the Union shell fell short among our men, but did no harm. On leaving the little woods, B and G became separated, leaving quite an interval between them, the first named company gaining distance to the, left in their hurried advance.

Judkins, of Company G, going forward with the New 'Yorkers, got ahead of the line, and took a position behind a fence in their front. While here, he became subject to fire in the rear, the balls striking the rails about him. Looking back he suddenly realized his danger and fell back to the line. His own company to the right had noticed his tall form, and taking him for a "Johnny," gave him a cross-fire at 400 yards, Private George A. Denniston putting in several dose shots, until ordered to stop firing in that direction by Lieut. Stevens in command, who justly concluded that our men were mistaken as to the military status of the man, thus no doubt saving his life. After a sharp skirmish for an hour, orders were received to fall back in good order, which movement was well executed by the entire line, without hurry, the men keeping up the fire until they were out of range, while the enemy poured in heavily, fortunately with little effect. It was a bitter cold morning, the men's fingers were too benumbed to quickly cap their pieces, and the

Sharpshooters resorted to the primers, which was seldom done excepting in cases of necessity. The enemy were observed striking their hands across their body after firing, to warm up, and taking considerable time to reload. Russell H. Rarrick, of Company B, was severely wounded, and Alexander J. Dupont, same company, on the left. On the right of the line which connected with the 1st corps, the Sharpshooters drove the enemy out of their rifle pits, doing considerable damage to the foe, taking some prisoners. While at this point the regiment suffered the loss of the commander, Lieut,-Col. Casper Trepp, who while taking observations of the situation in front, was shot through the head, the bullet entering at the red diamond on his hat. In his death the Sharpshooter service lost a careful and skillful officer, one who had become well known throughout the corps for his promptness and efficiency in executing movements intrusted to him. He had been very active that morning from long before daylight, in the disposition of his command, and was very particular to caution his men not to needlessly expose themselves, but when the order was given to go forward, to fail not to obey it. He appeared to me that morning to be unusually anxious, as if he feared dire results to his decimated regiment from this expected assault, whatever he may have thought about himself, and he may have had a premonition of his own fate, as he was at times quite restless and nervous. And yet he was the only one killed outright that day in his regiment, if a sure death wound may be called outright, although it was late that night when he finally expired. He was buried three times—on the field, on Botts' farm at Brandy Station, and finally at New York city. On the fall of this gallant officer, the command of the regiment devolved on acting field officer Capt. Marble.

Among the killed was Lieutenant-Colonel Trepp, of the First U. S. Sharpshooters, an officer of the highest merit, and one whose military knowledge and achievements have long been the admiration of all who knew him.—COL. EGAN.

The Second Sharpshooters were in on the left of the First Regiment, and also met with loss, including their gallant chaplain, Lorenzo Barber, who was severely wounded in the leg while on the skirmish line using a heavy telescope rifle—his favorite weapon. The chaplain was known as the "Fighting Parson," and early earned the title in the most patriotic sense. He had been out with his regiment in line of skirmishers on many occasions, using his rifle with effect, as has been noticed heretofore. He had the sympathy of the members of both regiments in his misfortune. On the fall of the chaplain, Lieut. Foote, of Company B, the left company of the entire Sharpshooter line, could scarcely be restrained from rushing forward, chafing with his men at the delay of the expected attack. They, however, endeavored to get satisfaction by keeping up the fire on every foe presenting himself for a target.

HIS LAST SHOT.

When the regiment first got into the line, they found themselves confronted by a rebel battery, off to their left quartering, near a farm house, and the question was asked, "how far it was across the valley to that battery? "Chaplain Barber, who had his telescope rifle sights marked for every 50 yards, cried out: "Hold on boys, I'll tell you how far it is." He saw some Virginia razor-back hogs near the farm house. Raising his sights to 650 yards he fired at a hog and wounded it. The men could hear it give a good squeal clear across the valley. Word was at once passed along the regimental line, "650 yards." It was but a few minutes before the Confederate gunners limbered up and got out of range. This was one of the last shots of Chaplain Barber as a Sharpshooter, and one of the finest shots in the U. S. army.

The order to storm, was countermanded, and the enemy therefore did not have an opportunity to use their artillery at this favorable place to mow down advancing Union troops. Gen. French (3d corps) had been opposed to an assault from his front, and it was finally determined by Gen. Meade to make French's attack dependent on the success of the two flank assaults. French's command on this day consisted only of Birney's division of the 3d, with two divisions of the 1st corps, and even with the prestige of success by the flanking corps, much doubt was entertained of his ability to take the strong works before him. But it seems Warren failed to go on with his assault, having concluded when he viewed the enemy's position by daylight, that it would be useless. So Meade countermanded the order, eventually deciding to withdraw and recross the Rapidan.

Col. Pierce reported the following losses in his "provisional brigade" at Mine Run, killed and wounded:

3d Michigan, total 10.

1st U. S. Sharpshooters, total 6.

2d U. S. Sharpshooters, total 3.

124th New York, total 5.

ANOTHER TOUGH MARCH.

The weather had turned very cold, especially at night, the troops were illy prepared to withstand the effects of the same, and perfectly content after their two fruitless fights to wind up this week's campaign in hurrying back to their warm log quarters at Brandy.

Soon after dark Dec. 1st, the Sharpshooters having been relieved from the picket lines during the morning; retiring to a piece of woods close by to rest and observe the strict orders to remain there quietly concealed from view, the troops began to fall back. It was a stinging cold night, and before getting fairly under way the men were kept standing for a full hour in the ranks awaiting orders to move on, with nothing to burn but patches of dried grass wherewith to warm their hands and feet, which was fired *of course* by some one unknown, although orders were repeatedly given to put out the same, in tones more vehement than pleasant. But, notwithstanding the rumored necessity of keeping "in the dark," an old log-building suddenly got into a blaze, probably the work of an *incendiary,* and as the boys moved off the red flames shot high in air, presenting a defiant beacon to the intrenched enemy over the Run. By means of quick marching, however, the men soon warmed up, and kept moving the entire night, arriving at the Rapidan at Culpeper Mine Ford, at daybreak, crossing the same on pontoons.

When this movement began, two columns of troops pushed on side by side at a rapid pace which soon increased into double quick, making the reverberating sounds from this heavy step roll off from the plank road through the surrounding forest, not unlike the rumblings of heaven's thunder. Meanwhile, the boys kept up a continuous chatting as they trotted merrily along throwing soldier's slang at each other—seemingly endeavoring to be the first to leave the broad highway on reaching the narrow wood road striking off to the left for the Ford. Each one seemed to understand that they had a hard march before them and that it was necessary to cross the river as early as possible, although many soon appeared to have forgotten it through their extreme weariness caused in a great degree by the cold weather, as the sequel will show.

In fact, it proved to be a night to be long remembered, many sleeping as they marched, and only half awaking when pushed against by those behind. A large number fell out by the roadside, to be soon roused up and started on again by the provost guard who succeeded, more easily than might have been the case but for the aid of a powerful auxiliary, in clearing the woods of—stragglers! must I call them? those tired, worn out veterans of many campaigns, too many of them, ah! as successless as this one, who, benumbed with the extreme cold, fell asleep in the ranks, dropping promiscuously along the road, dragging themselves from under the feet of those who still kept their place in the line of march, they were fast becoming *desperately* few, gained the cover of the woods and slept, as none but an old soldier knows how to sleep when, to use a phrase, "played out," too sound, in fact, to be awakened by anything short of a drove of cattle forced among them by the said provost.

The stern orders and loud demands to hurry on, the crash of fallen limbs and down wood, as the heavy cattle came roaring and bellowing on at the point of the bayonet, was too much for even tired if not pretty nigh demoralized soldiers, to withstand; so on they came cattle and soldiers, in grand confusion, stumbling forward, pitching headlong o'er the uneven surface in the pitchy darkness, without the line of march.

So it was; no regiment, no company, no squad, intact. The whole column was thinned out to that extent that in some regiments there were not guns enough on hand to stack arms, when they finally came to a halt over the river. The writer did stick it out, with the untiring Willard Isham by his side. They helped to awake each other from time to time, by sundry shakes not slightly given, but forcibly sudden.

The brave Van Buren, who had got ahead among other troops, completed the trio that crossed the bridge together.

NOTE.—*Of the two sergeants above named, and two better soldiers never wore the suit of blue, or in their case the rifle green, both survived the war, but Caleb M. VanBuren, after passing through 30 conflicts unscathed, lived to fall, with another gallant comrade George W. Griffin, who lost his foot in the last fighting before Petersburg, victims to the Indians' scalping knife on the western plains.*

And when they came to stack arms, but two guns *bayonet-less*, "lost in action," were insufficient to obey the order, and the men flung themselves to the hard ground in disgust, to sleep.

During the morning of the 2d the troops lay at rest near the Ford, those failing to keep up during the night coming in, in small squads. As they arrived they dropped to the ground and slept. The country they had but lately been through was known as the wilderness, therefore, when at noon, a band struck up the old tune,

"Oh! aint you mighty glad to get out of the wilderness?"

-the soldiers jumped up, and signified their approval of the same, considering the fatigues they had undergone "over yonder."

Capt. Marble being now responsible for the First Regiment, made every exertion possible to keep the men moving, a trying situation for that officer in the dense darkness, who, however, proved equal to the emergency, he having the satisfaction of reporting his command all present and accounted for, on re-assembling across the Rapidan.

But their fatigues did not end here. Another hard march was before them, over rough roads, which from the late raids had become in many places very wet and muddy, making the march doubly tiresome to these already tired soldiers. In the afternoon they moved on, halting three hours at dark in a piece of woods, the troops huddled together, as if anticipating the approach of foes. After which, they pushed on during the rest of the night, splashing through the mud holes, weary and worn, seemingly never to get to their journey's end. Frequently the soldiers would ask of some other soldiers, how far it was to Brandy, and for a long time the answer was only about "four miles," nor did these unsatisfactory replies change until near morning, when some one asserting it was "five miles," the boys kept still, plodding along in quiet after that—doing their own guessing. Finally at daybreak of the 3d they arrived at their camp on Botts' Farm, where they went into winter quarters after an extremely tough campaign of nearly eight days.

Mr. Botts didn't like the idea of their cutting off his timber or taking his rails, but it was done nevertheless, stealthily or otherwise. The soldiers thought that if Botts was a Union man, he should be glad to contribute so much for the cause; if a Confederate, the timber was by all the rights of war their property. But in after years, Gilman K. Crowell, of Company E, takes this considerate view of it: "John M. Botts had one of the finest places I saw while in Virginia. He would not give us any straw to make our beds; and looking at it from my present stand-point, I don't think we ought to blame him much, for the enemy had just stole all his grain and part of his stock, and if we had taken his straw he would have nothing for what little stock he had left. They had burned most all his fences, and I remember that we rebuilt some of them for him."

On the 11th of January, however, they broke camp and moving two miles, near Culpeper, encamped in a fine piece of hard timber where comfortable quarters were soon built, called "Camp Bullock," after a well-known Philadelphian who had presented every soldier in Birney's division with a pair of woolen mittens. Log cabins and board shanties with shelter-tent roof, good fire-places with brick and stone chimneys, were erected; the soldiers adapting themselves to every necessity, soon learning to do such work, to become carpenters and masons. It was not necessary to make details to cut down trees here. Volunteers were plenty, and knowing they had permission to chop for their needs, went at it like so many pioneers, with a will.

At this encampment some of the Wisconsin men traced a flight of bees to a big tree at the head of their street, close behind the officer's, tent, which they kept secret, patiently waiting until he became "officer of the day," when after making his rounds at night, being particular not to come that way again, the tree came down, and when the officer returned to his quarters next morning, on being relieved from duty, he found there, his share of the spoils in the shape of a large pan of honey. It proved to be a great bee tree, and several camp kettles full were obtained, from it. As for the tree, not a vestige remained at daylight on the spot where it had so long stood, being removed a sufficient distance to escape notice, strict orders then being in force against cutting off any of the camp trees. But with honey in sight, the average old vet would take all the chances of being discovered. When the regimental commander, Capt. Marble, called during the day, on being presented with a portion *of* this honey, he said: "Stevens, I don't suppose this honey came exactly from Wisconsin, but it is to my notion, just as sweet."

A new year proposition was made by the government to make veterans of all soldiers who had served two years or more, who would re-enlist, presenting them with $400 bounty and a 30-day furlough, the remainder of their original term being cancelled; also allowing regiments having a given proportion of re-enlistments, to go to their respective states and recruit up. But few of the First Sharpshooters accepted this offer, the number of original members being greatly reduced, and many of the recruits not having served two years. The Second Regiment, however re-enlisted almost to a man and went home, where they recruited up in their respective states before they returned to the front. They had suffered severely in many hard fought engagements, and deserved a respite, with a chance to breath the free clear air of their northern homes.

About this time Col. Berdan resigned, the only field officer left in the First Regiment being Major Hastings, who was absent on detached service in Washington, and did not forever after return to the regiment.

On the 6th of February at four in the morning, a portion of the Sharpshooters moved off with troops to the left towards the Rapidan, but took no part in the fight that occurred at Morton's Ford, they returning the night of the 7th, after another fatiguing march through rain and mud. The enemy had crossed several brigades at the Ford, where our 2d corps after a short engagement repulsed them capturing some of their number and causing their entire force to retreat back to the south side of the river. During this movement those of the Sharpshooters not participating, were out on picket where they were threatened by what were called, Scott's Little Fork Rangers, one of whom had sneaked up to one of our cavalrymen, in advance, and shot him through the body. The "murderer" probably wanted his horse but didn't get it. A skirmish followed between our cavalry squad and the above styled band. The Sharpshooter line under Lieutenant Stevens remained firm, having received special instructions to hold the position at all hazards, but were not attacked. It was an exciting time as the enemy were known to be hovering about, so that our men were kept constantly on the alert. Harrison De Long, of Company B, a well-known staunch comrade writes me: "That was the place where you gave me 'fits' for going to camp after the mail. I took my scolding good-naturedly, and the matter was soon ended." The boys used to take chances sometimes, notwithstanding orders were against them. But when a Sharpshooter wouldn't go for his mail when he heard there was a letter "from home," it was because there was no possible chance to do so.

Again at daybreak of the 28th we moved away with our division (having been preceded the day previous by the troops of the 6th corps, who passed through camp with bands playing, moving at a rapid pace), and marching through the town of Culpeper, company front, band playing, the weather being fine and roads good, we finally came to a halt at a small place called James City about two P. M., a distance of 14 miles south. Here we remained until the morning of March 2d, having been exposed in the meantime to an unexpected snowstorm,—a big one,—from which we were totally unprotected in the open field, as we were. The 6th corps was several miles in our front. Gen. Custer had passed by with a good raiding force of cavalry, and, penetrating within the enemy's lines, destroyed a rebel camp engaging them at different points; Kilpatrick pushing on towards Richmond, on the extreme left, where in that vicinity he scion arrived, on the outskirts of the city,—"hung his banners on the outer walls;"—but as Butler's troops from Yorktown had failed to connect, the cavalry was obliged to return without accomplishing the purpose of the expedition—to capture Richmond. Engaged in this daring raid some distance to the right of Gen. Kilpatrick, was a special cavalry force of 400, under Col. Ulric Dahlgren, who, getting into an ambuscade near Richmond, Dahlgren was slain and his small force demoralized and scattered, many being captured by the enemy. The Sharpshooters returned to their camp the afternoon of the 2d, after an unusually tiresome tramp through slush and mud, enough so indeed to materially dampen their ardor. But they soon got over it and were themselves again. It was such exposures that laid the seed to future and often incurable ailments, which in after years helped to swell the government pension list.

A MULE RACE.

During the dull days of the encampment some of the officers took a fancy to horse racing—short dashes. Among them was Capt. "Hank "Garrison, who had come into possession of a pretty fair saddle horse and a good runner known as the "yellow horse" on account of his light buckskin color, and which had won for the sportive captain a number of five dollar greenbacks. This set him to talking pretty loud about being able to beat any other horse in the brigade, and set some of the other officers to enter into a combination to take him down; so it was really Garrison *versus* the field. Finally one of the combine took up the captain's $25 challenge, and began to look about for "any good horse" that could be obtained in the brigade: At this juncture Col. Biles of the 99th Pennsylvania, came to his relief by sending over to camp a fine browny. The race occurred at the appointed time, but owing to the rain it was run in the mud. Just before it came off, Capt. Marble came to me laughing and said: "Hank paid the browny nigger 25 cents to hold the horse back, but Steve has fixed him he gave Hank's darky 50 cents to pull in the yellow horse."

"Then it's a mule race," I said.

"Just about!" and so it proved, for Hank's darky being the strongest puller, lost the race by a nose, as was finally determined at the finish, for they could scarcely be distinguished on the go, owing to the mud that completely enveloped them. So Steve won his $25, and Hank stopped his horse talk.

As spring rolled around, target shooting was again in order, and another match was in contemplation between the First and Second Regiments which, however, did not take place. Their skill was soon to be tried in a more needful direction where "gray" or "butternut" covered the human target. On March 27th 1st Sergt. Caleb N. Jacobs, of Company G, was transferred to the non-commissioned staff as sergeant-major of the First Regiment, *vice* Atwell, commissioned adjutant of the 36th Wisconsin. Sergt. James

S. Webster was then promoted to first sergeant, and other changes made in the Wisconsin company.

Gen. U. S. Grant having been placed in command of all the armies of the United States with the rank of lieutenant-general, made his headquarters with the Army of the Potomac, a part of which had been transferred to the West, with the five corps reduced in strength remaining, consolidated into three-2d, 5th and 6th, besides the cavalry. Of the infantry, the old 3d corps (1st and 2d divisions) became the 1st and 2d brigades of the 3d division under Birney, and two brigades of a 4th division under Mott, of the 2d corps commanded by Gen. Hancock; the Sharpshooters being in Birney's division, the First Regiment in the 2d brigade (Gen. Hays),the Second Regiment under Lt.-Col. Stoughton in the 1st brigade (Gen. Ward). They were, however, allowed to retain their respective "diamond" badges-1st division red, 2d division white; the badge of a 3d division being blue. The First Regiment was now commanded by Major Mattocks, of the 17th Maine, with Capt. Marble again acting as field officer.

On March 31st they left Camp Bullock, moving across the railroad into an old rebel camp near Brandy Station. Nothing particular transpired while here other than regular routine of duties, until April 2d, when they took part in the grand review by the newly appointed commander-in-chief, Gen. Grant, Gen. Meade commanding Army of the Potomac, and Hancock the 2d corps. On the 27th camp was broken up, the troops removed to fields where they pitched their shelters, under marching orders; all surplus camp and garrison equipage being turned over to the quartermaster. For some time previous heavy drills took place, six hours a day, while inspections and reviews were frequent. The old soldiers didn't like it ever so much—thought they didn't require it—but they had to stand it, and soon became in good condition for more rough marches and hard fighting.

When Gen. Hays took command of the brigade, he came to us prejudiced against the Sharpshooters, whose fame had reached him, doubting their ability to meet the requirements of leading and successful marksmen, to entitle them to the name and fame acquired throughout the Army of the Potomac; and he bluntly told Gen. Birney, who was one of our backers, that "the Sharpshooters were no better shots than ordinary infantry," and he "should therefore employ them in ordinary line of battle." In other words he was one of those old officers who evidently didn't believe in the Sharpshooter service; and would soon prove to Birney and staff, and other invited guests, that "the Sharpshooters were pets, and not particularly expert with the rifle." Of course our regiments heard of this, and didn't fancy Hays very much just then, while Capt. Marble in command of the First Regiment at once selected a detail "for a particular purpose," of "ten men in light marching order," who were ordered to report to brigade headquarters, with an invitation extended to our officers to "come and witness the test shooting determined upon."

Marble of course was careful to select reliable men, the least liable to become disconcerted no matter how difficult the test, as he was determined to guard against the possibility of a similar detail from some of Hays' "pets"—in other words he didn't propose to be taken at a disadvantage, but was ready to meet all comers on equal terms, in all manner of shooting and at all distances.

The result was, that Gen. Hays was completely surprised, his sour looks at us changed to "sweet smiles," in a speech acknowledging that he was "very much mistaken, and that henceforth he would be a Sharpshooter," at the same time ordering from Quartermaster

Marden, a pair of green pants in token of his appreciation of our men's proficiency in the use of the rifle; eventually, too soon after for the good of the cause, being killed with the same green pants on, dying a Sharpshooter at heart and in sentiment.

NINTH CAMPAIGN.

UNDER GRANT.

Major-General Meade was instructed that Lee's army would be his objective point; that wherever Lee went he would go also.—U. S. GRANT.

On the 3d of May the Sharpshooters packed up in the morning, and participating in the general movement of the army broke camp, the First Regiment with Hays' brigade, the Second with Ward's, and moving off at midnight, marching 20 miles, crossed the Rapidan at Ely's Ford at ten A.M. the following day. Having rested a sufficient time to allow the rest of the division to come up, they moved on, and after a steady march until towards the close of the afternoon, reached the old battlefield of Chancellorsville of the year previous, where they bivouacked for the night. While here, a number of articles were found formerly belonging to the regiment, among them their lost knapsacks which were mostly burned, strips only of them being left, and pieces of green clothing; also the graves of several of their former comrades. Human skulls and bones were scattered over the ground—grave reminders of the grim past. It was near the ground where the determined "80" drove back the "Stonewall men," where the Sharpshooters rested for the night.

The march was resumed on the morning of the 5th, our regiment being thrown out as flankers, passing through the Cedars, on towards Todd's Tavern, where they came to a halt. Firing being heard on the right, the troops moved back a short distance to the Brock road, when they were rushed rapidly forward, heavy fighting going on ahead; the din and clamor of which was plainly heard, in such tones of thunder as not to be misunderstood by the approaching columns.

BATTLE OF THE WILDERNESS.

May 5-6, 1864.

Arriving at the scene of action in the afternoon where the contending armies were hard at it, the First Sharpshooters deployed in skirmish line on the left of the Brock and Orange roads, and moving forward to ascertain the position of the enemy, soon found them in force mid terrific fire, whereby the right of the line composed of the Swiss and Vermonters suffered considerable loss in a few moments, while the major commanding—C. P. Mattocks, of 17th Maine,—was taken prisoner. It was a hot reception for the boys, but they endeavored to pay it back as earnestly. Finally, having accomplished the purpose for which they were sent forward, they were ordered back after a sharp skirmish, and relieved by other troops withdrew to the Brock road, where they remained until night behind rudely constructed breastworks. After dark they crossed the Orange road to the right, the battle for the day being over, and marching considerably about through the dark wood and swamp among the dead and wounded, at a late hour succeeded in rejoining their brigade which had been hotly engaged elsewhere, with the loss among many others, of their brave commander, Gen. Alex. Hays, who was instantly killed. We now rested, and poorly, the balance of the night, amid moans and groans in front and around us. Capt. John Wilson senior officer, commanded the regiment, on the capture of Major Mattocks who had been detailed to command us when the campaign opened. Capt. Marble was detailed for staff duty,—acting assistant adjutant general of the brigade,—which important position he retained during the balance of his term of service. The contest thus far had been a fierce one; the small trees and bushes were cut close to the ground by the bullets—mowed right down---but little if any artillery being used. The lines being close together in the thick woods enveloped by the dense smoke, the artillery couldn't be brought into play. Strictly defined, it was an infantry fight; where both sides struggled as stubbornly for the failing victory.

It is true, the batteries of the 2d corps, with one or two exceptions, were run up on some high ground on the extreme left of the corps and the Union line of battle, near the crossing of the Brock and Catharpin roads, and a portion of another battery (Ricketts') was placed at the Brock road junction with the Orange plank, but generally the artillery on both sides cut little figure in the contest.

Ricketts' battery, however, did good service and suffered much, having moved forward with the line of battle behind Getty's division of the 6th corps, now under Hancock's command, connecting on the right with Birney. Of this battery Gen. Hancock said:

"The section of Ricketts' battery which moved down the plank road when Birney and Getty attacked, suffered severely in men and horses. It was captured at one time during the fight, but was retaken under the direction of Capt. Butterfield, of Col. Carroll's staff, by detachments from the 14th Indiana and 8th Ohio volunteers of Carroll's brigade. It was then withdrawn and replaced by a section of Dow's (6th Maine) battery." He also speaks of this last battery, on the following day: "rendering valuable and effective service."

Gen. Birney called on the Second Sharpshooters late in the evening for volunteers to retake one of these guns that had been abandoned between the lines down the Orange road, whereupon Capt. Norton, of Company E, and plenty of men, rushed down fighting their way, and not only brought off the gun but took as well the harness off the dead horses, bringing it along.

At an early hour on the following morning (May 6), the First Sharpshooters deployed as skirmishers ahead, advancing westerly to the extreme front where they occupied and held an exposed position. The ground passed over contained many dead of the day previous; the wounded having been mostly carried off by the stretcher-bearers at work the entire night, using lighted candles to find the sufferers in that black, grim, dismal wood.

Our regiment finally recrossed the Orange road to the left, taking up a position in advance of the division, in a small opening, obtaining temporary cover behind rude breastworks constructed of half-rotten logs and brush. As the battle progressed, the fiery sun pouring down its hottest rays, the men with great drops of perspiration rolling from their faces, moved hurriedly forward to an advanced position, firing as rapidly as sight could be obtained through the thick smoke which soon covered the field. We had enough to do in hurried shooting—quick work—it being at the time Hill re-formed and came charging back, with Long-street's corps swinging around on our left, sending in a terrific fire on our flank and across our rear. It was terribly hot, the scorching sun, while the air was perfectly blue with bullets. On they came with their rebel yell—the most hideous music imaginable, when you know they 've got you if you don't get up and "get." In such places it is enough-to strike terror to the stoutest hearts. Shrieking shell and hissing bullets will develop a soldier's fullest senses—his eyes magnify, his ears expand—but unless he is flanked, or caught in the rear, he will hold on. But when they

> Howled in our ears Their hideous cries,

it required the greatest determination to withstand the effect and meet the onslaught. The Johnnies felt the same way, when we had them on the run. In this respect the Blue and the Gray were very alike. A very natural feeling, which proves that the human voice can on critical occasions,

> Strike more terror to the soul,
>
> Than more clamorous sounds of war.

The cry is, "here they come," and in unknown strength to charge our own weak lines, far to the front—as the Sharpshooters often were. But the trained soldier rarely gives way without orders, until the last possible moment. In this case we couldn't stand the pressure, and were forced hurriedly back along with the other troops behind us.

It was during this critical period that the brave and lamented Gen. Wadsworth was killed. His division (5th corps) was on the right of the road, connected with ours of the 2d corps on the left. But he had crossed over, and riding ahead to the Sharpshooter line urged us farther forward, although then away ahead of anything on that particular field. In answer to his loud demands, his peremptory orders, for he was excited as he rode the line with waving sword—a noble-looking white haired veteran—we still surged farther ahead, but not to exceed a hundred yards, when we met them, coming with a rush—the balls hissing hot and low. The general then rode into the road, where he was shot and captured, mortally wounded. Thus was lost one of the noblest spirits of the army.

The rebel General Longstreet was also wounded, in the throat, and carried back to die, but recovered to come at us again in future hot places—one of the Confederates' best officers. Gen. Jenkins of the enemy was at the same time killed in this vicinity.

The Second Sharpshooters went into this morning's fight on the right of the Vermont brigade which overlapped their line resting on the plank road, and fired into them. Capt. Albert Buxton, the tried and faithful commander of Company n, received his death wound while gallantly leading his men in.

Our regiments eventually took up a position behind the works along the Brock road. Hancock's corps went into action at five in the morning, driving Hill's troops a mile and a half before they rallied to return reinforced, assisted by Longstreet's flanking columns. It was the opinion of Gen. Hancock that the Confederates would have met with overwhelming defeat this day had his orders to his left wing been fully carried out. From information received he had apprehended an attack on his exposed extreme left, by way of the Catharpin road, from Longstreet, and it became necessary to keep the flank well-guarded to meet any such movement. He says:

"Barlow's division was placed in -position for that purpose, and my artillery was formed to cover the road leading from the Catharpin to the Brock road, along which it was supposed the enemy would advance. At seven A. M. (6th) I sent a staff officer to Gen. Gibbon, commanding the left of my line, informing him of our success on my right, and directing him to attack the enemy's right with Barlow's division, and to press to the right towards the Orange plank road. This order was only partially carried out. Frank's brigade of Barlow's division, was sent to feel the enemy's right, and after an obstinate contest succeeded in forming a connection with the left of Mott's division. I do not know why my order to attack with Barlow's division was not more fully carried out, but it was probably owing to the apprehended approach of Longstreet's corps on my left about that time; but had my left advanced as directed by me in several orders, I believe the overthrow of the enemy would have been assured. At all events, an attack on the enemy's right by the troops of

Barlow's division would have prevented the turning of the left of Mott's division, which occurred later in the day."

Relative to this desperate flank attack at midday, which eventually forced our corps back to the Brock road, Hancock said:

"The enemy now advanced upon Frank's brigade of Barlow's division, which joined the left of Mott's division. That brigade, *having* been heavily engaged in the earlier part of the day, had nearly exhausted its ammunition, and was compelled to retire before the enemy, whose attack was made with great vehemence. This was Longstreet's attack. Passing over Frank's brigade they struck the left of Mott's division, which in turn was forced back. Some confusion ensuing among the troops of that division, I endeavored to restore order and to re-form my line of battle along the Orange plank road, from its extreme advance to its junction with the Brock road, by throwing back my left, in order to hold my advanced position along that road and on its right, but was unable to effect this, owing to the partial disorganization of the troops, which was to be attributed to their having been engaged for many hours in a dense forest, under *a* heavy and murderous musketry fire, when their formation was partly lost. Gen. Birney, who was in command of that portion of the line, thought it advisable to withdraw the troops from the wood, where it was almost impossible to adjust our lines, and to re-form them in the breastworks along the Brock road on our original line of battle."

Late in the day, a desperate and almost successful charge was made by the enemy on to the Brock road works, the first line of which they entered, aided by the fire and smoke of the burning woods sweeping down our lines, thus covering their sudden approach; but the troops rallying, rushed forward and drove them back through the brush, the flag of the First Sharpshooters being conspicuously waved outside the works on the heels of the retreating rebs, by the brave color-bearer Sergeant Blakeslee, of Company C; while Color Sergeant J. Madison Tarbell, of Company E, Second Regiment, stood with his colors planted on the breastworks until the rebels stood theirs alongside, and until he received a shot through the arm and had to give up, though he hung to the flag.

The excitement was intense, and affairs looked desperate for a while; but when our soldiers found they had to do it—recover the lost ground—they did it nobly. It was now the Yanks' turn to shout, and it rose from regiments and brigades, high towards the heavens, a frightful piercing sound of determined valor.

Carroll's brigade of Gibbon's division, led the countercharge, by order of Gen. Birney, recapturing the breastworks, the First Sharpshooters being in line to the right, with them. The advance of the enemy checked, the tired troops rested for the night. Thus ended the battle of the Wilderness , proper, an engagement that cost hundreds of lives on both sides; and while the Union troops gained no point in their forward movement, yet as the enemy in this last grand charge had approached stealthily through the brush and' smoke almost to our lines, before they made their sudden dash, they failed to follow up their advantage by forcing the fighting after our men had fallen back over the open plain, and in some places in confusion, but remained at the works (in our immediate front) until our men rallied and easily drove them out and away—out of sight— with little loss, so that what there was of victory, was ours. They lacked the push at the critical moment, and lost the battle.

It always seemed surprising, coming out of a hot battle, how many were unharmed. With thousands of bullets continually passing through the ranks, the chances were slim enough to come out untouched, yet but comparatively a small proportion, as a general thing, of those engaged, get hit. It would be impossible to tell how many narrow escapes, or "close calls"—as the boys term it—occur. In such a fight, a soldier seldom knows how near he is to death until he is struck. There are times, however, when they had sufficient evidence that but a hair's breadth separated life and death, and some remarkable instances have been noted. One of this kind occurred in the forenoon before the hot work had fairly commenced. Three line officers stood talking by a sapling, on opposite sides, the other with his back squarely behind the tree looking to the rear. They were looking to see if our troops were coming forward.

The writer was on the south side, Capt. Nash on the north, and while engaged talking in low tones, watching front and rear, a single bullet spanged into the center of the tree, right through it. It was supposed that Lieut. J. L. Rilliet who covered the tree behind, was surely struck; but he very cooly replied, "if so, I don't feel it." Where the ball went, or how it could pass him, was a mystery; nor did we have a moment's time to solve it, as this apparent signal shot was instantly followed by a rattling volley, then the uproar, and the hissing of myriad balls showed the fight had begun.

Gen. Burnside, commanding the 9th corps, was guarding the approaches to Washington from the Rappahannock north, at the time the Army of the Potomac crossed the Rapidan, when he was ordered to move up his troops without delay, which was clone. Grant referring to Burn-side's promptness in this important reinforcement says: "By six o'clock of the morning of the (nil he (Burnside) was leading his corps into action near the Wilderness Tavern, some of his troops *having* marched a distance of over 30 miles, crossing both the Rappahannock and Rapidan rivers. Considering that a large proportion (probably two-thirds) of his command was composed of new troops, unaccustomed to marches and carrying the accouterments of a soldier, this was a remarkable March."

These accouterments consisted of the usual regulation supply. The Sharpshooters, as noticed at the time, had to undergo the same trials on leaving Camp of Instruction and' entering on to the Peninsula. Stuffed knapsacks, extra blankets, tent covers, rubbers and overcoats, all new troops had to endure.

THE ORANGE ROAD.

May 7, 1864.

On the morning of the 7th we were suddenly ordered forward to capture a battery. We were rushed down the Orange road far to the front, under shot and shell as we deployed out, and crossed to the left into a deep wood' close up to the rebel works situated on a hill. Here we were subjected to a severe fire of cannon and musketry, doing great damage, with little chance to retaliate, shooting upwards through the trees. The enemy had us in a bad spot—a complete corner where death awaited all. It was only a question of time, and short time at that, An infantry detachment coming up to our support on our left,. drew away some of the fire from us into this rash, rushing squad, and down they tumbled. But we had to get out of there. It was a useless attempt. When we went in, they told us we were going to capture a "jackass battery," but the jackass came near capturing us, or rather killing us all off. Men fell to the right and left on all sides, from the long-mouthed cannon and well-aimed muskets at short range. It seemed a useless slaughter, that might have been avoided by stealthy skirmishing without attracting attention, and with little or no loss been successful in ascertaining the movement afoot by the Confederates at this point, instead of the rush forward—all to capture a jackass battery well posted on a bluff; which with our slim force we couldn't do by so open an attack. It really required some strategy. If it was the intention to find out what was in front, we accomplished the purpose, paying dearly for the information.

The enemy had closed up behind his intrenchments, and Gen. Grant reported: "From this it was evident to my mind that the two days' fighting had satisfied him of his inability to further maintain the contest in the open field, notwithstanding his advantage of position, and that he would await an attack behind his works."

We were finally ordered back out of range, forming a line of pickets across the wood, where we remained on the 'constant and sharp lookout until night; our attempts to reach the fatal spot to recover the wounded or recognize the dead being prevented by the as alert enemy.

After the fight we were informed that the force coming 'down the road to our left, thus drawing the fire, was one of the "forlorn-hopes," or "straggler brigades," as the boys called them. As the campaigns and big battles increased, the provost guard were generally brought closer to the fighting lines, where stragglers and all soldiers falling back to the rear who couldn't "show blood" for a wound, were at once arrested and, formed into battalions, sent forward to the farthest front as a sort of forlorn hope,—but without the honors,—where they had to face the balls in the thickest of the fight; so that many no doubt fell unknown by name or regiment, which will account for the want of certainty in some cases, by company comrades, as such instances have occurred, in which missing men were lost in the described provost battalions. During the Wilderness-Petersburg campaign in all the numerous conflicts, the provost guard were right behind us, ready to do their duty in the manner stated, as the "sick and sorry" soldiers—and, we had them in every brigade—found out often to their sorrow.

In this action the Sharpshooters lost a number of as good men in a fight as stood in the Army of the Potomac. All told not less than a score went down on that reckless advance. Here again were close calls in order. Kirkham had his ear completely packed with the bark of, a tree, causing considerable blood to flow, the bullet having just missed him, and it was some time before he could get it sufficiently cleared out to bear again. While guarding this point during the day, with the battle-lines far behind us, we were occasionally reminded of the enemy in front, by certain whizzing music through the air—of the infernal order—as with a yell they fired ramrods at us. But we kept quiet, and watched.

After dark we were ordered to the Orange road on the verge of the fatal field of the previous morning, and stood guard all night, with vedettes in front. It was an ominous looking scene, the enemy known to be near, down the road, the Union army withdrawing and marching off to the left. A dreadful quiet prevailed during that black night—not a sound to be heard beyond our own whispers. We sat around on dead men for logs in the utter darkness, while the stench was suffocating. We were in the midst of the dead of the fight of the day before, where Longstreet made his flank charge. At daybreak we were ordered to fall back, being relieved by cavalry, and afterwards protected them as they came away—for the army had gone. Berdan's Sharpshooters were of the last to leave the Wilderness.

As we retired from the road, and crossed that fatal field, the ground was discovered completely covered with dead by the hundreds; and one remarkable thing about the appearance of the silent sleepers, was that the Northern men had pale faces, while the Southerners were of a chocolate color. They lay in all manner of positions, inter-mingled, Blue and Gray.

The question has been frequently asked: "How do men fall in battle?" It has even gone into the courts on the wit-ness stand, in important criminal cases. My answer to that is, to compare the soldiers on the battle field falling under fire, like the pins of a bowling alley when the ball strikes among them. They fall every way—forward, backward, sideways, gently sinking down, hurriedly pitching ahead, and all regardless of the way they are going, quick or slow, forward or backward. That is my answer as to how soldiers fall in battle. You can't tell anything about it. It often depends on the manner or the place where they are hit.

Sometimes they don't fall at all, until pushed over by their still living comrades. Stark in death they stand, as they were struck. It is natural to suppose, however, that when a soldier is running or charging forward and is struck dead, that he would pitch forward, but it does not always hap-pen so.

The Sharpshooters suffered considerable loss on this battle field. The First Regiment loss is as follows:

May 5-6.

Co. A.—1 killed, 2 wounded.

Co. B.—Wounded: Joseph Marr, mortal.

Co. C.—Killed: Lewis M. Beebe. Wounded: Cyrus W Wilcox. Captured : Jacob A. Ege.

Co. E.—Killed : Burnice Scales. Captured: G.W Straw-Co. F—Killed: Corp. David M. French, W J. Domag, E. E. Trask, Jacob Lacoy, and mortally wounded, A. C.

Cross, William Wilson. Wounded; M. Cunningham, Spaf-ford A. Wright, John C. Page. S. M. Butler, William McKeever. Captured: Sergt. Paul M. Thompson, J. H. Guthrie.

Co. G.—Wounded: First Sergt. James S. Webster, head, slight; Privates Michael Costelo, leg amputated, mortal; James Ragin, arm, slight. Captured: Sergt. James Durkee.

Co. H.—Captured: Corp. Martin V. Nichols, Private Orrin E. Doty.

Co. 1,—Killed: Albert N. Finch. Wounded: Samuel Ingling.

Co. K.—Killed: Sergt. Jasper McBain, shot in six places, died a prisoner two days later; Orville Parker.

MAY 7.

Co. A.—Killed: Corp. Ulrect. Wounded: five.

Co. C.—Wounded: Sergt. Frank H. Cobb, and a prisoner four months.

Co. D.—Wounded: John H. Phirney, mortal.

Co. F.—Killed: Edward Giddings, Joseph Hagan. Wounded: Lieut. H. E. Kinsman, Dustin R. Bareau, Henry Mattocks, Edward Lyman.

Co. G.—Killed: Corp. John A. Denniston. Wounded: Sergt. William W. Sweet, arm, severe; Private Israel Ingols-be, leg, mortal.

Co. H.—Mortally wounded: Lieut. Michael McGeough. Co. 1.— Killed: George R. Merrill.

As a, somewhat remarkable instance of lasting friendship springing up between mortal enemies, and continuing for years after the war, the following case is given: Sergt. Cobb, after he was wounded and left on the field, was picked up by some Alabamians, who recognized him as the Sharpshooter whom they had met in friendly conversation on picket in front of Fredericksburg in the spring of '63. They belonged to the 11th Alabama, and having crossed the Rappahannock several times exchanging papers and visiting Cobb and other of our boys (although strictly against orders either side), became warm friends, at the same time entering into an agreement, that should either of them, through the fortunes of war, fall into the other's hands, they should help them all they could. Sergt. Cobb said: "This meeting of these new-made friends again, on the Wilderness battle field a year after their first acquaintance, was an affecting scene." They carried him tenderly from the field, and did everything possible to make it easy for him, particularly when the surgeon told them ominously that "it was a question of but a short time with this Yankee at the longest," as his right side was badly shattered (a generally fatal wound), so that whatever was to be done must be then. The Alabama friends left Cobb with the surgeon, bidding him a sorrowful good-bye, with hopes for his recovery added, as their army moved off. For one month in the Wilderness hospital, and three months in a Lynchburg tobacco warehouse, did the gallant sergeant suffer with this terrible wound and the deadly gangrene. Then, on to Libby, where he was finally paroled, reaching home the winter following. Years after, through the earnest suggestion of his son, the veteran wrote an inquiring letter to a local Alabama paper published at the home of those Confederates, whose address he had never forgotten, and hearing from three of the four who had carried him from the battle field, a correspondence commenced which they have been keeping up as late as 1892, with the intention of arranging for one more meeting, or reunion, after nearly 30 years have passed.

Retiring silently through the brush to the Brock road, the Sharpshooters acted as rear guard, and protected the cavalry while falling back. The main body of the division having preceded them, they followed on as fast as circumstances would permit, halting and facing to the front from time to time, until the cavalry came up again, when the latter would halt and watch, while our men were pushing on. An important service which the Sharpshooters were frequently called on to perform. Skirmishing in advance, and protecting the retreat, often long distances from the main body, was their principal and hazardous duty. During this time William Wells, of Company F, was wounded and captured, subsequently dying in prison at Florence, S. C.

As our hard-fought troops marched back, down the Brock road, it was again in order to "swap guesses" as to whether we were to execute another retrograde movement—turn to the left at the Chancellorsville road, and recross the Rapidan; or if by keeping straight away to the south and along the enemy's lines—always found ready to oppose our advance—Grant was going to try the effect of farther attacks. They soon found out—in fact, before the first month expired they had many opportunities to find it out—that he was going to "fight it out on that line, if it took all summer."

But though knowing full well that a forward movement meant more hard fighting, more killed and wounded, they hurried on with light hearts ready for the worst, rather than go the old way. They had crossed the Rapidan for the last time.

Official return of Union loss at the Wilderness May 5-7, 1864: Killed: 2,246; wounded, 12,037; missing, 3,383; total, 17,666.

TODD'S TAVERN.

May 8-9, 1664.

Having rejoined the division at this place about noon, the First Sharpshooters were soon after placed in position on a timbered hill, where log breastworks were being erected. A sharp fight soon after occurred between the advanced lines and the enemy, on the plain below. The latter finally retired and during the night quietness prevailed, During the engagement Lieut: Perrin C. Judkins, Company G, acting aid on the brigade staff, while gallantly galloping to the front to encourage the troops to retain their position, was unhorsed by a rebel shell and thrown heavily on his head to the ground, rendering him insensible and causing death a few hours after. A. portion of the First Regiment had been thrown out across the Catharpin road, where some skirmishing occurred with the enemy's advance. During the forenoon a reconnoissance had been ordered by Gen. Hancock, consisting of a brigade of infantry, one of cavalry, and a battery, under Col. Miles, on the Catharpin road south, where they became engaged with the enemy near Corbin's bridge, and later in the day became more seriously -engaged with a rebel brigade, repulsing two of their attacks before returning to the main force at Todd's Tavern. On the morning of the 9th the Sharpshooters advanced to the front, and had a skirmish with rebel cavalry coming towards them on the road, the scouts sent out to reconnoiter following them as they fell back until ordered to return, when they continued the march to the left. While reconnoitering the front, the enemy's camp fires were found burning, thus showing that they had not been long gone.

Franklin Viall was sent with a detail of pioneers to bury Lieut. Judkins, and they dug a grave close to a private cemetery. But while preparing the remains at a house nearby, some other soldiers filled the grave with guns and equipments, which they were made to remove. Viall looked the unfortunate officer carefully over, but could find no indication of any contusion, bruise or wound. He said: "I understand Judkins was swept from his horse by a shell, while leading a regiment out of a place where they were entrapped and threatened with capture." The pioneers detailed with Comrade Viall belonged to that regiment, and they declared that Judkins' conduct was most heroic, and he was hailed as their deliverer from disaster.

YANKEE METHOD OF ELEVATING SIGHTS.

Some of the Vermonters tell how they were detached from the regiment for special sharpshooting, as they approached the high ground overlooking the valley of the Po, for the purpose of driving away a rebel signal party—some 1,500 yards off—as Gen. Hancock did not wish to have the enemy observe his movements. One of our batteries did open on them, but the distance was too great for canister, while "the saucy rebels only laughed at shell." Our Sharps rifles being sighted for 1,000 yards only, the green-coats resorted to an experiment by cutting and fitting sticks to increase the elevation, when a few expert shots tried what they could do, a staff-officer with his field-glass watching the result. It became soon apparent, however, from the way the men in the distant tree top—the improvised signal station—looked down, according to our officer's report, when the bullets began to whistle near them, that our riflemen were shooting under; so, longer sticks were fitted for sights, and now the rebels began to look above, showing that the balls went over. Cutting the sticks down a little, they were finally sighted about right, when the rebs began to dodge about, according to the officer with the glass, for our men could not distinguish them with the naked eye, but could see the tree and the flags. The result was, that as soon as the entire detail got to shooting, the surprised rebs abandoned their station in a hurry—their signaling proved a signal failure. This pleased Gen. Hancock very much, he having watched the shooting with much interest.

The country we had been in since crossing the Rapidan, was pretty heavily wooded, with but few openings or small fields. Heavy woods and thick underbrush were generally to be found, through which ran narrow roads, making oftentimes difficult marching, especially in hurried movements. After leaving Todd's Tavern, we struck a more open country, dotted here and there with farms and some pretentious residences.

FIGHTING AT PO RIVER.

May 9-11, 1864.

Arriving at the river Po, in the afternoon (May 9), where the artillery were engaged shelling the opposite woods and road on which the rebel trains were moving, we crossed in the evening, when after a crowded and very dusty march of a couple of miles only, scarcely seeing the files in front so thick was the dust, the column, worn out with fatigue, came to a halt for the balance of the night, resting under arms. It was in this vicinity in the morning that Gen. Sedgwick, commanding the 6th corps, was killed by the enemy's sharpshooters, having boldly exposed himself to their fire while reconnoitering their position. He was one of our very best officers, and the army mourned his fall.

Sharp fighting occurred late in the afternoon by a portion of the 2d corps while effecting a crossing of the river, particularly by Brooke's brigade of Barlow's division, and farther along by Birney's leading regiments, who met with considerable resistance from the enemy on the south side, protected as they were by a mill race. But though stoutly defended, our troops finally forced them back.

Falling in at an early hour of the 10th, after changing front several times we finally moved to the left, where heavy fighting was going on; and took up a position with the brigade under sharp artillery fire. In the battle in progress our troops met- with considerable loss, particularly Gen.

Barlow's division of the 2d corps, who, however, inflicted heavy blows on the enemy, repulsing his determined assaults twice. Gen. Gibbon's division also had a hand in—the Excelsior brigade, of New York, catching it bad. Gen. Warren's 5th corps had a hot fight and were forced back; while a special charging column under Col. Upton, sent out from the 6th corps, gained a temporary advantage, capturing a line with a lot of prisoners and a couple of cannon, which latter he was obliged to abandon. During the whole afternoon it was a severe engagement, and our losses were considerable; among them, Col. Stoughton, of the Second Sharpshooters, who while leading his regiment, received a gunshot wound, breaking two ribs and receiving other injuries, which compelled his retirement from the field until the 21st of June following. The regiment was in line of battle, the brigade in column of regiments. Col. Stoughton: "Every officer and man in the regiment perforated with alacrity every duty in this charge."

UPTON'S CHARGE.-" On the afternoon of the 10th an assault was determined, and a column of 12 regiments was organized, the command of which was assigned to me. The point of attack was at an angle of the enemy's works near the Scott house, about half a mile to the left of the Spottsylvania road. His intrenchments were of a formidable character, with abatis in front and surmounted by heavy logs, underneath which were loop-holes for musketry. In the re-entrant to the right of the house was a battery with traverses between the guns. There were also traverses at intervals along the entire work. About 100 yards to the rear was another line of works, partly completed and occupied by a second line of battle. The position was in an open field about 200 yards from a pine wood. The column of attack was formed in four lines of battle. The pieces of the first line were loaded and capped; those of the other lines were loaded but not capped; bayonets were fixed." Shortly after six P. M. "the lines rose, moved noiselessly to the edge of the wood, and then with a wild cheer and faces averted, rushed for the works. Through a terrible front and flank fire the column advanced, quickly gaining the parapet. Here occurred a deadly hand-to-hand conflict. The enemy sitting in their pits with, pieces upright, loaded, and with bayonets fixed, ready to impale the first who should leap over, absolutely refused to yield the ground. The first of our men who tried to surmount the works fell pierced through the head by musket-balls. Others seeing the fate of their comrades, held their pieces at arm's length and fired downward, while others, poising their pieces vertically, hurled them down upon the enemy, pinning them to the ground. Lieut. Johnson of the 121st New York, received a bayonet wound through the thigh. Private O'Donnell, 96th Pennsylvania, was pinned to the parapet, but was rescued by his comrades. A private of the 5th Maine, having bayoneted a rebel, was fired at by the captain, who missing his aim, in turn shared the same fate. The brave man fell by a shot from the rebel lieutenant. The struggle lasted but a few seconds. Numbers prevailed, and, like a restless wave, the column poured over the works, quickly putting *hors de combat* those who resisted, and sending to the rear those who surrendered. Pressing forward and 'expanding to the right and left, the second line of entrenchments, its line of battle, and the battery fell into our hands. The column of assault had accomplished its task. The enemy's lines were completely broken, and an opening had been made for the division which was to have supported on our left, but it did not arrive. Our loss in this assault was about 1,000 in killed, wounded and missing. The enemy lost at least 100 in killed at the first intrenchments, while a much heavier loss was sustained in his efforts to regain them. We captured between 1,000 and 1,200 prisoners, and several stand of colors."—EMORY UPTON.

While at this point, Gen. Meade and staff appeared on an eminence nearby, overlooking the scene of operations, and became subjected to a heavy fire from the rebel batteries.

Retaining their position until apparently satisfied regarding the movements before them, they retired. I think it was three times they galloped out of view behind the crest of the hill, and came up again, to meet more bursting shells. The third and last time they moved off. It was a dangerous place with their flags flying above them, so they might be excused if they didn't stay long—and they didn't, Gen, Grant was also seen moving about the field behind the lines *smoking his inevitable cigar,* but escaped unharmed from the deadly missiles flying over.

"During the heat of this contest the woods on the right and in rear of our troops took fire. The flames had now approached close to our line, rendering it almost impossible to retain the position longer. The last' bloody repulse of the enemy had quieted him for a time, and during this lull in the fight General Barlow directed Brooke and Brown to abandon their position and retire to the north bank of the Po. Their right and rear enveloped in the burning wood, their' front assailed by overwhelming numbers of the enemy, the withdrawal of the troops was attended with extreme difficulty and peril; but the movement was commenced at once,' the men displaying such coolness and steadiness as are· rarely exhibited in the presence of dangers so appalling. It seemed, indeed, that these gallant soldiers were devoted to destruction. The enemy, perceiving that our line was retiring, again advanced, but were again promptly checked by our troops, who fell back through the burning-forest with admirable order and deliberation, though in doing so many of them were killed and wounded, numbers of the latter perishing in the flames. One section of Arnold's battery had been pushed forward by Captain Arnold during the fight to within a short distance of Brooke's line, where it had done effective service. When ordered to retire the horses' attached to one of the pieces, becoming terrified by the fire and unmanageable, dragged the gun between two trees, where it became so firmly wedged that it could not be moved. They were compelled to abandon it. This was the first gun ever lost by the Second Corps.

I feel that I cannot speak too highly of the bravery, soldierly conduct, and discipline displayed by Brooke's and Brown's brigades on this occasion, Attacked by an entire division of the enemy (Heth's) they repeatedly beat him back, holding their ground with unyielding courage until they were ordered to withdraw, when they retired with such order and steadiness as to merit the highest praise. The enemy regarded this as a considerable victory, and General Heth published a congratulatory order to his troops, indorsed by General Hill and General Lee, praising them for their valor in driving us from our intrenched lines. Had not Barlow's fine division (then in full strength) received imperative orders to withdraw, Heth's division would have had no cause for congratulation. There were no more than two brigades of Barlow's division engaged at any one time." GEN. HANCOCK.

The First Sharpshooters ordered over to the right, ran on to a masked battery which opened on them at a short 200 yards with canister, humming right over their heads—we were just too close to catch it. Another shot would have swept us, when we were ordered behind the hill close by; we being unable to charge it, a deep gully and stream intervening. Under the hill we were soon exposed to a sharp flank fire of shot and shell, rendering necessary another change of position, not being able to respond with any effect—wasting ammunition was not to be thought of. Having fulfilled the duty required of us, guarding these different points of approach, we were finally moved to the left again and rested for the night behind rude works; having been exposed to heavy artillery fire the entire afternoon, with some loss. The Second Sharpshooters suffered considerably this day, the First Regiment having few casualties. During the day a dispatch was read that Butler and Smith had captured Petersburg; and that Sherman had whipped Johnston at Tunnel Hill and Dalton in Georgia. All of which was encouraging to hear, but all of which wasn't true.

Early on the morning of the 11th the Sharpshooters were again sent to the front, where they formed in squads around some buildings, and in shallow rifle pits hastily dug with bayonets and tin plates, the soil being sandy. As they worked like beavers for self-protection from their opponents' long-range cannon and concealed sharpshooters in the adjacent thickets, it was not long before they had heaps of dirt dotting the entire plain; but it was a rough place at best. Here they remained in position during the day actively engaged exchanging shots with the enemy, while fighting was going on right and left—principally cannonading, feeling each other. A heavy rain fell during the day, making things generally very muddy in places, and uncomfortable to the exposed troops. But notwithstanding the constant exposure to many dangerous missiles flying about, we suffered little loss; George W. Wiggins, of the New York Company "H," and Hiram P. Beede of Company E, being wounded.

While lying behind some rails, William Clelland, of Company K, asked permission to go after water. Sergt. R. W. Tyler told him that three men had been killed trying to get water from that spring, but if he wanted to take the chances he might. So Clelland crawled down to the spring only 10 rods away, filled his canteen and crawled out of the marsh into an orchard, where from behind a tree he raised up, when a rebel fired at him cutting a limb six inches from his head, but he was unable to return the compliment although he watched long for the opportunity, failing to locate the fellow, which was probably fortunate for the latter, as Clelland was a good shot. In the evening, under orders for "special duty" at division headquarters, the First Regiment was detached from their brigade, and, hurrying off, were engaged most of the night on the march over rough, wet roads, through thick woods and brush, rain falling heavily part of the time in straight, wire-like streaks, with naught but the struggling moon finally shining to catch glimpses through the general darkness, of their silent but hurried movement. Big, fiery shells occasionally crossed their path, fired at random by distant rebel batteries, seemingly anxious to make a noise to let us know they were still on hand. We didn't need such reminders—we knew too well, that we had to go, as usual, to their well-fortified positions to fight them.

Proceeding quietly and carefully with the division to the left, we came suddenly to a halt shortly before daylight in a field, the enemy being nearby behind a black wood, through which occasional "pop-pops" were heard from their pickets. But they didn't know of our arrival. With strict orders to make no noise, the troops rested a short time on the damp ground, scarcely as much as whispering their thoughts, although they would once in a while have their jokes, their quiet laugh, no matter what they thought was in store for them. The very stillness of the entire movement presaged a big fight, and they were there to take it in. And it may seem funny to those not posted, that the boys called it "fun."

HANCOCK'S CHARGE AT SPOTTSYLVANIA.

May 12, 1864.

Before the rising of the sun, the 2d corps approaching quietly the wood in front, made a daring charge on the enemy's works, (1,200 yards distant,) and so suddenly was it done that the rebels were completely surprised, and although they opened with canister and some sharp musketry, yet the Unionists quickly closed on them, flanking them on their right, and clubbing them down to a surrender; capturing one line of earthworks, a salient, 4,000 prisoners, including Maj.-Gen. Johnson and. Brig.-Gen. Steuart, and 20 cannon. The enemy were this time caught napping, rolling out of their tents in great disorder; the prisoners admitting they had been outwitted, and called it a "regular Stonewall movement." One wounded artillery man informed Cyrenius Alvord, that:

"You'uns came so quick, we'uns scarcely had time to shoot."

They did shoot, however, and our regiment, out as flankers on the right, had a number hit. Our troops occupied the captured works, the Wisconsin and some other companies advancing a short distance beyond; but finding the enemy in their front apparently well posted, were ordered back behind the line already taken, where they mixed in promiscuously with the other troops. These works were well made and capable of stout resistance. They left their tents standing, with ordnance and camp equipage, which fell into the hands of the Union forces. But the enemy were still in force in our front, and a desperate battle soon commenced; other corps coming up to assist us in the struggle. The captured cannon were turned upon them, the Sharpshooters taking part firing the same, but as they were not used to sighting such ponderous guns, few "center shots" were probably made; yet, with loud hurrahs the pieces were discharged, the shot and shell being sent towards rebeldom, high and low. It was one of those occasions where the fun came in.

The Union artillery soon getting in position, between the cannon's deep roar and the rattle of musketry, one deafening uproar was kept up the entire day. It was one continual roar from sunrise until sunset, and after a short intermission on until midnight. Again and again did the rebels charge the position, coming up like so many fiends, to be hurled back by showers of lead and crashing shell. I counted five different charges that day, the enemy running towards us at full speed, firing as they ran, and although they often reached the works, they couldn't get over. They fought desperately, running headlong to death and destruction. They had come to us, in this fight, and they certainly did it bravely. Our men would rise quick and fire low, throwing the muzzles downward, then drop back. At one time, on the right, they gained a temporary advantage, but were finally driven away with heavy loss. Their dead and wounded were actually "piled up "—the wounded often completely covered by the dead and dying. Although they fought with the greatest determination, they were as determinedly resisted. The artillery on both sides was constantly in play, with shell and shot flying murderously about. Mens' heads were knocked to atoms by iron, others were riddled through their bodies with lead. Goodly sized trees were cut off, and brush mowed low; altogether, a most bloody carnival occurred. One tree, directly in front of Company G., some two feet through, was shot completely away by bullets alone, leaving but a bare stump full of battered lead. This stump was afterwards taken up and sent to the patent office building at Washington. Notwithstanding the enemy strove so hard to regain their old position, they signally failed in so doing—the victory belonged to the Union troops. During the day and night heavy rain wired down again, and the soldiers at the front were hardly to be recognized by their powder-blackened faces, and clothes covered with mud from their caps to their shoes, while their guns soon became dirty and rusty, and at times almost noiseless when they exploded. Heart-rending scenes were on that field—the horrors of war were depicted on all sides. Men lay in all shapes, dying in position. Here, on their knees stiff and stark—there, another kneeling in the act of loading with his arms spread, shot while ramming the cartridge—on their backs, their faces, every way. A field officer's horse just behind the writer, struck with apiece of shell, was caught quickly by the officer, who with revolver at the head, sent the wounded animal out of suffering into eternity. A piece of the same shell struck down a Sharpshooter 50 feet in front of us—Lewis E. Crowell, Company E, (N. H.)—a particularly sorrowful death. The regiment had fallen back to replenish with ammunition, and while sitting under a tree with Capt. Andrews and others of his company, the unfortunate comrade was struck under the left shoulder. He was one of three brothers, members of this company, who were ever ready for duty when called upon. Sergt. Wyatt and Gilman K. Crowell, his brother, buried him on the field further back, in the best possible manner under the circumstances. These shells were coming on all sides thick and deadly. Such was Spottsylvania—one of the hardest day's fights of the war.

As an instance of the terrific power of bursting shells: See you, you man slowly limping to the rear? Wounded evidently in the thigh. Now he is hidden from view by the great expanse of flame and smoke of that suddenly exploding shell. This, however, soon clears away; but where is the wounded hobbler? That is what no one will ever tell. He is gone, apparently, to atoms—blown up and away into a thousand possible particles, leaving none so large as ever to be found. Not even a button or a shred of his garments. For such is the annihilative power of explosive shells. It does not often happen that men are struck that way—but when they are, they are surely *lost* in action.

The conduct of our soldiers in line of battle, was never better than in this day's fight. Every man seemed to be nerved with the same spirit of determination. With the utmost coolness the enlisted men went to work from the start, as if success depended on their individual action. The greatest care was given to the proper loading of their pieces, to aiming, and in firing; and though hurried shots were made, there was no flurry or undue excitement. Rather, a premeditated calculation in making, everything count in our favor,. There was very little talking, principally of caution, such as:

"Fire low, boys; don't forget that."

And when they rose to shoot, they jerked down the muzzles as they pulled,. They were behind those works to stay that day, not to be driven therefrom—such was the spirit in which they engaged in this fight.

There were two officers, however, who had imbibed too much, and in consequence, made fools of themselves. One, a Pennsylvania colonel, who had heretofore stood high with the men, on this occasion when the fighting commenced, rushed wildly on top of the works making an unnecessary and conspicuous target of himself, ordering everybody to follow,—"over and at them." As our orders were to hold our ground, no one followed his lead, despite his frantic yells and oaths—his brag. We expected to see him drop, and he, did get a couple of clips that turned him about, and finally forced him off, slightly wounded. He was trying to distinguish himself, and as he was put under arrest, he probably got "distinguished," or extinguished, as I don't recollect ever seeing that officer again.

The other one carried a star, a New York brigadier, who was pretty drunk and cross, for which "example" to the soldiers he paid the penalty of dismissal from the service. Company G didn't weep, as they had some trouble with that fellow before. He was going to "blow hard-tack through (Bill Sweet's) heart," once, when every rifle-hammer in the company cocked; he heard the click-click, and lowering his revolver, rode off swearing hard at us. No, they didn't weep when they heard he had left us.

Enlisted men had no liquor to "revive their spirits," in a hot fight, so that their valor was the result of sober honest pluck. Instead of taking stimulants to

"Screw their courage to the sticking point," they were obliged to rely on their sense of patriotism to stick and hang together, when facing death and danger. They were more to be depended on free from the effects of liquor, than had they been allowed its use. Whisky rations might do in cases of extreme fatigue, or exposure, or to ward off malaria, to revive for the time the fainting wounded, or in cases of sickness; but should not be issued to men going into a fight—that is when the soldier's head wants to be clear.

Between six and seven in the morning the 6th corps arrived, going into position at the salient on the right of the 2d, and later on became so hard pressed by the enemy, who seemed determined to recapture that part of the works, that Hancock was obliged to reinforce from the 2d corps a part of Wright's command.

. Again referring to Gen. Hancock's report: "The battle raged furiously and incessantly along the whole line from the right of the 6th corps to the left of Barlow's division. A cold drenching rain descended during this battle, in which the troops were constantly under heavy and destructive musketry fire for almost twenty hours. Our losses in killed and wounded were quite heavy, but we had inflicted a signal defeat upon the enemy. Ewell's corps of infantry was almost destroyed. The celebrated Stonewall brigade was captured nearly entire. The losses of the enemy during the day in killed, wounded and captured must have amounted to at least 10,000 men. On the morning of the 13th of May it was discovered that the enemy had retired to his second line of works, about one half-mile in rear of the line we had carried on the previous day, thus yielding to us the palm of victory. Owing to the losses in action and the expiration of the term of service of many regiments of

Mott's division (Fourth), it had become so reduced in numbers that I issued an order on the 13th of May consolidating it into a brigade, and assigned it to Birney's division."

On the 13th in the evening, they were sent out to establish new picket lines on the right, which was successfully accomplished, when the regiment re turned to headquarters. On the 14th, up early going to the front through deep mud. Entering the wood they formed line on the farther side of same and were engaged all day watching the foe and in sharpshooting, again meeting with some loss. During the day heavy cannonading was carried on all along the lines, some heavy rain also pouring down. At dark they were relieved. On the 15th they moved a short distance at daylight to the left, being again' sent to front under sharp fire, taking position in rude rifle pits and behind trees, still engaged as sharpshooters. The enemy opened on them during the day with artillery, causing a force of infantry on picket, to fall back in disorder. The Sharpshooters, however held their position until dark, the relief arriving to find the picket for the day skedaddled; the Sharpshooters were then ordered back. During the artillery fire which was close, several men were hit by splinters from the logs and trees, while George W. Griffin, a slight but brave youth, had a shell pass through the top of his tall felt hat, one he had picked up and worn in lieu of a cap. This made the boys laugh, yell in derision, but none laughed louder than he. On the afternoon of the 16th both regiments were sent out to retake a line on the right, which had been abandoned. Moving forward under fire, they drove the rebels back and obtained possession of the works, which they held until relieved by infantry at nine in the evening. On the next day heavy firing occurred on the right, during the afternoon. We received this day in our corps a considerable number of new troops, said to be 8,000 in all, consisting principally of a division of what was called "heavy artillery," a branch of service which, while it took, amazingly in the later enlistments, did not confine their efforts to handling ponderous siege guns in fortifications, but required also, when the service demanded, that they should carry muskets and fight with them, in line of battle. So in this way, these "heavies" had to help us out; and they were a great acquisition, some of the regiments numbering as high as 1,800 men. Of course, they brought with them into the field the full complement of a soldier; as a result, the old boys never looked far for a good blanket or new overcoat when night came around, thrown wide and scattered far by the new men after they got into their first fight. The division was under command' of Gen. Tyler. The "Corcoran Legion" of infantry were with them, going into Gibbon's division. On the 18th the, enemy opened with artillery and musketry on our left, Han-i cock's 1st and 2d divisions being severely engaged for several l hours; there was also heavy artillery firing on the right during the day.

"Gibbon's and Barlow's divisions traversed the same ground which we had fought so desperately on six days since, and as but a portion of the dead of that day's (12th) contest had been buried, the stench which arose from them was so sickening and terrible that many of the men and officers became deathly sick from it. The appearance of the dead who had been exposed to the sun so long was horrible in the extreme as we marched past and over them—. sight never to be forgotten by those who witnessed it."—GEN. HANCOCK.

About noon the Sharpshooters moved to the right, where they remained in position among the pines until night, when they finally moved off again "to the left," resting at daylight of the 19th in a large open field beyond the Court House, near the river Ny.

HARRIS HOUSE.

May 19, 1864

Late in the afternoon Gen. Tyler's "heavy "division, stationed on the Fredericksburg road at a point called "Harris House," was attacked severely by Ewell's corps who continued the fight up to nine P. M., when the enemy were forced to retreat across the Ny; two brigades of Birney having gone in on the right, with some 5th corps troops on the left of Tyler, assisting greatly in the rebels' repulse. A part of the Second. Sharpshooters were engaged in this affair, of which Lieut. Wm. H. Humphrey, of Company E, laconically remarks: "May 19, Gen. Birney gave the company a day off. We were near his headquarters, when up the road in our rear we heard firing, 'fall in, Sharpshooters;' we go on the double-quick and drive back Ewell's rebels—Company E having two wounded, and that is all the rest we got." Birney's brigades captured 500 prisoners, during this evening and the morning of the 20th.

"The loss of the enemy in this action in killed and wounded was severe. About 400 prisoners fell into our hands. This was the first engagement in which the troops of General Tyler's division had participated. They conducted themselves handsomely, firmly sustaining the shock of the enemy's attack, until the arrival of Birney and the troops of the 5th corps."—HANCOCK.

The official return of casualties in the Union forces at and around Spottsylvania May 8-21, 1864, show—Killed: 2,725; wounded: 13,416; missing 2,258; total: 18,399.

FIRST SHARPSHOOTERS.

Co. C.—Killed: Frank R. Edgerton, Daniel Tillapaugh. Co. E.—Killed: Lewis E. Crowell.

Co. F.—Killed: Henry Mattocks, Thomas Brown, John Bowen. Wounded: Amos A. Smith, J. E. Chase.

Co. G.—Wounded: Corp. Wesley Armfield, leg, slight; Privates George A. Denniston, head, mortal; William Mc-Quivey, right arm.

Co. H.—Wounded: Harvey Mathews.

Co. K.—Killed: Darius Hall. Wounded: William Clelland, right hip; Calvin Smith, right breast; George H. Smith, right leg.

On the 21st the general movement to the left was resumed. Crossing the Richmond & Fredericksburg railway they halted for a short time about noon, the day being hot and the men fatigued, having traveled over 20 miles before getting breakfast. Passing Milford Station in the afternoon they came to a halt two miles south, and in the evening our men were sent out to establish the picket lines, where they remained until the next morning, during which time some firing occurred on the right of the line. The 22d they were again in the front on picket, but were relieved at dark, the troops in the rear fortifying. On the 23d they moved on, passing by Chesterfield a couple of miles south, where they took part in another engagement.

BATTLE OF NORTH ANNA.

May 28-28, 1864.

Companies B and G, First Regiment, were ordered out to support a battery, where they remained until dark under artillery fire from both sides, being in advance of the Union gunners, and making long-range shots with the telescope rifle, a *few* of which were carried in the regiment, and were known by the name of "the heavies." On their right, the 2d and 3d brigades, under Cols. Pierce and Egan, became hotly engaged in a charge, driving the enemy back and obtaining a position on the river bank. The progress of this affair was carefully watched from a half-fallen tree by Franklin Viall, a true and ever-ready soldier, who reported from his high position as follows:

"Now they're at it! Halloo! our men got it that time. But they rally again, and now they are in it hot and heavy. Halloo! there goes a line back. I can't tell which one, the smoke's too thick. But it makes no difference, for either the enemy are falling back, or our men advancing—Hurrah, boys! it's all right, now! The stars and stripes wave over the river bank."

And jumping from his elevated position to the ground, he took his place in the skirmish line. The next morning (24th) before daybreak we were placed behind breastworks at the river, built during the night, the enemy being posted under cover opposite, with a redoubt containing more troops on a rise of ground behind them. Soon after sunrise sharpshooting began, and was kept up at intervals until eight o'clock, when troops began to cross over a bridge the rebels had been unable to destroy, the railway bridge to our left being in flames. The rebel artillery now opened from the right furiously, but the crossing was effected with little injury and the redoubt captured under fire, with some artillery and several hundred prisoners, the Second Regiment who led the charge meeting with serious casualties. The artillery firing during the movement was kept up on both sides without intermission. The First Sharpshooters soon after crossed and advanced beyond the captured works to a shady grove, near a large and considerably dilapidated mansion known as Fox's house, which at times was under fire from the rebel pickets and sharpshooters. To stop this shooting, Capt. John Wilson commanding First Regiment detailed Lieut. Stevens with 40 men, who were sent out on the left of the line of infantry skirmishers and advanced over a large field several hundred yards, under a close and heavy fire from the enemy. Here the lieutenant was ordered to swing his men around and hold some log buildings or quarters near the Confederate lines, from whence this persistent firing had been kept up. Rushing forward on double-quick, firing rapidly as they ran, the place was soon occupied on the heels of the retreating foe, and held until late in the day. While here, sharp exchanges took place at distances varying from 300 to 1,000 yards, resulting in close shooting on both sides. But we had accomplished the purpose for which we were sent out, the stopping of rebel bullets in and around Fox's place. During the day a Union force appeared on the left of our detail, and by a rapid movement put a body of the enemy to flight while trying to cross the railroad which ran along close to the left of our position at the huts, the Johnnies running wildly back to the ridge where their batteries were planted. Our men getting out of ammunition were finally relieved by another detachment, after repeated signals for aid, with the enemy threatening, and liable at any moment to crowd them out from behind the rude buts; when they fell back under the rebel fire to the regiment at Fox's.

At this place the officer in charge ran the gauntlet of scores of bullets traversing the open ground, to get three hang-back fellows up to the exact front. As our campaigns increased the orders became more severe, particularly in regard to straggling; and for which the line officer commanding the company was held responsible. So that when it came to going back over a battle field under fire, to recover and bring forward one or more of his command, who had dropped out of sight behind a big log or other pretty safe place, if the officer didn't exactly swear at his luck—and he probably did—he at least gave forcible notice that it was no joke to be made a special target of, by yanking the delinquents out from their snug cover.

The line officer (who in many cases came from the ranks themselves) incurred the hardships of the enlisted men, besides had the responsibility upon them for the proper performance of the duties assigned, and often has it happened that they have been picked off by the enemy, simply because of the double danger encountered, in movements brought about by the failure through carelessness or otherwise of the men, to follow the strict letter of their instructions. This is where the regular soldier was supposed to be superior to the volunteer; not in all cases, or probably very many, but some of the latter were to be found in all organizations who knew better than their officers, and as a result, were too decidedly heedless of orders, to be depended on. Such men required watching. On the other hand, there were men in the volunteer service, and I may safely say a large majority, that could not be surpassed in military behavior, under the hottest fires of the hardest battles.

The enemy had been busily engaged shelling the troops around the Fox grounds, where breastworks were being thrown up in the field by our soldiers. Some of these shells passed through the grove where the regimental reserve had remained, and where several noted Union generals had congregated. The central figure of the group was Gen. Hancock, whose tall, handsome and commanding person looked every inch the brave soldier he had long before proven himself to be. On his left stood honest, though sometime unfortunate, Burnside; on the right the gallant division commander, Birney; while immediately in front facing them was Crittenden. An earnest consultation took place, the rebel shell passing occasionally over their heads as if hunting for somebody. Of course they were closely observed by the green-coated riflemen, who tried to discern from their looks and gestures, rather than to hear their low-toned conversation, what was the coming programme. Finally, they broke up the council and at once repaired to the house preparatory to mounting and away!—all but Hancock—it was his headquarters. And not a moment too soon did they leave their meeting place, for right there is where these four Union generals just missed being shattered to death, as they had scarcely moved around to the front of the house, when a searching shell passing through a Sharpshooter's knapsack, landed in the exact spot they had a moment before occupied, exploding with terrific force, but luckily harmless.

This knapsack belonged to Richard W. Tyler, of Company K, who had set it against a tree in the front of the garden, and he looked in vain for the smallest fragment, to say nothing of his lost letters, sundry daguerreotypes (we had no photographs then), and other articles of more or less value. All were gone forever. After the startling nature of the explosion and the miraculous escape had passed by, the comrades had a big laugh at Dick and his misfortune. But Sergt. Tyler was soon after placed in a position whereby he did not have to draw another knapsack, on account of the faithful, and I may add gallant, Lieut. C. W. Thorp, being forced to resign on surgeon's certificate the next day, the 25th, having previously been seriously sick with typhoid fever, the effects of which no doubt remained; and Tyler was promoted first lieutenant and assumed command of the company, in the absence of Capt. Nash, who had been captured by the enemy while acting as staff officer.

While expecting to receive orders to charge the enemy's position, at about sunset a drenching rain poured down and the wind blew with great violence, causing further operations for the day to cease. On the 25th the First Sharpshooters rejoined their brigade, remaining quiet in the field behind works that had been hurriedly built. While here,

Quartermaster Marden arrived at the front with the regimental teams with provisions and clothing, which was a welcome sight to the command, especially as he brought them letters from home. But he was not wholly unexpected, because the boys knew Marden would come just as soon as it was possible for him to do so—for our quartermaster was a hard worker in the interest of the regiment, and suffered his share of the hardships with the soldiers.

On the 26th in the afternoon heavy firing occurred right and left; in the evening the Sharpshooters moved quietly off to the right, into a deep wood, relieving Burnside's men on picket, where they remained until midnight, the darkness being so intense it was with great difficulty they found their way out; and then not until Wilson and Stevens had first traced the way, after almost running on to the rebel lines, made manifest by a low but determined "halt! "which they didn't do, however, but left the puzzled Johnny to discover nothing in his front but fast retreating steps. And there Capt. Wilson for once admitted he was scared, not for himself but for the regiment, for they were lost. This particular scene of picket duty, in that black, lonely wood, fits so well with the following choice composition illustrative of the trials of the sentinel on picket, the most important duty performed by a soldier, that I borrow it for the occasion from Love's "Wisconsin in the War of the Rebellion "—by the way, one of the completest state histories ever written. These worthy lines are supposed to have originated with Lieut. George Bleyer, 24th Wis. Vols., killed at Stone River; and will no doubt prove a most interesting as well as exciting description of picket duty; which, however, does not always end so happily.

ON PICKET.

'Tis midnight; in a lonely strip of wood
With darkness draped—a pall of solitude—
I walk my beat with measured step and slow,
Then, like a drunkard, stagger to and fro,
Intoxicated by the drugs of sleep;
My eyes are heavy, yet strict vigils keep;
Imagination fills my drowsy brain
With scenes of battles—fields of maimed and slain;
The stumps and bushes into phantoms grow,
The shadows shape themselves into the foe.
There is no moon, and not a star I *see,*
Altho' I know they shine on shrub and tree,
By the faint streaks of silvery, wandering light,
That now and then bewilder sense and sight.
Like the poor felon in his dungeon deep,
I pray each beam my company to keep,
And light my lone and solitary place.
How long will morning screen her rpsy face?
Hark! hear that crash among the bush and leaves-
Still, still, my nervous heart, your throbbing heaves!
You flutter like some frightened captive bird.
Hush! for your throbs by others may be heard,
And thus betray the covert where I stand,
Grasping my musket with a firmer hand;
My drowsy eyes open wide and peer
Into the gloom. Again the noise I hear;
And now a form of tall, gigantic size,
From out the earth, as 'twere, I see arise.
Slowly it moves, but with its forward strides
Into a human form and shape it glides.

> My heart beats slow again, my speech I've found,
> My challenge stern the ghostly woods resound;
> It proves a "friend," and not a wily foe
> The secret talisman it whispers low;
> I let it pass toward the sleepy camp:
> A *soldier from a chicken forage tramp.*

Rejoining the command after much difficulty, they fell back and recrossed the river among the last of the Union forces shortly before daylight. The troops in the meantime had been tearing up the Richmond & Fredericksburg railroad for several miles, bending rails, burning ties, etc. At an early hour on the morning of the 27th, the Union army having all recrossed the North Anna, the bridge was burned and the troops moved off again to the left, laughing at the rebel cheers on the opposite side of the stream as they charged the deserted works.

The march resumed in the afternoon, the road being lined with dead horses for many miles, the result of some sharp cavalry skirmishing ahead of the advancing columns. The carcasses were tumbled about in all manner of shapes, presenting a sight almost sickening,_ even to the veteran soldier; while occasionally dead men were found on either side, covered with dust and dirt to that extent as at times to scarcely, distinguish the blue from the gray. After marching until midnight, the road crowded with teams and troop-, we rested in field until daylight of the 28th, when, marching again until late in the afternoon, the Sharpshooters crossed the Pamunkey at Hanovertown, halting nearby in a field where they remained until noon of the following day. Advancing then to cross-roads near Salem Church, halting on the Mechanicsville road some eight miles from the latter place, they commenced fortifying. After building a good line of works they left them, and changing position several times in the evening, finally rested under arms in the field.

While proceeding on this march, still on the line of the North Anna, a squad of Sharpshooters under Sergt. Eli Cook, of Company 1, were called on to operate against the enemy's batteries that had been run on to a favorable position to enfilade the road. Cook's command took their position in tree tops, behind rocks and stumps, without having been seen. Presently a rifle report from a high tree caused the rebel cannoniers to respond, and the work began from 400 to 600 yards range—close enough for our men to get in good shots. Three full batteries opened on them one round, when Berdan's men had them ranged and sighted. They would try to load their pieces by reaching up under the muzzle, but the boys could send a Sharps rifle ball so completely in the muzzles of their cannon, at this distance, that they could not load. They stuck up one battery flag, and this was at once shot away and our men just yelled. They tried every possible way to get in a shot, but as the Sharpshooters had orders not to let them load again, their cannon became subject to the will of Sergt. Cook's force, who kept them quiet until our passing troops had gone on, when the riflemen crawled from view, and pushing on joined the command.

THE TOTOPOTOMOY

May 30, 31, June 1.

Falling in before daybreak of the 30th, the First Sharpshooters were finally posted on the edge of a ravine within 300 yards of the rebel works, which position was taken up after daylight. Temporary breastworks of rails were hastily built, under the enemy's fire, and the men were kept busy sharpshooting until late in the afternoon when they were relieved. Considerable fighting occurred during the day, and at night heavy cannonading, our side sending over a number of mortar shells. Late in the evening Brooke's brigade made a dash to our left, carrying a line of the enemy's rifle pits. On the 31st we crossed a small stream known as Swift Run, occupying the enemy's line,—a series of trenches,—the Second Regiment having skirmished ahead. Lieut. Humphrey reports: "We were told by Gen. Grant in person, to go across the creek, if we had to surrender when we got there, but we did not surrender; we took 137 of the 27th North Carolina prisoners and held the works that night."

Capt. Wilson galloping up, subject to the enemy's fire from the woods in front, ordered the First Sharpshooters out of the works, when deploying out over the open field to the left, under heavy fire front and flank, they rapidly advanced in skirmish line, actually running towards the enemy, and reached the position assigned them on the Richmond road capturing several soldiers of Breckinridge's command. Under the severe fire from the woods on their left, while crossing the plain several were hit in the movement, while the ground under their rapid feet and otherwise about them, was continually dusted by the hundreds of spattering bullets from the rebel force in the forest. Capt. Wilson gallantly led the regiment, mounted, receiving a rattling fire about him as he galloped to and fro issuing his orders. Occupying this position far down the road in the advance, with a dc tail under Lieut. Stevens still farther ahead, to the left, dos(up to the enemy in the woods, within speaking distance, causing close shooting and much danger, they remained under fire the entire day, and not until eleven o'clock that night were they ordered back to a field in the rear, to sup and rest. A few hours later they moved into a pine wood, where they remained until daylight of June 1st, when they were hurried into line owing to the reported- advance of the enemy on the right, over the grounds vacated the night before by the 6th corps, which at the time was unoccupied. Skirmishing through the timber they reached the empty breastworks, forming line to the right of the division, having captured a number of unarmed men who had come over they said to get some "fresh beef," which was lying where slaughtered, left by the troops that were withdrawn during the night. In front to our right, in plain view with their flags above them, was observed a small body of the enemy, reported by Capt. Wilson to be "Billy Mahone's men," and during the day he was very anxious to move on them to attempt their capture, although he had no orders to do so, but he finally abandoned the enterprise. Remaining where they were until dark, with occasional exchange of shots by the vedettes, they then moved off via Salem Cross Roads, arriving at Cold Harbor in the forenoon of June 2d. Capt. Aschmann had a narrow escape on the 30th, by a shot across-his chin, whereby he lost his goatee. He was "awful mad" when hit, for fear the goatee wouldn't grow out again.

CASUALTIES.

Co. A.—Wounded: Capt. Aschmann, chin, slight.

Co. B.—Killed: Thaddeus Hadden; Francis Snyder, mortal wound.

Co. E.—Wounded: Lieut. Isaac Davis, George A. Collins. Co. H.—Wounded: John Snyder, mortally.

Co. K.—Wounded: Lewis C. Bitton, slight, wouldn't leave company.

BATTLE OF COLD HARBOR
June 1-5, 1864.

Heavy fighting at this point had taken place before the Sharpshooters arrived. In fact, Gen. Sheridan's cavalry forces had succeeded in occupying the position here as long back as the 21st of May, after an obstinate fight with the enemy's cavalry and infantry combined, and with orders to hold on, they did so until the morning of June 1st, when a desperate attack was, made to retake the place, the enemy being repulsed, our cavalry fighting nobly. The 6th corps under Wright, who came into command by the death of Sedgwick, now coming up from the right, and from the left reinforcements from the Army of the James under Baldy Smith—Lee also reinforcing his lines—a severe battle followed. The attack was made by, the two Union corps, and an advanced line taken with several hundred prisoners. Farther, however, they could not go, the interior breastworks being too strong for them. In this assault the Union army lost 2,000 killed and wounded, but the position secured was held. Hancock's corps coming in later, took no part in this day's fight. The next day was occupied in preparing for another and still greater attack. On the 3d, when the great battle of the engagement here was fought—a battle that cost us many lives, and was _barren of any successful result farther than to hold our ground—Hancock's corps at daybreak, at the given signal, rushed over their works, for our troops had intrenched,—they had learned to fortify on this campaign,—Barlow's division on the left, with Gibbon and Birney, bayonets fixed, ready for a grand charge. Gen. Barlow's troops had a clean sweep at first,. driving everything before them, making some captures—men and guns. But soon they met such disastrous volleys, such a storm of balls, that in 10 minutes time they were-beaten, and recoiling under the terrible fire—nothing abating—Barlow's line got back behind a ridge, those that could, many lying in front in a depressed roadway unable to get out, but held there for hours—till night—by the exulting enemy. Meanwhile Gibbon's men, supported by Birney, made a gallant effort to cross the rebel works, Gibbon's brigades charging close up, almost on top of them. The intrenched enemy behind had the advantage, as we did of them at Spottsylvania, and our men had to fall back.

Gibbon's line was unfortunately cut in two by a marsh, which widened as the line, neared the enemy's works. The country over which he advanced was cut up by ravines. The line moved gallantly forward, however, until close to the enemy's works, but was not able to advance farther under the destructive fire.—HANCOCK.

Col. Smyth, commanding 3d brigade, 2d division, says: "At half past four A. M. June 3d, I was ordered to attack the enemy. I formed my brigade in line of battle and advanced, and charged the enemy's works. When the command arrived at from 60 to 100 yards from the enemy's works the ranks had become so thinned and the fire from the enemy's artillery and musketry was so destructive that the men were compelled to halt and seek such shelter as presented itself. In this position the command soon erected a rude breastwork. At nine A. M. Berdan's Sharpshooters and a battalion of the First Massachusetts Heavy Artillery reported to me. I deployed part of the Sharpshooters in front as skirmishers, and held the battalion of 1st Mass. Heavy Artillery in reserve."

In closing his report of the 4th epoch of the campaign, Gen. Hancock said of the 2d corps: "The first report of casualties after the action, which was unusually short, hardly an hour in duration, showed a loss of 3,024. Among officers the loss had been without precedent. I had to mourn the loss of those who had hitherto been foremost and most daring and brilliant in action. When it is remembered that I had only my two smallest divisions actually engaged, it will be seen that the loss in commanders was unusually severe. It was a blow to the corps from which it did not soon recover."

The 6th corps and Smith's troops also found their brave attacks useless, the principal impression they made was in their own losses. Burnside later on had got a flank movement, but before he could execute it, Gen. Meade ordered further operations for the day to cease. A famous writer speaking of this charge, tells how "in the short space of 10 minutes, 12,000 Union soldiers lay writhing on the sod."

Particularly was this the case with Barlow's first line, Miles' and Brooke's brigades, who rushed right up to the rebel guns, a new regiment (7th New York Heavy Artillery) 1,600 strong, being the first on the works, capturing 300 prisoners, one color and four cannon; while the second line stopped short behind the sunken road—they quickly surveyed it as a death trap and came to a decided halt. The 7th heavy artillery regiment lost heavily, while the total loss of both brigades—the first line—was about 1,300, or about 1,500 for. Barlow's division. Gibbon's loss on the right, was over 1,600; Birney about 200, making a totality of over 3,000 in the 2d corps; with an official Union loss at Cold Harbor and vicinity, June 2-15, of 12,738: Killed, 1,845, wounded 9,077, missing 1,816. Gen. Meade wished to have the attack renewed in the evening, but Gen. Hancock advised against it as being a useless effort.

The Confederates occupied the ground held by the 5th corps two years before, at Gaines' Mill, while Meade's troops were now in the rebel places. Then, Porter held his position with half the number of his opponents, in an open fight without breastworks—little used those days—now, Lee had fortified, and very strongly, so that the battle was but a repetition of loss of life without any perceptible gain to the Union arms except that the Confederates, whose losses were slight as compared to ours,—as 100 is to 1,000,—could less afford to lose men than our side with a great northern reserve still remaining to be drawn from.

After the morning's assault of the 3d of June, Birney's division being now in reserve, the Sharpshooters were engaged during the day in front of Gen. Gibbon's division fighting the enemy's musketry and artillery, while the troops in their rear were employed in constructing additional breastworks. Some sharp fighting, however, was going on at other points on the line. While on duty here the writer was knocked flat to the ground by a glancing shot across his right shoulder, but as it didn't draw blood the boys of his command yelled: "You can't go back on that, you've got to stay," and I did stay. In fact, I long ago learned that in such a place as that, the safest place was with the company unless at least, you could "show blood." It was only another of those miraculous escapes, for had the ball struck me square in the shoulder I never would have written these lines. In the evening the Sharpshooters were recalled from the front, and while forming the regiment in a small field were suddenly exposed to a terrible fire of shot and shell, front, flank and rear, the shells exploding close over them, for they lay flat, being caught in a position they could not escape from. It was during the disastrous charge of the enemy on the Union lines at dusk. After it was over, they retired a short distance to the rear to rest for the night. On the 4th and 5th they were employed on the same dangerous duty, were greatly exposed, suffering more or less loss. On the 4th one of our men, Emery Munsell, carrying a 28 pound telescope rifle, was unceremoniously knocked head-first into the brush by a retreating horseman, during a sudden and well-directed discharge from the enemy's line. Munsell for a few moments felt as if he was wounded in fifty places, and would liked to have given the runaway some of the same kind of wounds. He didn't swear any—he "didn't have time."

On the evening of the 5th they moved to the left, through heavy brush and woods in close proximity to the rebel lines, halting late at night 100 yards from the enemy's pickets, near Barker's Mills, remaining under arms till daylight. Surely the situations were trying, for the Sharpshooters had now been more or less under fire, 24 days out of 31.

CASUALTIES.

Co. F.—Killed: Joseph Bickford; Alvin Babcock, mortally wounded, and three others slight. Almon D. Griffin, wounded on picket June 12:

Co. G.—Killed: Private Conrad Murat. Wounded Lieut. C. A. Stevens, right shoulder, slight; Corp. Franklin Viall and Private Alvin Sherman, scalp wounds, slight.

Co. H.—Wounded: Private Aaron H. Fuller.

Co. I.—Killed Sergt. Benjamin Shay and James Curtis. Wounded; Ryon E. Williams.

Co. K.—Wounded: Lewis C. Bitton, lost right foot by solid shot.

PUNISHING A LIBELER.

While halting near Barker's Mills a novel scene occurred on the 8th of June. A newspaper reporter rode under guard, along the lines, with a hard-tack box strapped on his back bearing this inscription: "Libeller of the Press." A mounted bugler rode in front sounding the call "Attention!" The reporter, who had been ordered out of the army for saying what he ought not, in his sensational dispatches—violating existing orders—was greeted by the soldiers with enquiries for the "latest news," with a desire to "send him to the front," also with numerous other remarks tending to provoke his deepest disgust. This was a case of being retired in disgrace, similar to that of the "poor old soldier" who gets drummed out. The man narrowly escaped being shot by order of Gen. Burnside for some previous act prejudicial to military methods; and to Gen. Grant, from whom he had stolen by means of sneaking up, the result of private consultations with Meade during the Wilderness battles, this correspondent Swinton, owed his life, and could afford to be extremely thankful for a mitigation of the sentence whereby he was only to be expelled from the army, with orders never to return.

Remaining near Barker's Mills, their old camping ground two years before, until the night of the 12th, during which time clothes and rations were issued, they finally moved away quietly, still to the left, crossing the Chickahominy at Long Bridge early on the 13th, and marching by the old "field" at Charles City Cross Roads (Glendale), reached the Court House at night where they rested till the following day. On the afternoon of the 14th the Sharpshooters crossed James river by steamboat at Wilcox Landing, halting a short distance above in a brushy, field for the night, being out of rations. It was now plain to be seen that Grant could not attack Richmond over McClellan's old ground as he wished to, but would operate south of the rebel capital on the line of the James and Appomattox, with Petersburg (23 miles from Richmond) his chief point of attack.

It was well understood by both Gens. Butler and Meade before starting on the campaign that it was my intention to put both their armies south of the James river in case of failure to destroy Lee without it.—U. S. GRANT.

SIEGE OF PETERSBURG.

The fighting around Petersburg comprised many battles and at different points, extending from the Appomattox river east of the city and southerly four or five miles, and these actions wherein the Sharpshooters were engaged are principally distinguished by the names given as they occurred.

On the 15th at eleven A. M. we received orders to march, the expected rations not having arrived, and after a hot, dusty tramp, arrived after dark in the vicinity of Petersburg, after the fighting for the day by the troops of the Army of the James was over.

According to Gen. Grant, it appears that Hancock was uninformed of what he was expected to do on crossing the

James, although Gen. Meade had been directed to push him forward to back up Baldy Smith in his attack that day on the works before Petersburg. Thus, the waiting for the necessary rations ordered by Gen. Grant from Bermuda Hundred which failed to come, kept him back just long enough to be too late. Grant says if Hancock had been notified, he with his usual promptness would have reached Petersburg by four P. M. An unfortunate mistake, which if it had not occurred might have been the saving of many lives in decreased battles.

Early on the morning of the 16th the Sharpshooters proceeded hurriedly to dispatch their simple breakfast of coffee, their haversacks being short of eatables, with not even a cracker to be had; they having but four hours sleep following the march from James river and about the works along the front of Petersburg, from eleven A. M. to one A. M.—14 hours. It was not long before the enemy commenced throwing shell, with little damage. During the past night the rebel troops were heard arriving from the vicinity of Richmond by railway, so that it was evident they were in force in our front. Had the 2d corps arrived in time to have taken part in the fighting of the day previous, it is quite possible that Petersburg would have fallen into Union hands before Lee could have reinforced the place. At an early hour of the 16th the division artillery opened with rifled Parrots on the city, which could be seen two miles away, while troops on the right, near the Appomattox, caused the rebel pickets to hurriedly retire over a large field to their lines immediately in front of the city; the Union forces now occupying lines captured the day previous by the troops under Butler, white and black.

HARRISON'S CREEK.

June 16, 1864.

The First Sharpshooters, 175 strong under command of Capt. John Wilson, while holding a position on a road leading to Petersburg, received orders to double-quick down the same to assist in the discomfiture of the retiring Confederates. Obeying promptly, the men hurried forward until brought in close proximity to the rebel riflemen posted along the small stream above named. At this place they remained until the afternoon guarding the road and having sharp exchanges at short range with the enemy, meeting with some loss on our side. The enemy were finally driven out of their advanced rifle pits at this point after much resistance; the fences and other obstructions being removed by our reserve, the ground was cleared,. ready for any assault that might be determined on by our corps commander. One of the first men shot on taking this position was James Heath, of Michigan, who carried a 34-pound telescope rifle, the heaviest in the regiment, and which, as he went down, fell with a heavy blow in the middle of the road. This rifle was immediately turned over to James Ragin, of Wisconsin, who was sent to the rear by Capt. Wilson, to put it in thorough repair before attempting to use it. The giving of these telescopic rifles but few of which were now carried, at this period of our service, was in the nature of a mark of honor, as the Sharpshooter thus armed was considered an independent character, used only for special service, with the privilege of going to any part of the line where in his own judgment he could do the most good. It is therefore sufficient, in naming the men carrying these ponderous rifles, to show that they were among our most trusty soldiers and best shots. A small party of scouts under Lieut: Stevens having been sent out, later on, to the left of the road proceeded under sharp, close fire to the, designated position, but finding the enemy in much greater force close at hand, both in their immediate front and on the flank, from whom they received a warm reception, it was determined to report back the condition of affairs, the detail not' being strong enough to hold their ground any length of time, especially should an advance be made, which was threatened. The officer reporting back in person under a storm of bullets "barking his clothes," for they could see every movement, after a short consultation he received orders to withdraw his party, which was fortunately done without loss. Later in the day, the regiment moved to the left of the road, where the detail had previously been, and with this necessary strength, at once established an advanced line at this important point, close up to the rebel works,—not a hundred yards between them,—and about sunset became suddenly subjected to a severe attack. But notwithstanding the hundreds of balls flying about them, they held their ground without flinching, although their cover was only a small slope of ground. The brigade came up soon after under Col. Macallister, a bold leader, and checked the enemy, the firing being very heavy on both sides until long after night had come upon them, the long lines of flashing guns on either side giving a grand but terrific aspect to the scene. The Sharpshooters after the night fight was over, were sent to the rear to rest, and to procure rations brought up during the afternoon, of which they were greatly in need, the first received since leaving Cold Harbor.

CASUALTIES.

Co. B.—Wounded: Sergt. Thomas Smith, in leg, mortal; John W. Kenny, arm; Stephen C. James, right arm; John McCauley.

Co. C.—James Heath, killed.

Co. F.—Caspar B. Kent, killed.

On June 17th Companies B, E, and G were sent to the front of Gen. Barlow's division, where they were engaged in sharpshooting until nightfall. Company F was also out further to the left, in hastily prepared intrenchments, where they had hot work with the enemy, whose rifle pits were said to be but 50 yards in their front, shooting upwards of 100 rounds per man. It proved an exciting day for the Vermonters, who were kept busy dodging the rebel bullets and sending back good shots in return. It was close work, and the Sharpshooters had plenty of it before Petersburg. Running out of cartridges, Capt. Merriman sent Sergt. Cassius Peck after more, and twice he passed over the places of danger commanded by rebel guns, getting two haversacks filled, which enabled Company F to hold their greatly threatened position.

During the afternoon a portion of the 9th corps on the left of the three first named companies, made a daring charge on to the rebel works, but failing, they retired, crowding back over our own works in considerable disorder, leaving their dead and wounded in the cornfields in long rows, to mark their destructive course in their futile attempt. Soon again, however, another assault was ordered, this time by the combined forces of Hancock and Burnside (2d and 9th corps), which resulted in driving the enemy away, capturing their fronting lines; an important gain to our side, although at fearful cost in casualties—over 3,000 killed and wounded. At dark the Sharpshooters were called in, short of ammunition, retiring to the field behind the works, where they re-formed with the other companies, lying on their arms for the night, exposed to stray bullets which frequently came among them, causing the loss of one killed and several wounded in the regiment.

The casualties this day were as follows:

Sergt.-Major Caleb N. Jacobs, shot in left arm and side. Co. B.—James D. Seward, killed.

Co. F.—Corp. Charles B. Mead, killed; Henry E. Barnum, mortally wounded; John Quinlan, wounded.

Sergeant-Major Jacobs was mortally wounded on the front lines while taking observations. I sent him back in charge of T. A. Kirkham and another man, with a note to the provost-guard, to let Kirkham pass with Jacobs to the Surgeon, but they wouldn't allow it, and ordered Kirkham back to his company. During the night Jacobs died, but had lived long enough to send a message to his mother and sister as follows:

"Tell them I enlisted to save my country, and if need be, to die for my country. Tell them I never regretted that I enlisted. I am glad I have served my country, and do not regret to die for it."

Such were the last and noble words of one of the best and bravest men we had in the service, and who was in all respects a true patriot and a splendid soldier, who had worked up gradually from the ranks to the head of the noncommissioned staff.

On the death of Jacobs, Sergt. Charles J. Buchanan, of Company D, was promoted sergeant-major, and on August 12th was commissioned first lieutenant, he having the highest testimonials, and, as before indicated, had always been ready for duty when called, was never sick or wounded, and bad never missed an action of his company. Here was an illustration of what boys would amount to, as soldiers; for "Buck," as he was familiarly known and generally called in the regiment, was one of the youngest members, having enlisted at the tender age of 17. Without ever knowing what hardship was at home, for he had been a law student, he readily broke in to a soldier's life, becoming one of the best marchers, enduring his share of all the hard trials the soldiers were subjected to. They went in "boys," but they soon became men—and men of endurance. And yet, there were not so many boys enlisted, particularly in '61-'62, as some might think. At least, this was the case in Companies D and G; for out of a total in Company D of 64 members, only 16 enlisted under age, 38 were over 21, 8 over 30, and 2 over 40, making an average of 24$^{1}/4$ years. In Company G, out of a total of 152 enrolled, only 22 enlisted under age, nearly one-half of whom were over 20. While, counting by decades, there were 100 over 21, 25 over 30, and 5 above 40. There were 60 between 24 and 30, and but 40 from 21 to 23; the average age being 26 years, which I believe would hold good in the two regiments.

So, the "boys" were pretty good boys after all, worthy defenders of their country, and "Buck" was one of them. After the war he was offered by Gen. Hancock a commission in the regular army, but respectfully declined, preferring to practice law, which he has since done to date.

Without any wish to disparage in any manner the good qualities of other companies in either regiment, or to appear invidious by comparison, the writer is constrained to remark in this connection— principally on account of the fact that Company D was the smallest company numerically, attaining hardly the minimum requirement, and because of more being said individually or otherwise of other companies—that this company enjoyed the reputation of having a superior lot of men. Though few in numbers they were a host in themselves, who never failed to make good their calling and election to the Sharpshooter service. In every action in which they were engaged, they always did whatever was required of them cheerfully and acceptably, thus contributing materially to the success so nobly earned and so steadfastly maintained by the regiment.

Company D never received any recruits, which was owing, as Capt. Buchanan has justly said, "largely, to that miserable policy which so generally obtained during most of the war, of raising new and inexperienced battalions instead of filling up, the wasted ranks of veteran organizations. It seemed to be of far more importance that the political favorites at home, though novices in war, should be preferred over those who had won their positions and enviable records by bravery in the face of the enemy. The policy was wrong, as well as disastrous. Had the armies at the front been kept fully recruited, as they might easily have been," (had it been insisted on), "who shall say that our forces would not have been far more efficient everywhere, and consequently, the war brought to an end far more quickly than it was." A policy, however, that has been carried on to a great extent since the war, in the matter of political favors, wherein the poor soldier, who battled at the front, must stand aside for wealth and a false, un-American aristocracy.

HARE'S FARM.

June 18-20, 1864.

On the 18th, advancing from the line of works taken from the enemy the night previous, our Sharpshooters were posted in and around the premises of O.P. Hare, a noted Virginia turfite, whose race-course and training grounds called "Newmarket" were soon despoiled of all semblance of their former glories by the tramping of armed men, the galloping of war-like steeds, and the wheeling of heavy batteries. Here our men remained until the night of the 21st, using their rifles faithfully, often within 60 yards of the enemy's rifle pits, at different points along the line. The charge near the Hare House by a Union brigade on the 18th, resulted in disaster, although the Sharpshooters at the house were busily engaged assisting them with their rifles. Casualties with us this day were:

Wounded: Adjutant E. R. Blakeslee.

Co. A.—Wounded: Lewis Koester.

Co. B.—Killed: Daniel Vandebogert.

Co. F.—Killed: Edward Lyman.

Co. H.—Killed: William R. Hicks.

Co. I.—Killed: Robert Sheldon.

Co. K.—Killed: James Stephens.

On the 19th Companies E and G occupied a position in and around the house, the brigade building a line of works across the garden. Hare's house was evidently left by the late occupants in a hurry, as a large amount of books and papers principally referring to sporting items, furniture of different kinds, carpets, etc., were found scattered about. The walls of the building were completely perforated with bullet holes, while larger ones were being daily made by round shot and shell. The windows of-the carpeted basement opened on one side in full view of the rebel pits in front, and as the basement itself made a very comfortable rifle pit, with chairs of mahogany to sit on, a number of the riflemen took possession of the same for the day. Among them was Emery Munsell, who was seated in an arm-chair with his 28-pounder, making long-range shots, several of which were thrown at random towards Petersburg, in hopes of attracting the notice of the editor of the *Express* while seated in his evidently uneasy chair, where he could have found a truthful item about the Sharpshooter& as an equivalent to the lying one he invented on the death of Durkee before Yorktown; as the Union Sharpshooters were actually established in a "carpeted rifle pit" (but furnished by the enemy) with "comfortable arm-chairs to sit in," and "mahogany tables to eat off of; "although the wine cellar which was close at hand, contained naught but empty bottles.

While the New Hampshire captain (Andrews), and Wisconsin lieutenant (Stevens), were seated at one of Hare's tables at half past six o'clock the morning of the 19th, eating their simple breakfast of hard-tack and coffee, the rebel bullets whizzed through the windows over their heads into the opposite wall, showing conclusively that they had range of the place although they did no harm, yet succeeded in raising considerable dust inside as the broken plaster fell to the floor. The Sharpshooting party, however, silenced them in the course of the morning.

The shooting between the rebel riflemen and the Sharpshooters at this place, was carried on at times at extremely short-range, with much determination.. As an Alabama rebel afterwards remarked: "It was only necessary to hold up your hand to receive a furlough." On one occasion, he 'stated, his comrade did so, and receiving a ball through his arm, started, as he expressed it, "for bum," but soon after leaving the pit he received another shot in the rear, whereupon he wheeled about exclaiming with an oath: "I didn't ask for an extension."

The rifle pits were generally approached before daylight, and for hours in the hot sun would the rifleman lie watching his antagonist in his front, frequently exchanging shots. After dark they would fall back behind the breastworks for the night. At times an agreement would be entered into between the parties to cease firing, while one of the occupants of the pit on either side, would start a small fire and make coffee. Such agreement would -be in about the manner following:

"Well, Yank! Ain't it pretty near breakfast time? We'uns are getting hungry."

"All right, Johnny! Down with your shooting irons." Sufficient time having elapsed to obtain the meal, firing would be resumed, giving notice, thus:

"Hurrah there, Johnny! Time's up!"

"All right, Yank! pitch in!"

And the sharp crack of their rifles would resound as a reminder that business had commenced again.

ONE WAY TO KILL A JOHNNY.

On one of these occasions a rebel soldier was rather slow about responding to the call of time. He was in plain view of a Sharpshooter, who saw him seated by a little fire a few feet from the pit, slowly blowing his coffee, and munching his corn cake.

"I say, you fellow! Get up from the table. You'll eat too much," cried the Sharpshooter.

"Yes! I'm at my post," responded the lying rebel, unaware of his being seen.

"Don't lie, you tar-heels!" accompanied by a shot, was the rejoinder, as the bullet went spinning into the fire throwing the ashes into the coffee, and causing Johnny to jump into his hole quickly, creating laughter on both sides. But a great struggle and commotion was noticed in the pit where soon all was still, when a loud mouthed Johnny rising full length yelled above all the rifles:

"By jove! You've killed him!"

"How's that! "asked our men.

"He's choked to death on the corn bread."

The "telescopic" men were supposed to perform the fine work of the regiment, such as making close shots at long-range, using their telescopes to make objects dim to the naked eye, perfectly plain and distinct, and some exciting specimens of marksmanship was the result. While engaged around Hare House, an incident occurred showing how even an old soldier will sometimes become demoralized. James

Ragin had settled into his position and having obtained range at 300 yards, was closely watching his opponent, who was covered by a tree, and had gradually reduced his shots to about once in a half-hour. Ragin's rifle firmly resting on top of the pit, was sighted for the spot where the rebel showed himself when disposed to try a shot. A movement was discovered, the grayback stepped a little to one side of his tree, bringing down his piece preparatory to sending in another round. Now was the time, and Ragin pulled. In an instant his opponent jumped back quickly, flinging his gun from him to the ground. As he shortly after, however, stepped out and picked it up, hurriedly firing a return shot, the Sharpshooter concluded that it was at least a "close call," and that the fellow was badly scared, if not hurt. It was Jim's opinion, that: "That shot must have barked the fellow's clothes, if not actually skinned him," and he just roared at the performance. The following day Ragin got "barked." A rebel rifleman in a pit 400 yards off, commenced shooting through a small opening to the great annoyance of the Union soldiers moving about in rear of the breastworks. Ragin getting range on the fellow, a few shots silenced him effectually, and for several hours after no shooting was done from that quarter, when Ragin noticed that another man was sent into the pit to take the place of the one he had already "shut np." This fellow proved to be a tough customer, evidently a splendid marksman. The contest soon commenced, and for a long time the Wisconsin man exchanged shots with him, Ragin putting his balls into the opening almost every time, throwing the dirt down in the back of the pit, while his opponent dusted Jim frequently. The rebel evidently used a telescope, his bullets always striking in about the same place on top of the Sharpshooter's pit. Finally, an almost simultaneous exchange took place, Ragin shooting through the opening, and receiving a clip through the hair close to the scalp, inflicting no injury. It was a close shave for the veteran, but he was used to such things, therefore failed to show the slightest emotion. His opponent *never fired again,* and quietness reigned supreme for the balance of the day in that pit.

There were many such episodes occurring almost daily during this siege, the shooting being done often at much greater distances than here given. And that the enemy entertained the greatest respect for the marksmanship of the "Yankee Sharpshooters," the following story is introduced as an illustration:

KILLED BY A FORCED BALL.

"The narrowest escape I ever had," said a well-known lieutenant of police the other night, "was in front of Petersburg. My regiment was in Pickett's division of Longstreet's corps,' he continued, "and another fellow and I were in a trench together. We were at the front of the line. The other fellow went by his first name, Dick. The trench was about six feet deep and there was a groove cut in the top of the front, through which we did our shooting at the Yankees. When we wanted to pop away we'd lay the gun-barrel along the groove, get quick sight on the enemy, pull the trigger and then jump down. Dick was a pig-headed sort of a chap. I had told him a dozen times he didn't have sense enough to hold his head on his shoulders.

"There was a lot of Yankee sharpshooters, in front of us, and I cautioned Dick to look out how he exposed himself. I tell you it was dangerous for even so much as a man's ear to get in sight of those fellows. I heard the bullets whistling lively over our trench, and I knew by the sound that they were, 'forced bails.' A forced ball, you know, is a bullet from a breech-loader. It is a little bigger than the diameter of the gun-barrel, and consequently it goes out with greater force than the ball from a muzzle-loader. The way we could distinguish between the two kinds of guns was that, if it was a breech-loader, the bullet got to you before the report, but if it was a muzzle-loader the report got to you before the ball. Most all of the Yanks used the breech-Loaders, and you can just bet your boots we were mighty careful how we got in their way.

"As I was saying, the bullets were whistling pretty lively over our trench. I was loaded and was about to put my gun in the groove and try to pick off a blue coat. Dick was standing in front of the groove putting in a charge. He had his eye at the breech of his gun examining it, and the side of his head was turned toward the groove. While he was standing there—it was not more than half a minute altogether—one of the 'forced' balls came singing through the groove and bored a hole clear through his head as big as a walnut. He fell dead. I stepped across to him, and in doing so passed in front of the groove. Just as I got on the other side of the trench another bullet passed through the groove and buried itself in the rear wall of the trench. Two other balls followed it and buried themselves in the identical hole made by the first bullet. The sharpshooter who did that neat job was a half mile away."

"Pretty good shooting," suggested one of the listeners.

"I should say so," said the lieutenant, with an expressive shrug of the shoulders. "Some of those Yankee sharpshooters were marvelous. They had little telescopes on their rifles that would fetch a man up close until he seemed to be only about 100 yards away from the muzzle. I've seen them pick a man off who was a mile away. They could hit so far you couldn't hear the report of the gun. You wouldn't have any idea anybody was in sight of you, and all of a sudden, with everything as silent as the grave and not a sound of a gun, here would come skipping along one of those 'forced' balls and cut a hole clear through you.

"How we used to lay for these sharpshooters, though," he said, chuckling at the remembrance. "We'd keep a look-out for every little puff of smoke. The sharpshooters, you know, mostly climbed trees and hid themselves in the branches. So every time they'd shoot there'd be a tell-tale puff of smoke come out of the tree. Just as soon as we'd see one of those little puffs of smoke the entire battery would rain shot and shell into that tree, and we'd make it so hot for the sharpshooter that he'd either tumble or crawl out, dead or alive. The best shooters were in the Union army. Most of them came from the west, and many of them had been scouts in the Indian country. They rarely missed a man at a distance of a mile. Indeed, they could hit any object as big as a pie-plate that far away."—Balti-more Herald, (Nov. 3, 1886).

The lieutenant made at least one slight mistake in saying that most of our Sharpshooters came from the west.

On the night of the 20th being relieved by Burnside's men, the Sharpshooters with their division changed position after dark, moving off to the left the following day towards the Weldon railroad, halting for the night in the rough woods near the picket lines. The section we had marched through was covered with deep woods, tangled brush, creeks and swamps, making the movement tedious and unsatisfactory. The position taken up was several miles south of Petersburg, with the intention of cutting the Weldon Road and wresting its possession from the intrenched enemy; for which purpose were brought together the combined forces of the 2d and 6th corps.

JERUSALEM PLANK ROAD.

June 21-22, 1864.

Col. Stoughton who had been absent on account of wounds received at Po river, had joined his regiment and assumed command the morning of June 21st; and in the flank movement to cut the Weldon railroad begun that day by Hancock's corps, the Second Sharpshooters became engaged. Col. Stoughton says: "The Second Regiment was put to the front to encounter the described squadron of Fitz Hugh Lee's cavalry. Col. McDougal who commanded the brigade, and to whom I reported, sent our regiment in and we soon found ourselves largely outnumbered and reported to Col. McDougal, when he replied: "Go on, there is nothing in your front." So I pushed on. Presently report came from Companies A and B both, that their line was being overlapped, and in danger of being captured. I directed them to break to the rear their respective flanks, and the firing was beginning to be sharp. I heard what I supposed was support coming on my left and rear, and in attempting to adjust and join the line, fell into the hands of the 2d N. C. cavalry, dismounted., At the same time the colonel and orderly of the 2d N. C. cavalry were both captured by Lieut. Shoup and some of the men. Five of our regiment were captured besides myself, "—among them, Capt. Samuel F. Murray. Col. Stoughton did not return to the regiment, being mustered out seven months thereafter, soon after the end of his imprisonment and parole.

Sharp firing had occurred in front during the night of the 21st, which was continued in the morning (22d). The 6th corps, following the 2d, not getting up in time, a considerable gap intervening on the left of Barlow's division and the right of the 6th, in the afternoon Barlow's lines were severely attacked and successfully flanked, the enemy having good roads to come in on, thus facilitating quick: movements. The result was, we were driven in, the troops doubled up, falling back in confusion, the line of works taken by the foe with four pieces of artillery, with the other divisions of the 2d corps forced back from their positions_ The corps rallying, retook its original line, driving the Confederates off. But the mischief had been done in the first attack, and our corps lost heavily, particularly in captured men, held by the enemy.

Three companies of the First Sharpshooters, A, F and I, in advance on the extreme left, were obliged to leave with considerable loss, on finding the rebels swinging around in their rear. A special detail of 10 men had been sent out in charge of Sergt. Eli Cook with orders direct from the general in command of the line to "move your men through that piece of woods and you will be in range of a rebel battery that is sending shell through our ranks causing much annoyance to me." Pushing carefully through the timber Cook's command found four belching cannon 400 yards distant. Getting right down to business the Sharpshooters soon had the big guns quiet—not a living man could stand and load them for a full half-hour. So intent were these riflemen to perform the part in the battle assigned them, that the enemy had swung clear around behind unnoticed, within 15 yards, before our boys knew of their danger. They were completely cut off, but determined not to surrender without a struggle, they dashed into the scattered rebel line and six out of the eleven breaking through, returned to the regiment. Company F also suffered greatly. Owing to the losses sustained since the commencement of the Wilderness campaign, this gallant company had been reduced from 47 members to 10 left for duty, 35 having been killed or wounded and two uninjured taken prisoners.

While this was going on, the other companies were in reserve, but under rapid and close shelling. Immediately behind them on their horses, the Sharpshooters lying on the ground, were several generals with their staff, and it was noticeable that every time a shell came over, most of the aids dodged and ducked as if they were unused to them, while the generals sat perfectly unmoved, except Gen. Griffin, who was constantly turning his head and watching where the shell exploded. About sunset these companies were sent forward in skirmish line over a large opening or field to within 100 yards of a thick wood where the enemy were posted, who suddenly opened on them sharply. Our men taking cover in a ditch, from that point briskly responded to the rattling musketry, pouring in thick and fast their bullets closely about them. The left of our line had swung around almost into the timber when the enemy opened, causing them to fall back to the ditch where the right and center had stopped. The fighting was kept up on both sides with much spirit, the Sharpshooters holding their ground until a brigade came up on a charge. As these troops rushed down the sloping field we had a good chance looking back, to -see a line of infantry coming at full charge, with their bayonets before them. The interest, however, was soon lost from the startling fact, that some of them were sufficiently excited to cause their pieces to discharge in a rather careless manner. At least, the Sharpshooters in front of them had good cause to think so, as the muskets being pointed high and low, their flashing shots came whizzing close over our heads and in the ground behind and at our side; so that our men watching their every movement, their reckless firing, yelled above the noise to "stop that firing, you infernal fools." However, they were soon over us, and gradually forcing the hidden enemy back from the edge of the thicket, established an advanced line. The action ceased soon after dark, when the Sharpshooters engaged, assembled in the rear with their regiment. Although the enemy's fire was rapid and at short range, yet but few were hit in the brigade and none in the Sharpshooters. On the following day we moved to the rear of the breastworks, being used by detail for special sharpshooting purposes.

CASUALTIES.

Co. A.—Captured: John Fehr, Frederic Teller.

Co. D.—Wounded: Capt. John E. Hetherington, in hand, severe.

Co. F.—Killed: Barney Leddy, Peter Lafflin. Wounded: Sergt. L. D. Grover, David Clark, Walter P. Morgan, captured, and died of wound.

Co. I.—Missing: R. D. Mills and P. Luttes.

Capt. John E. Hetherington was born Jan. 7, 1840, in Cherry Valley, N. Y., and was one of the original members of Company D, 1st U. S. S. S. Rising rapidly from the ranks he succeeded to the command of his company at the battle of Gettysburg. It was from no boyish freak that he enlisted, but from a deliberate sense of duty, that he left the most extensive bee business in the United States. His service as a Union soldier comprised all the principal actions of the Army of the Potomac up to the time of receiving this his last wound, before Petersburg; and he had been especially mentioned to the Secretary of War for "bravery and meritorious conduct" in the front ranks before the enemy. For two years after his discharge it was a question whether he would live, but he gradually regained a large part of his former vigor. As a resident of Cherry Valley, N. Y., he was one of the organizers of the New York Bee-Keepers Association, said to be the oldest of the kind in the country, and of which he was at one period its president. His lectures on Bee-Keeping before farmers' clubs in central New York, made him very popular, and had much to do with their success in raising bees, Capt. Hetherington being high authority on everything pertaining to bee culture, and he is credited with being (in 1892) the most extensive bee keeper in the world. He stands high in the Presbyterian church, of which he and his family are members. His religion is of a practical, working kind, that bears immediate fruit; that raises the fallen, feeds the hungry, cares believes there is a divine those to our fellowmen. Mason for the sick. At the same time he side to religion, with duties beyond He is an active Good Templar and Captain Hetherington's sword was shattered by a bullet, and a piece of the weapon driven through his hand. The engraving shows this piece lying by the broken sword, while the portrait shows the position of the sword and hand. He had thrown his rubber blanket across the hilt of his sword, and that over his shoulder. Providentially the bullet, so well-directed, found a lodgment in his sword and hand, instead of his heart, which lay just beneath. A distinguished general of the English army on seeing this sword, said he had seen many of the heir-looms of prominent British families, and the relics sent home from 20 years of active service, and added: "Among them all there are none that I consider as fine a personal relic as this broken sword." Capt. Hetherington had thrown it away as being of no further use to him; but it was preserved by his men. He commanded the regiment one day in the field, before he was wounded, by request of Capt. Wilson, who was unwell. In personal appearance the captain is tall and commanding, and looks like the accomplished soldier he was so well known to be.

An order was promulgated to us shortly after this fight, by the peerless Hancock, which I understand was not published in the newspapers at the time, relative to the 2d corps having acted so badly in the first part of the engagement, which I insert, as it may not be entirely uninteresting to the survivors of the two regiments who remember Hancock as he then was, every inch a soldier, or to that other class who disdain not, but rather love to read rebellion history. It should not be forgotten, however, that the 2d corps at that time, was not the 2d corps of old; as a large proportion of the veterans had been lost to service by death and deserved discharge, so that without the accession of latter-day recruits who had never been under fire, and many of whom were reputed worthless characters at home, however they may have, and I believe did vindicate themselves afterwards, the 2d corps could hardly have existed—for want of numbers. The order read as follows:

HEADQUARTERS SECOND ARMY CORPS. NEAR PETERSBURG, VA., June 27, 1864.

GENERAL ORDERS]

No. 22.

Major-General Hancock resumes command of the 2d corps. In so doing he desires to express his regret that during his absence from the command it suffered a disaster from the hands of the enemy, which, under the circumstances, seriously tarnished its fame. The abandonment of the line by brigades and regiments without orders and without firing a shot, and the surrender to the enemy of entire regiments by their commanders without resistance, was disgraceful and admits of no defense. It should be recollected that those officers who surrender their commands on the plea of saving the lives of their men, but, in reality to save their own, will be held in contempt by the very men they surrender. A little firmness in defending themselves would have given time to have brought up troops to their assistance and would have enabled us to gain a success. The guilty will not be allowed to go unpunished, and those officers who surrendered their commands to the enemy without fighting will be brought to trial when opportunity offers.

The reputation of the Corps has been deservedly so high in the army, and throughout the country, that it was not deemed possible that such a disaster could occur to it.

It is necessary that the stigma cast upon it should be removed, and it can be done if the brave officers and soldiers of this command will only do as well as they have habitually done since this eventful campaign commenced. The war is one of endurance. Our numbers are greater than those of the enemy, and it is only required that each one should do his duty in this crisis, when so much is at stake for the future of each individual, to insure success. It is necessary to be patient and watchful. Each officer and soldier should feel that the fate of the army depends upon his personal vigilance. Hereafter those skulkers who abandon the field on the plea of carrying off the wounded, which, in action, none but the Ambulance Corps are allowed to do, and those who run away while their comrades are fighting, will be shot down by the Provost Guard, who are required to execute this order.

By command of Maj. Gen'l Hancock.

FRANCIS A. WALKER, Asst. Adjt. Gen'l.

On the 24th, the Second Sharpshooters being out on the front line, at an early hour in the morning heavy cannonading was heard on the right, and soon after in front in the vicinity of the "Chimneys" on the Jerusalem plank road. Two companies of Sharpshooters from the First Regiment having been sent for to operate against the rebel artillerists, who were engaged firing into Union regiments that were moving about, Companies G and H, under Lieut. Stevens, were ordered to go, and under instructions from Capt. Wilson, regimental commander, approached carefully the position designated, keeping under cover of the woods out of sight of the enemy's pickets, as some of our troops advancing over the open plain to the front lines were subjected to this firing, with considerable loss. Reaching the outer lines close up to the enemy, position was obtained under fire in rifle pits and behind deserted works, with a portion of the detachment in reserve. The rebel battery remained silent for the balance of the day, kept quiet by our men; but occasional exchanges took place from the rifle pits, the Sharpshooters having obtained proper range soon after taking their posts, whereby they could send in their shots to the rebel pits when occasion required. The position on the left of the line having been occupied afterwards by other troops, those of the Sharpshooters placed there were recalled and sent to the reserve nearby. One of our men, Corp. Andrew Kirkham, of Company G, failing to hear the order, remained at his post all day until found in the evening and brought back; he having performed good service in silencing the enemy's pits in his front, to the great satisfaction of our infantry moving about in his rear. In the evening the command received orders to withdraw and rejoin the regiment.

During the morning Ragin had been posted by Capt. Wilson, at the special request of an artillery officer, at his battery a half-mile in rear of the advanced line taken up by the Sharpshooter detachment. This battery had been subjected to considerable artillery fire from the enemy, and it was the wish of the officer in command to witness Ragin's skill in long-range shooting. After firing a few shots, however, the enemy responded with shell and bullets, which did not suit the artilleryman, who thereupon in a profane and excited manner ordered Ragin away, when the latter instantly followed up and rejoined his company, anything but pleased at the manner in which he had been treated after complying with the officer's request to "give 'em a few shots." The Sharpshooter was hit twice in this affair, shoulder and breast, slightly, by spent ball and piece of shell. Notwithstanding he felt hurt at the summary manner in which he had been ordered off, Ragin could not refrain from laughing at the "scared officer with his red face."

From this time until July 26th, the men were employed in picket and fatigue duties at different points to which they were from time to time, with their division, moved. The firing in the meantime along the lines, had been kept up with little intermission night and day, between the opposing pickets, while the artillery was also kept busy, especially when bodies of troops moved about, readily discovered by the clouds of dust, the weather being dry as well as extremely warm. At the date mentioned, participating in the movement of the 2d corps, they broke camp in the evening, marching rapidly and silently by the City Point road, crossing the Appomattox on pontoons at Point of Rocks near Bermuda Hundred, and pressing steadily forward, after a fatiguing march of 18 miles crossed the James river also by pontoon bridge, at Jones' Landing near Curl's Neck, at three o'clock the following morning. On this tramp they passed for a long distance through a dense green forest of heavy pines, the darkness being so intense that torches were purposely lit and posted along the route, thereby presenting an illuminated scene both grand and impressive, the whole column forming an extensive as well as novel torch-light procession. The pinus covering on the ground though soft and easy to the now noiseless feet, was at times so slippery as to make it difficult to keep in the ranks, so that unexpected thumps on the head from rifle barrels were not infrequent. After a short rest after their forced march, the men were astir at an early hour of the 27th, and the greatly scattered troops collected in their proper places, many having fallen out on the latter part of the march.

DEEP BOTTOM.

July 27-28, 1864.

It was early the morning of July 27th when the artillery opened, Brown's and Sleeper's batteries, which was soon followed by skirmishing across Strawberry Plains where the enemy had taken position. After some sharp fighting, Barlow's division in the lead, the rebels were driven back with the loss of four 20-pound Parrott guns, recaptured Union guns which they had been using against us, an important work and a number of prisoners; during which time the Sharpshooters were held in reserve under the fire of the enemy's guns. In the afternoon they moved across the plains to a deep wood, where they were employed as Sharpshooters and skirmishers on the right, guarding that flank. Here they were held in position until night-fall when, the firing having ceased, they were assembled and remained under arms in the woods overnight. On the next day the gun-boat Mendota was busily engaged throwing 100-pound shell into the enemy's position with great apparent effect, while the troops were fortifying. In the meantime, a large force of cavalry under Sheridan, were reconnoitering on the right. In the evening the Sharpshooters, with their division now commanded by Gen. Mott, were quietly withdrawn, and recrossing the James, returned by another forced march over the Appomattox, halting at four A. M. of the 29th beyond the City Point railroad, in rear of the right of the line before Petersburg, having marched a distance of 14 miles.

The movement at Deep Bottom was a diversion by Gen. Grant, to induce Lee to withdraw a large portion of his Petersburg army to reinforce his reduced force north of the James, to prevent their being cut off, at the same time secure Richmond, 10 miles distant, which was threatened. Han-cock's corps and a portion of Butler's troops co-operated in the design, while a large force of cavalry were to destroy railway communications north of Richmond, and otherwise harass the enemy in that vicinity. Besides, there was a mine to be exploded in Burnside's front before Petersburg, therefore to make the succeeding attack more successful, a reduction of the enemy's force in front was a great desideratum. But the Deep Bottom affair was not the success hoped for, as Lee could move quicker by rail than the Union troops could afoot. At least, the success was not apparent to ordinary soldiers' minds, however satisfied Grant may have been with the result.

Resting where they had halted during the day, hid from the view of the enemy behind some sandy hillocks, where they were treated to a visit by Gen. Grant in person, with whom the Sharpshooters had an inspiring chat, after dark they approached cautiously to the right of Hare's house, and relieving the 19th Wisconsin of the 18th corps, occupied their works. Three companies, B, G, and K, under command of Lieut. Stevens as picket officer, were immediately placed in the rifle pits in front, where they remained within a short distance of the enemy's line until half-past three in the morning, when they were quietly withdrawn behind the breastworks through intricate winding paths in the heavy brush and fallen trees in front of the same no firing taking place except the enemy's mortar shells, which could be plainly seen, like a fiery comet, in the darkness, as they rose high in air from Fort Clifton on the opposite bank of the Appomattox, situated on high ground in a position commanding the works now occupied by the Sharpshooters and their brigade

It was a night of great excitement, impressed as were our troops with the certainty of another terrible conflict. The very death-like stillness that was insisted on and which prevailed, presaged too plainly to the veteran soldier's mind something awful to occur. It was death in all its horrors pertaining to the battle-field, to many, and who of them watching that fearful night would count among the slain, was a matter of the gravest conjecture. But tired nature's balm, sleep, came to them finally, and with the exception of the watchful sentinels on the front lines, the great army lay in hopeful repose.

BURNSIDE'S MINE,
AND ASSAULT ON PETERSBURG.

July 30, 1864.

The-advanced position held by Burnside's corps was within 150 yards of the enemy's fort, called Elliott's Salient, located in front of Cemetery Hill, a crest of ground commanding Petersburg, which Gen. Grant wished to secure. The occupation of this ridge by the Union batteries would have placed Petersburg at his mercy. Behind Burnside's line was a hollow formation out of sight of the Confederates. Here it was that the mining commenced, the purpose being to dig a tunnel under the level ground intervening to the center of the rebel fort. A Pennsylvania regiment (48th) contained a number of miners, from whom came the suggestion that a mine could be successfully laid under the fort. The matter was talked over by the men, until Col. Pleasants, their regimental commander, became interested, also the division general, Potter; finally Burnside took it up, and after laying the matter before his engineers concluded to give it a trial; Gen. Meade consenting with little hope, however, that it would succeed. It was commenced June 25th, and after much difficulty in removing the earth, carrying it away in cracker boxes for want of something better through the persistent efforts of the tired and worn out miners the work was completed July 23d. The tunnel was over 500 feet in length, the mine being planted directly under the fort. This was charged with 8,000 pounds of powder, to be exploded July 30th before daybreak, with an assault by

Burnside's troops in advance, followed by the other corps—in all, a force of not less than 50,000 men.

It was Gen. Burnside's wish to have Gen. Ferrero's colored division take the lead, they having been trained for weeks previous for this especial service, while the white soldiers had in the meantime been arduously engaged on the front lines, incurring considerable loss. In fact, during the whole time of the mining operations, an incessant firing was kept upon Burnside's front. But Gen. Meade was opposed to having the colored troops go first, so was Grant, principally because of the charge that would afterwards be made in case of failure in the enterprise, that they were sent ahead to be sacrificed. Of course a great howl would have gone up throughout the north that this was the case—that the negroes were sent into a death trap to save our white troops. The choice was then left to the three white divisions of the 9th corps, to be selected by lot, and it fell upon Ledlie's to take the lead.

"We had but one division of colored troops in the whole army about Petersburg at that time, and I do not think it would have been proper to put them in front for nothing but success would have justified it."—GRANT.

The mine not exploding at the time expected, it was feared by the officers in the rear, at headquarters, Grant, Meade and others, that it was a failure. Over an hour passed by,

>And still no earthy sound
>
>To quake the morning air.

The connecting fuse had been lit, but was finally discovered by a member of the mining regiment, Sergt. Reese, who coolly volunteered to go in, to have gone out within a short distance of the magazine. Relighting it, he hurried out just as the explosion came, sending Elliott's fort high in the air, leaving a great pit or crater burning in its place. This hole measured 150x60 feet, and 30 feet deep. It was the death trap. The mine exploded at twenty minutes to five A. M. with a dull, rumbling sound, shaking everything animate or inanimate far around. Soldiers fell down, others lying prone were shaken upward to fall again, as if perfectly lifeless. Thus were they shocked by this frightful concussion. The stunning effect over, the Union artillery planted along the line, at once opened on Cemetery Hill and beyond, so that between the explosion and the terrific cannonading, the rebels became terror stricken and, those that could, fled wildly to the rear. It is known that 400 of them, South Carolinians, were lost in the demolished fort, with several cannon. Then Ledlie's men ran forward, the best they could, considering that they had to climb their own works—there being no opening—filing down through the thick abatis in front, crooked trees and sharp sticks, by winding ways, to the plain. The result was it took too much time to get the troops over, then instead of going forward in line of battle, they rushed on by the flank, stringing along, without formation, headlong into the crater. The white soldiers knew little or nothing about this movement, until they were ordered to go forward after the explosion, and without a clear understanding of what was expected of them, ran ahead, and undoubtedly did the best they could. Some of the troops passing the crater, gained the crest; among them a portion of the colored division following, by whom a few hundred prisoners were taken. But they were so disconnected, so unsupported, that they were obliged to fall back, and into the crater they went. So much time was lost in getting the troops forward, that the enemy rallied, coming forward in great numbers, and in good order, aided by their artillery trained to play on the opening between the crater and our works behind, whereby they soon swept the ground of all living persons, so that the opportunity was lost and the movement resulted in a lamentable and disastrous failure. Upwards of 4,000 Union soldiers were lost in the assault, killed wounded and captured. The men in the crater were so completely hemmed in they could not escape, preferring rather to remain than to take the chances of a retreat through the fire of the rebel batteries. For a time, a hand-to-hand fight occurred at the crater, the enemy rushing down, firing rapidly into the bloody chasm, while the shells from mortars and cannon exploded among our doomed men. Twice indeed the rebels were repulsed in their assaults, but it did no other good than to keep them off for the time being. Everywhere was confusion, on all sides death and destruction. Finally, orders were given to recall the troops, to stop the now useless slaughter.. To get back was the difficulty now, many refusing to attempt it, while of those who did, numbers were shot down in their tracks. The cannonading during this time, for it lasted from about five until noon, was of the most deafening and continuous character. It was like the roll of musketry increased in sound. With the exception of Burnside's troops, but one division, from the 18th corps, went into the fight, who made a gallant struggle to retrieve the fortunes of the day. The same may be said of Potter's and Willcox's divisions of the 9th corps. The other corps were waiting for orders that never came—they simply took the enemy's shell that came over, and watched the result.

The Second Sharpshooters were deployed in front of the enemy's batteries on the right, keeping them silent, and were complimented by their brigade general therefor.

The First Sharpshooters were in the meantime under severe fire from the rebel batteries planted at Fort Clifton, which had range of their works, sending long Whitworths amongst them, causing sometimes a resort to the bomb-proofs, while bullets from the front kept the too inquisitive down, we having no orders to fire back, in fact, the contrary—we were to keep quiet, and we did. We had orders, however, to be ready to move across the front at any moment. This was countermanded in the afternoon, with notice that further operations for the day would be suspended, when the firing gradually ceased on both sides. The Sharpshooters, notwithstanding, met with some loss in wounded, among them James Ragin of Wisconsin, shot in the left arm. The 34-pound telescope-rifle I then turned over to Frederick H. Johnson, of Company B, another very deserving soldier. Fred was one of the youngest members of Capt. Wilson's company, enlisting from New York city. He was always with his company, did effective service at Chancellorsville and Gettysburg, and was one of its "reliables," therefor the compliment of the regimental commander having turned over to him one of the telescope guns, which he invariably used with good effect.

During the night they left this position, having been relieved, proceeding to the rear of the front lines, where with their division they were held in reserve. On the evening of August 5th they moved suddenly after dark without packing up, but after going three-fourths of a mile returned, excitement abating, which was caused by a Confederate failure in springing a mine,—they having gone into the mining business,—their engineers being several yards too short in their estimate. In fact, their wily generals had a grave suspicion when Burnside's mine was under way, of something of the kind being attempted, and had commenced one of their own, running a few yards outside the course of the Union tunnel.

August 12th they again broke camp as part of Han-cock's corps marching to City Point, on the James river, seven miles distant. The dust was heavy, which with the extreme heat of the day, had a weakening effect on the men, many of the soldiers falling out of the ranks, with cases of sunstroke reported. Arrived near the City Point landing during the evening, after much halting on the way, where they remained overnight until the afternoon of the 13th. Considerable speculation occurred amongst the officers and men as to where we were going when the steamboats swung around to load on the troops, especially when we steamed down the river. All manner of places were suggested, principally north. But as we didn't go many miles before coming to a stop, mid-stream, it was getting to be looked upon as a ruse, to deceive any lurking enemy on the rebel shore. This was assured when about eight P. M. a tug came along side with orders to start up stream at ten o'clock for Deep Bottom. This was done, the troops being landed at daylight the next morning at the scene of our former movement the north side of the James. Grant's plan was to threaten Lee on his flanks, either in front of Richmond or south of Petersburg, to prevent his sending reinforcements to Gen. Early in the Shenandoah—soon to be whipped out by Sheridan, sent there to command the Union troops. The troops sent across the James to menace Lee's left, consisted of the 2d corps, 10th corps and Gregg's cavalry division.

Not long after the landing was effected, a portion of our troops engaged the enemy in front beyond Strawberry Plains. Our brigade moved forward to the farther side of the plains remaining there during the day and overnight; the artillery and musketry plainly to be heard in the battle then raging, in which a part of the 10th corps captured a number of prisoners, several cannon and mortars.

DEEP RUN,
OR FOUR—MILE CREEK.

August 15-16, 1864.

The morning of August 15th, the brigade being ordered to report to Gen. Birney now commanding the 10th corps, moved forward to the extreme right, and in the afternoon went into action in the neighborhood of Deep Run or Four-Mile Creek, the First Sharpshooters advancing ahead as skirmishers through small but thick pines, pushing the enemy back over a mile, following them up closely, eventually obtaining a position on the Charles City road. A line of cavalry skirmishers were on the right, also a regiment of infantry on the left of the Sharpshooter line. On reaching the road, the right of our line were suddenly confronted with a rebel line of infantry who fired a volley into Company A and the dismounted cavalry, inflicting considerable loss, particularly in the cavalry; while in Company A Capt. Aschmann fell wounded, but the enemy were soon driven off. It was a hot afternoon, and the firing being rapid on both sides, as we advanced the Sharpshooters lost a number of good men, mostly in wounded. Owing to the close growth of the young trees it was almost impossible to distinguish the enemy in the Sharpshooters front, they lying close to the ground and after delivering their well-aimed fire, hustling back to farther favorable positions from which to sight on our men as the latter advanced steadily on them—a perilous adventure bravely accomplished. During this sharp disadvantageous skirmish, to the Sharpshooters, the regimental colors were gallantly pressed forward on to the concealed enemy, in charge of Corp. Andrew Kirkham.

On the 16th sharp fighting occurred the entire day. In the morning the Sharpshooters were sent out as flankers, passing through a huckleberry swamp where the boys made a faint attempt to enjoy themselves, into heavy timber; thence moving forward through heavy slashing of pine trees and brush, difficult to climb through, they succeeded in capturing a line of works on the heels of the retreating foe, where they halted, having captured 25 of the Johnnies. This position the Sharpshooters held for a considerable time, during which sharp exchanges occurred with the enemy, posted behind another line of works beyond an open field in our front. Other troops finally came to them and after some severe fighting, becoming flanked by the enemy in force, they were obliged to fall back from their exposed position, under a very hot fire, through the thick slashing; the Sharpshooters reopening as they took their place again on the right flank. In this affair they met with more loss, among others, Capt. Andrews and Lieut. Tyler, both severely wounded, and a great loss to the regiment. A portion of the 10th corps, among them some negro troops, were behind the works to the left of the Sharpshooters, and they also fell back. Among the losses in the brigade which were reported heavy in this fight, was the commander of the same, Col. Craig, who was killed. Later in the afternoon we were ordered to report to Gen. Birney for further "special duty." Capt. Wilson soon had the regiment moving forward to the new position, and through the dense smoke of the artillery which settled close to the earth, obtained a position on the crest of a high hill in the woods near the Run, where they were employed until dark sharpshooting, when they were withdrawn. Taking no farther part in the fighting still in progress, they left the field on the night of the 18th, and moved back over the James and Appomattox by pontoons, with their division. Gen. Birney gave the Sharpshooters great praise for "gallant and meritorious service" performed while under his command.

CASUALTIES.

Co. A.—Wounded: Capt. Rudolph Aschmann, right leg amputated; also one enlisted man injured, Emil Harmuth.

Co. C.—Wounded: Adjt. E. R. Blakeslee, slight; John M. Booth, captured.

Co. E.—Wounded: Capt. Wm. G. Andrews, arm, severe; First Sergt. Charles E. Spencer, Sergt. David C. Wyatt.

Co. G.—Wounded: Private Levi Ingolsbe, mortal.

Co. 1.—Killed: Franklin Dolton. Wounded: Elisha R. Philo.

Co. K.—Wounded: First Lieut. Richard W. Tyler, arm amputated; Edwin B. Parks, slight.

The Second Regiment marched towards Richmond and flanked a four-gun battery which was taken on a charge in which they were engaged, capturing a lot of prisoners and ammunition. The regiment was kept busy during the entire movement.

This was the last action in which the First Regiment of Sharpshooters took part, the term of service being about to expire with several of the companies, so that in a short time the regiment would be virtually disbanded as an organization. But there was yet considerable duty for them to perform, principally on the picket lines, before they were mustered out.

Having got back before Petersburg again, on the morning of the 19th they were posted on picket on the left of the Jerusalem Plank Road at "Fort Hell," near the Chimneys, which latter were now pretty much destroyed, where they remained until the 24th, being at the time within 60 yards of the enemy. An agreement had been entered into between the opposing pickets at this place, that no firing should occur unless ordered, then notice should be given. As a consequence of this arrangement the pickets could walk their beats unmolested, instead of being cooped up, or huddled together, in the rifle pits, often half-full of water from frequent heavy rains. Artillery firing, however, was kept up, with little intermission. Along these outer lines were bomb-proofs, which were used to protect the troops from the rebel fire, especially the mortar shells. Company F on the 21st, while out in the pits, got into a sharp fight, driving the Johnnies from their pits in front, capturing 40 of them; although there were but 10 of the company to do it. While at this point heavy fighting had been going on, to our left, in the vicinity of the Weldon railroad way south of Petersburg, with success to the Union arms, principally of Warren's corps, who although hard pressed in his almost isolated position, and at times severely flanked by the enraged Confederates whereby he lost quite heavily, bravely held his ground which remained thereafter in his possession; there being at the time but few troops in the rear of the Sharpshooters—a thin far-stretched line—and their division; the balance of the corps having gone under Hancock with a brigade of cavalry some miles south of the Weldon road fight, to Reams' Station, where on the 25th after repulsing the enemy, they were forced back with loss of their line of works and three batteries, one of which was recaptured. During the darkness Hancock withdrew from before the superior forces of the enemy. In this deplorable affair, out of 8,000 men all told, Hancock lost over 2,400, of which nearly 1,800 were "missing;" the most of whom were supposed to have been captured very easily, from the fact that bounty jumping recruits hardly relished hard fighting, therefore were incapable of stout resistance to the fierce onslaughts of the enemy.

Leaving their picket line the Sharpshooters encamped in pine woods on the left of their previous position. A few days before, the First Sharpshooters as an organization commenced breaking up, when the Swiss company, "A," a mere squad left (a dozen only), were mustered out, August 18th, and departed for their homes. This was followed by the muster out of Company C, Aug. 20th; Lieut. Edwin A. Wilson, their last company commander—and a good one—says "the overwhelming number of five of the original 101 who enlisted Aug. 21, 1861," were with him when the day for muster out finally came. On August 28th the muster out of Company B followed, another handful of battle-scarred men; Lieut. Theodore Wilson commanding, the first lieutenant Frank S. Wells having been on staff duty for a considerable time previous, while the captain, John Wilson, had been regimental commander.

On the afternoon of the 25th the regiment moved to the left again towards Reams Station, where the fighting above noticed had been going on, and obtained a position for the night on the flank, where they lay guarding the same until the following morning, when they returned to their former place at the pines. The firing in the meantime had been heavy, especially in cannonading. Shortly after, they were posted behind breastworks on the front line where they remained, often subject to severe fire, employed in daily picket duty, the picket lines of the opposing forces being from 60 to 150 yards apart.

ALL ABOUT A LONG-EARED, LONG-NOSED, LONG-TAILED MULE.

A series of scenes, with a comical commencement and a tragical ending, occurred at this encampment, wherein a mule was the chief actor. This mule had been confiscated by the officer keeping the same, sometime previous, or rather had strayed over to the officer's quarters, and being captured by his man Friday, was made to earn its hard-tack and such other provender as could be picked up, by carrying blankets, rations, etc., during the many sudden marches that were occurring in this vicinity. It was against orders to allow any pack-horse or mule to go beyond a certain point, and the provost guard was pretty sure to stop them. On a certain occasion (1st Deep Bottom), when it came to turning back this mule, our man leading pointing to a couple of telescope-rifles placed on the mule's back for a blind, with an assurance, and I may reasonably add, cheek, almost as great as the mule's, rather demanded that he be not interfered with as "them guns must go forward." The provost officer, informed as to the regiment owning "them guns," had no more to say except to tell his men to "let that mule go through—never stop that animal—those rifles are its passport," etc. After that, on similar occasions it was sufficient to say; "Sharpshooter Mule!" and it went right along loaded down with "extras" for the boys, to the very front. The mule was large and very tough, and although fodder was often scarce, muley appeared to have but little appetite. In fact, seemed to accustom itself to the hard times for all stray stock, as no regular rations could be drawn for horses or mules not on the list of those entitled to keep the same; therefore the luckless animal picked up by company officers, stood in a fair way to starve if it couldn't accommodate itself to circumstances, satisfied with gnawing hard-tack boxes, and accepting such scraps as the boys would throw in its way. As for fresh grass—none grew under the countless soldiers' feet. But this particular muley would not hunt for more profitable quarters, preferring rather to be around among the boys, especially when the camp-fires were burning, and the coffee and meats cooking over the coals. There muley would stand, right in the way before the fire, its long nose snuffing up the fumes of the broiling meats or steaming coffee, while the curling smoke would circle in blue cloudlets around its ponderous head, but causing muley to flinch?—never! In truth, it would snuff it all down with as much composure as a Turk would inhale the aromatic fragrance from his meerschaum, no matter how thick it came. Occasionally one of those lengthy ears would flap over onto some stooping soldier's head, brushing off hat or cap into the fire, frequently upsetting the coffee and peppering the meat with ashes. 'T was no use to whip that mule, to beat it, or drive it away. It would be sure to be back to the fire before the soldier, and plant that long nose where the smoke was the thickest. Finally, it was resolved that this particular mule, kind and gentle though it was, molesting none except in the comical manner stated, unless an occasional switch of the tail would sometimes spread carelessly over some luckless tormentor's face; 't was resolved that muley was a nuisance. So, the lieutenant taking pity on the poor brute, made arrangements one evening to send it off to City Point, 12 miles distant; and after a formal leave-taking by the company, poor muley departed, although mulish about setting out. The absence of the mule at that evening's supper was favorably noticed by the boys, and a "good riddance to bad rubbage," was the general verdict. City Point, as before stated, was 12 miles distant, on James river, the road thereto being crowded more or less by scattering troops, with teamsters and teams without number, running thence through different camps, past patrol guards, amid jostling wagons which generally crowded the roads within the lines night and day, and it was certainly at that time considerable of an undertaking; yet, on that same night, the mule arrived there in due time, after a good feed was loosely corralled, and left to ruminate the balance of the night on the ups and downs in a muley's career. But, on awakening the following morning, the new master was surprised to find his beast of burden vamosed. Just as much surprised as were the members of the Sharpshooter company, to find, that same next morning, standing at the head of the company street near the cook's tent, their old friend, muley, waiting as was its usual custom, for the fire to be started. No! muley couldn't stand the change in its condition, although it was from a worse to a better one, but must plod its way back to the boys of Company G. So again for awhile did muley hang around, nosing the smoke, flapping its lengthy ears, switching the long tail. Another consultation took place, at which it was decided to take muley some two miles along the lines to an opening in the breastworks, then after passing out to the front towards rebeldom, to move back to a point opposite camp and there let muley go—the breastworks it was thought would prove a barrier to its appearance again. A detail being made, muley once more took its departure amid the congratulations of the boys. The programme was carried out to the letter; muley was cast loose about a mile from camp, with a long line of breastworks as a bar to its reappearance. There, the detail left muley, and started back to camp climbing the breastworks, taking a direct line to "quarters." Now, how 't was done, is not known, but sure enough when the detail after a hurried march got back to the company, there stood inevitable muley at the head of the company street, having arrived just in time to take its old accustomed place, when the returning detail appeared entering the foot of the street. But the next day poor muley's fate was everlastingly fixed. The company officer being out to the front on the picket lines, a senior captain at the time in command of the handful of men left to represent what was once one of the fullest regiments in the field, ordered the mule to be taken without the lines, beyond the breastworks, where the Sharps rifles finished its career instanter. Unfortunate muley fell a victim to its love for the boys, and the thick smoke of the company camp-fires.

The army mule took an important part at times in the great battles in progress, impressed into the heat of the fight, by bringing ammunition to the front; boxes of cartridges being slung either side the body with one or more on top, making a pretty heavy load. Particularly was this the case in the last half of the war. It was noticeable that great care was observed on reaching that part of the field "under fire," that muley was not struck by shot or blown up by exploding shell, and the cartridges scattered and lost. But as one of the great curiosities in the army was a dead mule,

I presume that but few were sacrificed in that way. Mules were also used to carry coils of telegraph wire, which were run out and laid close to the army lines from one bivouac or camp to another, men being on duty for that especial purpose, with operators assigned to the different headquarters, particularly corps, who were thus in quick communication with the general commanding. Under Grant, in our last campaigns, this telegraph service kept pace with the different movements.

During this time while we were in position behind the works as before stated, heavy artillery practice was almost constantly indulged in on both sides along the lines, while frequent discharges of musketry were heard; the Sharpshooters being often rolled out under arms, in anticipation of an attack. For awhile the opposing pickets were on very friendly terms, those of the enemy coming over, trading tobacco for coffee, sugar, etc., and exchanging newspapers. The artillerists having entered into no such agreement, frequently blazing forth over their heads the heavy shot and bursting shell. During this period the enemy deserted in large numbers, principally at night, although oftentimes coolly walking over in the daytime, giving themselves up. They were mostly in our front, from the 8th and 9th Alabama regiments. Considerable information was furnished by the rebel newspapers, which were daily obtained at the picket lines. Lieut. Stevens, of G, received the Richmond Sentinel from two deserters whom he sent to the rear, one morning while out in charge of a number of posts, dated that day, Sept. 3d, containing the news of the nomination at Chicago the day previous of McClellan for President, in advance of the northern papers, which latter arrived that evening confirming the same. The two deserters, on my asking what their officers thought of these desertions, replied very independently: "We don't exactly know, and we don't exactly care a—, for we came over to stay, and with your permission we are going north "—and north they went.

On this occasion the pickets were on particularly friendly terms, advantage of which was taken to distribute copies of the President's proclamation relative to deserters, which had a good effect. For, as before stated, many desertions from the enemy occurred. There were many, however, who seemed to distrust Lincoln the president, and wanted to hear from Grant the general. If he promised them the same terms, they were ready to come over. So, what purported to be Grant's proclamation was read to them, to their apparent utmost satisfaction. During this friendly spell, jokes and sharp hits were good naturedly indulged in, and the following episode soon became known along the line:

HOW A JOHNNY TRICKED A YANK.

In the forenoon of this day, the extreme post of the Sharpshooter detachment was the scene of considerable amusement at the expense of one of the group, who had got sold in the following manner. A rebel from a rifle-pit opposite, a hundred yards distant, had called over to "see the boys "as he expressed it, and having traded sufficiently in hard tobacco—big thick plugs a foot long—for coffee and sugar which he stowed carefully away in a couple of stockings—packed full—promised to give the Yank in question, "five dollars in gold," if he would go back to the Union sutler and buy him that amount of provisions; which arrangement was agreed to, when the reb made off to his own side of the plain. The northern soldier taking advantage of the prevailing quietness, stole away from his post and proceeding to the sutler a mile or more to the rear, made purchases to the extent of a five dollar greenback. With his hands full of canned fruit, condensed milk, butter, cheese, bolognas, etc., he hurried back to the front. According to the agreement with the Confederate, he was to advance half-way over the intervening ground and laying down the supplies, return to his post. After which Mr. Johnny would saunter carelessly along that way, avoiding observation as much as possible from his officers, to prevent being ordered back, and on reaching the spot take possession of the stores, then return to his pit after leaving the gold piece on a chip, which his Yankee friend, calling around soon after, would consign to his pocket. All these little arrangements appeared to be carried out, and the programme seemed a success. Yank left the sutler stores, Johnny came forward and got them, but when Yank returned to the place again and found on a chip, in place of a five dollar gold piece, a worn out chew of tobacco, he was forced to come to the sage conclusion that he had been badly sold—to pay him for violating existing orders regarding furnishing supplies to the enemy.

The supplies for the Union troops were brought by teams from City Point, two days rations being issued at a time. To facilitate matters the lieutenant-general caused to be built a railroad along the lines from City point landing, which was rapidly finished the entire length. It wasn't as broad gauged as a trunk line, but it served the purpose for which it was intended.

On the night of Sept. 4th considerable excitement was occasioned, especially with the enemy, by the firing of a double-shotted salute by the Union batteries, of 100 guns, in honor of the capture of Atlanta by the forces under Gen. Sherman., This caused a great commotion among the Confederates who thought it the commencement of a general assault, and they soon responded with interest, sending over a dozen mortar shells at a time, besides numberless other missiles from their cannon. A network of fiery balls could be plainly seen as they sped through the air, which with the numerous flashes and bright, expansive explosions, presented a scene never to be forgotten.

The night of the 10th the 1st brigade stationed on the right of the 2d, at Fort Hell, were ordered forward to capture and occupy the enemy's rifle pits, notice having previously been given them to evacuate the same as they were necessary to straighten out the Union lines, besides were too close to our works to suit the general in command. Making a sudden dash with the 20th Indiana, the charge was successfully accomplished, the enemy being taken by surprise. A number of prisoners (56) were taken, no firing occurring during the movement. As soon as it became known, however, the enemy opened heavily until daylight of the 11th, and during that day sharp skirmishing followed. The Second Sharpshooters took a prominent part in this affair and had two killed, while the First Regiment, with their brigade, were held in readiness to repel any counter-attack that might be made by the enemy in their front. The telescopic rifles, however, were sent to the front during the afternoon of the 11th to operate on the rebel gunners. After shooting at each other most of the following day, the pickets by mutual consent ceased firing, when immediately the top of the rifle pits on both sides was covered with soldiers, some smoking, others talking and laughing. Soon after, an officer was observed running along the lines of the enemy, when a rebel soldier standing up in plain view, notified our men that they had received orders to keep up their firing, in this significant manner:

"Lookout! Lookout! Yank!"

Down went both parties into their respective holes, when firing was instantly resumed, and kept up along the lines with little intermission during the balance of the term of service of the First Sharpshooters as an organization, frequently resulting in casualties among the troops in rear of the works, especially after dark, many being shot in their beds.

On one occasion several of the companies out in front, were ordered to take possession of a position that had heretofore been considered neutral on account of a well thereon, where Yank and Johnny had often met unarmed and drank each other's health. Soon after daylight the fracas began, by the Sharpshooters dashing forward and taking the place, capturing 85 of the enemy, and fortifying. For several days efforts were made to retake the ground, on account of this well, but we continued to hold it.

On the 21st a grand salute of 100 guns was opened by Gen. Butler on our extreme right, for the great victory in the Valley of the Shenandoah by the troops under Phil Sheridan, causing another grand rumpus among the F. F. V.'s. The next day, Sept. 22d, Company G was mustered out, 12 in number. Previous to this date, during the month, E, F and H, received their honorable discharge; leaving but three companies, D, I and K, First Regiment, whose term had not expired; D being mustered out November 22d, I and K later. Of the latter companies Eli Cook as first sergeant, and Lieut. Thomas B. Humphrey, who had gradually risen from the ranks to his well-deserved position, commanded their respective companies. These remaining companies with the recruits and veterans, formed for a while a consolidated battalion, until December 31st, when they were transferred to the Second Regiment, excepting those from Michigan, who went direct to the 5th infantry of that state. Subsequently, the Second Regiment remaining intact until February

20, 1865, a general break up and transfer took place of those whose term had not expired, to some of their respective state regiments: the New Yorkers to the

124th New York; Company G, (1st), going to the 36th Wisconsin; Company A, (2d), to the 1st Minnesota, etc. During this time they took part as sharpshooters and skirmishers, in several more important affairs: Hatcher's Run, Boydton Road, and a skirmish at or near the Weldon road. So that in all, they were engaged in 65 actions.

Charles H. Berner, of Company B, speaks particularly of the handsome manner in which they were treated by the officers and men of the 124th New York; and the same may be said of the other state regiments towards other companies.

Misfortune and sorrow seldom comes singly, and this was exemplified during the war in the many cases known to exist where families surrendered the lives of more than one member, as an offering to patriotism and the cause of the Union. Instances could be given almost innumerable. In the writer's company, the aged and crippled widow Dennis-ton of Fox Lake, Wis., lost her three boys, all she had, one killed and two dying eventually from wounds received. The Melvin family lost two by death from fever, with one discharged from same cause. Two Ingolsbe brothers were killed—all Wisconsin men. Also, in many cases, soldiers seemed to be continually getting hit, some of them wounded several times in the course of their term of service, while there were others who escaped entirely in scores of battles. Harrison DeLong, of Hopkins, Mich., (Company B), tells how he lost two of his tent mates twice—J. W. Chidsey, who "was a splendid soldier, one of the best in Company B," killed at Locust Grove; and R. H. Rarick, wounded at Mine Run. And again, James D. Seward, killed at Petersburg, and H. A. Seward, a brother, wounded and "crippled" at Spottsylvania. Of course there wasn't anything fair about it, for so many to get more than their share, while others went scot free; except that we fully recognize the claim that all is fair in war.

In October the Sharpshooters were very active on the front lines. On the 2d of the month, the Second Regiment while on the skirmish line had a sharp fight and broke one line of works near Poplar Grove church; later in the month, the 27th, they skirmished all day, capturing 50 prisoners near Stony Creek, as I am informed by Comrade Edwin Aldritt, an old stand-by of Company A, writing from his home on the shores of Lake Minnetonka, in Minnesota.. Some of the boys called this day's work the battle of the

Bull Pen. On the same day the First Regiment battalion went into the action at Hatcher's Run, deploying as skirmishers, and advancing through the woods met a brigade of the enemy lying in ambush for our boys. They opened fire on the Sharpshooters, then charged them. A hand-to-hand fight took place, and while a Confederate was taking to the rear Norton M. Stannard and John W. Howard, of

Company I, who had been captured, Alonzo Woodruff, of the same company, sprang forward and with his Sharps rifle killed the rebel by a blow on the head. In the effort to get free Howard fell wounded, being left on the field, the others escaping. Howard was reported killed, but some years after the war, turned up alive and applied for a pension, and it was a long time before the Department became satisfied he was the right man. In this affair seven recruits-were killed or wounded.

There were also lost during the siege of Petersburg the following named members of the First Regiment:

Co. A.—Killed: Adam Friedmann, July 30.

Co. B.—Captured at Hatcher's Run: Harrison Frailick, died in rebel prison.

Co. C.—Killed: William H. Thompson, Daniel Tilapaugh.

Co. E.—Mortal wound: Edwin French.

Co. F.—Killed: Daniel E. Bessie, Charles Danforth..

Wounded: Carlos E. Mead, A. W. Bemis, Volney W. Jencks, Jay S. Percy.

Co. G.—Killed: Wm. McQuivey. Wounded: Geo. W. Griffin, foot amputated, and Charles W. Baker.

Co. H.—Missing: July 17th, Lewis H. Soule, supposed to have been captured.

ANOTHER MINE FIZZLE.

Eli Cook, of Company I, tells the story: "October 31, 1864, Berdan's First Sharpshooters (with the 105th Pennsylvania and 5th Michigan) were ordered to Fort Davis to do garrison duty. The regiment remained there until Nov. 29th. Deserters came in quite frequently, and reported that the enemy were mining one of our large forts near the Jerusalem plank road. Further reports led to the fact that Fort Sedgwick was the one that was mined. This was the farthest fort in advance on this part of the line. It was located on the right-hand side of the Jerusalem plank road, 25 rods to the right and front of Fort Davis. The rebel rifle pits were 15 rods in front of Sedgwick. The rebel fort, Mahone, Was on the opposite side of the plank road, 40 rods from our lines. Fort Sedgwick was the one known as "Fort Hell," while Mahone opposite was called "Fort Damnation." So close were the rebs that if we showed signs of work on Fort Sedgwick, they would order us down or would fire, and we had to obey their orders. On Nov. 17th orders came to have a detail of Sharpshooters ready to march at three the next morning. This detail was composed of 14 men front Company I, who were ordered to pack up and march to Fort Sedgwick, there to receive farther orders. On entering this large fort to our surprise there was not a man to be seen in or around it. It was vacant. All the cannon and munitions had been removed, and our orders were to allow no man to enter the fort without a permit. All kinds 4 rumors were afloat with us, as to what was to happen farther. Now came orders for regular guard-mounting, drill with guns at right shoulder arms—to deceive the enemy

—to build 20 or more fires night and morning, and to keep up a general appearance of a strong force. No officer of the day made his appearance, nor did we have to turn out for the grand rounds—there wasn't any rounds to turn out for. The 14 Sharpshooters were the conspicuous figures of this sham show of strength, and we made the most of it, but really had an easy time while there. Finally a small working party made their appearance in the outer trench of Fort Sedgwick, when we were ordered to watch the enemy in our front, very closely night and day, while the working party were sinking three shafts in this outer trench. They went down to the depth of 22 feet; at the bottom of each shaft a tight barrel was placed, the earth tamped solid about the same. The heads of the barrels were removed and a string stretched tight across the top of each barrel so, the miners claimed, they could hear the stroke of the picks by the enemy, by placing their ears to this string, a distance of 16 feet through solid earth. The boys were wild with excitement, some saying: `To-morrow morning the rebs will spring the mine just as we have our coffee ready, and spill it. Others illustrated how their heels would go up in the air at four in the morning. A report was circulated that our commanding officer declared that the rebel powder would get damp, flash in the pan, and do no damage to the fort. Then our miners claimed to have cut off the rebel lead, also that one magazine was placed under Fort Sedgwick. But it didn't explode, the attempt was another fizzle. On the 24th the heavy artillery was stationed in the fort, and a mortar battery and a regiment took our place, we returning to our regiment at Fort Davis, when all the Sharpshooters packed up and went with Gen. Warren on the raid to tear up the Weldon railroad."

With this I complete my history of the organization known as the Berdan Sharpshooters, an organization composed of the most expert riflemen that could be obtained in the Union states, whose skill as marksmen was acknowledged to be superior to that of the best troops in the world; proven on the front line in most every battle and skirmish of importance, in which the infantry of the Army of the Potomac were engaged; who rendered more of the enemy's best troops *hors de combat* than any other regiment in the field.

In his "Regimental Losses in the Civil War," Col. Fox thus speaks of them: "The unique regiments of the war. Berdan's United States Sharpshooters were the best known of any regiments in the army. It would have been difficult to have raised in any one state a regiment equal to Berdan's requirements. The class of men selected were also of a high grade in physical qualifications and intelligence. They were continually in demand as skirmishers on account of their wonderful proficiency as such, and they undoubtedly killed more men than any other regiment in the army. In skirmishing they had no equal."

On the final disbandment Gen. DeTrobriand issued the following valedictory order:

HEADQUARTERS 3D DIV. 2D ARMY CORPS,

February 16, 1865.

GENERAL ORDER

No. 12.

The United States Sharpshooters, including the first and second consolidated battalions, being about to be broken up as a distinct organization in compliance with orders from the War Department, the brigadier-general commanding the division will not take leave of them without acknowledging their good and efficient service during about three years in the field. The United States Sharpshooters leave behind them a glorious record in the Army of the Potomac since the first operations against Yorktown in

1862 up to Hatcher's Run, and few are the battles or engagements where they did not make their mark. The brigadier-general commanding, who had them under his command during most of the campaigns of 1863 and 1864, would be the last to forget their brave deeds during that period, and he feels assured that in the different organizations to which they may belong severally, officers and men will show themselves worthy of their old reputation; with them the past will answer for the future.

By command of Brig. Gen. R. DeTrobriand.

W. K. DRIVER, A. A. G.

It seems certainly proper for me to add here, that Charles N. Race, of Owosso, Mich., of Company K, who was one of the youngest soldiers in the Union service, having mustered in 1862 at the age of

14, was the only Berdan Sharpshooter of the original members remaining as a sharpshooter until the end of the war, July 17, 1865.

THE LAST CAMPAIGN

FROM RICHMOND TO APPOMATTOX.

The spring of 1865 found the Union army before Petersburg ready again for the fray. Their winter's rest, so much needed; broken only by detailed duties on the front lines as pickets,_ and by a second fight at Hatcher's Run in February, participated in by the 2d and 5th corps, whereby our lines south of Petersburg were extended farther west, after a sharp conflict lasting two days; had recuperated them, and when the time came for further active operations, they were in a fitting condition for the now final struggle.

Gen. Sherman, who had made his famous march across the cotton states, was approaching through the Carolinas, driving all opposition away. Sheridan also had again appeared before the Army of the Potomac, after clearing out 'the Shenandoah Valley and intervening country north of Richmond to James river. In the meantime Lee was getting uneasy; he evidently wished to desert Petersburg and the line of the James, thence retreating southerly to form a junction with Gen. Johnston. This Gen. Grant determined if possible to prevent. In the latter part of March he published an order to his generals to prepare for a combined attack on the Confederate right wing, which rested southwesterly from Petersburg in the vicinity of Five Forks where several roads came together, distant six miles from the Union left, held by Warren and his devoted 5th corps. This movement was ordered to be made March 29th. But the wily Confederate commander was anticipating such a move sooner or later, and for the' purpose of delaying it until he could get safely away, he determined to hazard the chances of an assault right into Grant's center—on the lines confronting him at Petersburg—hoping thereby to force an abandonment of the extended Union wings to protect our center, which he hoped to' penetrate and thus divide the Union army; then in the confusion following, withdraw and evacuate Petersburg before our troops could reach him.

For this purpose an attack was made by the rebel Gen. Gordon, very early the morning of March 25th, on that part of the 9th corps stationed at a point called Fort Steadman, near the scene of Burnside's mine explosion, which for a time succeeded. But Gen. Parke, in command of the Union troops at that point, after a short but severe, resistance, aided greatly by his artillery right and left, successfully repulsed all their attempts, to the damage of the Confederates of over 3,000 soldiers lost, two-thirds of whom were captured. To make matters worse for Lee, later in the day the 2d and 6th corps, which had come up from our left, made a desperate attack on the rebel lines in front, and carried them with nearly 1,000 prisoners. It is stated that President Lincoln was present—a happy witness of the recapture of Fort Steadman.

The grand movement by the Army of the Potomac was commenced by Sheridan on the 28th at the head of 10,000 cavalry, who quickly passed around Petersburg south and west to Dinwiddie Court House on the Boydton plank road, meeting with little opposition, and that easily overcome. Before daylight on the morning of the 29th, the 5th corps under Warren, composed of over 15,000 troops, moved southwesterly to the Quaker road, thence turning north,

Griffin's division in advance, met the enemy and after a sharp engagement drove him back behind his intrenchments. The 2d corps now came up when Lee found himself checkmated, in imminent danger of being cut off from his supplies, or to effect an escape from Petersburg 15 miles from this field of action. Determined to do the best under the circumstances, he withdrew his troops from the Petersburg front all but a thin line, and 'with 17,000 men advanced during the night of the 29th to reinforce his position in front of Warren, and take the chances of a general engagement. He was favored in this movement by a heavy rain coming on, which proved to the disadvantage of the Union corps, owing to the swampy nature of the lands they were now in, with the roads converted into immense mud puddles, so that they could do but little all day the 30th. This enabled Lee over better ground to get up with his Petersburg columns on the morning of the 31st, occupying a new advanced position, on the White Oak road leading towards Five

Forks. On the 31st a sharp fight took place between Warren's corps and the enemy, which was at first in favor of the latter, owing principally to the fact that Gen. Warren could not in that swampy region get his corps together, whereby Ayres' division in front was forced back behind the others with considerable loss. A part of the 2d corps coming in on the flank, checked the Confederates; later on, Warren attacking with' his whole force, met with great success, taking a number of prisoners, causing the enemy to fall back.

A more important point in Gen. Lee's mind was to hold Five Forks where Gen. Sheridan's cavalry had obtained a foothold, whipping the rebel cavalry there stationed. To attain this end, so important to him, he took his troops away from, the 5th corps, and reinforced by his cavalry, beat back Sheridan's force after a hard fight towards Dinwiddie Court House, where Sheridan made a determined stand, dismounting his men and stopped the enemy's farther pursuit. During a portion of the night they lay close together, towards morning the enemy began to fall back, and at daylight April 1st, when Warren's corps—ordered to report to Sheridan—appeared on their flank, they retreated to their works at the Forks, followed closely by some of our cavalry. Gen. Sheridan now made his preparations for a grand assault on the Confederate position, but it was not until late in the afternoon that the attack began. The fight was opened by Gen. Warren, whose corps—decimated by previous losses—after a hard struggle in woods and openings succeeded in driving the enemy back, from point to point, capturing meanwhile large numbers of the rebel infantry; one division, Johnson's, being completely swept away, leaving but a remnant of Gen. Pickett's to escape the same fate. In this great victory Warren was assisted by the cavalry, particularly in pursuing the fleeing Johnnies. Gen. Warren having captured the position at Five Forks, dashed ahead of his troops, when he was met by a rebel volley unhorsing him, killing the animal, also killing and wounding several of his aids. Warren, more fortunate, escaped. The Confederates lost 6,000 prisoners in this action, besides a heavy list of killed and wounded.

The news of the victory having reached Grant, an order was issued for the troops fronting Petersburg; who during the fighting at the

Forks had been quiet, making no demonstrations, but watching sharp their front; to be ready for a direct assault on the morning of April 2d, while during the entire night a general cannonading was kept up all around Petersburg by the Union artillery. It was "business" now, for the Yanks, and desperation for the Johnnies. Both sides felt just that way. It was the beginning of the end to the Confederacy. Things looked dark for Secession, and bright for the Union. The Union army, thus encouraged, were more determined than ever to capture 'Petersburg. They had tried it many times in the past ten months and had failed, often with heavy losses. Now they felt it must be done. Therefore when the assault commenced at daybreak, the troops' of the 9th corps rushed forward with an ardor unsurpassed by any previous attempts, carrying line after line before them until they got within good artillery range, when, sending their heavy shots into the city, it caused the utmost dismay not only to the citizens, but to the Confederate commanders as well.

Lee finding our men getting closer with every attack, sent Hill forward to investigate, but he never returned to report. He ran into an ambuscade of blue _coats who to his imperative demand to surrender, shot him down. This was a great loss to the Confederate cause, for Gen. Hill was a thorough fighter.

Meanwhile the 6th corps to the left of the 9th aided afterwards by a part of the 2d and 18th corps, came up and swept everything before them, taking many prisoners and penetrating their lines of battle divided the rebel army, their right wing flying across Hatcher's run, northerly, to a point on the Southside railway called Southerland. Sheridan's command during this time was not idle, his cavalry and the 5th corps after destroying railroad communications, appearing at Southerland on the flank of the Confederate right. And that evening Miles' division of the 2d corps attacked these troops, utterly routing them with many prisoners taken, driving them off towards the Appomattox over which they succeeded in escaping, after being hard pushed.

In front of Petersburg three hours' determined fighting had done the work, and Lee must either retreat or give up. This latter alternative he would not do so long as there was one more chance. So he resolved when night came to evacuate Petersburg, likewise Richmond; thus bringing together all his scattered troops, in hopes of being able to unite his forces with those of Gen. Johnston, now crowded by Sherman.

When it became known that Richmond was lost, the people thereof, albeit it was Sunday, ran riot. Stores and houses were pillaged, men crazed with liquor formed in great mobs, and the hitherto peaceful city in a few short hours was turned into a veritable pandemonium. All night this lasted, mills were burned, arsenals and gun-boats blown up, and to add to the fearful excitement a great fire raged burning blocks of buildings, forcing the people back in one dense throng, to escape the stifling smoke and approaching flames.

In their hurry to get away from Richmond, many things of value to them were lost, including a large stack of Confederate scrip which they were forced to burn. For some time back they had suffered very much for the want of provisions, and it was admitted they had paid as high as $1,500 for a barrel of flour, and $300 for a cord of wood. But this was not the "dollar of their daddies "—the Union dollar— only gray paper unbacked by silver, the best they had. In Love's history the following quoted statement is made:

One old lady, a relative of John Randolph, who, with her husband, had yielded nearly their all to the Confederacy, said: "Sir, I have suffered with disease more than Job ever did; my two angel babes went to heaven long ago; I have taken many sick and wounded Southern soldiers to my house during the war; I have seen the ambulances filled with our wounded men pass by my door after battle, and witnessed the blood streaming down to the ground; but, sir, in all my sufferings and trials during these thirty years past, I have never shed a tear till last Monday morning. When I saw your Yankee troops pass along our streets, I sat down and wept."

And yet, many of the whites were glad to see the Blue Coats; they had got tired of the reign of terror under which they had lived; while the darkies were joyful and happy at the result.

The Union army before Petersburg was made aware of what was transpiring the retreat of Lee—long before daylight, by the constant explosions going on, all along the line of the James, from Petersburg to the -rebel capitol. At daylight the 9th -corps advanced without opposition—the enemy had gone—and 'twas not long before the flag of the Union was raised on high, floating over Petersburg. And soon after sunrise, Gen. Weitzel's troops entered Richmond with bands playing, and the stars and stripes waved over the city from the capitol building.

Thus far, so good, but Lee was hurrying away and Grant must hurriedly follow him; so the Union army was at once set in motion, the morning of the 3d. Lee had the advantage of a long start and reasonably hoped to reach Danville without hindrance. The race between the two armies was along the line of the Appomattox river, Lee on the north side, Grant south of the stream. But Lee, after crossing the Appomattox near the Danville railroad, was detained two days at Amelia Court House a few miles west of the crossing, to forage for rations, of which he was entirely out, for his now famished troops—fatigued and starving. This delay enabled Sheridan's cavalry and the 5th corps, joined afterwards by the 2d, to get, ahead of Lee and cut him off from the route he had intended to take, south westerly to Danville. Finding Sheridan's troops across his path at Burkesville, intrenched, Gen. Lee changed his course directly west to Appomattox Court House situated half-way between the head-waters of the Appomattox and the James river north of it, hoping thereby to reach Lynchburg near the Blue Ridge mountains. In this latter attempt he was foiled. His supply trains were first cut off by our cavalry, some 190 wagons being destroyed including ammunition, with a number of pieces of artillery and some prisoners taken. The next attack was at Sailor's Creek, April 6th, nearly halfway to Appomattox Court House, where Sheridan's cavalry in force under Crook, Custer and Devin, destroyed several hundred more wagons, cutting off Ewell's corps and the decimated division of Pickett, upon whom soon after came the 2d and the 6th corps, which, with the aid of Custer's division, finally forced the isolated Confederates to surrender, officers and men-7,000 in all.

There were other attacks by small forces of the Army of the Potomac, which in several instances failed in their _purpose, the hard-pressed Confederates, like the lion at bay, despite their worn out and demoralized condition—for there were many stragglers—making a surprising and gallant defense.

But at Appomattox Station on the Southside railroad, Custer's cavalry gained an important victory late at night of the 8th, wherein he succeeded in cutting off a number of cars loaded with provisions, together with 25 field-pieces and a lot' of wagons, besides routing a Confederate brigade found there.

The next day Lee pushed on, when learning that the Union troops were ahead, he sent Gen. Gordon to reconnoiter. The latter finding a large force of infantry and cavalry in his front, effectually blocking the farther advance of the Confederate column, sent out a flag of truce to Sheridan, and reported back to Lee. That ended it. That after-noon—April 9th—Lee surrendered to Grant. At Appomattox Court House the terms as dictated by Gen. Grant, were agreed upon as follows:

"The rolls of all the officers and men to be made in duplicate, one copy to be given to me, the other to be retained by such officers as you may designate. The officers to give their individual paroles not to take up arms against the government of the United States until properly exchanged, and each company or regimental officer to sign a like parole for the men of their commands. The arms, artillery and public property to be parked and stacked, and turned over to the officers appointed by me to receive them. This will not embrace the side-arms of the officers, nor their private horses or baggage. This done, each officer and man will be allowed to return to their homes, not to be disturbed by the United States authority so long as they observe their paroles and the laws where they may reside."

The terms of surrender were very lenient, and were so considered by Gen. Lee. And when Gen. Grant afterwards allowed every enlisted man owning a horse to take him home, Lee was greatly pleased, feeling sure such magnanimity would have a most happy effect on the Confederate soldiers. Three days thereafter, April 12, 1865, just four years from the firing of the first gun of Secession—on Fort Sumter—the Confederate army of Virginia laid down its arms and departed for their homes. And on the 26th of April, Johnston surrendered to Sherman in North Carolina near Raleigh.

Gen. Grant in his memoirs has this to say of the Army of the Potomac:

"The Army of the Potomac has every reason to be proud of its four years record in the suppression of the rebellion. The army it had to fight was the protection to the capitol of a people which was attempting to found a nation upon the territory of the United States. Its loss would be the loss of the cause. Every energy, therefore, was put forth by the Confederacy to protect and maintain their capital. Everything else would go if it went. Lee's army had to be strengthened to enable it to maintain its position, no matter what territory was wrested from the South in another quarter."

And in his official report he pays the following generous compliment to Gen. Meade:

"I may here state, that in commanding all the armies as I did, I tried, as far as possible, to leave General Meade in independent command of the Army of the Potomac. My instructions for that army were all through him, and were general in their nature, leaving all the details and the execution to him. The campaigns that followed proved him to be the right man in the right place. His commanding always in the presence of an officer superior to him in rank, has drawn from him much of that public attention that his zeal and ability entitle him to, and which he would otherwise have received.

Previous to this (May 13, 1864), the following among many other promotions were recommended by Gen. Grant:

"Gen. Meade has more than met my most sanguine expectations. He and Sherman are the fittest officers for large commands I have come in contact with. If their services can be rewarded by promotion to the rank of major-generals in the regular army the honor would be worthily bestowed, and I would feel personally gratified. I would not like to see one of these promotions at this time without seeing both."—U. S. GRANT, Lieutenant-General.

In his memoirs he thus speaks of Lee: "General Lee, who had led the Army of Northern Virginia in all these contests, was a very highly estimated man in the Confederate army and states, and filled also a very high place in the estimation of the people and press of the Northern states. His praise was sounded throughout the entire North after every action he was engaged in; the number of his forces was also lowered and that of the National forces exaggerated. He was a large, austere man, and I judge difficult of approach to his subordinates. To be extolled by the entire press of the South after every engagement, and by a portion of the press North with equal vehemence, was calculated to give him the entire confidence of his troops and to make him feared by his antagonists. It was not an uncommon thing for my staff-officers to hear from Eastern officers: 'Well, Grant has never met Bobby Lee yet.' There were good and true officers who believe now that the Army of Northern Virginia was superior to the Army of the Potomac-man to wan. I do not believe so, except as the advantages spoken of made them so. Before the end I believe the difference was the other Way The Army of Northern Virginia became despondent and saw the end. It did not please them. The National army saw the same, thing, and were encouraged by it."

The advantages alluded to were described as follows: "He (Lee) was on the defensive, and in a country in which every stream, every road, every obstacle-to the movement of troops and every natural defense was familiar to him and his army. The citizens were all friendly to him and his cause, and could and did furnish him with accurate reports of our every move. Rear guards were not necessary for him, and having always a railroad at his back, large wagon trains were not required. All circumstances considered we did not have any advantage in numbers."

Exaggeration on behalf of the Confederates and against the Army of the Potomac, kept up on every possible occasion by the press and people at home—"up North"—it is claimed, had its effect in forcing "good and true officers" out of the service.

REGIMENTAL STATISTICS.

To give anything like a complete record of the losses of either regiment is seemingly impossible, owing to the failure to obtain the necessary 18 complete company rosters, some of which are not on file in the adjutant-general's offices of their respective states; so that a comparative showing of ratio on lasses as between the companies, or as a whole in either regiment, I am unable to give. An approximate result is given by taking from the First Regiment one company from the east and west as follows:

Company F (Vermont), killed 18 per cent.

Company G (Wisconsin), killed 16 per cent.

In the Second Regiment I find two companies, E and H (Vermont) which average about 13 per cent.

Col. Fox in his "Regimental Losses" says of our Sharpshooters, whom he classifies among "three hundred fighting regiments" of the service, thus: First Regiment, total enrollment, 1,392.

Killed 153-10:9 per cent.

Total killed and wounded, 5461

Second Regiment, total enrollment, 1, 178.

Killed 125—10.6 per cent.

Total killed and wounded, 462.

It should also be taken into consideration, that there were quite a number of men in most every company who never saw a day of active service, but were discharged in Washington, or died there, and these should not rightfully be counted in the ratio of any regiment.

APPENDIX

WOUNDED AND A PRISONER.

The experience of Ames Winchell, of Company D, 1st U. S. S. S., while a prisoner of war, after his severe wound *received at* the battle of Gaines' Mill. A heartrending narrative of suffering, much of which could have been prevented by reasonable care by his captors.

After stating the fact of his being wounded, as noticed on page 113 of the preceding history, Comrade Winchell proceeds: I was taken prisoner about an hour after being shot, a rifle ball striking my left arm midway between the elbow and shoulder, passing through the bone, splintering it up fine. I walked 100 rods afterwards—had to—carrying my gun, but received a little help the last few steps. The hospital to which I was going was the basement of a brick house about three feet lower than the level ground. A file of Johnnies passed in, asking each one of the prisoners what was the matter, and those found to be uninjured were walked out and off. While the battle was raging two Union shell struck the house, one passing clear through; the other entered the chimney and came down upon the hearth near where I lay. Balls came clicking through the windows utterly regardless of the hospital flag on top. My pillow was a man's leg that was cut off near the hip joint, but the surgeon in charge obliged me by putting my haversack in its place, to my great relief. This doctor, after telling me my arm would be taken off at the shoulder, and after putting his thumb through the bullet hole, bandaged splints on and went off with a large knife I gave him, which he said he would like to have—said he was going out on the battle field; this was the last I saw of him. But there were left with us poor fellows, some 500 wounded in all shapes, a Union surgeon, Dr. White, of a Massachusetts regiment and a student or assistant, a lieutenant. I remember one poor fellow shot in the bowels, lying only a few feet from me, the surgeon said: "Young man, you will be dead before to-morrow morning;" he replied: "I shan't, I am not fit to die, and shan't die;" but the surgeon saying: "You will." passed on. Ere the morning dawned, his upturned glassy eyes proved the doctor had told the truth. All night I could hear the cries of "water, water," and the moans of the weak and dying. The next morning I was carried out of the bloody basement and laid on the ground near the doorway in the sun beside three dead comrades, and soon was accosted by a rebel officer who said: "Well, we have got you;" I replied "Yes, and that is not much," and to his promise that "by G— we have got McClellan on the run and will have him in less than three days, or drive his army into the James," I said: "If you do, there are plenty in the north that will come, and in less than three months they will have as large an army again." On informing him of the regiment I belonged to and where we were on the field, that we shot officers if they came in our front, he said: "By G—, that accounts for so many of our officers being killed, there was one in every four at that point." He soon left me, and now, the sun getting rather warm, I crawled into the yard to a scrub, oak tree where, picking up some scattering straw and old staves for a pillow, I lay 16 days among vermin, fleas, mosquitos, maggots and flies, and oh! the last mentioned were the worst. I can feel my arm ache yet, so tired was I keeping them away. On the night of the 28th a Johnny who said he was one of Mosby's guerrillas and had just come on from West Virginia, let me have his tent cloth and rubber poncho, which I kept most of the time after, while there. One of this reb's stories was as follows:

"While scouting in West Virginia with their horses all the time going over fences and ditches at a bound, one day they met a lot of Yanks, and during the fight one of his comrades got on a chase after one of them, and finally killed him; then dismounting to go through his pockets, he pulled out a picture, and behold! it was that of his own mother, and looking again saw his brother lie weltering at his side. Nothing would induce him to stay longer with Mosby."

There was a detail of 20 rebs to care for us, from different regiments. They did not touch a thing of any one; the only fault I could find with them was that they would not get a drop of water at night, arid they kept telling us they were going to White House Landing and numerous other, good places; and at other times they would blurt out: "If you d—d Yanks had not burned Bottom's Bridge you would have been sent into your lines; "this kept us all on our mettle, all the while. They talked freely, and many said they would not have been in the Confederate service, but were obliged to, or do worse.

The days passed slowly by, the booming of cannon could be heard each day a little farther off, how we wished it would be nearer. Every time I asked our surgeons to do something for me they would say, "yes, as soon as we get through with a few bad cases." Four days had gone by with nothing done to my wound, and I gave up asking them, losing all hope. Nothing to eat but a small piece of biscuit, and two or three black raspberries. But about noon July 1st, Surgeon White came to me and said: "Young man, are you going to have your arm taken off, or are you going to lie here and let the maggots eat you up." I asked if he had any chloroform or quinine or whisky, to which he replied "no, and I have no time to dillydally with you. I finally said it was hard, but to go ahead and take it off. He got hold of my arm, pulled the bandage off, pushed his thumb through the wound and told me to "come on." and helping me up we walked to the amputation table where they were taking off a young man's arm near the elbow. He lay there like a man, and when they had finished, Surgeon White asked if I could keep as still as he did, that "he is a soldier, every inch of him." I replied that we could tell better when this job was through. They put me on the table, cut off blouse and shirt sleeves filled with maggots, and after a lot of preliminary (cruel) poking and careless feeling around my arm and shoulder—it appeared rough to me—they made me sit up in a chair, and wanted to hold my legs, but I said "no, I won't kick you, but steady my shoulders," then set my teeth together and clinched my hand into my hair, and told them to go on. After cutting the top part of my arm and taking out the bone, they wanted me to rest an hour or so; to which I refused; as they had mangled my arm I wanted but one job of it, for I was just as ready, I said, to kick the bucket then as in another hour. To this they replied: "He's pretty spunky, let's make a good job of it." Then they finished it, while I gasped for breath and the lower jaw dropped in spite of my firm clinch. I was then led away a short distance and left to lie on the hot sand—like a bake oven— and could feel the hairs crawl on my head as large apparently as my fingers. Burning with fiery pain, flushed with the fiery hot bed of sand, I arose wild with the pain and extreme heat, and began to look for a cooler place to lie down to die, as I then thought I would; went up a stairway nearby and entered a room where men were lying on the floor. There was one bed and one man lying on it, and I sat on the foot of it pulled off my shoes and crawled beside him. Neither spoke, but if I had just entered into a furnace I would not have burned with more pain and fever. I lay here but a few moments; wild and nearly delirious, when I got up and went out, not stopping for my shoes, to the little oak tree and my old straw nest, where I rolled and groaned with burning pains until a captain of the 14th Regulars told me to take a little of his advice, to lie down and keep still, that the rolling only made me feel worse. I at first wouldn't be consoled, but cried in my agony that, "I wished to God I never had my arm taken off, I could stand it but a short time longer." He said then: "Young man, I wish I bad as good a chance to get well as you have, for I am shot clear through the body "(the ball passed through his chest going out near his spine), "I can't get anything done for me, although I have offered $300 for a team to take me to Richmond, only nine miles, but I cannot get any one. If I could only get to Richmond I think I could get help." How this captain came out I can't say, I presume he died; and but for his advice I am sure I would. I heeded what he said, and in a short time the burning pain had left me, and I could stand straight up and show myself. (The illustration shows how-be looked after his wound began to heal)

My wearing apparel was a crown of a straw hat, shirt was a tent cloth, pants a pair of army drawers, shoes I picked up on a deserted battle field, and that would just let my foot in a little over half-way; I curled the heels down and they did very well.

It rained three days and nights while I was under that tree and I got wet through. Surgeon White praised my spunk, as he called it, and treated me to a half gill of brandy which, considering my wet state, helped me, In about 12 days' time teams came and took away the slightly wounded to Richmond; and on the 16th day the rest of us were given a wagon ride seven miles to Savage Station. They drove on a trot over corduroy roads and all, in our wagon at least, which carried a dozen of us, regardless of the poor fellows lying on their back with thigh bones broken and other helpless injuries; too helpless to resist the unnecessary and cruel jolting; and heedless of the moans and cries begging the driver not to drive so fast, but the hard hearted wretch refused to slacken his pace.

I shall pass by the sickening details of the rotten meat soups, and other hard experiences, although on one occasion while hunting for an unfortunate comrade from a Massachusetts battery who was wounded twice, hip and ankle, but never found again, I ran onto some Johnnies baking pan cakes, and asked if they would not please *give* me one. They turned one with a slap onto a plate and handed it to me. I sat down on a box and ate it, and never in my whole life did anything taste so good. I walked back and said, "will you not please to give me one half of another, that tasted so good," they did not keep me long waiting before it was on the plate. There were two benighted souls from the Emerald Isle dressed in our blue, detailed from Libby prison to look after us—but thank God not all of the same stamp as these precious rascals, Union men though they claimed to be, came from Old Ireland. These two were detailed to help, us—or rather to persecute us—the water they had standing in a barrel was thick with flies; here they would fill our canteens half flies every time, so we would shut our teeth and drink, then spit out the old drowned out flies. A week at this station, sick at heart, unable to eat the villainous food,—the soups,—and with daily, hourly witnessing the fresh sand heaps appearing over another unfortunate Union soldier; for death was busy in our midst, and as I looked at the long and increasing row, I asked God to spare me long enough to get where lived His and my people, and where the star spangled banner floated.

From this place after 14 days' stay, we were conveyed by freight cars to, Richmond, nine miles, jolted on our backs, where the two aforementioned: sons from—not of Erin I am sure—told me I would have to jump out and walk to another train three blocks off, which I at first refused but finally gave in, after seeing a lot of the mangled freight taken off in the direction of Libby, where I didn't want to go, so with the help of these two aforesaid sons of h—I got out of the car and endeavored to walk to the "next train." My wearing apparel as before described attracted attention,

-as I plodded through the streets of Richmond, and on going past Libby prison a number of heads peeped out of the south end second story windows, and they wished me "good luck and lots of it," for which I meekly thanked them and passed on. Another block further I was called across the street, "come over here, Yank," where I met a party of Confed--crates who asked me "who was it mean enough to send you in this way," to which I answered it was two of our own men that made me walk. They pushed a knapsack along and made me sit down and rest,—these rebels did that, and other kindly acts, showing they had a heart too, if they were rebs,—swore I should have a conveyance and not walk another step. Then after some chaffing about war prospects in which they seemed to think if they gave up, Uncle Sam would hang them for traitors, which I assured them would not be done—that Lincoln's word could be depended on every time—and after a boy stepped up and matte me a present of a pie, with "never mind if you haven't any money, I don't want any from you," for which I thanked him with tears, they lifted me carefully into a wagon and I was soon on the cars again, regular passenger coaches, where the -conductor allowed me and another one-armed comrade to occupy two seats, to stretch out. Reached Petersburg, 32 miles, changed cars—now freight cars—to City Point. Hear a Union steamboat came along floating that fairest of the fairest, our glorious Old Flag. Oh, those stars looked like -spots of gold, and my feelings of joy can better be imagined than described. In all three boats came up and loaded on the exchanged soldiers. The one I sailed in was named "Daniel Webster "—heroic statesman—and was run in the interest of the sanitary commission. Clean garments were furnished us the first thing after taking our names, etc. At Fortress Monroe we -stopped long enough to take off a number who had died on the way. Arrived at Philadelphia July 30, 1862, and entered the West Philadelphia hospital, if such I could really call it, as this institution was run by contract, and I will not tell what I have picked out of rice soup, etc., here; but will tell what I told a visitor who was very anxious to know whether Stonewall

Jackson would get into the city or not, which was that, with all due gratitude towards the good people of that great loyal city, I would like to have Stonewall get just near enough to throw a few 100-pound shots into the center of this so-called hospital. He went away shocked, not giving me a chance to tell why. For notwithstanding all the nice things, the dainties sent there for the "poor soldiers," you could see posted conspicuously on the walls and doors: "People bringing anything here for the soldiers, are forbidden to give to them, but to give to the charity committee who will distribute." I never saw any of the Blue Coats get any. Where did it go to? Look right in the center of this building under the dome. There are chairs filled with 200 medical students—to learn how army doctors practice on Uncle Sam's boys—and right there is where your fruit has gone, and your nice cakes; and right there is where I wanted Stone-wall's big shells to explode, not to harm, however, the big hearted people of Philadelphia. This I can't say for the red taped, big headed, stuck up fools, that required the poor sick soldiers to come to "Attention! "and rise up every time those *practicing* army surgeons and their dude scholars came in to the ward. Sept. 18, 1862, I left them, with my honor—able discharge.

BIOGRAPHICAL SKETCHES

GEN. H. BERDAN.

The originator of the Sharpshooter organization was born in the town of Phelps, in Ontario county, and State of New York, Sept. 6, 1824, and was educated practically and scientifically for a mechanical engineer, and became well known through his inventions, some of Which are in use in all civilized countries. His military record as a Sharpshooter I have attempted to give impartially in the preceding pages. After the war, he was appointed by President Johnson, by and with the consent of the U. S. Senate, Brigadier-General of Volunteers by brevet, to rank from March 13, 1865, "for gallant and meritorious services in the battle of Chancellorsville." Also appointed by the President major-general by brevet for "gallant and meritorious services at the battle of Gettysburg," but it lacked confirmation by the senate before the passage of the act against more brevets out of active service. While in service he received an official communication from Gen. Hooker, then commanding the Potomac Army, to reply to one from President Lincoln asking: "Whether or no, it would help or hurt, to order Col. Berdan to take a larger command." To which the latter replied: "It would hurt," fearing the Sharpshooters would be put into another brigade in case he accepted, as Secretary Stanton refused to allow him to take at least the First Regiment with him. After the war closed, his inventive genius brought forth several important subjects. The breech-loading system for firearms, having through the success of his Sharpshooters proven to be an important improvement on the old styles, it was soon adopted, not only with the rifle but also with shot-guns, by all the manufacturers of the country as well as foreign nations, so that in a few years the old muzzle-loading system became obsolete. Believing that he could improve the system, General Berdan after introducing the Berdan central-fire cartridge with the primer inserted outside, so extensively used since in cartridge shells in all countries, invented a rifle which he took to Europe, the governments of Russia, Germany and others purchasing the same, and arming their troops with this gun--the Berdan rifle. Relative to the first use of breech-loaders, the following from his speech at Gettysburg in 1888 is appropriate here:

"You are as well known among military men in Europe as you are in this country, and you are regarded as the men who taught the world the superiority of breech-loaders over muzzle-loaders. Some of you may not be aware of the fact that the Sharpshooters was the first command that fired breech-loaders at any enemy, because while Prussia had the breechloader called the needle-gun, yet it had never been tested in action. It was, left for our corps, therefore, to prove the importance of this arm of the service."

Since his return from Europe to Washington, after some years absence, Gen. Berdan invented a" Range-Finder," which measures distance up to six miles, with 17 deviations, and in less than one minute. Also, the "Mechanical Fuse," so constructed as to utilize the rotary motion of the shell when passing through the air, so as to cause the shell to explode when it has made the number of revolutions at which the fuse has been set. This has been successfully tried by the ordnance department, and reported on favors ably. He met his old command 22 years after the war, on the occasion of the 25th anniversary of the battle of Gettysburg, on that memorable field, and where arrangements were made for the erection of monuments to the Sharpshooters. It was his wish to have one general monument, but the different states from whence" the Sharpshooters came, had already voted appropriations to be included among the respective state troops engaged at Gettysburg, and as a result the battlefield is dotted over with these monuments to the Sharpshooter companies. He again met his command at Boston at the Grand Army Encampment in 1890, where an organization composed of over 200 members from both regiments, was effected, to be known as "The Survivors' Association of Berdan Sharpshooters," with Gen. Berdan as its first president, Major E. T. Rowell vice-president, H. A. Redfield secretary and treasurer, and D. P. Craig assistant secretary.

HON. DANIEL PERRY

Better known while in the Sharpshooters as the "Tall Corporal on the Right," and first corporal of Company F. First Regiment, after the close of the war became a graduate of Albany law school, class of 1867-1868. Removed to Missouri and was Principal of Public Schools at Maysville, that state, in 1880; and from 1881 to 1883 held the office of County Superintendent of Schools of De Kalb county; Public Administrator of said county 1883 to 1885, and Mayor of Maysville in 1884, where he still resides practicing his profession of lawyer, also abstractor and real estate dealer.

GEN. WM. Y. W. RIPLEY

Lieut. Col. Ripley of the 1st U. S. Sharpshooters was born in Middlebury, state of Vermont, December 31, 1832, and was therefore 29 years old at the period of which I write. In 1837 his father removed to Rutland, Vt., which has ever since been Gen. Ripley's home. In 1857 he took an active interest in the reorganization of the. National Guard of Vermont, then in a sad state of decadence, and was commissioned a First Lieutenant the same, and shortly after promoted to Captain. When President Lincoln' issued his call for 75,000 troops to serve three months, Capt. Ripley's company was one of ten selected from the various regiments and consolidated into one to be called the First Vermont Volunteers. He served with his regiment at Fortress Monroe, and was present with them at an armed movement of troops into Virginia on May 23, 1861, which was the first reconnoissance of Union troops on rebel soil—the movement of Ellsworth into Alexandria taking place the next day. Capt. Ripley commanded the first detachment of troops to throw up intrenchments in Virginia at Newport News, on May 270.861. Was present with his company at Great Bethel in the engagement of June 10th, and was mustered out with his regiment August 15th. Immediately after his return to civil life he was offered in succession the Lieut. Colonelcy of the First Vermont Cavalry, a Lieutenant Colonelcy in the Regular Army, his choice of various field positions in the infantry regiments then forming in his native state, and the Lieut. Colonelcy of the First United States Sharpshooters. This last suited his inclinations best of all, as he was himself a notably good shot with the rifle, and a firm believer in the efficacy of his favorite weapon in' the hands of skillful men. He therefore accepted this appointment, joined the regiment at Camp of Instruction in November 1861, succeeding Col. Mears as Instructor as stated in the history, and which position he retained until we broke camp in March, 1862. Col. Ripley was present at all the battles in which the regimental organization took part on the Peninsula Campaign, as I have described in their proper order, down to the closing hour of the battle of Malvern Hill when he fell severely wounded; and when the army retired from that victorious field, Col. Ripley was left behind at the field hospital, but was brought off by a few devoted members at great personal risk, who hearing he had been left behind, returned to his rescue, and safely conveyed him to Harrison's Landing. He was next appointed by the Governor of Vermont to be Colonel of the Tenth Vermont Vols then organizing and was discharged to accept this position. His wound, however, proved so serious that he was kept on crutches for nearly two years and was unable to assume the active duties of the position. While yet an invalid from his wounds, the State of Vermont influenced partly by the hostile attitude of England, whose Canadian provinces lie adjacent to Vermont on the north, and partly by the desire to be fully prepared for whatever might happen to our armies in the field, commissioned Col. Ripley a Major General of Volunteers, and authorized him to raise ten regiments of infantry, one of cavalry and two battalions of artillery, Under this authority he raised, armed, completely equipped and thoroughly drilled a force of 10,000 men, who could have been assembled, thoroughly prepared for the field, in twelve hours. Happily, however, their services were never required either for offense or defense, and on the closing of the war, no occasion remaining for the maintenance of so large a body of troops, they were disbanded, and General Ripley retired to private life. Since that time he has been extensively engaged in business in Vermont until 1887 when he retired from active business life, but yet retains the position of President of the Rutland County National Bank in Rutland where he resides. His affection for the survivors of his gallant regiments is unabated, and none are more welcome visitors than those who can say; "I belonged to the First Sharpshooters."

MAJOR JOHN WILSON

Was born in Albany, July 11, 1835. In 1849 at the tender age of 14, he went to California, and there met Gen. McPherson, who was then only a subaltern, but nevertheless attracted young Wilson's attention, and on an occasion there he remarked that if the country ever needed McPherson's services he would not be found wanting; thus showing that young as he was, Jack could form pretty correct opinions from personal actions and appearances. When the late war broke out he was commissioned First Lieutenant Company B, 1st U. S. S. S., being mustered in with his company Aug. 29, 1861, and on the resignation of Capt. Martin, became captain. Served his full three year term, being mustered out in the field before Petersburg, August 28, 1864, as regimental commander. He was really promoted to major of volunteers by the governor of New York Dec. 19, 1868, with rank from Nov. 30, 1863, but could not muster in as such. It is not saying a whit too much, nor is it detrimental to others, for me to endorse the words of a comrade, and from another company, in saying that Capt Jack, as the boys familiarly called him, was one of the best officers in the service. After muster out, Major Wilson was appointed assistant state agent for New York, stationed' at Washington. Was also somewhat active in Albany republican politics, and was a prominent member of the old Knickerbocker Club there, enjoying the friendship of the Hastings family. He lost his health in the service, and died April 22, 1869, in his 34th year—a young man, just getting into his prime.

CAPTAIN RICHARD WOLSEY TYLER, U. S. ARMY.

Born in Wayne County, Michigan, January 1st, 1842. Enlisted in Company K, First. Regiment U. S. Sharpshooters at Detroit, Dec. 26th, 1861. Served as duty Sergeant and 1st Sergeant to May 25th, '64. Promoted Second Lieutenant May 25fh, '64, and 1st Lieutenant Aug. 4th, '64; resigned Nov. 9th, '64. Appointed 2d Lieutenant V. R. C. Oct. 25, '64; accepted Nov. 10th, '64; Breveted Captain March 13, '65; mustered out Oct. 15, '66. 1st Lieutenant 44th U. S. Infantry

July 28, '66; accepted Oct, 15, '66. Unassigned May 27, '69. Retired with rank of Captain Dec. 15, '70, for disability in line of duty and loss of left arm. Was breveted Captain in the Regular Army for gallantry at the battle of Deep Bottom, and promoted from The volunteer service to a higher grade in the Regular Army at the close of the war, upon his military record alone, by Gen. U. S. Grant.

Service: In field (War of the Rebellion) from '61 to '65, with troops, and on special duty at War Department from '65 to '68; with troops at Norfolk, Va., in '69, and again on special duty at War Department in 1870 until retired. Was sent by direction of Gen. Grant to inspect Bull Run battle field in 1866, and afterwards in charge of a corps of men to gather up the remains of the Union dead there and remove the same to Arlington National Cemetery, where they were placed in what is now known as the "Tomb of the Unknown." Was detailed for special duty between Baltimore and Washington for the apprehension and arrest (if found) of J. Wilkes Booth, after the assassination of President Lincoln, and afterwards on duty as Officer of the Day and guard at the trials of the assassins, and also at the trial of "Wirz," who was convicted by a Military-Commission convened at the Capitol, and hung for. Cruelty to Union prisoners at Andersonville. Participated in upwards of thirty battles and skirmishes in which the regiment was engaged; received the gun-shot wound through left leg below the knee (bone fractured) at Second Bull Run; also gun-shot in left arm at Second Deep Bottom (Deep Run), resulting in amputation at middle third above elbow. Was sent to Judiciary Square Hospital, Washington, after Second Bull Run, and to Turner Lane Hospital, Philadelphia, after Second Deep Bottom.

History: By a suit in his own behalf commenced in 1881, in Which he made the principal arguments in the U. S. Court of Claims, also in the United States Supreme Court, was established the right of officers of the Army to reckon time after retirement the same as active service, in computing longevity pay. These cases are reported in 16th C. C. 223 and 105 U. S. S. C. 244. He was admitted to practice in the U. S. Supreme Court in May, 1887, and resides now in the City of Washington, D. C.

MAJOR CHARLES J. BUCHANAN

Having fulfilled his duty to his country as a volunteer soldier in three years arduous service, Buchanan in 1865 accepted an appointment to a clerkship in -the Quartermaster-General's office at Washington, and for a while was stationed at Fort Snelling, in Minnesota. He resigned this position after about a year to complete his academic studies which his enlistment had interrupted. In 1867, Gen. Hancock offered him a lieutenancy in the Regular Army, which he declined, as I have before stated. This same year, President Johnson appointed him a Cadet to the U. S. Military Academy at West Point. Here Buchanan made the most of his time, and repeatedly declares that his first year at West Point was worth all the other schooling he ever had. In October, 1870, he resigned his cadetship to resume the study of law, this having been his intention from the first. He at once entered the law office of Smith, Bancroft & Moak at Albany, N. Y., for this purpose. In 1875 he was admitted to membership in this distinguished firm, which had a large practice in all the courts. Buchanan has been first vice president of the Young Men's Association, a literary institution founded by Amos Dean, and has refused the presidency of this organization. I(e is a trustee of the Albany Law School, and Secretary of i s Board of Trustees; and is also a Director of he National Savings Bank of Albany. He has been for nine years one of the Commissioners of Washington Park, and is Treasurer of this Commission. Is a member of the Buchanan and St. Andrew's Societies, and is also Judge Advocate of the Third Brigade of the New York National Guard with the rank of Major. His home is at Albany, where he is hard at work in his professional-ranks, enjoying the fruits of long and faithful service in military and civil life.

JOHN T. SCHERIVIERHORN

Formerly First Sergeant of Company H, 1st U. S. S. S., was born in the City of Schenectady, N.Y., April 26, 1836. Enlisted as a Sharpshooter Sept. 17, 1861, wounded at Gettysburg as noted, but stayed by his company to the end of their term, being mustered out in the field before Petersburg as cr)m-pany commander Sept. 16,

1864. Resided since then for a number, of years in Norfolk, Virginia, engaged in marine engineer building; and at present (1892) is in the employ of the GP. Allis company at Milwaukee.

MAJOR GEORGE E. ALBEE.

A member of the Wisconsin company (G) of Sharpshooters in 1862, who was discharged account of wounds received at Second Bull Run, after the war gained national reputation as an expert marksmen a:lilting American riflemen; as the winner of the Rapidity' and Accuracy contest at Creed-: moor in 1862, distance 200 yards; having with a Hotchkiss rifle as a single loader fired 19 shots in 60 seconds, making the highest score, 50; 20 shots a minute, scoring 62; and again 19 shots, scoring 60, defeating all competitors, with different kinds of rifles, and winning the Lorillard gold medal: In 1891, Major Albee made the highest individual score in 2d Reg. Conn. Nit. Guard rifle Match at New Haven at 200 and 500 yards. Thus showing that his initiatory lessons in sharpshooting as an active member in the-field of the U S. Sharpshooters attained for him good results in the future, as he says: "Any success I have had in the profession of arms is due to the: fact that I was properly started in Company G, 1st U. S. Sharpshooters.": Major Albee's military record is comprised in the following branches of the service:.,

Private Cd. 'G" 1st U. S. Sharpshooters; 1862.

Private 3d Wisconsin Battery, 1863.

2d Lieut. 36th Wisconsin Vols., 1864..

c, 1st Lieut. 36th Wisconsin Vols., 1865.. z; 2d Lieut. 36th U. S". Colored Troops, 1866:

'2d Lieut. 41St U. S. Infantry, 1867.

1st Lieut. 41st U. 6-Infantry, 1568.

1st Lieut. 24th U. S. Infantry, 1869.

1st Lieut. U. S. Army retired list, 1878:

Captain National Blues, "D" Co.,keit., C. N.G.; 1891:

MAW and Brigade Inspector of Rifle Practice Conn. Nat. Guard, 1892..)

Brevet Major-General J. J. Reynolds, commanding department of Texas, writes from San Antonia, Jan'y 24, 1872: "Lieut. Geo. E. ALBEE, 24th Inty, has served with me in Texas since the summer of 1867. I can from personal observation bear testimony that he has been among the very foremost in zeal, enterprise and devotion to duty, *especially conspicuous* for the number of Indian expeditions in which he has been engaged. During the last year he has been on duty at Department Headquarters as aide-de-camp, the various duties of which position he has discharged in the most satisfactory manner. Lieut. Albee is among the most deserving young officers in this department as is shown by his *record of services* during and since the rebellion.

HON. H. J. PECK

Harrison J. Peck, was born in Clarendon, Rutland County; Vermont; on the 23d of November, 1842, and spent the early years of his life on his father's farm. 'He was educated at New Hampton Institute, Fairfax, Vermont. He was attending school there when he enlisted Sept. 11, 1861, in the First Regiment Berdan Sharpshooters. He attended Albany Law School, where he graduated. He came to Minnesota in 1865, and purchased the Shakopee Argus; which he published until 1866, when he sold the paper and, went to Montana, where he remained until the winter -of 1868, when he returned to Minnesota., Since then he has devoted his entire attention to the practice of his profession, and for years has been recognized as one of the leading lawyers of the state, and especially as a criminal lawyer. He has held the office of City Attorney, and Was for eight years Mayor of the city of Shakopee. He 'was County Attorney of his county four years and for two terms State Senator.. 'He 'is a member of the Grand Lodge of Masons of the state. In politics he is a democrat.

GILMAN K. CROWELL

Was born in Hopkinton, N. H., pec. 3, 1838, where he lived and was employed as a farmer, until the breaking out of the rebellion. Was one of three brothers who enlisted in Company B, Berdan's First Regiment U. S. Sharpshooters,. Aug.. 28, 1862, as a recruit. ,Served with the company until Oct. 9; 1864, when he was discharged as a supernumerary non-commissioned officer. Was slightly wounded in the "Battle of the Wilderness, May 6, 1864: In Feb., 1865, again entered the service by serving in the quartermaster's department at Nashville, Tenn., and was discharged there-, from in May, 1865. At the close of the war he again resumed farming, until the Spring of 1866, when he removed to Concord, N. H., where *he* entered the; service of the Concord Railroad as Conductor. He was elected a member of the City Council in 1888, re-ejected in 1890, and for the last two years has held the position of president of that body.

COL FRANCIS PETELER

Col. Peteler was born in Bavaria, in 1828, and came to the United States when he was but 12 years old and alone, in 1840. He enlisted in the spring of 1847 in Company A, 8th U. B. Infantry, and served under Scott in the Mexican War. Removed from New York city to Minnesota in 1853. Raised the company of Sharpshooters known as Company A, Second Regiment, which were mustered in at Fort Snelling Oct. 5, 1861, and which he commanded until after arrival at Washington, where he became Lieutenant-Colonel of the regiment. During the time he was absent from his regiment owing to the outbreak of the Indians under Little Crow, and while yet at Fort Abercrombie, but on the point of leaving to return to his regiment on the Potomac, he was the recipient of resolutions front the officers and soldiers of the garrison, complimentary to him as an energetic and efficient commander, and in recognition of his success in banishing from Fort Abercrombie the vice of intemperance—" that fruitful source of disorder and insubordination," and for inaugurating it its stead "order, discipline and sobriety;" closing with fervent wishes for success "in his new field of operations against the assassins who have conspired to destroy our nationality, and with it those free institutions of which we are so justly proud." Since the war, Col. Peteler lived on a farm in Hennepin county,

Minnesota, up to 1870, and since then has been a railway contractor and manufacturer of railway portable dump cars, etc. He has now with his sons shops on five acres of ground near Prospect Park, in southeast Minneapolis, and resides in that city.

PHILIP E. SANDS

At the time he enlisted in Company B, 1st U. S. Sharpshooters, July 10, 1861, was a locomotive engineer running a passenger on the Harlem road of New York city, by trade a machinist and 29 years of age. His father was a provost marshal of the 9th congressional district, later on. Sands was wounded at Malvern Hill, Gettysburg, Locust Grove and the Wilderness, and died at Alexandria from the effects of the last wound, amputation of leg, some months after, being buried at Greenwood cemetery. He had been a corporal, a sergeant and finally first sergeant. Was well liked by all, and was one of Company B's best men.

COL. HOMER R. STOUGHTON

The military-history of this officer has been pretty completely given throughout the work, and these sketches are more for the purpose of showing something of after-army life, when the soldier becomes again a citizen. There is one thing,, however, I will mention with his soldier's career: that is when the regiment re-enlisted as veterans, the non-commissioned officers and privates presented to Lieut.-Col. Stoughton a beautiful sword, belt and sash, with the numerous battles in which the regiment bad been engaged up to Jan, 1, 1864, inscribed thereon, which bespoke more than words the feelings of the men who shot the rifles, towards their commanding officer. Col Stoughton's civil life since the war has without doubt been a very busy one. Having entered the army from a railroad position, he naturally returned to the railway service after leaving the army, in 1865, on going back to Vermont, his native state, where he became agent at Randolph for the "Central Vermont R. R." from 1865 to 1872. Was postmaster from 1866 to 1872, a Republican committee man in town and county. Was transferred in '72 to same position on the "New London Northern,'. stationed at Palmer, Mass. In April, 1876, he went to Reading, Mich,, in charge of a wringer company remaining through 1877, and was a member of the city council of that place. Went back to Palmer beginning of '78 as railway agent again until 1883, when be was made freight agent at New London, Conn., until Jan. 1, 1885; then accepted a position with the "Shelby Iron Company "at Shelby, Alabama, and was elected Director and made General Manager in April of that year, arid Vice President in 1886, which positions he held until the property changed owners in 1890, but continued general manager until April 1, 1891. In May, '91, was made general manager of the "Florence Land Mining and Mfg. Co." at Florence, Ala., which he vacated in May, 1892. At present Col. Stoughton is engaged in the real estate business in Cleveland, Ohio. For a number of years he has been au active worker as teacher and superintendent of Sunday schools in the Congregational churches, with which he has been connected since 1868. The colonel has settled with his family, wife and seven children in Oberlin, in the hope of giving all a fine education in the excellent institutions there located.

CAPT. FRANK E. MARBLE

Capt. Marble was among the first who enlisted at Madison, Wis., early in September, '61, at the age of 22 years, in Company G, of the First Regiment of the Sharpshooters, and before leaving Camp Randall was elected by the company First Lieutenant. On the death of Capt. Drew, Lieut. Marble became captain. His military career has been closely identified throughout the history with the First Regiment, which he for a time commanded. Since the war he has been located at Lynn, Mass., as a U. S. Pension agent. His home, however, is at Syracuse, N. Y. Capt. Marble and family,—wife, son and daughter—are always glad to see the old soldier comrades, to whom their hospitality is unbounded. The Captain is a member of the Loyal Legion, as well as of the G. A. R.

JOHN WILLIAM KENNY

Was born in Albany. Was working with Charles E. Graves and George Campbell learning the tinsmith trade when the war broke out. Campbell enlisted first, then Graves, then Kenny. During all the campaigns from the Peninsula to Petersburg, Comrade Kenny took a very honorable part. Was slightly wounded at Glendale and at Gettysburg. On June 16, 1864, at Harrison's Creek before Petersburg, he was badly wounded in the left arm, and was sent north to hospital in Rhode Island, where he remained' until discharged Sept. 16, 1864, on surgeon's certificate of disability; and in consequence of his wounds could not do anything for a long time, but went to work at his trade as soon as be could being unable to enlist again, so went back to the shop he had left when he volunteered. Some 12 years thereafter he became superintendent of the Albany Stamping Works, where he was when this book was issued: He has made a good citizen, just as every sharpshooter ought to. Has an interesting family of a wife and I believe about three daughters, and a son who is a member of Company B, 10th battalion, N. Y. National Guard, one of their team of sharpshooters. Comrade Kenny is also interested in a photograph establishment at Bath on the Hudson, and has contributed for this history a number of enlarged proofs from card, photos and old style tintypes, which were well done.

HON. THOMAS MCCAUL

This worthy comrade was born in New York city Jan. 18, 1838, and lived with his parents for a considerable time prior to the breaking out of the rebellion at Fox Lake, Wis., from which place be enlisted on the fill of Fort Sumter in the Citizens Guard of that town, known as Company A, 2d Wisconsin, for a three months' term. In September following (17th) he joined the rifle company known as Company G, Berdan Sharpshooters, Serving as a private therein until his discharge Feb. 22, 1863, on account of gunshot wound in thigh received at 2d Bull Run. His service as a Sharpshooter has been mentioned in the preceding pages; and in recognition of the same, Gov. Fairchild issued to him a captain's commission "for gallant service in rallying retreating troops at Charles City Cross Roads." Immediately after the close of the war, he served at Fort Laramie as Forage Master and Master of Transportation, until March, 1866. Married April 24, 1866, Miss Agnes H. Williams of Watkins, N. Y. Removed to Tomah, Wis., in 1867, and became a considerable property holder. Elected to legislature in 1874 as a democrat from a republican district. In 1883 was, elected the first mayor of the new city of Tomah. A whole souled, active -citizen, who forgets not his comrades of the tented field.

CAPT. FRANCIS D. SWEETSER

Formerly of Company E, 2d U. S. S. S. writes from Brentwood, California, since this history was placed in the hands of the printer, and too late to be inserted at the proper places in the work, first: That "California Joe" (Truman Head) died and was buried in the G. A. R. plat at San Francisco, where he had been an Inspector of U. S. Customs, while Capt. Sweetser was U. S. Boarding Officer at that Port. He says: "He was always the same old California Joe, and went by no other name, except upon the pay rolls." Also an incident that occurred on the line of the Rappahannock when Capt. Sweetser was a lieutenant and in command of Company E, where a rebel cavalry officer was caught by Lietit Sweetser and a bugler from another company. The rebel tried to obtain special favors by giving a Masonic sign. To which Lieut. Sweetser replied harshly: "this is a pretty time and place for you to talk about rank, with a lie on your lips at the same time." Capt. Sweetser is Post Commander of the largest Grand Army Post on the Pacific coast, (Lincoln, No.1), and has frequently been engaged organizing Posts in other parts of the state.

THE ISHAM BROTHERS

Albert S. Isham was born in Hamburg, N. Y., Sept. 17, 1840, and in 1844 went to Wisconsin with his parents to live in Dane county on a farm, and where as he grew up he "was occupied until the war broke out, when he enlisted in Company G, of the Sharpshooters Sept. 5, 1861, at Madison, and did effective service in the field with his company' through the many campaigns and engagements to and including Chancellorsville, in which, battle as I have stated he was severely wounded; from the effects of this wound he was eventually discharged, but was unable to perform manual labor for two years thereafter. Having married Miss Juliette Park, of Vermont, he bought a farm at Black Earth, Wis., living on it until 1867, when he sold out and removed to Iowa, purchasing 160 acres of prairie which he improved and farmed for nine years, When he again sold out, going back to Wisconsin. Gave up farming, going into the hardware business at Clinton, meeting with success up to the present time. His family consists of himself, wife and two married daughters. Of course he is a good Grand Army than, and also a good citizen, as he was a good soldier, as I have testified in the preceding history.

Willard M. Isham was also born at Hamburg, Sept. 22, 1841, and joined the company (G) Sept. 19, 1861, serving through all manner of hardships until the final muster out Sept. 22, 1864. After the war, one of his first steps was to get married and then settle down to business, his wife being a Miss Arnold, of Blue Mounds, Wis. In 1869 he moved to Iowa where he has resided ever since in different towns in that state, at present being at Des Moines, connected with the mercantile trade. He has two sons. These two Isham brothers, as they were known in war days, served their country faithfully and fearlessly. Of modest, uncomplaining dispositions, clean dress and appearance, excellent habits, and always ready to respond for duty, they left the service with a military record unsurpassed. At Gettysburg, Willard at great personal risk to himself, voluntarily carried away to a point behind the battle line out of danger, a helplessly wounded comrade, returning immediately to his place in the front.

EUGENE PAINE

Was born at Brookfield, Vt., March 6, 1839. Enlisted at Randolph that state Sept. 11, 1861, in Company F., 1st U. S. S. S., and was discharged Sept. 13, 1864. Was wounded at Locust Grove as before shown, when he was sent to hospital at Alexandria. Removed west in 1868, locating at Iowa City, where he engaged in the coal business, with which he has been connected for the past 23 years. He is also a prominent member of the "Comrades of Battlefield "order, and is fully entitled to the honorable distinction of veteran.

LEWIS J. ALLEN

Whose military history has been fairly given herein, was born on Gull Prairie, Mich., March 4, 1840, during a temporary sojourn of his parents, who were Vermonters, and returned to the latter state in 1842, bringing up their family amid the Green Mountains. Young Allen, who had been a carpenter by occupation during the previous five years, enlisted at the age of 21 on Sept. 2, 1861, in Company F, of the First Regiment of our Sharpshooters, and was made one of the Sergeants on its organization and muster-in. Passing through the Peninsula Campaign safely and honor.. ably, he was eventually sent on recruiting service to Vermont, as a reward for services at Hanover Court House, rejoining his company after being wounded and participating in its last charge in the evening of May 27, 1862. Returned from this last service the 10th of October following, with 47 recruits for his company, and from that time on served steadily and faithfully with company and regiment until his muster-out before Petersburg Oct. 9, 1864, as First Sergeant, although he had been commissioned Second Lieutenant January 22d preceding, when he had become a Veteran Volunteer by re-enlistment but could not muster owing to the reduced strength of members. Lieut. Allen narrowly escaped instant death at Totopotomoy Creek May 30, 1864, by an exploding shell wrecking his rifle pit, passing through within a few inches of his hip and inflicting injuries that have lasted through life. Since discharge from service he has resided at Battle Creek in the, state of Michigan, following the insurance business, a notary public, conveyancer, etc. He also holds a prominent position, being second in command, in the order known as the Comrades of Battle.

CHAPLAIN BARBER

Lorenzo Barber, who was chaplain of the Second Regiment, was, as I have heretofore stated, known, and I may add far and wide, as the Fighting Parson, and likewise as one of the best shots in the army. His record as a soldier is inferior to that of no member connected with our especial service. He was a Sharpshooter in fact, and a truer patriot never lived on American soil. What more need be said, additional to what is contained in this history? And yet I will add three incidents, two of which properly belong in the preceding pages but are not there, having come to my knowledge a little too late: At the time of the scattering of the Confederate cavalry at

Rappahannock Station by the Second Regiment, as related on page 167, Col. Peteler called for two volunteers to go into the cornfield, whereupon Chaplain Barber, John M. Powers, and I think one of the Livingstons of Company A stepped out and went into the cornfield to the right of the line, and when the rebels jumped off their horses into the field, the Chaplain, Powers and the other man were all mixed up with the rebels; at one time two rebs had the Chaplain, at another the Chaplain had two reb prisoners, and three rebs had Powers prisoner, but they all got away from each other. Powers was injured from the run and never rejoined the company, and the chaplain in retiring simply said ` Good Gracious!" While on the way to Gettysburg the Chaplain, who held the position of regimental mail agent or carrier, was 'gobbled up at Emmitsburg by the enemy's cavalry,' mail bag and all, but succeeded in effecting his escape, although be lost the mail which was rifled in his presence. In lieu thereof I understand he brought along with him two prisoners, however he managed to do it. The last and most serious, in fact lamentably fatal incident, or rather accident which it was, occurred some years after the war, whereby Chaplain Barber, while returning from a hunting expedition (for he was a great sportsman), accidentally shot himself, and in a rather careless way too, a charge of shot entering his body, from which he died, I have understood, at his home in Troy, N. Y. Thus ended the life of a most worthy minister, a perfect gentleman, and a truly Christian soldier.

MAJOR. WM. P. SHREVE

Entering the service as a member of Company H, Second Regiment U. S. Sharpshooters, from the state of Vermont, he became Quartermaster Sergeant of the regiment, but in Dec., '62, was commissioned First Lieutenant. When Col. Berdan was made Chief of Sharpshooters, Lieut. Shreve, and Lieut. Calef of the Second;- Were detailed on his staff. Lieut. Shreve also became Mustering Officer while at Brandy, when the veterans were re-enlisting. He was known to be a most conscientious officer, and in every engagement riding over the field carrying orders regardless of danger.

With him duty was always first. He was complimented by Gens. Ward and Birney frequently for his gallant bearing and promptness. Is now engaged, in business in Boston in a large jewelry establishment.

ELI COOK

This well known member of the Sharpshooters, was born in Richland county, Ohio, Aug. 24, 1842, but migrated With his parents to Eaton county, Michigan, in 1834 by "ox-team express," a slow but strictly honest way of traveling,—where they settled on a farm in a section known then as the wilderness. Here the farm was cleared up, and Eli helped to do it while growing up to manhood. His education was furnished by the public schools of the counties of the respective states where, he lived. The War of the Rebellion being fairly under way, Eli attempted at first to enlist in December, '61, in the 1st light artillery of Michigan, but couldn't get in.) Heard about the Sharpshooters, and borrowing four dollars, started for the front on a forced march of 30 miles to the railroad at Jackson. Had: never seen the inside of a car until he took the train from Jackson to Detroit, where he joined Capt. A. Milan Willett's company, afterwards Company of Berdan's regiment; being mustered in, Feb: 16; '62. , Served with honor and distinction every day until Jan. 5, 1865, with the exception of a few days off duty at Washington with sickness, and left service as First Sergeant of his company, which he frequently commanded. It seemed to be perfectly natural for Comrade Cook to be a good and dutiful soldier, as his great-grandfather fought in the Revolutionary war, and his grandfather Eli Cook in the war of 1812, and was wounded at Plattsburgh. On leaving the Sharpshooter service, our soldier comrade went back to his father's farm in Michigan but in 1866 tried to find a better place farther west

Not doing so, returned to Eaton county and has devoted his time since to agricultural pursuits, and been very fortunate, having one of the best farms of 120 acres in that section. Of course he got married (July 3, 1867), and to a Miss Elizabeth French, has three children, two daughters and one son. It is one of Eli Cook's greatest pleasures to meet and greet his old comrades of the Sharpshooters.

CHARLES A. STEVENS

Born in New York city March 27, 1835. Studied law three years in the office of J. Bancroft Stevens, a brother. Director and teacher of Ottignon's Gymnasium in 1860. Was in ",Bleeding Kansas" in 1854, when "Yankee Town" was covered with "anti-waterproof tents," through which rain poured like a sieve. Present at the first election held there. Was the deputy postmaster of Kansas City in the winter and spring of 1855, in sole charge. Went to Minnesota in August, '55. Lived on a pre-emption claim several years in the big woods of Le Sueur. In Fox Lake, Wis., when Sumter was fired on, and enlisted in the Citizens Guard, Capt. Geo. H. Stevens, a brother, which company became "A "of 2d Wisconsin. This was for the short term. Re-enlisted on Sept. 2, 1861, among the first, in Company G, Berdan Sharpshooters (so known); was the first Orderly Sergeant (by vote of company Appointed acting lieutenant by Col. Ripley March 27, '62, on Great-Bethel reconnoissance; and again at the battle of Gaines' Mill by Cols. Matheson (California Regiment) and by Col. Berdan. Was the first one sent off on recruiting service from the regiment, from Harrison's Landing after the Seven Days. Was promoted to Second Lieutenant from July 4, 1862, and in October following to 'First Lieutenant, becoming Company Commander when Capt. Marble became Field Officer; was also at times acting Sergeant-Major and Adjutant. Passed safely through 32 actions. Returning to Wisconsin was appointed Captain of Wisconsin Volunteers by Governor Lewis,; and afterwards raising a:company for the state was tendered the captaincy thereof, but declined, to go into Hancock's Veteran Volunteers where he commanded Company -A, 9th Regiment, until the final muster out in April, 1866. Prior thereto had purchased and published the "Fox Lake Record," a weekly newspaper. Returned to Minnesota in summer of 1866, and later on became an employe of the "Milwaukee & St. Paul," and also "Sioux City "Railway companies, in all for a period of ten years, as elevator and station agent, superintendent of elevators and acting traveling auditor, bookkeeper, etc. In 1877 began the publication of the

"Shakopee Courier," and has been a country editor ever since; and am also now a country squire. That's me.

SHARPSHOOTER MONUMENTS

ON THE FIELD OF GETTYSBURG

On this memorable field are to be found scattered far and wide, monuments, of every conceivable description, erected to commemorate the service of the different state troops fighting for the Union, in this battle. And not the least among them in point of conspicuous beauty of finish, and high-towering grandeur, in finest granite and marble designs, are those erected at different important points on the battle field to the United States Sharpshooters. O[r] them I here give brief sketches, with liberal extracts relating to the dedication ceremonies.

THE NEW YORK MONUMENT

An organization perfected by the survivors of the four New York Companies, A, B, D and H, known as the Veteran Association, with John W. Coates as president, Charles E. Graves vice-president, Charles J. Buchanan secretary, and Charles Donnelly treasurer, assembled at Gettysburg July 1889, to dedicate their monument, costing $1,500, at the advanced spot occupied by Companies D, 'E, F and I, near Pitzer's Run. After prayer by the chaplain Robert P. Tunnard (Co. B), and appropriate opening address by Vice President Graves, who presided, Comrade Chas. J. Buchanan was introduced as the orator for the occasion.

THE ORATION

"Can a stronger contrast be imagined than the quiet and glow this midsummer scene and the struggle which took place on this spot twenty-sin years ago? These woods today have that calm which' belongs· to the earth, but which was denied to them when we first made their acquaintance. It hardly seems possible that such a long period has intervened since we fought over this ground. In that interval time has wrought marked changes in us, but we who have assembled to dedicate this monument insist that we are still Sharpshooters, and our hearts beat as lightly now as they did years since when we touched elbows together in our then common cause.

We go back, in memory, this morning, to our 'soldier days, and recur to that patriotic brotherhood then formed and cemented, whose ties bound us firmer than we at that time knew or even dreamed. When the sound of artillery reached us at Emmitsburg, from this direction, on the morning of July 1, 1863, it was evident to all who heard it that the battle was at hand which would determine whether freedom or slavery should prevail on this continent. As our feet touched northern sod and we snuffed the breezes fresh from our native hills, our drooping spirits arose as if touched by magic. The very air we breathed seemed laden with patriotism and devotion. , Our old-time ardor and zeal for the cause to which we had pledged our fortunes and perilled our lives came back to us, renewed and invigorated, and nerved us with ten-fold courage.

Buford's challenge was the first real salutation the Confederates had received from our army since its unfortunate and unexpected defeat at Chancellorsville. As this cannonade shifted and gradually subsided, every one of us knew that, whatever troops of ours had been engaged were worsted, for it was apparent from the hurried march we made that our immediate presence here was necessary and imperative. The fact that our seven army corps were widely scattered, and not within supporting distance of one another, *gave* us no concern. We soon learned that the rebels were concentrating rapidly and were moving down upon us with clock-like precision from the north. Our only salvation was to unite instanter and present to them an unbroken front from the south, and we did it with like celerity. When the war began we set our faces southward, but now, for the first time, we had reversed our direction, and were to receive an attack in a free state and from the north, Our enemy's temerity had enabled him to suddenly put himself between us and our homes. It is matter of record that the legions of Kearny, Hooker and Whipple, composing the old 3d army corps, were hastened hither as soon as it was known that fighting was in progress, without orders, and, in fact, against orders. Gen. Sickles, though miles away, with the instinct of the true soldier, knew that there was naught to do but for our army to hasten hither, and that the point of concentration was whence the cannonade indicated. The

3d corps reached this field after the first day's battle had ceased, coming most of the distance from Emmitsburg on the double-quick. We went into camp the night of July 1, 1863, near Little Round Top, knowing that the battle before was hardly commenced, and that our opportunity to participate in the fight would be promptly afforded On the morrow. Our course Was clear 'as noonday, and we had been in loo many close campaigns to fear or falter at such a crisis. Wearied with our long and tedious march, we slept as soundly that night as if no conflict awaited as if peace, instead of war, was our inheritance. The next day was destined to severely test the mettle of the old 3d corps as it had never before been tried. During the morning of the 2d of July there were busy preparations and hot haste everywhere, but there seemed to be no reliable information as to what were the enemy's strength, dispositions and intentions on the Union left. Gen. Sickles fretted and chafed under the constraint imposed upon him, and, apprehending the enemy's purpose here, could not long brook this uncertainty in front, and therefore promptly determined to ascertain by whom and how he was threatened. It fell to our regiment to obtain this desired information in a way of which I shall speak in a moment. " The recollections of our old comradeship crowd upon us this morning, and we say to ourselves in all sincerity, thank God that we are permitted to peaceably assemble upon this great battle field after so long a separation, to do honor to those who here fell in their country's cause. What hallowed associations are around us! What glorious memories confront us recalled by these rocks and woods, these ravines and runs! We come hither to clasp hands over the remains of comrades fallen here in our great struggle for national existence.

>"Their bones are dust,
>
>Their good swords rust,
>
>Their souls are with the saints, we trust."

This monument is erected to the brave men of our regiment who fell on this field, but especially to those of our four New York companies who here gave up their lives. The fact that our granite memorial is not upon a more familiar or pretentious part of the battle field is no objection to its location, The quiet and seclusion of its site commend themselves to our better judgment, and here we may always come to renew our courage and loyalty to our country. It will be a continual reminder to those who come after us as well as to the survivors of these four companies, so long as any of them remain, that the great state of New York will never fail to recognize the brave deeds and heroic actions of her sons wheresoever and by whomsoever of them performed. The men who died here that our nation might live belonged to and were elements of that same great cause which solicited and obtained their services voluntarily. Without their aid republican institutions, for the time being, at least, would have perished in America. They never fail who are forced to yield or who die in a conflict for the right. May this monument be a lasting memorial, not of the strife and antagonism of the war, but of the principles thereby settled and of the peace following the same, and may it continue to be an enduring reminder of a Union saved and perpetuated to the whole country, north and south, by the valor and patriotism of our volunteer regiments, and be recognized as such through all coming generations. The universe looks with admiration upon and approves: of our thus honoring those members of Our command who fell at Gettysburg. Would that I could speak in trumpet tones and in more fitting language of their great and memorable services. Their honor and patriotism were as solid as the foundation upon which this monument rests; their characters and heroism were as pure as the heaven to which it points."

THE NEW HAMPSHIRE MONUMENT

This monument is made of Concord granite, and was dedicated July 2, 1886. It is located a few rods north of the clump of trees near where Gen. Hancock was wounded at the time Pickett made his famous charge, July 3, 1863. It is the only spot where the three New Hampshire companies were together during that famous battle. It cost $700, the state of New Hampshire appropriating $500, the balance being made up by the surviving comrades. The building committee consisted of one from each company: G. K. Crowell, Company E, (1st), Major E. T. Rowell, Company F, and H. A.

Redfield, Company G, (2d). Great credit is due the ones who came forward and raised the $200 necessary to complete the monument.

THE WISCONSIN MONUMENT

This handsome monument is placed at the edge of the Emmitsburg road in front of the "Rodger House," and 200 yards in rear of where the company, the farthest advanced on that part of the field was in line of skirmishers, as indicated by, a stone marker. The figure of the Sharpshooter is life-size, on gray granite,, five feet high. The base is red granite (Wisconsin marble), and sits on a foundation of granite from the battle field. The amount appropriated by the state of Wisconsin for this monument was $500. The committee appointed to select the site, and superintend the erection and dedication of Company G's monument, was James S. Webster, Joseph K. Hawes and Charles W. Baker. The dedication took place July2, 1888, Capt. Frank E. Marble of Lynn, Mass., delivering the oration, extracts from which are here given:

"We have assembled here today, charged with the solemn and impressive duty of dedicating a monument, as a memorial to the valor of Company G. Berdan's First Regiment, U. S. Sharpshooters, to commemorate the death of our comrades who fell on the field of Gettysburg; to commemorate the death of those who fell on the score of other battle fields in which the company participated; to commemorate the death of those who died of wounds or disease in the cause of liberty and unity during the great struggle of the civil war of 1861, and to commemorate those who survived, to further teach the lessons and enjoy the fruits of that liberty, patriotism and national unity, which their arms had achieved during that fratricidal strife. We are charged with the duty, so far as that duty can be accomplished by our company as an association, of completing and giving a final and lasting tone to a great principle that had been already proclaimed as a vital principle in the growth and prosperity of this great nation, but which had been assailed by an invidious foe, who had espoused the opposite belief that was hostile to national unity, and who had declared their ability, their willingness and their determination to defend their faith to the death.

This principle had passed the stage of debate—its leaders bad closed their eyes to farther reasoning, and had committed their hopes to the wage of battle. The contest had been long begun, when, twenty-five years ago, a struggle between two mighty contending armies began on the fair fields of Gettysburg, which was burdened with the destinies of a nation, and the result of which made this day, with the vast concourse of people and these ceremonies, possible. The duty assigned me, though it must recall much of hardship and suffering and sadness, is nevertheless a pleasant one; for out of the suffering and sadness comes the rejoicing of one country and one flag.

Out of the night of woe come the brightness and hope and joy of the morning. Our mission is that of peace, which has long been blossoming in the full light and warmth of the nation's summer day of prosperity.

"It remains for me to speak of a portion of the union army, which as an organization and as to numbers was so small in comparison that but for its greatness in deeds it could scarcely be recognized as an atom in the greatness and extent of our army during that war. And that "atom" fought on this field, and helped by its heroic deeds to make that history about which so many volumes have been written. It is for this, that the monument now before ns has been chiseled in granite and erected here as a memorial, to teach future generations the value of patriotism as measured by its cost in hardships and blood. I wish I might recall in language such a history of Company G as dwells within my memory—as wells up in my heart when I close my eyes to the world around me and live over again those days that tried men's souls. Numberless are the scenes that crowd in upon my mind when I go back to 1861 to '65 and live over again the days and scenes of my army life, that became inwrought and changed the whole perfecting themselves in the skirmish drill that made them deservedly famous on every field,—for their ability to deploy as skirmishers, at double quick, under a galling fire over any kind of open or wooded country and every man drop into his place in line five paces apart. Following the movements of the company up to this battle, Capt. Marble proceeds:

"But at the time we made this memorial a possibility to be erected to the valor of Company G, the rebel hosts had left their own soil,—invaded the free state of Pennsylvania, and as a final incentive—a final struggle, they were to try and win a decisive victory away from their homes, on their enemy's soil, as a further inducement for - sympathizing England to acknowledge the independence of the so-called southern confederacy, and thus to make treason respectable and transform it into successful revolution. The clouds of war had hung dark and heavy over our distracted country. The "boys in blue," with our green coats interspersed, had been waging battle for long days and months, and the months had crept up to years, under the deep and damning shadow of those clouds,—had taken defeat and disappointment with stoical philosophy, while the clouds grew darker, more grim and more threatening. It was thus we marched to the fields of Gettysburg,—the fields that were fair and bright with the abundance and wealth of the husbandman's toil,—beautiful as the garden of the Lord with the fruits of His providence. Here we received an inspiration to repel an invasion aimed at our own homes. Here we were to meet the enemy, and fight within the borders of a state rich in historic -recollections of our first congress, and they were fondly cherished. This was soil which we re-consecrated, as it had long before been consecrated by the memories of the Declaration of Independence, which is, as has been well said, "the grandest document that ever heralded the birth of a nation." Here a rift came in these darkening clouds, made by crashing thunderbolts of mighty battle, and through that rift beamed the sunlight of victory and liberty and union, whose warming and cheering rays flooded the whole land as by a miraculous power, carrying its resplendent light and warmth to the hearts of a throbbing, nation. "

I close Capt. Marble's address with a eulogy on the military character and services of Capt. Edward Drew: "For 13 years he had belonged to one of the finest independent military companies of the United States which had given exhibition drills in the principal cities of the north; and he assured me that during that time there had never a day passed, except Sundays, but that he had had a sword or a musket in his hands for the purpose of drill. With such a captain in command of Company G it is no boast to assert that it stood at the front as being the best drilled company in the regiment. The officers and sergeants of the regiment were for awhile placed under his instruction, so that the other companies might have the benefit of his knowledge and experience, and there is no doubt but that the efficiency of the regiment was greatly increased by his presence, ability and skill, which he always exerted for the benefit of all. At Charles City Cross Roads, he gave up his life for his country's cause. His loss was keenly felt by every member of Company C by whom he was loved as tenderly as a father. And

> 'He loved as we loved, yet he parted
> From all that man's spirit can prize;
> Left woman and child broken-hearted
> Staring up to the pitiless skies;
> Left the tumult of youth the sweet guerdon
> Hope promised to conquer from fate,
> Gave all, for the agonized burden
> Of death for the flag and the state.'

THE VERMONT MONUMENTS

The monument to Company F, First Regiment, was designed and made of Vermont marble, by Ripley & Sons of Rutland, who contributed heavily towards the expense of it, their special interest in it being due to the fact that the company formed a portion of the command of Lieut. Col. Wm. Y. W. Ripley of the First U. S. Sharpshooters. It appears that the State Commission had only $500 at their disposal for this monument, and as a better structure was desired, Ripley & Sons agreed to build a monument worth $1,200 for the $500, thus contributing $700, on account of the especial desire of Gen. Ripley to suitably commemorate his old command; which generous offer was accepted. The monument is over 20 feet high, made of the best Rutland marble, the only Vermont monument of that material, others being granite or bronze. The monument to Companies E and H, Second Regiment, stands by the roadside near the "Slyder House," and is of rough granite finished upon the face, showing the Vermont coat of arms, the Sharps and target rifles, and a hornet's nest, representative of the name given the Second Sharpshooters by the assaulting column of the enemy July 2d. The Michigan Companies, C, I and K, have erected their monument on Little Round Top.

THE END.

Get your FREE EBOOK—join our mailing list to get notified of great new (old) books and the latest blog posts.

BIG BYTE BOOKS is your source for great lost history!

Printed in Great Britain
by Amazon